'This is an excellent text book. It combines theory, practice of entrepreneurship and great examples in a very accessible way. The inclusion of teaching points makes it a valuable resource for both students and lecturers.'

Professor Helen Lawton Smith, Birbeck, University of London, UK

'This modern textbook offers support to teachers as they facilitate student learning processes, allowing students to develop their knowledge and skills in a new way. The mix of theories, models, cases and exercises offer a good foundation for learning what entrepreneurship is all about and creates a mind-set for executing.'

Erik Lindberg, Associate Professor USBE, Umeå, Sweden

'This is an excellent textbook for entrepreneurship students and educators alike. Packed with easy to follow prose, illustrative case examples, and workbooks to implement student ideas, Greene's textbook has set the standard for others to follow.'

Niall G MacKenzie, Adam Smith Business School, University of Glasgow, UK

'A comprehensive and contemporary text offering an excellent overview of entrepreneurship, small business and enterprise issues. The insightful integration of critical theory and practical cases with additional teaching material aimed at student-centred learning offers invaluable material for those teaching undergraduate and postgraduate students within Business and Management. This text combines a solid academic approach with innovative learning approaches from a leading entrepreneurship scholar.'

Professor Susan Marlow, University of Birmingham, UK

'This highly informative book provides a comprehensive examination of current theory and practices on entrepreneurship in different contexts. Systematic and user-friendly, this book enables readers to critically analyse complex problems and practically navigate the start-up journey from idea through to implementation. The book is ideal for students with an interest in the connections between practical and theoretical knowledge about various entrepreneurial activities, which are here illuminated through case studies and research insights.'

Professor Boris Urban, University of the Witwatersrand, South Africa

'One of the most comprehensive entrepreneurship textbooks, successfully bridging both theory and practice. It practically guides readers through how to start up, offering in-depth coverage of the key entrepreneurship theories. It is an invaluable and accessible resource for students, teachers and practitioners.'

Dr Xiaodan Yu, Nottingham University Business School, China

'Highly recommended. Leading scholar Francis Greene provides a lucid and enjoyable overview of the main themes of contemporary entrepreneurship, skilfully blending together insights from theory and practice.'

Professor Alexander Coad, CENTRUM PUCP, Peru

'Bridging theory and practice, this book provides a comprehensive examination of entrepreneurship. Francis Green has successfully integrated evidenced-based thinking and captured the current developments in the field, covering different aspects, such as entrepreneurial contexts, start-up pathways, scaling and exit. Covering every aspect of entrepreneurship theories and including case studies, activities and class discussion, this book is an excellent addition to existing entrepreneurship textbooks.'

Dr Shova Thapa Karki, University of Sussex, UK

'Francis Greene's new book is a fabulous platform for both students and entrepreneurs looking to manage the fraught process of establishing and growing a business. It pulls in and summarises the work of key practitioners and thinkers in this subject and present the tools for success in a practical and user-friendly way alongside excellent case studies. Highly recommended.'

Mark Copsey, Leeds Beckett University, UK

ENTREPRENEURSHIP

THEORY AND PRACTICE

FRANCIS J. GREENE

macmillan international
HIGHER EDUCATION

RED GLOBE PRESS

First published 2020 by
RED GLOBE PRESS

Red Globe Press in the UK is an imprint of Macmillan Education Limited, registered in England, company number 01755588, of 4 Crinan Street, London, N1 9XW.

Red Globe Press® is a registered trademark in the United States, the United Kingdom, Europe and other countries.

ISBN 978-1-137-58955-2 paperback

This book is printed on paper suitable for recycling and made from fully managed and sustained forest sources. Logging, pulping and manufacturing processes are expected to conform to the environmental regulations of the country of origin.

A catalogue record for this book is available from the British Library.

A catalog record for this book is available from the Library of Congress.

Brief Contents

Long Contents

List of Figures

PART 1: ENTREPRENEURIAL FOUNDATIONS

PART 2: PLANNING THE START-UP JOURNEY

PART 3: FINANCING THE VENTURE

PART 4: BEYOND START-UP

PART 5: INTRODUCTION TO THE WORKBOOKS

List of Tables

PART 4: BEYOND START-UP

PART 5: INTRODUCTION TO THE WORKBOOKS

Preface

Most entrepreneurship texts are either theoretical or 'how to' guides. Very few successfully bridge theory and practice.

This book is different. It integrates theory and practice.

For undergraduate and postgraduate students, there are three key benefits:

1. **It is rigorous.** In-depth reviews of the key areas of entrepreneurship research and in-chapter 'assessment tips' and 'academic insights' all make it easier to research and structure assignments.
2. **It is relevant and modern.** It uses the latest research, tools and techniques to practically walk you through how to pitch and plan a start-up. Two workbooks at the end of the book and numerous practical in-chapter 'Entrepreneurship in action' exercises provide practical ways of applying your learning.
3. **It is accessible.** It is written in plain English. Chapters begin and end with a summary of your learning. Concepts, ideas and activities are clearly explained. There are numerous in-chapter entrepreneurial case studies from across the globe that show key features of entrepreneurial practice.

This book also has other benefits for aspiring entrepreneurs on their start-up journey:

- It provides you with a tried and tested methodology for your start-up journey. It shows you how to make low-risk, low-cost investments to develop your business idea first before committing more resources and time to assess the viability of your start-up.
- It helps you to think through the likely sources of external finance you might need to start and develop your business idea.
- It gives you insights into the likely challenges you will face in growing your business and keeping it afloat.

For educators, other key benefits are:

1. It is a reference guide. Each chapter has a thorough, modern and relevant review of the literature. The book has nearly 900 endnotes, with the vast bulk of these being key citations from across start-up, growth, finance, failure and public policy. There are also many cases from a wide range of industries, sectors and countries, designed to equip lecturers and students with richly diverse and multifaceted examples of entrepreneurship in the real world.
2. It provokes discussion. Throughout the book, there are discussion and assessment questions that bring to life many of the key controversies in entrepreneurship research and practice and stimulate critical thinking skills.
3. It is adaptable, with a varied and flexible pedagogy. It supports courses and modules which need a firm theoretical framing; guides courses and modules that aim for practical understandings; and introduces students to entrepreneurial finance, business closure and policymaking. Further resources will be provided on the companion website, including videos, a test bank and a comprehensive set of lecture slides.

Author's Acknowledgements

There are a number of people whom I would like to thank who have helped me to develop and write this book over the last five years.

First, I would like to thank all of the entrepreneurs and undergraduate and postgraduate students whom I have taught over the last 20 years for allowing me to test and develop my thinking and practice.

I would also like to thank the team at Palgrave. My Commissioning Editor Isabelle Cheng, and before her Andrew Malvern, have stuck with the process and have been unfailingly helpful and supportive. Peter Atkinson and Milly Weaver also provided key insights and directions that helped sharpen the book. Thanks also go to Dr Stefania Romano and the large number of academic reviewers who have read and commented on earlier drafts of this book.

Along the way, I have been helped by students such as Konstantin Kamp, Abbie Greene, Jasper Epsom, Ahmed Abd-Elhamid and Amrita Ahluwalia, who have all read and commented on parts of the text. In particular, I would like to thank Derek Main for all of his help and guidance. He is a star.

Finally, I would like to thank my wife, Anna, for her support and love. The book is dedicated to her.

About the Author

Professor Francis J. Greene is Chair of Entrepreneurship at the University of Edinburgh Business School, Scotland. He previously worked at Durham, Warwick and Birmingham Universities and has taught in Europe, Australia and Hong Kong. He has spent over 20 years teaching practical and theoretical entrepreneurship courses. He has also authored two other books and numerous articles, book chapters and reports that range across entrepreneurial start-up, growth, failure, finance and entrepreneurial support. In his applied work, he seeks to improve understandings of entrepreneurship for individual businesses and stakeholders, such as financiers, support agencies and policymakers.

Digital Resources

Visit the book's companion website at (macmillanihe.com/greene-entrepreneurship) for extra resources to enhance your teaching and learning.

Teaching Resources

- Instructor videos, with suggestions of how to teach using this book
- A set of Microsoft® PowerPoint slides for each chapter
- A test bank of multiple choice questions

Learning Resources

- Video interviews and lectures for revision and further study

Guided Tour of the Book

Learning Outcomes

In this chapter, you will learn:

- Why entrepreneurship is vital for econo
- The definitions of entrepreneurship.
- How entrepreneurial activity can be me

Learning Outcomes

The opening page of each chapter provides a short summary of what is covered in the chapter. The learning outcomes will help you to organise your learning and track your progress.

Discussion questions

Regularly interspersed throughout each chapter, these questions help you to reflect on and absorb the material at hand.

Discussion questions:

- Although this definition is popular, can yo entrepreneurship distinct from strategic also looks at the process of creating and entrepreneurship different?
- Is it more sensible to equate entrepreneurs
- Are opportunities found or created?
- How do entrepreneurs recombine resourc

Academic insight: Changing and Mark II

The role of entrants in stimulating innovation reasons for studying entrepreneurship. The innovation occurred was due to chance. Some resources. Europe had the horse, South Americ cannot be tamed. This stymied innovation in A

Academic insight

These boxes cover key academic writings on entrepreneurship, reinforced with discussion questions.

Case Studies

Mini-cases throughout each chapter feature different types of enterprises from around the world. Discussion questions at the end of each case study give you a chance to reflect further

Case study: Is there an identikit entrepreneur?

The identikit picture of a successful entrepreneur is an immigrant high-tech start-up makes them rich.

Fitting this mould are brothers, Patrick and John Collison. They moved as teenagers to the USA to go to university. While at univ to help sellers on marketplaces such as eBay list their items more this for $5 million. Afterwards, having dropped out of university, th payments business Stripe in response to their frustrations in using scale Stripe, the brothers raised $450 million in successive fund D), allowing them to set up offices across the globe, employ 900 valuation of $9.2 billion. This made both of the brothers, at least

Assessment tip: Crossing the T's and d

In all academic writing, there are constraints. A
the journal's style guide and word limit. If they
You face similar constraints in your academ
font types and sizes, setting margins, providin
conventions. They matter because one of the w
look at a bibliography. If this is messy and inco
the actual writing. To standardise your referen

Assessment tips

These will help you to improve your performance while studying and when taking exams.

Entrepreneurship in Action

These practical exercises in Chapters 4-12 will help you to explore your own start up ideas.

Entrepreneurship in Action

- Investigate a successful entrepreneur. D
or is it more to do with being passionate
- Interview an entrepreneur. Ask them w
entrepreneur. Was it to do with a recog
entrepreneurship, because they had str
experiences or because they had strong

ASSESSMENT QUESTIONS

1. What is the best way of assessing entrepreneurial e
2. Identify three common factors associated with bus
factors is the most likely to explain business termin
3. Does the outside environment have a greater in
entrepreneur's background?
4. Does entrepreneurial experience promote business
5. Discuss what factors influence family business succ
6. Do family businesses outperform non-family busin

Review and Revise

The end of each chapter has a number of features to help you consolidate what you have learned, including a chapter learning summary, assessment questions and suggestions for further reading.

Workbooks

Two workbooks at the end of the book have a number of practical exercises designed to help you determine the feasibility of a start-up and then to plan and present your start-up.

WORKBOOK 1

START-UP DESIRA
AND FEASIBILITY

Case Study Grid

Chapter	Organisation	Country	Industry Covered	Main Topics	Page
1	Grameen Bank	Bangladesh	Social enterprise	Entrepreneurial motivation; Schumpeterian vs Kirznerian entrepreneurs	9
1	Vibe Bar	UK	Entertainment	Entrepreneurial uncertainty	19
2	Coffix	New Zealand	Food and drink	Finding opportunities in well-established markets	33
3	Apple	USA	Personal computing	Entrepreneurial motivations; founding of Apple	45
3	GF Biotechnology	Italy	Alternative energy	Entrepreneurial motivations	46
3	Professionals	Greece	Professional services	Effects of tax evasion	49
4	Rome2rio	Australia	Travel services	Turning frustrations into business opportunities	74
4	Baubax	USA	Clothing	Using SCAMPER to come up with new ideas	78

Chapter	Organisation	Country	Industry Covered	Main Topics	Page
4	Waldo Emerson	USA 	Rodent control	Importance of promoting products and services	81
4	Hewlett Packard	USA 	IT	Bootstrapping the business	82
4	Listerine	USA 	Personal hygiene	Intellectual property protection	85
4	Subway	USA 	Food retailing	Franchise business model	86
5	Innocent drinks	UK 	Smoothies	Using the Business Model Canvas to understand your business model	100
5	Ice Hotel	Sweden 	Hotels	Effectuation and business creation	113
5	Dropbox	USA 	Cloud storage	Lean start-up, building a minimum viable product	117
5	Patrick Cameron	New Zealand 	Hairstyling	Building a scalable business model	118
6	Big Heart	Sweden 	App development	Turning problems into opportunities	128
6	Instabugs	Egypt 	Software	How talking to customers can lead to product development	129

Chapter	Organisation	Country	Industry Covered	Main Topics	Page
6	Rêve En Vert	UK	Fashion retailing	Developing a niche; identifying your target customers	131
6	The Cook Kitchen	UK	Food retailing	Segmenting and focusing on your target customer	133
6	Kar-Go	UK	Logistics	Importance of explaining how your product or service works	136
6	Golf4you.com	Germany	Leisure activities	Solving a market need; identifying how to grow the business	141
6	Modomojo	Germany	Fashion retailing	Finding an entrepreneurial solution to a customer problem	142
6	Black Hops	Australia	Drinks	Sales channels; pricing; competition	144
6	Paytm	India	e-payments	Disruptive ways of changing markets	145
6	Pets.com	USA	Pet food	Importance of capturing customer value and developing a sales strategy	147
6	School Notices	UK	e-platforms	Turning multi-sided markets into an advantage	148

Chapter	Organisation	Country	Industry Covered	Main Topics	Page
7	Tabur Marine	UK 	Leisure activities	Difficulty in protecting intellectual property	159
7	Trunki	UK 	Travel goods	Issues in protecting design rights	160
7	Textilis	Sweden 	Fabrics and cloth	Issues in protecting design rights	161
7	Dropbox	USA 	Cloud storage	Developing an entrepreneurial team; importance of the team to gaining venture capital finance	163
7	Facebook	USA 	Social media	Team formation and idea protection	164
7	Pretty Young Professional	USA 	Career support	Team formation, team ownership issues	165
7	Snapchat	USA 	Social media	Team formation, team ownership issues; sharing equity	167
7	Microsoft	USA 	Personal computing	Team formation, team ownership issues; sharing equity	169
7	Careem	United Arab Emirates 	Taxi services	Why competition is a good thing	171

Chapter	Organisation	Country	Industry Covered	Main Topics	Page
7	Mr. Cesar	Brazil	Dog food	Using Blue Ocean strategy to find a new niche in a competitive market	174
8	Jiayuan.com	China	Dating services	Understanding your gross profits, break-even point and sales conversion rate	199
8	Take Eat Easy	Belgium	Food delivery	Finance needed for growth; importance of the break-even point	202
8	Halal cosmetics	Oman	Beauty products	Dangers of over-trading	203
8	Sunbeam	USA	Kitchen appliances	Poor accountancy practices	204
8	Boo.com/ Better places	UK/Israel	e-retailing/ transport	Importance of the cash burn rate to business survival	207
9	Heel the World	Ghana	Fashion design and manufacture	Bootstrapping the business	216
9	Fetchr	United Arab Emirates	Logistics/last mile delivery	Challenges in raising external finance; need for successive funding rounds to grow a business	220

Chapter	Organisation	Country	Industry Covered	Main Topics	Page
9	AdGrok	USA 	e-platform	Challenges, costs and advantages in using business angel finance	226
10	Stripe/ Dangote	USA/Nigeria 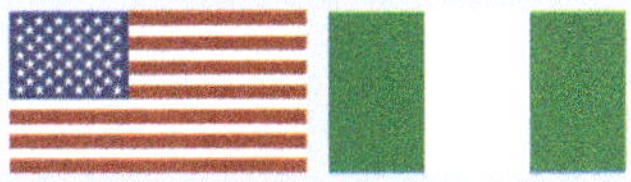	Online payments/food	Challenges in identifying an identikit picture of a fast growth entrepreneur	246
10	Bulb	UK 	Energy services	Building the business; overcoming growth pains	251
10	Rolls-Royce	UK 	Aircraft maintenance	Innovative business model; building a sustained competitive advantage	256
10	Valve Corporation	USA 	Gaming	High performance workplaces	259
10	Fraser Doherty	UK 	Food	Importance of finding a fast-growing market place	262
10	Canva	Australia 	Design	Importance of geography to gaining external finance	264
10	Rovio Entertainment	Finland 	Gaming	Importance of luck to business success	265
11	Majoy	China 	Gaming	Consequences of business failure	281

Chapter	Organisation	Country	Industry Covered	Main Topics	Page
11	Apple	USA	Personal computing	Dark entrepreneurial traits	282
11	Royal Bank of Scotland	UK	Banking	Dark entrepreneurial traits	282
11	Fairchild Semiconductor	USA	Electronics	Importance of geography; how business closure leads to new businesses	283
11	Jamie's Italian	UK	Restaurants	Challenges for businesses to stay competitive and relevant	286
11	Kongō Gumi	Japan	Construction	Difficulty of maintaining a family business	291
11	Hōshi Ryokan	Japan	Hotels	Business succession issues; blood heirs vs adopted heirs	292
11	Gina Rinehart	Australia	Mining	Family business conflict	293
12	Policymakers	Various	Government	Challenges in designing good entrepreneurship policies	306
12	Local governments	Brazil	Municipalities	Institutional barriers to business creation and development	309
12	QPay	Australia	e-payments	Importance of government help to business development	312

Chapter	Organisation	Country	Industry Covered	Main Topics	Page
12	Simón de Cirene	Chile 	Business support	Advantages of business advice and mentoring	313
12	El Mashroua	Egypt 	Entertainment	Impact of entertainment on entrepreneurial attitudes and behaviours	314
12	CréaJeunes	France 	Business support	Challenges in providing support for young disadvantaged people	315

PART 1

Entrepreneurial Foundations

CHAPTER 1

Entrepreneurship in Focus

Learning Outcomes

In this chapter, you will learn:

- Why entrepreneurship is vital for economies.
- The definitions of entrepreneurship.
- How entrepreneurial activity can be measured.
- The important differences between large and small businesses.

Mini Contents List

1.1 WHY IS ENTREPRENEURSHIP VITAL?

1.1.1 *Entrepreneurship is part of our everyday lives*

Across the globe, more of us try to set up a business than have children. In countries such as Australia, Sweden, Singapore and the United Kingdom (UK), more people start up than get married.[1]

1.1.2 *Entrepreneurship gives you a holistic perspective on the fundamentals of business practice*

At least 95 per cent of all businesses around the world are small enterprises. If you are a European, by the time you are 40 you have about a one in eight chance of being an entrepreneur. Even if entrepreneurship is not for you, there is a good chance that you will work for an entrepreneur at some point in your life.[2]

Gaining a better grasp of how entrepreneurship works is an excellent basis for understanding how individual business activities such as finance, operations, marketing and sales fit together in any business.

1.1.3 *Entrepreneurship drives economic growth*

Most new jobs come from new entrepreneurs.[3] Globally renowned start-ups such as Twitter (founded in 2006) and Instagram (2010) have redefined, challenged and broken up markets.[4] This ability to challenge existing business practices contributes to economic development. By 2014, Apple's output was equivalent to 0.5 per cent of total United States (USA) economic growth. If it were a country, its revenues would place it somewhere between Slovakia and Oman.[5]

1.2 HOW THIS BOOK HELPS YOU UNDERSTAND AND PRACTISE ENTREPRENEURSHIP

Most books on entrepreneurship are either biographies of entrepreneurs or 'how to' guides about how you can start or grow a business. They can be useful but are often limited if you want to understand the evidence base on entrepreneurship. For that, you usually need to read lots of academic articles or reviews. However, these often tell you little about the practical aspects of entrepreneurship.

This book bridges this gap by being 'research-led, practice-orientated'. It applies the latest evidence-based thinking on entrepreneurship to the practice of entrepreneurship. This approach gives you:

- A detailed understanding of key topics in entrepreneurship (entrepreneurial characteristics, start-up, entrepreneurial finance, business growth, venture closure and entrepreneurship policy) backed up by comprehensive reviews of the academic literature.
- 'Assessment tips' in each chapter to develop your academic writing.
- Practical and theoretical knowledge about entrepreneurial activities through 66 case studies and in-chapter 'academic insights'.
- An up-to-date, tried and tested methodology for creating and developing a new venture that builds on the Business Model Canvas to help you with your start-up plans and presentations.
- Seventy-four in-chapter 'Entrepreneurship in action' practical exercises that develop your entrepreneurial activities.
- Two workbooks that practically guide your start-up planning journey from an idea through to a plan.

1.3 WHAT IS MEANT BY ENTREPRENEURSHIP?

There is no agreed definition of entrepreneurship. Economists, psychologists and management researchers all have their own perspectives. Entrepreneurship is an elastic term, meaning different things to different people depending on the situation. However, there are three key components of a good definition of entrepreneurship: risk and uncertainty, the entrepreneur and entrepreneurial contexts.

1.3.1 *Risk and uncertainty*

Making decisions under uncertainty is the first element of a good definition of entrepreneurship. This is rooted in a crucial distinction that the American economist Frank Knight (1885–1972) made between risk and uncertainty. He understood that we calculate risks based on experience. Weather forecasters cannot be certain whether it will rain next week but they can use their records to estimate how likely it is to rain. Equally, a poker player does not exactly know what cards their opponent holds, but they can determine probabilities because there are only 52 cards in a normal poker card deck.

For Knight, uncertainty differs from risk because prior experience does not provide any useful guidance on how to deal with it. With uncertainty, 'it is impossible to form a group of instances because the situation dealt with is in a high degree unique'.[6] If asked to think about what the world will look like in 20 years' time, our only options are to guess or just say that no one can forecast so far ahead. Without knowledge of what all the possible futures could be, no one can determine their probabilities. Entrepreneurs face similar uncertain situations. At the outset of their new venture, they cannot be certain whether it will succeed because their product, market and customers are untested.

Knight's distinction between risk and uncertainty has two main implications:

1. You cannot manage uncertainty, but you can manage risk.
2. Entrepreneurship is a process of transforming 'unknowns' into quantifiable risks. Central to this process is that the entrepreneur 'undertakes' (the literal meaning of entrepreneurship from the French word *entreprendre*) to bring forward solutions that solve problems that can provide benefits both to the entrepreneur and society.

Discussion question: Can you think of other examples of risk and uncertainty?

1.3.2 *The importance of the entrepreneur: Schumpeter and Kirzner*

Tackling the characteristics of the entrepreneur is the second key element of a good definition of entrepreneurship. There are many different views of entrepreneurial characteristics. Most of these stem from the thinking of two economists, Joseph Schumpeter (1883–1950) and Israel Kirzner (1930–) (Table 1.1).

Schumpeter was an Austrian economist who is important because he explained why entrepreneurship was central to the development of capitalism. He suggested that entrepreneurs are 'characterized by supernormal qualities of intellect and will'.[7] He also saw them as innovators. Their role 'does not essentially consist in either inventing anything or otherwise creating the conditions which the enterprise exploits. It consists in getting things done.'[8] Entrepreneurs achieve this by implementing 'change within markets through the carrying out of new combinations'. He identified five ways of introducing innovations:

1. *Introduction of a new method of production:* Henry Ford's introduction of the mass production line for cars is one such example. Another is gene splicing methods that cure inherited diseases by altering specific parts of human DNA.
2. *Opening up of a new market.* Current examples include marketplaces such as eBay, Amazon and Etsy, which have led to significant changes in how we shop. In the past, we used to go to shops to inspect and then buy things. Now we go to the shops, inspect what we want and then buy it from the internet.
3. *The conquest of a new source of supply of raw materials or half-manufactured goods.* The scientist, Andre Geim, has won two well-known prizes in this life. His first was the IG Nobel prize for using magnets to levitate frogs. He won this prize because it is for science that makes people laugh and then think.[9] His second prize was for the discovery of graphene, a carbon honeycomb which is 100 times thinner and stronger than steel. For that, he won the Nobel Prize for Physics.
4. *The creation of a new type of industrial organisation.* In the non-profit sector, charities traditionally raised grants and donations to fund their needs and meet social objectives. Nowadays, a more common not-for-profit organisational form is a social enterprise. These are more likely to rely on generating profitable trading activities to support social goals.
5. *Introduction of a new good or significant improvement.* Driverless cars could mean anything from greater opportunities for personal travel for blind people to the creation of 'mobile automotive offices'.

Schumpeter felt that because entrepreneurs were agents of change, their activities were likely to lead to 'gales of creative destruction' in markets. Innovation for Schumpeter is 'radical innovation'. These are 'competence destroying' because they 'creatively destroy' existing markets.[10] Take the move from fuel-powered engines in cars to electric motors. This switch is creative because it brings far lower emissions and potentially lower maintenance costs. But it is also destructive to fuel engine manufacturers who may go out of business and to their workers who may lose well-paid and secure jobs.

Schumpeter recognised that radical innovators are rare. Few innovators have had such a dramatic influence on society as Thomas Edison. His contribution to the commercialisation of electricity means that we can all today enjoy electric lights, listen to music and watch films.

Another word commonly associated with being an entrepreneur is 'arbitrageur' (Table 1.1). Arbitrage happens when an individual realises there is a difference in price for a product or service between one market and another and exploits the opportunity for profit. IKEA founder Ingvar Kamprad started his entrepreneurial career buying matchsticks in bulk from the Swedish capital Stockholm, breaking them down to smaller batches and selling them at a higher price in his local village.

Kirzner termed this ability to recombine existing information into something profitable as 'entrepreneurial alertness'.[11] He saw this ability as a central feature of the entrepreneur. However, entrepreneurs do not need specific skills or characteristics; they just need to be alert to opportunities. These opportunities come from 'errors' in markets such as customers getting poor service or having to pay high prices. This suggests that opportunities exist 'out there' in the world waiting to be discovered and it is the role of the entrepreneur to find them and in doing so bring markets back into equilibrium. Entrepreneurs are imitators who spot an opportunity and subsequently attempt to make a profit. Kirzner's contribution, therefore, was to point out how individuals could act entrepreneurially.

Table 1.1 Key differences between Schumpeter and Kirzner

	Schumpeter	Kirzner
Who is an entrepreneur?	An *innovator* who introduces radically new products, services or processes to the market	An *arbitrageur* who brings incremental changes to the market
What knowledge do they need?	*New* knowledge	*Existing* knowledge
What do they do?	*Create* opportunities for exploiting knowledge	*Discover* new profitable opportunities arising from differences in prices between one market and another
What is their role in society?	To fundamentally disrupt markets and break existing routines (*disequilibria*)	To bring markets back to *equilibrium* (even if only temporarily)
How common is entrepreneurship?	Opportunities to introduce new radical innovations are *rare*	Opportunities to exploit incremental changes in knowledge are *common*

Discussion question: Who do you agree with – Schumpeter or Kirzner? Why?

1.3.3 Entrepreneurial contexts

Examining the context in which individuals make decisions under uncertainty is the third key element to a good definition of entrepreneurship. Context is important because entrepreneurship is not solely the expression of individual personality.

When William Gartner examined the question 'Who is the entrepreneur?' he found it difficult to work out what an 'entrepreneurial' personality was.[12] If someone has Schumpeterian 'supernormal qualities of intellect and will', does that mean they behave entrepreneurially when they do their shopping or feed their cat? Gartner suggested that instead of examining 'who' the entrepreneur was, it is better to work out 'what' they do in particular situations.

Gartner suggested that the 'unit of analysis' should focus on entrepreneurial behaviours – how ideas turn into start-up propositions, how teams and organisations are formed and how resources are acquired and combined – rather than the dispositions of the entrepreneur.

The emphasis on the individual neglects the wider social nature of entrepreneurship. Commercial opportunities do not exist in a vacuum. Opportunities do not just exist 'out there', waiting to be discovered by a detached and solitary entrepreneur. Instead, opportunities are socially constructed by people working together to give meaning to the identification and realisation of opportunities.[13]

Context also points to different types of entrepreneurship. Schumpeter and Kirzner focused on the economic role of the entrepreneur rather than whether they owned a business. However, a popular definition of an entrepreneur is that it is someone who is involved with venture creation. This led Gartner to conclude that 'Entrepreneurship is the creation of organizations'; 'it is a role that individuals undertake to create organizations'.[14]

Academic insight: Scott Shane and Sankaran Venkataraman's definition of the field of entrepreneurship

One of the most common and popular academic definitions of entrepreneurship is that entrepreneurship is 'the scholarly examination of how, by whom and with what effects opportunities to create future goods and services are discovered, evaluated and exploited.'[15]

Their definition has four key assumptions:

1) Entrepreneurial opportunities exist – but are not known to everyone.
2) People have different perceptions of the monetary and non-monetary value of an opportunity.
3) Some people will choose to pursue these opportunities.
4) Acting on these opportunities results in both profitable and unprofitable outcomes.

This definition argues that there is a 'nexus' or connection between opportunities and individuals. Opportunities exist waiting to be exploited; entrepreneurship is a process of discovery, evaluation and exploitation, and the role of the entrepreneur is to find new means of recombining resources.

Discussion questions:

- Although this definition is popular, can you identify challenges? For example, is entrepreneurship distinct from strategic management? Strategic management also looks at the process of creating and sustaining value. How is the field of entrepreneurship different?
- Is it more sensible to equate entrepreneurship to start-ups?
- Are opportunities found or created?
- How do entrepreneurs recombine resources: are entrepreneurs those who create novel ways of recombining resources (Schumpeter) or do they optimise existing ways of recombining resources (Kirzner)?

Equally, very few start-ups are radical Schumpeterian innovators. Most start-up product or process innovations are incremental 'order-of-magnitude improvements in price/performance that build on existing know-how within product classes'.[16] For example, the former UK Prime Minister, Margaret Thatcher, started her working career as a chemist. She was part of a research team that increased the amount of air in ice cream. This allowed ice cream manufacturers to cut their raw material costs while continuing to churn out the same volume of ice cream.

Just concentrating on start-ups also neglects other important aspects of entrepreneurial activity. Amancio Ortega Gaona is not an entrepreneur because he founded Zara but because he grew the fashion retailer from a single shop in Spain to an international conglomerate. Entrepreneurship also exists in corporate settings, involving 'individuals or groups of individuals, acting independently or as part of a corporate system, who create new organizations, or instigate renewal or innovation within an existing organization'.[17]

Corporate entrepreneurs might decide to set up a start-up from within their large business or independently (corporate venturing).[18] Another route is to renew an existing business by developing new innovative ways of meeting customer needs (strategic entrepreneurship). When Steve Jobs co-founded Apple, he was seen as an entrepreneur. But when he returned to the company in 1997 following 12 years away from the company, he might be better seen as a corporate entrepreneur who embarked on a process of strategic renewal and innovation (strategic entrepreneurship), which involved setting up new parts of the multinational technology company's business (corporate venturing).

Much of the discussion about entrepreneurship happens in the context of profit-driven business. However, many new ventures are established to meet social needs. Social entrepreneurship can be defined as 'individuals who are starting or currently leading any kind of activity, organisation or initiative that has a particularly social, environmental or community objective'.[19]

Case Study: What sort of entrepreneur is Muhammad Yunus?

Muhammad Yunus began lending small amounts of his own money to help people start a business to support their families during the 1974 famine in Bangladesh. His idea grew into Grameen Bank (literally the 'Bank of Villages'), a revolutionary social enterprise that provides credit to help poor people set up and run their own business. Grameen Bank invests in the business aspirations of people who – owing to their lack of assets – would otherwise be ignored by traditional lenders. Although it makes a profit, the main objective of the Grameen Bank is to lift people out of poverty. It now operates throughout Bangladesh and in other poor countries.[20]

Discussion questions:

- Is Yunus a Schumpeterian entrepreneur who has radically transformed society?
- Is he more like a Kirznerian entrepreneur who identified an existing problem and brought forward a solution for solving this need?
- The impetus underlying Yunus's motivation for setting up the Grameen Bank was to solve a societal problem rather than creating a vehicle for personal wealth: is this entrepreneurship?[21]

1.4 HOW IS ENTREPRENEURSHIP MEASURED?

Entrepreneurship can be assessed by counting the number of individuals in business or the number of businesses. Keeping score is important. For entrepreneurs, there are a number of public support schemes providing finance or business assistance (Chapter 12, pp. 311–316). To gain access to this support, some businesses choose to stay 'small'.[22] Policymakers and researchers also want to rank the entrepreneurial activities of regions and countries to benchmark entrepreneurial performance.

Assessment tip: Your unit of analysis is important

Assessments often ask for a discussion or a critical examination of 'entrepreneurship'. This means having a clear understanding of what the 'unit of analysis' is. Is it, for example, the individual or the business? Defining your units of analysis is good academic practice. Academic papers often explicitly define what terms mean, helping the reader to work out the focus of the paper. This is often particularly important in entrepreneurship studies because of the elastic and contested nature of 'entrepreneurship'.

1.4.1 The self-employed

Estimating the number of individuals engaged in entrepreneurship typically means counting the self-employed. These people work 'where the remuneration is directly dependent upon the profits (or the potential for profits) derived from the goods or services produced'.[23] Self-employment is a measure of entrepreneurship because it involves organising resources, identifying and exploiting opportunities and making decisions in dynamic and uncertain settings.[24]

Policymakers and researchers use self-employment as a proxy measure of entrepreneurial activity because it is one of the few standardised ways of comparing entrepreneurial activity across countries and regions. However, there are two reasons why it is a poor measure of the *quality* of entrepreneurial activity:

1. Some self-employed people are 'necessity entrepreneurs'. They may have only chosen entrepreneurship because they have no other way of getting work. Necessity entrepreneurs might not grow their business or be able to stay in self-employment for long. This is in contrast to 'opportunity entrepreneurs', who are motivated to grow their business.
2. Statistics on self-employment only count those formally registered as being self-employed. However, many people work for themselves without formally registering themselves as being self-employed.

1.4.2 Five common features of entrepreneurial activity

Despite its drawbacks, using self-employment as a proxy reveals five consistent features of entrepreneurial activity:

1. **Entrepreneurial activity varies markedly in richer countries.** Figure 1.1 shows that a little more than one in-20 USA workers are self-employed. This rises to just around one in eight in European countries such as the Netherlands. In Italy, Korea and Chile, anything from one in five to one-quarter of the workforce is self-employed. In Mexico, Turkey and Greece, it is one in three.

Figure 1.1 Self-employment rates in selected developed economies (data.oecd.org/emp/self-employment-rate.htm, author's calculations)

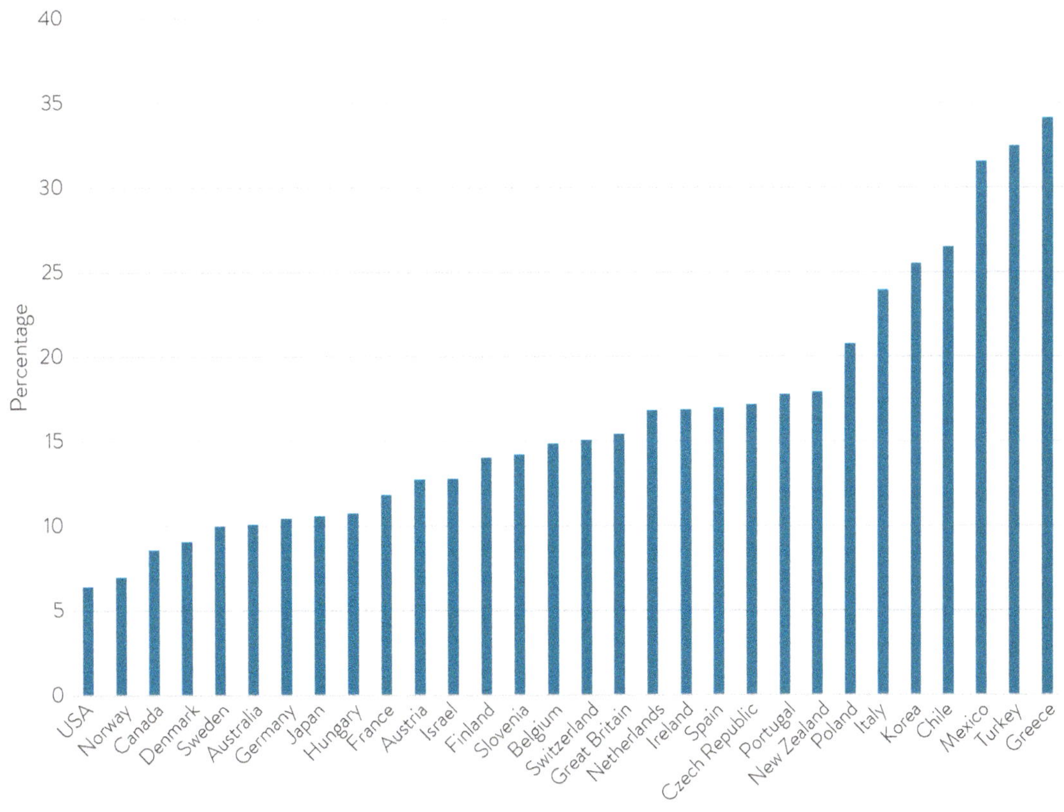

Source: Data compiled from data.oecd.org

> **Discussion questions:**
> - Why are self-employment rates so low in the USA? Isn't the USA supposed to be the land of entrepreneurship?
> - Why is self-employment so high in countries like Greece? Does this imply that Greece is a more entrepreneurial country than very many other rich countries?

2. **Entrepreneurial patterns vary over time in richer countries.** Figure 1.2 shows that the UK and the Netherlands have seen rising levels of self-employment. In contrast, in the USA and Norway, self-employment has been broadly flat or has declined.

Figure 1.2 Self-employment rates in the Netherlands, Norway, USA and UK (data.oecd.org/emp/self-employment-rate.htm, author's calculations)

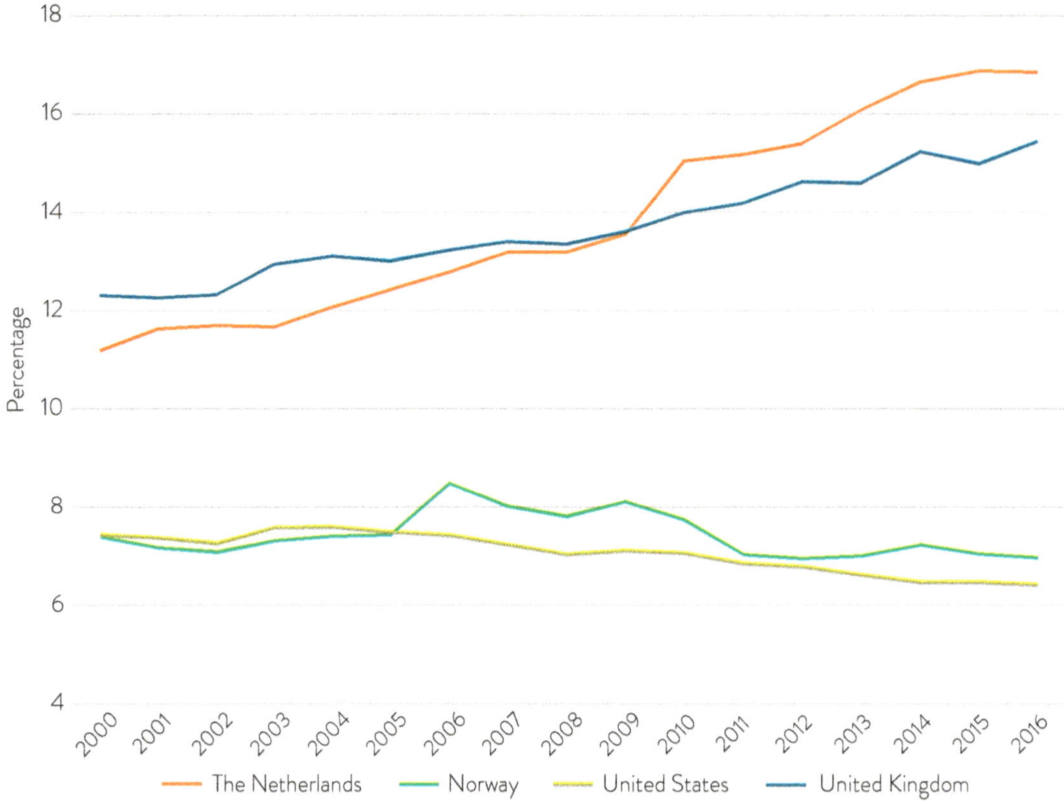

Source: Data compiled from data.oecd.org

Academic insight: Has there been an entrepreneurial revolution?

David Audretsch and Roy Thurik argue that large firms dominated richer economies until the 1980s.[25] These companies enjoyed economies of scale and scope, were more efficient and provided long-term job security for many workers. By contrast, small businesses paid their workers less, were less innovative and less productive. In the era of the 'managed economy', the number of small businesses was in long-term decline.

From the 1980s onwards, people in richer economies became wealthier, while changing tastes and a desire for variety created new niches for small firms. At the same time, it became easier to produce goods efficiently at a lower scale. The world became more connected through the development of new information and communication technologies, and the pace of globalisation increased. As a result, Audretsch and Thurik argue wealthier countries became 'entrepreneurial economies', driven forward by the innovations of job and wealth-creating small businesses.

However, there are flaws in this argument. Not all rich countries have seen large increases in their business populations. The overall number of enterprises in some countries has fallen. More telling is that small businesses remain less productive, pay their workers less and produce fewer innovations than large businesses.

1

A more critical and radical explanation is that there has been a transfer of the risks from large to small businesses. One illustration of this is the changes in the pharmaceutical industry. In the 1980s, giant drug companies employed thousands of scientists to develop new drugs. Today drug discovery is commonly driven by start-ups. This works for large multinational drug companies because they know that start-ups generally lack the resources to manufacture, market and distribute new drugs. Subsequently, start-ups bear all the risk of inventing new drugs while surrendering control of the commercialisation of their new drug to 'big pharma'.

Discussion question: Has there been a shift towards the entrepreneurial economy? Does this constitute a revolution?

3. **Men are more likely to be entrepreneurially active than women.** Figure 1.3 shows the differences between men and women self-employment rates in a range of rich countries. The biggest difference is in Ireland where 23 per cent of men are self-employed, compared to 8 per cent of women. In Figure 1.3, this equates to the 15 per cent difference. Canada and Chile have near equal rates of men and women in self-employment. In Turkey and Mexico, women are more likely to be self-employed than men.

Figure 1.3 Self-employment rates of men and women in richer countries (data.oecd.org/emp/self-employment-rate.htm, author's calculations)

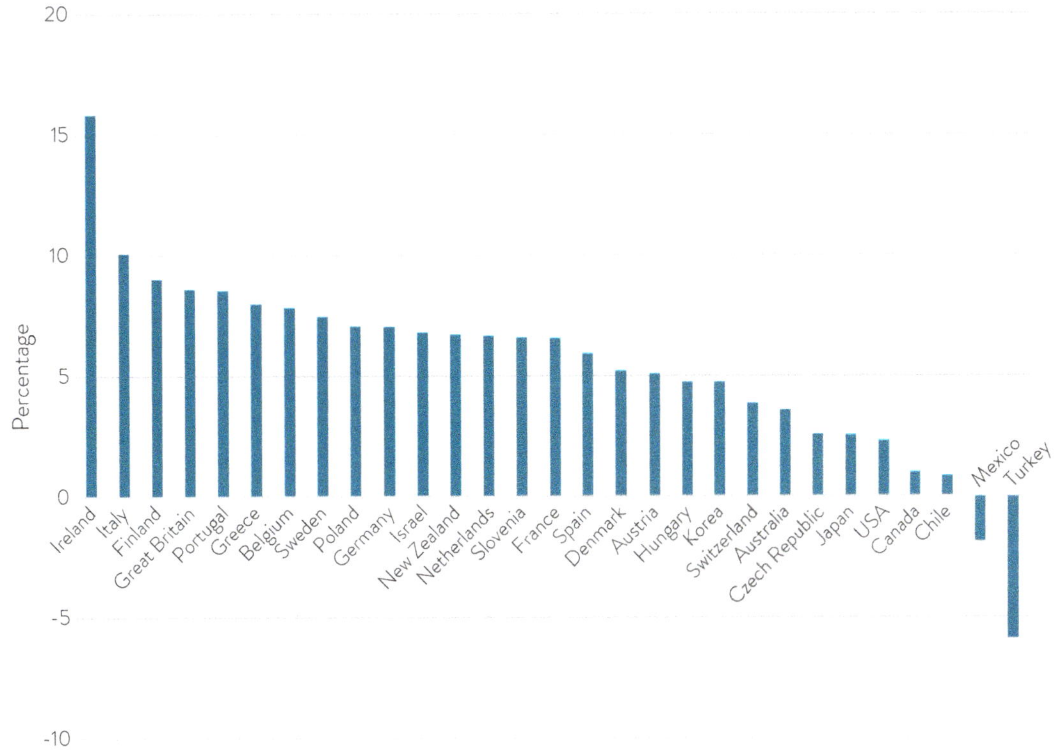

Source: Data compiled from data.oecd.org

Discussion questions:

- Why are there differences in the self-employment rates of men and women?
- Why are there higher rates of female self-employment in countries such as Turkey and Mexico? Do women have better life chances to men in these countries?

4. **Entrepreneurial activity is higher in poorer countries.** Self-employment in Côte d'Ivoire (Ivory Coast) was 80.5 per cent in 2012.[26] While this may have a little to do with differences in the ways some countries collect self-employment data, the bigger picture is that self-employment rates are associated with income levels.[27] In general, the less wealthy a country is, the greater the percentage of the labour force that is self-employed. Figure 1.4 shows that in high-income countries 13 per cent of people work for themselves or employ others. In low-income countries, 53 per cent of people either work for themselves or employ others.

Figure 1.4 Percentage of workers in employment and self-employment

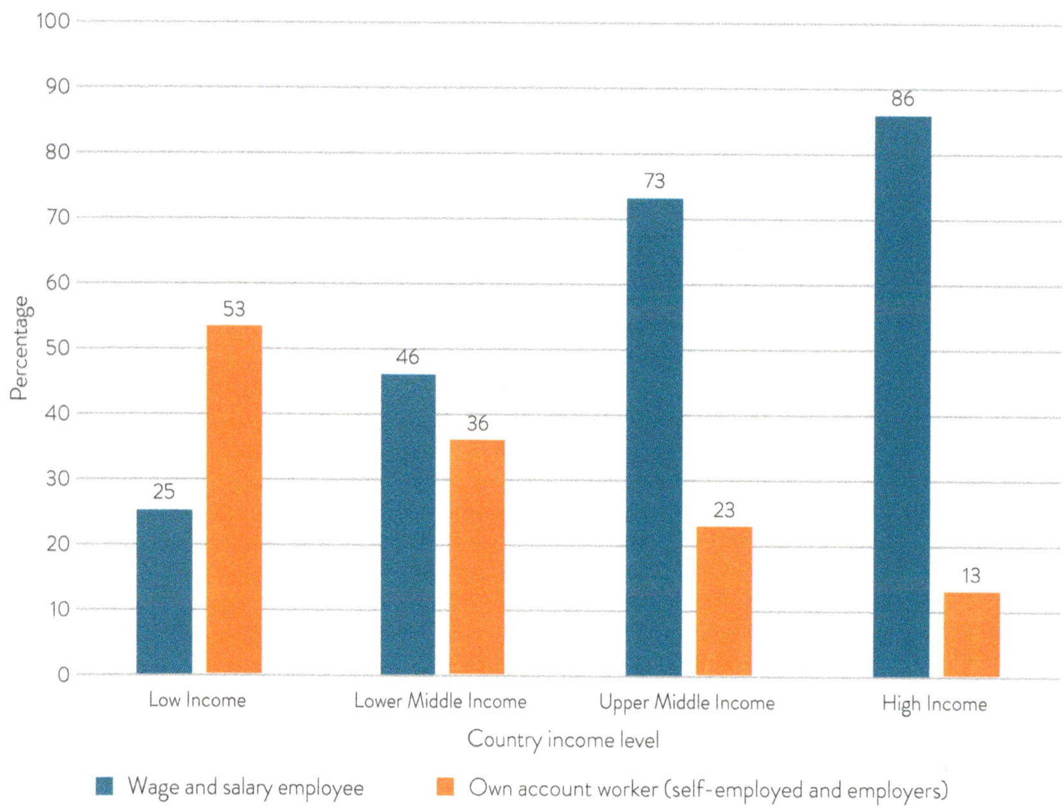

Source: Data compiled from Gindling and Newhouse (2014, Table 2)

Discussion questions:

- Is it fair to assume that most self-employed people in poorer countries are 'necessity entrepreneurs'? Why would there be high numbers of these types of entrepreneurs?
- Why do richer countries have lower self-employment rates than poorer countries?
- Is self-employment a good measure of entrepreneurial activity?

5. **Many self-employed people operate in hyper-competitive markets.** Self-employed workers are often concentrated in sectors that have few obstacles to entry and only require a limited amount of start-up capital. They typically choose sectors where there are few cost advantages to having a bigger operation and are disproportionately likely to be plumbers, electricians, restaurateurs, doctors, dentists, hairdressers, gardeners and small-scale retailers.[28]

Academic insight: Entrepreneurship in the animal kingdom

© PHOTODISCCC

The economist David Birch categorised businesses in three ways: elephants, mice and gazelles. Elephants are large firms. He felt that they were dominant in their marketplace but were slow and often lacking in innovation. Dick Smith was once a dominant force in Australia electronics retailing until it went bankrupt because it could not respond quickly enough to changes in the market.[29]

Birch's second group of animals are mice. These are the vast majority of smaller businesses. This is because the average small business has a short life span and provides little in the way of innovation, jobs or economic growth.[30] They also pay less and provide less training. 'Mice' tend to be the self-employed or small businesses such as hairdressers, car repairers or convenience stores.

The third group of animals in this business kingdom are gazelles. These are small but grow very quickly (more than 20 per cent per year) and are most likely to contribute to employment, productivity and economic growth. A variant of gazelles is 'unicorns' (new start-ups that grow to be valued at more than $1 billion). Gazelles (and unicorns) tend to be rare and hard to spot. Examples of these include Didi Chuxing, the Chinese ride-sharing company set up by Cheng Wei; the German car trading platform, Auto1 group, set up by Christian Bertermann and Hakan Koç; and Spotify, the Swedish music streaming service set up by Daniel Ek and Martin Lorentzon.

Discussion questions:

- Is this system of categorisation useful?
- Is it fair to describe large companies as 'elephants'?
- What would happen to your community if there were far fewer 'mice'?
- When we talk about entrepreneurship are we really talking just about 'gazelles'?
- Is it useful to draw a distinction between a small business owner and an entrepreneur? If so, in what ways can you distinguish between these two groups?

1.4.3 Measuring businesses

Counting the scale of entrepreneurial activity can also be done by looking at the size and distribution of businesses. This is important since limited companies rather than the self-employed – are more likely to create jobs and economic growth (Chapter 10, p. 247). Across 23 developed economies, business ownership increased from 30 million to 49 million over the period 1972–2008.[31] However, this masks wide differences between countries. Germany, the USA and the UK saw increases in their business population, while France's declined.

1.4.4 Counting the enterprise population

There is no agreed definition of a 'small' business. 'Smallness' is measured by assessing business sales, assets or, most commonly, number of employees. Thresholds vary between countries. Small businesses can be businesses with fewer than 20 employees (Australia), fewer than 250 employees (European Union) or fewer than 500 employees (the USA and Canada). They are often also known as Small and Medium-sized Enterprises (SMEs). In the European Union, SMEs are classified into three broad size groupings: micro-businesses (0–9 employees), small businesses (10–49 employees) and medium-sized businesses (50–249).[32]

Globally, 94.15 per cent of companies are micro-businesses, 4.98 per cent are small and 0.67 per cent are medium. This means that only 0.2 of businesses around the world are large. To put this into perspective, in Germany – Europe's biggest economy – there are only about 10,000 large businesses.

However, as these measures only count formal businesses, they can underestimate total entrepreneurial activity. In poorer economies, rates of informal work (work with no social protection) are high, ranging from around 80 per cent in East Asia to 45 per cent of all workers in the Middle East and North Africa.[33]

1.5 WHAT ARE THE DIFFERENCES BETWEEN LARGE AND SMALL BUSINESSES?

Another way of distinguishing small businesses is to work out how they think, act and behave differently from larger companies. This is important because small businesses are not scaled-down versions of larger firms. Table 1.2 shows some of the significant ways in which they differ.

Table 1.2 Key differences between small and large businesses

Aspect	Small business	Large business	What difference does it make?
Relative risk of failure	High	Low	Small businesses focus on short-term survival and improving their cash flows rather than their profits. Means that some will want to grow quickly to avoid failure. External funders are selective in who they choose to fund.
Uncertainty	Price taker; more likely to face external uncertainty; small number of customers.	Price maker; relatively greater internal uncertainty; large numbers of customers.	Smaller businesses tend to set prices based on competitors and focus on quality benefits such as convenience or service rather than cost advantages. Will fail if they lose and cannot replace their customers.
Management style	Owner-manager operated; informal undocumented management style; varied motivations for being in business such as family focused; lifestyle orientated, growth motivated.	Separation of ownership and management; formal procedural management style focus on shareholder value.	Have fewer business procedures in place; less formal training; rely on informal recruitment channels; unless a growing business will want to 'satisfice' rather than 'optimise' and be more of a 'lifestyle' business that the owner hopes will provide a comfortable living for them and their family.
Brand value	No brand value other than perhaps in their local community.	Focused on growing and protecting brands.	Small businesses spend relatively little on marketing whilst growing businesses want to build a brand.
Staff	Pay lower wages and provide fewer fringe benefits; higher job satisfaction rates.	Higher wages and better fringe benefits; lower job satisfaction rates.	Small and growing businesses are more likely to attract those attracted by a team ethic. There is a spectrum of small business workplaces: at one end, they can provide a happy environment while at the other end, they may be exploitative.
Strategy	Flexible, responsive to the customer, and innovative.	Focus on cost advantages, invests heavily in its resources, such as people.	Smaller sized businesses tend to focus on local markets. Growing businesses aim to disrupt existing marketplaces, export and focus on commercialising an innovation rather than just adopting an innovation.

Table 1.2 continued

Aspect	Small business	Large business	What difference does it make?
Financing	A limited number of sources. Small businesses prefer to use their own funds and are wary of using external financiers, such as banks or venture capitalists. Growth orientated businesses usually have to access external finance at some point.	A wide number of sources, such as debt funding from their bank or going to the stock market.	Small businesses 'bootstrap' resources; can struggle to get external finance; pay higher interest rates. Fast growth businesses can also struggle to access appropriate and affordable sources of external finance.

© Getty/Daniel Grizelj

Small and large businesses face different types of uncertainty. A large multinational firm with a significant market share and a well-known brand is less likely than a small business to experience *external* market or customer uncertainty. It is more likely to devote substantial resources to its operations, logistics and marketing. As it often benefits from economies of scale such as being able to buy in bulk at a reduced cost, it is also more likely to set prices ('price maker').

However, a multinational is more likely than a small business to experience *internal* uncertainty. Its size and geographic spread make it difficult for staff to buy into its strategy, mission and vision. Although it can invest in internal processes and communication mechanisms to support this, it is unlikely its leadership team will ever know the majority of employees by name or be able to monitor their work. A large firm can rely on middle management to bridge this gap, but this does not always help and may lead to further problems.[34]

Small businesses often lack the market share, brand recognition and economies of scale that larger companies enjoy. In the face of greater outside competition, they are more likely to face *external* uncertainty and have to be responsive to prices in the marketplace ('price takers'). They are also more likely to adopt a flexible strategy, one that focuses on service or convenience rather than on price. This can create problems if they are dependent on a small number of customers. If the tastes of these customers change, this can have dire consequences for the business.

Compared to large firms, small enterprises are less likely to face *internal* uncertainty, as their leadership is more visible and accessible. Entrepreneurs can also 'manage by walking about', which makes it easier to build worker understandings of their aims and goals. Although small business employees are often paid less, they have higher job satisfaction rates than comparable workers in large firms.[35] The self-employed are also more likely to be more content than employees, although this satisfaction can decline over time and differs between opportunity and necessity entrepreneurs and between poorer and richer countries.[36]

Small businesses remain more likely to fail than larger ones.[38] Another major difference between small and large ventures is their motivation for staying in business. Most small businesses are set up to meet non-monetary needs, such as someone wanting to be their own boss. Most of these entrepreneurs do not intend to grow their business beyond meeting their lifestyle needs, so rely on their personal resources to fund their venture.[39]

Small enterprises with growth ambitions often face a different challenge. If they are in the 'pre-revenue' (no sales yet) stage, they can struggle to secure external funding and be forced to stretch their resources or seek innovative ways of using their resources (bootstrapping) to develop their business.

In contrast, large firms often have access to multiple sources of funding from debt, such as bank lending through to equity financing from issuing shares in the business in return for money injections into the business.

Discussion question: What keywords best describe small, growing and large businesses?

Case Study: How red tape wrapped up the Vibe Bar

© iStock Unreleased

Alan Miller's Vibe Bar began from humble beginnings in a neglected corner of East London: 'When we started out in Brick Lane, we were told by many that nobody would visit, that it was a "no go" zone. But after getting in very early, the Vibe Bar acted as a sort of catalyst.' During its 20-year history, Vibe became one of the pre-eminent night-time destinations in this part of London and played a key role in transforming the area into a thriving and creative business hub. However, external changes beyond Miller's control ultimately led to the bar's closure: 'police officers working with licensing have made it very clear that things such as Temporary Event Notices, a type of licence that was used by many of the Brick Lane clubs to go on beyond 1 am, would no longer be permitted. Alongside that were a raft of other measures that contributed to my decision to shut Vibe Bar.'[37]

1.6 WHAT YOU HAVE LEARNED IN THIS CHAPTER

This chapter has introduced you to the idea that entrepreneurship plays an important role in our lives. You have also learned that entrepreneurship is a multidimensional phenomenon that has three core features:

1) Entrepreneurs make decisions under uncertainty.
2) The characteristics of the entrepreneur are important.
3) Contexts underscore entrepreneurial activity.

There remains, however, a lack of consensus about how to define entrepreneurship. This reflects that entrepreneurship is a slippery concept that is difficult to pin down.[40] Consequently, because it is often stretched to cover different individuals and contexts, you have to take care in how you choose to define entrepreneurship.

There is greater clarity about how you can count entrepreneurial activities such as self-employment or business ownership. Despite its problems, you were shown that examining self-employment rates reveals five consistent features of entrepreneurial activity. You can also classify businesses by size by dividing them into micro, small and medium-sized businesses. This, again, helps because it reflects the heterogeneity of entrepreneurial activity and enables you to compare entrepreneurship across regions and countries.

Finally, this chapter showed you that small businesses are not scaled-down versions of large companies. A key difference is that large firms are more likely to be price makers and are more likely to face internal uncertainty. By contrast, small businesses are more likely to be price takers and have relatively greater exposure to external uncertainty.

ASSESSMENT QUESTIONS

1. What are the key differences between large and small businesses?
2. Explain the difference between risk and uncertainty. Critically evaluate how differences between internal and external uncertainty influence small business activities and behaviours.
3. Describe the key differences between Schumpeter and Kirzner's views of the entrepreneur. Who better describes entrepreneurs?

4. Write up a case study of an entrepreneur. Are they more like the entrepreneur described by Kirzner or Schumpeter? Why is this?
5. Are entrepreneurs defined more by their characteristics or their behaviours?
6. Why is it difficult to define entrepreneurship?

FURTHER READING

Gartner, W. B. (1988). Who is an entrepreneur? Is the wrong question. *American Journal of Small Business*, *12*(4), 11–32.

Gindling, T. H., & Newhouse, D. (2014). Self-employment in the developing world. *World Development*, *56*, 313–331, Table 2.

Nightingale, P., & Coad, A. (2014). Muppets and gazelles: Political and methodological biases in entrepreneurship research. *Industrial and Corporate Change*, *23*(1), 113–143.

Shane, S., & Venkataraman, S. (2000). The promise of entrepreneurship as a field of research. *Academy of Management Review*, *25*(1), 217–226.

Notes

1 In Australia, there were 121,197 marriages registered in 2014. In the same year, there were 281,553 businesses set up. (www.abs.gov.au/AUSSTATS/abs@.nsf/DetailsPage/3310.02017?OpenDocument; (www.abs.gov.au/ausstats/abs@.nsf/DetailsPage/8165.0June%202014%20to%20June%202018?OpenDocument). In Sweden, there were 53,817 marriages and 68,113 new businesses in 2017 (www.scb.se/en/finding-statistics/statistics-by-subject-area/population/population-composition/population-statistics/pong/tables-and-graphs/yearly-statistics--the-whole-country/summary-of-population-statistics/; www.thelocal.se/20180102/this-is-how-many-new-businesses-were-started-in-sweden-in-2017). In Singapore, there were 28,212 marriages and 124,226 start-ups in 2017 (www.singstat.gov.sg/find-data/search-by-theme/population/marital-status-marriages-and-divorces/latest-data; www.singstat.gov.sg/find-data/search-by-theme/industry/formation-and-cessation-of-business-entities/latest-data – authors own calculation for start-up statistics for 2017). In the UK, there were 247,372 marriages and 350,305 start-ups (http://www.ons.gov.uk/peoplepopulationandcommunity/birthsdeathsandmarriages/marriagecohabitationandcivilpartnerships/bulletins/marriagesinenglandandwalesprovisional/2015; http://www.ons.gov.uk/businessindustryandtrade/business/activitysizeandlocation/datasets/businessdemographyreferencetable).

There were around 140 million children born in 2010 (ourworldindata.org/fertility-rate) and an estimated 250 million people trying to set up a business (Reynolds, P. D., & Curtin, R. T. (Eds.), (2011). *New business creation: An international overview*. New York: Springer).

2 In richer countries, anything between 40 and 80 per cent of the *current* labour force work in a small business: Criscuolo, C., Gal, P. N., & Menon, C. (2014). *The dynamics of employment growth: New evidence from 18 countries*. CEP Discussion Paper No. 1274, London. June.

3 Haltiwanger, J., Jarmin, R. S., & Miranda, J. (2013) Who creates jobs? Small versus large versus young. *Review of Economics and Statistics*, *95*(2), 347–361.

4 Ibid.

5 Financial Times. (2015). If Apple was a country. https://ftalphaville.ft.com/2015/01/28/2103622/if-apple-were-a-country.

6 Knight, F. (1921). *Risk, Uncertainty and Profit*. Boston, MA: Houghton Mifflin, p. 223.

7 Schumpeter, J. (1934). *The theory of economic development: An inquiry into profits, capital, credit, interest, and the business cycle* (trans. Redvers Opie, p. 38). Cambridge, MA: Harvard University Press, p. 38.

8 Schumpeter, J. (1942) *Capitalism Socialism, and Democracy*. New York: Harper and Row, p. 132.

9 www.improbable.com/ig/.

10 Tushman, M. L., & Anderson, P. (1986). Technological discontinuities and organizational environments. *Administrative Science Quarterly*, *31*, 439–465.

11 Israel, K. (1973) *Competition and entrepreneurship*. Chicago: The University of Chicago Press.

12 Gartner, W. B. (1989). Who is an entrepreneur? Is the wrong question. *Entrepreneurship Theory and Practice*, Summer, 47–67.

13 Fletcher, D. E. (2006). Entrepreneurial processes and the social construction of opportunity.

Entrepreneurship & Regional Development, 18(5), 421–440; Wood, M. S., & McKinley, W. (2010). The production of entrepreneurial opportunity: a constructivist perspective. *Strategic Entrepreneurship Journal, 4*(1), 66–84.

14 Gartner (1989), ibid., pp. 62 and 64.

15 Shane, S., & Venkataraman, S. (2000). The promise of entrepreneurship as a field of research. *Academy of Management Review, 25*(1), 217–226.

16 Tushman & Anderson (1986), ibid.

17 Sharma, P., & Chrisman, J. J. (1999). Toward a reconciliation of the definitional issues in the field of corporate entrepreneurship. *Entrepreneurship: Theory and Practice, 23*(3), 11–28, p. 17.

18 Kuratko, D. F., & Audretsch, D. B. (2013). Clarifying the domains of corporate entrepreneurship. *International Entrepreneurship and Management Journal, 9*(3), 323–335.

19 Bosma, N., Schøtt, Th., Terjesen, S. A., & Kew, P. (2016). *Global entrepreneurship monitor 2015 to 2016: Special topic report on social entrepreneurship* (p. 5). Babson: GEM.

20 Banerjee, A. V., Banerjee, A., & Duflo, E. (2011). *Poor economics: A radical rethinking of the way to fight global poverty.* Public Affairs.

21 www.grameen-info.org/about-us/.

22 Tsuruta, D. (2018) SME policies as a barrier to growth of SMEs. *Small Business Economics*, pp. 1-40.

23 https://stats.oecd.org/glossary/detail.asp?ID=2426.

24 Patzelt, H., & Shepherd, D. A. (2011). Negative emotions of an entrepreneurial career: Self-employment and regulatory coping behaviors. *Journal of Business Venturing, 26*(2), 226–238.

25 Audretsch, D., & Thurik, R. (2000). Capitalism and democracy in the 21st century: from the managed to the entrepreneurial economy. *Journal of Evolutionary Economics, 10*(1), 17–34.

26 https://data.worldbank.org/indicator/SL.EMP.SELF.ZS?locations=CI.

27 Gindling, T. H., & Newhouse, D. (2014). Self-employment in the developing world. *World Development, 56*, 313–331.

28 Hurst, E., & Pugsley, B. W. (2011). *What do small businesses do?* (Working Paper w17041). Cambridge, MA: National Bureau of Economic Research.

29 https://businessinsider.com.au/dick-smiths-administrators-have-outlined-the-8-underlying-causes-of-the-companys-collapse-2016-7.

30 Nightingale, P., & Coad, A. (2014). Muppets and gazelles: Political and methodological biases in entrepreneurship research. *Industrial and Corporate Change, 23*(1), 113–143.

31 Van Stel, A., Cieslik, J., & Hartog, C. M. (2010). *Measuring business ownership across countries and over time: Extending the COMPENDIA data base*, Scales Research Reports, H201019 (EIM Business and Policy Research) The Hague: Netherlands.

32 EU Commission. (2015). *SME definition.* https://ec.europa.eu/growth/smes/business-friendly-environment/sme-definition/index_en.htm.

33 www.wiego.org/informal-economy/statistical-picture.

34 Harris, L. C., & Ogbonna, E. (2010). Hiding customer complaints: studying the motivations and forms of service employees' complaint concealment behaviours. *British Journal of Management, 21*(2), 262–279.

35 Benz, M., & Frey, B. S. (2008). Being independent is a great thing: Subjective evaluations of self-employment and hierarchy. *Economica, 75*(298), 362–383; Larsson, J. P., & Thulin, P. (2018). Independent by necessity? The life satisfaction of necessity and opportunity entrepreneurs in 70 countries, *Small Business Economics*, 1–14.

36 Georgellis, Y., & Yusuf, A. (2016). Is becoming self-employed a panacea for job satisfaction? Longitudinal evidence from work to self-employment transitions. *Journal of Small Business Management, 54*, 53–76; Hanglberger, D., & Merz, J. (2015). Does self-employment really raise job satisfaction? Adaptation and anticipation effects on self-employment and general job changes. *Journal for Labour Market Research, 48*(4), 287; Kwon, I., & Sohn, K. (2017). Job dissatisfaction of the self-employed in Indonesia. *Small Business Economics, 49*(1), 233–249; Binder, M., & Coad, A. (2013). Life satisfaction and self-employment: a matching approach. *Small Business Economics, 40*(4), 1009–1033.

37 www.vice.com/en_uk/article/mv5wv3/were-closing-the-vibe-bar.

38 OECD. (2014). *Entrepreneurship at a glance.* Paris: OECD, Figure, 2.1.

39 Hurst & Pugsley (2011), ibid.

40 Penrose, E. T. (1995 [1959]). *The theory of the growth of the firm.* Oxford: Oxford University Press, p. 33.

CHAPTER 2

What Makes an Entrepreneur? Traits and Biases

Learning Outcomes

In this chapter, you will learn:

- Which personality traits are associated with entrepreneurship.
- The role that entrepreneurial intentions play in a start-up.
- How cognitive biases influence entrepreneurship.

Mini Contents List

2.1 INTRODUCTION

In 1977 a university dropout was arrested for running a red light and driving without a licence in the US city of Albuquerque, New Mexico. This was not his first traffic offence. His 'mug shot' was taken and he had to post bail. This young man was Bill Gates, the founder of Microsoft.[1] His behaviour shows a willingness to take risks – a propensity that may explain why, for a time at least, he became the world's richest man.[2]

In this chapter, you will examine how psychological traits influence people's choice to become entrepreneurs. Traits are psychological dispositions that remain stable across different contexts. A trait-based approach argues that entrepreneurs such as Bill Gates choose entrepreneurship because it fits in with their personality dispositions.[3] The three main traits are:

1. A propensity to take risks.
2. Locus of control (how much a person believes they have control over their lives).
3. A need for achievement.

You will also consider if some other traits, the 'big five' personality traits and human cognition influence entrepreneurial activity. Cognitive approaches – how individuals remember, perceive and think about situations – emphasise that the expression of personality is a product of both personality and an individual's context.[4] So, rather than there being fixed and stable entrepreneurial traits, cognitive approaches point to intentions and actions that vary depending on the situation faced by the entrepreneur. Two key approaches are Ajzen's theory of planned behaviour and Bandura's notion of the importance of self-efficacy. You will also see that Kahneman and Tversky's 'prospect' theory provides insights into how people cognitively edit and frame information and why resulting cognitive biases such as over optimism and over confidence are important in explaining entrepreneurial activities.

2.2 PSYCHOLOGICAL TRAITS

2.2.1 Risk-taking

You might choose entrepreneurship because you are more tolerant of risk. Risk-taking can be defined as a greater willingness to pursue uncertain decisions or courses of action even if there is uncertainty about success or failure.[5] The argument is that if you are a risk-taker you choose entrepreneurship because it gives expression to your personality and because you are better able to cope with uncertainty.

There is evidence of a positive correlation between risk-taking and entrepreneurship.[6] Young people who do risky things, such as breaking rules, dealing drugs and other antisocial behaviours, are more likely to be entrepreneurs later on in life.[7]

Meta-analytic studies – which combine evidence from many prior studies – reveal a small but positive association between risk-taking and entrepreneurship, with entrepreneurs being more risk-loving than managers, having stronger entrepreneurial intentions and being more likely to create businesses.[8]

However, there are good reasons for being sceptical about a strong relationship between risk-taking and entrepreneurship. One is methodological. Risk is measured in different ways, such as by assessing experimental and hypothetical risk situations and by using self-report surveys. This makes it difficult to compare results. In addition, some of the meta-analytic evidence draws on a crude distinction between entrepreneurs (the self-employed) and non-entrepreneurs (employees, managers). Such methodological issues can lead to the criticism of 'garbage in, garbage out'.

Another criticism is that entrepreneurs might *say* they are risk-takers but actually *behave* in similar ways to managers and employees.[9] One experiment, for example, found that the risk preferences of 700 randomly selected Chinese entrepreneurs differed little from a control sample of 200 non-entrepreneurs.[10]

Perhaps a more important reason to be cautious about assuming a strong association between risk and entrepreneurship is that it may misrepresent the start-up process. A key to a successful start-up process is turning uncertainties into manageable risks by better understanding customers, suppliers and competitors (see Chapter 1, p. 5) . Entrepreneurs do not seek out risks. Instead, they appear to accept risks grudgingly and prefer to focus on potential rewards. As one entrepreneur put it: 'My idea of risk and reward is for me to get the reward and for others to take the risks.'[11]

Discussion question:

- Are entrepreneurs more likely to have a psychological disposition towards taking risks?

© Getty Images/Klaus Vedfelt

Assessment tip: Description versus analysis

One of the challenges in academic writing is the difference between writing descriptively and analytically. Describing involves telling the reader about facts. Facts might be who wrote a study, when it was written, how many people took part and what its findings were. Describing is often necessary but remains only a small part of academic writing.

Writing analytically is more important. You have to weigh up, analyse, argue for and against and evaluate the evidence to develop an argument. One way of thinking about this is to imagine being part of a debate. To take part, you need some facts (description), but much more important is how you link the evidence, see strengths and weaknesses, think of alternatives and are careful about what you can and cannot say.

Take the question (see the end of this chapter): 'Is risk-taking central to entrepreneurship?'

An immediate challenge with this question is to define the meaning of 'risk-taking' and 'entrepreneurship' to guide the reader. A descriptive answer will list facts from studies on risk-taking. This is often a long summary of sources that itemise studies that are either for or against risk-taking being an entrepreneurial trait. But this approach leaves the reader with few clues as to where the balance of evidence lies and, crucially, if risk-taking is central to entrepreneurship.

Contrast this with the key features of an analytical answer:

- **Organises and synthesises source material** – what are the fundamental reasons for existing disagreements about why risk-taking may or may not play a central role in entrepreneurship?
- **Makes links and suggests alternative perspectives** – where do opposing arguments agree about the role that risk-taking plays in entrepreneurship? How does risk perceptions influence risk-taking? How do different entrepreneurial contexts and different types of entrepreneurs impact on entrepreneurial risk-taking?
- **Analyses where arguments are strong and identifies their weaknesses and omissions** – does an argument draw on methodologically flawed source material? Is the argument partial? Where is its logic strong and where does it fall down?
- **Evaluates arguments** – which of the opposing arguments is stronger and why? Like a judge, you have to weigh up the evidence and come to a judgement. The reader is often not particularly interested in the 'truth' of your answer; usually of more concern is the quality of your argument. Does it stick to evidence or rely on opinion? Is it a careful judgement that recognises the strengths and weaknesses of arguments? Are there holes in your logic?
- **Has implications** – any writing should mean something to someone. Usually, in entrepreneurial settings, an essay has implications for entrepreneurs, for academics or for policymakers. One challenge in identifying routes forward is the temptation to fall into opinion. You might advocate better entrepreneurial training for entrepreneurs to help evaluate risks, but how do you know if entrepreneurial training actually works?

2.2.2 Locus of control

A second trait associated with entrepreneurship is a person's locus (literally place or location) of control. The psychologist Julian Rotter defined locus of control as a 'generalised expectation that the outcome of an event is either within or beyond a person's control'.[12] He argued that if you believe you are the author of your own fortune (or misfortune) you have a high *internal* locus of control.

In contrast, those who have a high *external* locus of control believe events and outcomes are due to fate or luck. Because entrepreneurs have to be purposeful and self-directed, the expectation is that they will have a high internal locus of control.

Some meta-analyses find that entrepreneurs have a higher internal locus of control, although the association is small.[13] However, context-independent self-evaluations such as 'locus of control' have fallen out of fashion because there is now a better recognition of the role context plays in shaping entrepreneurial behaviours.

2.2.3 Need for achievement (nAch)

The psychologist, David McClelland, argued that if you have high levels of achievement motivation (nAch) you seek out contexts that provide moderate levels of risk-taking, allow you to take individual responsibility and give you direct feedback on your actions.[14] Meta-analyses suggest a small positive association between nAch and entrepreneurship.[15]

Discussion question:

- Wanting to achieve and believing that you can achieve are perhaps necessary conditions for starting up or growing a business. However, are they sufficient on their own to make an entrepreneur succeed?

2.2.4 The 'big five' and other psychological traits

Other personality traits associated with entrepreneurship include *stress tolerance*, the *need for autonomy* and a *tolerance for ambiguity*. The logic behind why these are important is that if someone can better cope with stress, actively seek out personal responsibilities and can cope with incomplete information they are better suited to entrepreneurship.[16]

Despite a huge range of studies, the evidence on whether, and if so why, entrepreneurs have particular traits remains weak. It is difficult to identify a single trait or combination of traits to explain the entrepreneurial 'personality'.[17] Proving an association (showing two factors are related) is not the same as causation (that one factor caused another). Entrepreneurs might rate high on stress tolerance or be tolerant of ambiguity because they have chosen an occupation that is both stressful and requires having to deal with ambiguity.

Faced with the multidimensional nature of people's personalities, trait-based approaches have increasingly made use of 'OCEAN', or the 'big five' personality dimensions:

1. Openness.
2. Conscientiousness.
3. Extraversion.
4. Agreeableness.
5. Neuroticism.

Measuring these dimensions is done by assessing levels of agreement with statements such as:

1. 'I have a vivid imagination' (Openness).
2. 'I like order' (Conscientiousness).
3. 'I talk to a lot of different people at parties' (Extraversion).
4. 'I am not really interested in others' (Agreeableness).
5. 'I am easily disturbed' (Neuroticism).

A meta-analysis of the 'big five' attributes found entrepreneurs were more likely than managers to score highly on Conscientiousness, Openness and Extraversion but less well on Agreeableness and Neuroticism. Another study found that Openness, Conscientiousness, Extraversion and Neuroticism had positive effects on entrepreneurial intentions and business profitability and operational effectiveness, while Agreeableness had a negative impact.[18]

Entrepreneurship in Action

- Take one of the free tests to measure your entrepreneurial dispositions (e.g. https://discovermyprofile.com/entrepreneurship.html).
- If you score higher on one or more of the 'big five' attributes associated positively or negatively with entrepreneurship, what does this say about how well you are suited to entrepreneurship or how your business might perform?

Academic insight: Is there a biological basis for entrepreneurship?

© Getty Images/iStockphoto

One of the emerging areas of entrepreneurship research is how biology influences entrepreneurial activity. This is rooted in the popular idea that entrepreneurs are born, not made. Entrepreneurship also runs in families: if your parents are self-employed, you are more likely to be self-employed (Chapter 3, p. 55). Risk propensities are similar between generations, and the children of self-employed parents tend to have higher risk-seeking tolerances.[19] Risk-taking can vary depending on your birth order: Han and Greene showed that last or middle borns are more likely to be entrepreneurs later on in life, while other studies have associated entrepreneurship with behavioural disorders such as Attention Deficit and Hyperactivity Disorder.[20]

Nicolaou and others have also investigated if there is a genetic basis of entrepreneurship. They examined if identical and non-identical twins had different chances of becoming entrepreneurs and found that a sizeable proportion of the variance in the likelihood of becoming self-employed was explained by genetic factors.[21] They have also argued that genetic factors are associated with entrepreneurial intentions, the 'big five' traits and creativity.[22]

However, it is still extremely difficult to identify whether an 'entrepreneurial gene' exists. For that to happen, large-scale genome-wide association studies are needed to examine all our genomes together rather than one by one.[23] This avoids 'false positives' (results that are positive but only because of statistical variation). Findings are not encouraging: Van der Loos and his colleagues studied 50,627 people but failed to find a genetic association with entrepreneurship.[24] The wider problem is that often the only source of large-scale data on entrepreneurship is self-employment, even though this is a crude measure of entrepreneurship (Chapter 1, p. 10).

Another route to understanding the biological basis of entrepreneurship is to examine hormones such as testosterone. This is a prime candidate because of its links with risk-taking. Some studies have found a small positive link between having higher levels of testosterone and entrepreneurial activity.[25] However, this often relies on an imprecise measure of testosterone (such as the ratio between the size of the second and fourth finger), small samples or on cross-sectional (snapshot) data.[26] This presents causal problems: is an association between entrepreneurship (self-employment) and testosterone due to high testosterone levels or is it because entrepreneurship induces high testosterone levels?

Current evidence suggests there is only a modest effect of biology on entrepreneurship. However, our understanding of the relationship may change as science continues to advance.

Discussion questions:

- Do you think that entrepreneurs are born or made?
- Is there a psychological 'identikit' picture of an entrepreneur?
- Examine the size ratio between your ring finger and your index finger. If there is a large difference between the size of these two fingers, do you agree that (a) it means you have greater levels of testosterone?; and (b) it increases your chances of being an entrepreneur?
- Much of the research on testosterone's link with entrepreneurship only looks at men. Men have higher levels of testosterone than women. Do you think that this explains the difference between men and women self-employment rates (Chapter 1, p. 13)?

2.3 PLANNED BEHAVIOURS AND SELF-EFFICACY

2.3.1 Planned behaviourt

Ajzen's theory of planned behaviour (Figure 2.1) argues that if we want to understand why someone acts in the way that they do, we have to examine their intentions.[27] For Ajzen, intentions – a person's readiness to behave in a certain way – are influenced by three factors:

- Their attitude to the behaviour (how hard they will try to achieve a particular behaviour).
- Perceived social norms (social pressures to achieve the behaviour).
- Their perceived behavioural control (how likely they believe that the behaviour is achievable).

Ajzen predicts that if you want to achieve something, believe you can do it and feel supported by your social network to succeed, you form positive intentionalities towards that activity. However, his theory does not examine how emotions or moods influence intentionalities. Applications of his theory are often reliant on cross-sectional data that takes 'snapshots' of entrepreneurial intentions.[28] This makes it difficult to disentangle causal relationships. The focus is also on students, who might say that they want to be an entrepreneur but actually choose employment when they leave university.

Figure 2.1 Ajzen's theory of planned behaviour

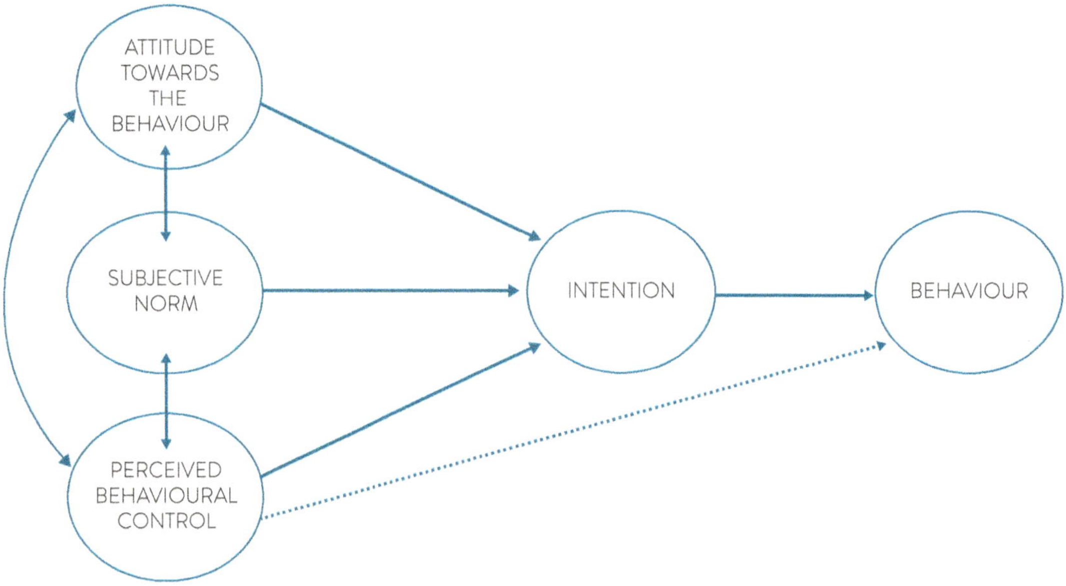

Few studies link intentions to actual entrepreneurial behaviour, although there is some evidence that entrepreneurial intentions do lead to entrepreneurial behaviours.[29]

2.3.2 Self-efficacy

Ajzen's concept of perceived behavioural control is closely related to Bandura's concept of self-efficacy. Self-efficacy is defined as being 'concerned with judgments of how well one can execute courses of action required to deal with prospective situations'.[30]

Superficially, self-efficacy is also similar to locus of control as both focus on how perceived control influences intentions and actions. The difference is that while locus of control is a trait that is independent of the situation, self-efficacy is situation dependent. You might believe that you have an aptitude for entrepreneurship but still believe that you are a poor driver, gardener or athlete. For Bandura, if you have high levels of self-efficacy, you believe that you can master challenges. Consequently, you commit to goals and weather any setbacks. In contrast, if you have low self-efficacy, you avoid the task, and if you have to pursue the task, you often do it half-heartedly and with little belief in achieving success.

As Figure 2.2 shows, Bandura suggests that self-efficacy has four sources:

- Knowledge and feelings gained from direct past experience.
- Vicarious learning from self and others.
- Social persuasion.
- Emotional status.

Bandura suggests the most likely way of building self-efficacy in a particular domain is having experience of successfully completing a task in that area. This builds resilience. Another route is observing others who achieve success.[31] If they are similar to you and they can complete a task, you will believe in your ability to do it. If it is not possible to observe others (vicarious learning) or rely

Figure 2.2 Bandura's concept of self-efficacy

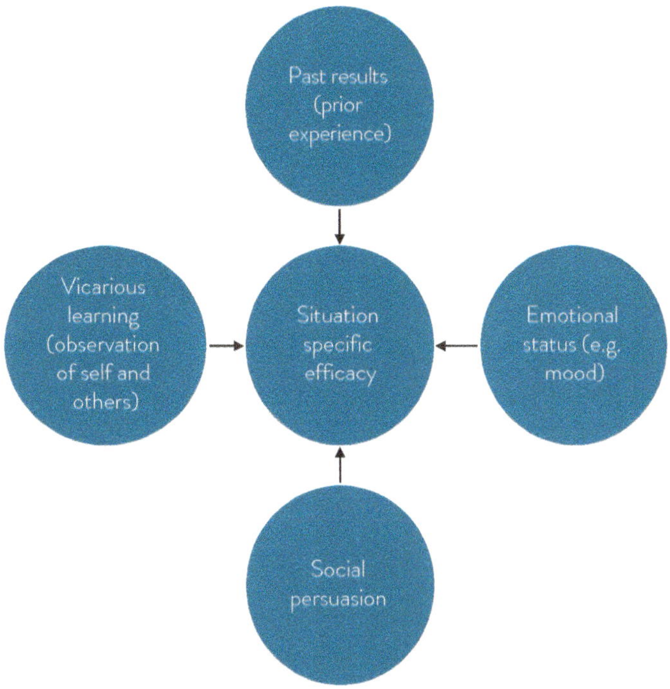

on past results (mastery experience), self-efficacy is likely to increase if you are in a positive mood or because you have experienced coaching and positive feedback.

Self-efficacy has led to the notion of entrepreneurial self-efficacy. This is a measure of 'a person's belief in their ability to successfully launch an entrepreneurial venture'.[32] It covers perceived capabilities in marketing, innovation, management, risk-taking and financial control. High levels of entrepreneurial self-efficacy appear to help set and achieve 'stretch goals' such as venture creation.[33]

Passion is also associated with achieving entrepreneurial goals because it aids task persistence or 'grit' and helps with developing strategies to achieve goals.[34]

These approaches recognise that we have flexible notions of intentions and self-efficacy. Self-efficacy suggests that we learn from our experiences and from others and that we are affected by our emotions and moods. If we lack passion or entrepreneurial self-efficacy – regardless of our actual capabilities – we are less likely to become entrepreneurs. One implication, therefore, is that if society wants to encourage entrepreneurship, it should provide education and training to develop an entrepreneurial mindset ('the ability to rapidly sense, act, and mobilize, even under highly uncertain conditions').[35]

Intentions, however, are a necessary but not sufficient condition for choosing entrepreneurship: just because you have strong intentions or passion does not mean that you are necessarily going to succeed in starting up or growing your business. Similarly, the relationship between passion and goal achievement can go both ways: effort spent on creating a start-up also impacts on passion and on the chances of creating a new business.[36] The emphasis also tends to be on the individual 'heroic' entrepreneur. This ignores team start-ups and downplays negative personality factors such as greed, ruthlessness, obsessive control and dishonesty.[37]

Discussion questions:

- Do you think that you can teach people to have an 'entrepreneurial mindset'? If so, what do you think your government should be doing to help?
- Ajzen's theory of planned behaviour acknowledges the importance of social networks in forming positive attitudes towards entrepreneurship. Do you think an entrepreneur's social network is just as important as their own beliefs and how hard they are prepared to work?
- Do you think that an entrepreneur's sense of control is innate (locus of control) or situation specific (self-efficacy)?

Indeed, a simpler explanation for why a person starts a business is because it is in their interest (see Chapter 3, pp. 44–49). This suggests that an entrepreneur should focus less on if they have the 'right' personality or drive towards entrepreneurship and more on having the appropriate training, support and finance in place before they start.

Entrepreneurship in Action

- Investigate a successful entrepreneur. Do you think that they have particular traits or is it more to do with being passionate or having an 'entrepreneurial mindset'?
- Interview an entrepreneur. Ask them what stimulated them towards becoming an entrepreneur. Was it to do with a recognition that their personality was suited to entrepreneurship, because they had strong role models, because they had relevant experiences or because they had strong entrepreneurial motivations?

2.4 COGNITIVE BIASES

2.4.1 Prospect theory

Prospect theory examines how we make decisions under uncertainty. It is based on the idea that humans have two basic ways of processing information: System 1 thinking (quick, automatic thinking) and System 2 thinking (slow, deliberative, analytical thinking). Automatic thinking is being able to locate where an unusual sound comes from. Deliberative thinking is counting how many times the word 'the' appears on this page.

The psychologists Amos Tversky and Daniel Kahneman argue that although we are capable of System 2 thinking, much of our decision-making – particularly under uncertainty – relies on System 1 thinking. This distinction is at the heart of prospect theory, which is descriptive (how people act) rather than normative (how people ought to act).[38]

2.4.2 Editing information

Prospect theory suggests there are two phases to our decision-making in uncertain contexts. The first is to edit information. Information about decisions is often incomplete, noisy and complex, so we use three simplifying strategies or heuristics (rules of thumb):

1. *Representative heuristic.* This rule of thumb is the tendency to use an earlier 'representative prototype' from your experience of a person, event or action to make judgements. Consider this description:
   - Alberto is good with numbers and likes to spend his spare time playing chess. Is Alberto an accountant or a salesman?

If you thought accountant, this indicates that you used representative (stereotypical) information. If you thought salesman, you might have realised that there are many more salesmen in the world than there are accountants.

This has implications for entrepreneurship. Venture capitalists use 'what success looks like' stereotypes. This results in them being more likely to fund experienced entrepreneurs.[39] Behaviours and attitudes based on negative stereotypes may also explain why women are less likely to start up.[40]

2. *Availability heuristic.* To ease and speed decision-making, we use easily recalled information. Take two individuals: one who spends all of their leisure time watching the news and another who only watches shopping channels. If they are asked how society has changed in recent years, the first person might say that crime, terrorism and corruption are on the increase, while the second person might say that the rate of new product innovation, particularly in kitchenware, is phenomenal.

Similarly, an entrepreneur may truncate their search for information, believing that they have enough information to make a judgement. Alternatively, they may find out that an entrepreneur has made a fortune by selling a novel 'superfood'. This may lead them to believe that a copy-cat business could be successful.

Case Study: Copy-cat businesses – Coffix's answer to overpriced coffee

© Alamy Stock Photo

Most copy-cat businesses struggle. Microsoft created Zune to compete with Apple's iTunes. Like iTunes, Zune provided users with the opportunity to download and listen to music. Despite spending millions on development and marketing, it never gained customer traction and was quietly closed down by Microsoft.

Occasionally, a copy-cat product or service works out. Mirela Martinescu set up New Zealand coffee chain Coffix to tap into the country's almost unquenchable thirst for coffee. But because entry costs are low and demand is high, the market is extremely competitive. She also noted that prices were high. So Martinescu's idea was to sell each type of her coffee – flat whites, cappuccinos, lattes and so on – for just one fixed price. In doing so, she undercut her competition and successfully franchised Coffix.

Entrepreneurship in Action

- Go to your local shopping area and identify which businesses are independent. How many of them are hairdressers, independent coffee shops and so on?
- How many of them look like copy-cat businesses that broadly offer the same range of services or products?
- Are there any independent businesses in your local shopping area doing anything different?

3. *Anchoring and adjustment heuristic.* Suppose there are two individuals. Independent and unknown to each other, one is presented with a bottle of champagne and asked two questions:

   (a) Is the champagne more or less likely to be worth £60?; and
   (b) How much would they pay for it?

A second person faces the same situation but is told that the champagne is worth £15. Again, they are asked how much they would pay for it.

These prices (£15 or £60) are 'anchors', and we use them to make guesses about the value of a good or service. If we are told the champagne costs £60, we are likely to base our guess on this anchor. But if we are told it is worth £15, we use this as the anchor price.

Anchoring matters in entrepreneurial contexts. For example, valuing a business is notoriously difficult and can come down to what the seller and the prospective buyer think it is worth. Reaching an agreement might be difficult if a buyer and seller use radically different anchors to frame negotiations about the value of the business.

We use cognitive heuristics to frame choices because they economise on decision-making. We use three main heuristics – representative, availability and anchoring and adjustment. Using these can lead to systematic biases because how choices are presented influences the choices we make. If you wanted to open a gym and worked out that you needed each customer to pay $350 for you to make a profit, is it better to advertise that the annual cost is $350 or to say that membership costs less than $1 a day?

2.4.3 Evaluating choices

Once we have edited or 'framed' our choices, we evaluate them in two ways. First, we consider whether the choice facing us will result in a gain or a loss, relative to a reference point such as our values, aspirations or personal experiences.

Here is an example. In this first scenario, you only have the choice of:

1. A certain $240 win.
2. A 25 per cent chance of winning $1000 and a 75 per cent chance of winning nothing.

You have to choose. Which of these two choices do you prefer?

In the second scenario, your choice is between:

1. A certain $750 loss.
2. A 75 per cent chance of losing $1000 and a 25 per cent chance of losing nothing.

Again, you must choose. Which of these two choices do you prefer?[41]

Although the expected probabilities are the same in both these scenarios, we are more likely to choose the certain gain in the first scenario and gamble in the second scenario. When we have a chance of a gain, we tend to be risk-averse. In a loss situation, we tend to be risk-loving.

Second, we overweigh small probabilities. We are happy to take the (almost) certain loss of buying a lottery ticket for the virtually non-existent chance of a huge gain. Similarly, we take out insurance against lightning (another almost sure loss) to prevent the small chance of being struck by lightning in the future.

The influence of framing, that risk propensities depend on whether we expect a gain or loss, and that we weigh probabilities differently, have led to the identification of cognitive biases. We are

prone to *confirmation bias* (only seeking out information that confirms our particular beliefs) and *hindsight bias* (the tendency to over estimate our ability to predict an event after it has occurred).

This can lead entrepreneurs to seek out information that only confirms beliefs such as that their market is buoyant. Hindsight bias is also common: entrepreneurs were asked to predict the chances of their business failing before and after it failed. It turns out that they were optimistic about their business prospects while their business was still running. However, once it had closed, they said that they 'knew all along' that closure was going to occur.[42]

2.4.4 Over optimism and over confidence

Two other biases are particularly prevalent among entrepreneurs: over optimism and over confidence. Over optimism is the tendency to believe that negative events are less likely to occur and, by implication, that positive events are more likely.[43] This is a common bias. Ask a newly wedded couple how long they think they will be married, you might get: 'We are so happy, we will be together forever.' A realist might, however, say: 'I reckon that we have about a 50 per cent chance of not divorcing' Although the second comment is closer to the truth in the USA, individuals still expect divorce to happen to others and not to them.[44]

Entrepreneurs are 'super-optimists'. When asked, 81 per cent of entrepreneurs said their chances of success were more than 70 per cent while one-third of them thought they were 100 per cent likely to be successful.[45] While this also reflects a bias towards self-justifying actions, entrepreneurs remain super-optimists, particularly in relation to their life expectancy, their future sales, abilities and survival chances.[46] This is particularly true if they believe they are able, that outcomes are within their control and they have an emotional commitment to their start-up. These are all common features of entrepreneurship: entrepreneurs have to commit financial resources, back their ability and emotionally invest in a new business, even though the information about their chances of success is both incomplete and unclear.[47]

Closely related to over optimism is over confidence. This occurs in three main ways:

1. Over estimating our ability to conduct a task.
2. Over estimating our performance relative to others (the 'I am better than the average' effect).
3. Over precision in judgements about the accuracy of our beliefs.

Although these effects are different, they are often muddled together, often alongside over-optimism.[48]

Those who are more over confident about their abilities are more likely to become entrepreneurs. They are also more prone to suffer 'competition neglect'.[49] An entrepreneur might set up a new restaurant but ignore that there are already a number of established restaurants in the area. This can lead to the early termination of a business. Over confidence can also stifle innovation. If entrepreneurs are more certain in their judgements, they tend to exploit an existing product rather than explore a new product.[50]

The negative consequence of over confidence is that it leads entrepreneurs to underfund their new business, thereby threatening its viability.[51] Entrepreneurs may also stick with a business that does not produce economic returns because of a mistaken belief that business prospects will improve.[52]

Further, over optimism can lead to lower entrepreneurial income levels and choosing sectors that are 'easy' to enter, even if these sectors are hyper-competitive and have thin average profits.[53] It also has wider impacts. It might drive out 'realistic' entrepreneurs who would be better able to take advantage of a business opportunity.[54] Equally, if banks cannot distinguish between those who are rational and those who have 'irrational exuberance', they may restrict credit to 'rational' entrepreneurs.[55]

On the upside, over optimistic entrepreneurs are less likely to follow their peers and therefore provide greater novelty in the marketplace.[56] Such biases also promote entrepreneurial effort and persistence because if someone believes that a goal is attainable and desirable, they are more likely to work hard to achieve it.

In situations where accurate information is hard to come by or incomplete, entrepreneurs use cognitive 'rules of thumb' to economise their decision-making. Being a 'super optimist' creates challenges. Yet having unrealistic expectations about the future and individual personal abilities is perhaps a necessary condition for entrepreneurial entry because 'the people who have the greatest influence on the lives of others are likely to be optimistic and overconfident, and to take more risks than they realize'.[57]

Discussion questions:

- If our risk appetite varies depending on whether or not we face a gain or a loss situation, what does this say about risk-taking being a personality trait?
- Would pessimists make better entrepreneurs?

Go to Exercise W 1.1: Do your personality attributes incline you towards entrepreneurship?

2.5 WHAT YOU HAVE LEARNED IN THIS CHAPTER

This chapter has shown you that there are psychological explanations for why some individuals choose entrepreneurship and others do not. You have learned that there are three main personality traits associated with entrepreneurial activities: risk-taking, locus of control and the need for achievement. These remain popular explanations because they chime with the idea that entrepreneurship is risky and the entrepreneur has to be a self-starter to succeed. The actual evidence, however, indicates that entrepreneurs tend not to be risk-lovers but prefer to take informed risks.

The chapter then showed that entrepreneurial intentions and self-efficacy are important. These differ from traits because they suggest that the situation or context is important in explaining why some people choose an activity. There is some evidence that people who form stronger motivations towards entrepreneurship and have greater levels of self-efficacy are more likely to choose entrepreneurship.

Subsequently, you have considered how cognitive biases influence entrepreneurial activities. Prospect theory suggests that in situations of uncertainty, we are prone to using heuristic rules of thumb to edit information. How the information is framed also influences the decisions we make. This shows that risk-taking is not just to do with personality traits but also varies, depending on whether we believe that we face a winning or losing situation. Finally, you have been shown that particular cognitive biases are important, with entrepreneurs being more likely to be 'super-optimists'.

ASSESSMENT QUESTIONS

1. Identify three core traits associated with entrepreneurs. Do you think that these traits provide insights into why some people but not others choose entrepreneurship?
2. What are the main cognitive biases associated with entrepreneurship? What implications do these cognitive biases have for the understanding of entrepreneurship?
3. Is risk-taking central to entrepreneurship?
4. Explain Ajzen's theory of planned behaviour. What implications does it have for understanding start-up activity?
5. What role does biology play in entrepreneurial activities?
6. Explain Bandura's notion of self-efficacy. Do you think that it provides a good explanation for entrepreneurial activity?

FURTHER READING

Greene, F. J., Han, L., Martin, S., Zhang, S., & Wittert, G. (2014). Testosterone is associated with self-employment among Australian men. *Economics & Human Biology*, 13, 76–84.

Hayward, M. L. A., Shepherd, D. A., & Griffin, D. (2006). A hubris theory of entrepreneurship. *Management Science*, 52(2), 160–172.

Kahneman, D. (2011). *Thinking, fast and slow*. London: Macmillan.

Kautonen, T., van Gelderen, M., & Fink, M. (2015). Robustness of the theory of planned behavior in predicting entrepreneurial intentions and actions. *Entrepreneurship Theory and Practice*, 39(3), 655–674.

Nicolaou, N., Shane, S., Cherkas, L., Hunkin, J., & Spector, T. D. (2008). Is the tendency to engage in entrepreneurship genetic? *Management Science*, 54(1), 167–179.

Zhao, H., Seibert, S. E., & Lumpkin, G. T. (2010). The relationship of personality to entrepreneurial intentions and performance: A meta-analytic review. *Journal of Management*, 36(2), 381–404.

Notes

1 www.mugshots.org/misc/bill-gates.html.

2 www.forbes.com/billionaire (2016).

3 Markman, G. D., & Baron, R. A. (2003). Person–entrepreneurship fit: Why some people are more successful as entrepreneurs than others. *Human Resource Management Review, 13*(2), 281–301.

4 Mischel, W. (1968). *Personality and assessment*. New York: Wiley.

5 Zhao, H., Seibert, S. E., & Lumpkin, G. T. (2010). The relationship of personality to entrepreneurial intentions and performance: A meta-analytic review. *Journal of Management, 36*(2), 381–404.

6 Colombier, N., Boemont, L. D., Loheac, Y., & Masclet, D. (2008). Risk aversion: An experiment with self-employed workers and salaried workers. *Applied Economics Letters, 15*(10), 791–795; Ekelund, J., Johansson, E., Jarvelin, M. R., & Lichtermann, D. (2005). Self-employment and risk aversion – Evidence from psychological test data. *Labour Economics, 12*(5), 649–659.

7 Fairlie, R. W. (2002). Drug dealing and legitimate self-employment. *Journal of Labor Economics, 20*(3), 538–567; Obschonka, M., Andersson, H., Silbereisen, R. K., & Sverke, M. (2013). Rule-breaking, crime, and entrepreneurship: A replication and extension study with 37-year longitudinal data. *Journal of Vocational Behavior, 83*(3), 386–396.

8 Stewart, W. H., & Roth, P. L. (2001). Risk propensity differences between entrepreneurs and managers: A meta-analytic review. *Journal of Applied Psychology, 86*(1), 145–153; Zhao et al. (2010), ibid.; Zhao, H., & Seibert, S. E. (2006). The big five personality

dimensions and entrepreneurial status: A meta-analytical review. *Journal of Applied Psychology, 91*(2), 259–271; Rauch, A., & Frese, M. (2007). Let's put the person back into entrepreneurship research: A meta-analysis on the relationship between business owners' personality traits, business creation, and success. *European Journal of Work and Organizational Psychology, 16*(4), 353–385.

9 Koudstaal, M., Sloof, R., & Van Praag, M. (2015). Risk, uncertainty, and entrepreneurship: Evidence from a lab-in-the-field experiment. *Management Science, 62*(10), 2897–2915.

10 Holm, H. J., Opper, S., & Nee, V. (2013). Entrepreneurs under uncertainty: An economic experiment in China. *Management Science, 59*(7), 1671–1687.

11 Stevenson, H. H. (1983). *A perspective on entrepreneurship* (pp. 1–13, p. 2). Cambridge, MA: Harvard Business School.

12 Rotter, J. B. (1966). Generalised expectancies for internal versus external control of reinforcement. *Psychological Monographs: General and Applied, 80*(1), 1–28, p. 1.

13 Rauch & Frese (2007), ibid.

14 McClelland, D. C. (1961). *The achieving society.* Princeton, NJ: Van Nostrand.

15 Collins, C. J., Hanges, P. J., & Locke, E. A. (2004). The relationship of achievement motivation to entrepreneurial behavior: A meta-analysis. *Human Performance, 17*(1), 95–117; Stewart, W. H., & Roth, P. L. (2007). A meta-analysis of achievement motivation differences between entrepreneurs and managers. *Journal of Small Business Management, 45*(4), 401–421.

16 Rauch & Frese (2007), ibid.

17 Chell, E. (2008). *The entrepreneurial personality: A social construction.* London: Routledge.

18 Zhao & Seibert (2006), ibid.; Zhao et al. (2010), ibid.

19 Hryshko, D., Luengo-Prado, M. J., & Sorensen, B. E. (2011). Childhood determinants of risk aversion: The long shadow of compulsory education. *Quantitative Economics, 2*(1), 37–72; Charles, K. K., & Hurst, E. (2003). The correlation of wealth across generations. *Journal of Political Economy, 111*(6), 1155–1182; De Paolo, M. (2013). The determinants of risk aversion: The role of intergenerational transmission. *German Economic Review, 14*(2), 214–234.

20 Han, L., & Greene, F. J. (2016). Are "born to rebel" last-borns more likely to be self-employed? *Personality and Individual Differences, 101*, 270–275; Wiklund, J., Yu, W., Tucker, R., & Marino, L. D. (2017). ADHD, impulsivity and entrepreneurship. *Journal of Business Venturing, 32*(6), 627–656; Canits, I., Bernoster, I., Mukerjee, J., Bonnet, J., Rizzo, U., & Rosique-Blasco, M. (2018). Attention-deficit/hyperactivity disorder (ADHD) symptoms and academic entrepreneurial preference: Is there an association? *Small Business Economics, 53*(2), 369–380; Verheul, I., Rietdijk, W., Block, J., Franken, I., Larsson, H., & Thurik, R. (2016). The association between attention-deficit/hyperactivity (ADHD) symptoms and self-employment. *European Journal of Epidemiology, 31*(8), 793–801; Lerner, D. A., Verheul, I., & Thurik, R. (2018). Entrepreneurship and attention deficit/hyperactivity disorder: A large-scale study involving the clinical condition of ADHD. *Small Business Economics, 53*(2), 381–392.

21 Nicolaou, N., Shane, S., Cherkas, L., Hunkin, J., & Spector, T. D. (2008). Is the tendency to engage in entrepreneurship genetic? *Management Science, 54*(1), 167–179.

22 Nicolaou, N., & Shane, S. (2010). Entrepreneurship and occupational choice: Genetic and environmental influences. *Journal of Economic Behavior & Organization, 76*(1), 3–14; Shane, S., Nicolaou, N., Cherkas, L., & Spector, T. D. (2010). Genetics, the big five, and the tendency to be self-employed. *Journal of Applied Psychology, 95*(6), 1154–1162; Shane, S., & Nicolaou, N. (2015). Creative personality, opportunity recognition and the tendency to start businesses: A study of their genetic predispositions. *Journal of Business Venturing, 30*(3), 407–419.

23 Van der Loos, M. J., Koellinger, P. D., Groenen, P. J., Rietveld, C. A., Rivadeneira, F., van Rooij, F. J., et al. (2011). Candidate gene studies and the quest for the entrepreneurial gene. *Small Business Economics, 37*(3), 269–275.

24 Van der Loos, M. J., Rietveld, C. A., Eklund, N., Koellinger, P. D., Rivadeneira, F., Abecasis, G. R., et al. (2013). The molecular genetic architecture of self-employment. *Plos One, 8*(4), e60542.

25 Greene, F. J., Han, L., Martin, S., Zhang, S., & Wittert, G. (2014). Testosterone is associated with self-employment among Australian men. *Economics & Human Biology, 13*, 76–84; White, R. E., Thornhill, S., & Hampson, E. (2006). Entrepreneurs and evolutionary biology: The relationship between testosterone and new venture creation. *Organizational Behavior and Human Decision Processes, 100*(1), 21–34; Bönte, W., Procher, V. D., & Urbig, D. (2015). Biology and selection into entrepreneurship – The relevance of prenatal testosterone exposure. *Entrepreneurship Theory and Practice, 40*(5), 1121–1148; Unger, J. M., Rauch, A., Weis, S. E., & Frese, M. (2015). Biology (prenatal testosterone), psychology (achievement need) and entrepreneurial impact. *Journal of Business Venturing Insights, 4*, 1–5; Nicolaou, N., Patel, P. C., Wolfe, M. T. (2017). Testosterone and tendency to engage in self-employment. *Management Science, 64*(4), 1825–1841.

26 Van der Loos, M. J., Haring, R., Rietveld, C. A., Baumeister, S. E., Groenen, P. J., Hofman, A., et al. (2013). Serum testosterone levels in males are not associated with entrepreneurial behavior in two independent observational studies. *Physiology & Behavior, 119*, 110–114.

27 Ajzen, I. (1991). The theory of planned behavior. *Organizational Behavior and Human Decision Processes, 50*(2), 179–211.

28 Krueger, N. F., Reilly, M. D., & Carsrud, A. L. (2000). Competing models of entrepreneurial intentions. *Journal of Business Venturing, 15*(5–6), 411–432; Schlaegel, C., & Koenig, M. (2014). Determinants of entrepreneurial intent: A meta-analytic test and integration of competing models. *Entrepreneurship Theory and Practice, 38*(2), 291–332.

29 Kautonen, T., Gelderen, M., & Fink, M. (2015). Robustness of the theory of planned behavior in predicting entrepreneurial intentions and actions. *Entrepreneurship Theory and Practice, 39*(3), 655–674.

30 Bandura, A. (1982). Self-efficacy mechanism in human agency. *American Psychologist, 37*(2), 122.

31 Zozimo, R., Jack, S., & Hamilton, E. (2017). Entrepreneurial learning from observing role models. *Entrepreneurship & Regional Development, 29*(9–10), 889–911; Bosma, N., Hessels, J., Schutjens, V., Van Praag, M., & Verheul, I. (2012). Entrepreneurship and role models. *Journal of Economic Psychology, 33*(2), 410–424.

32 McGee, J. E., Peterson, M., Mueller, S. L., & Sequeira, J. M. (2009). Entrepreneurial self-efficacy: Refining the measure. *Entrepreneurship Theory and Practice, 33*(4), 965–988.

33 Miao, C., Qian, S., & Ma, D. (2017). The relationship between entrepreneurial self-efficacy and firm performance: A meta-analysis of main and moderator effects. *Journal of Small Business Management, 55*(1), 87–107.

34 Cardon, M. S., Wincent, J., Singh, J., & Drnovsek, M. (2009). The nature and experience of entrepreneurial passion. *Academy of Management Review, 34*(3), 511–532; Latham, G. P., & Locke, E. (1990). *A theory of goal setting and task performance.* Englewood Cliffs, NJ: Prentice-Hall; Mueller, B. A., Wolfe, M. T., & Syed, I. (2017). Passion and grit: An exploration of the pathways leading to venture success. *Journal of Business Venturing, 32*(3), 260–279.

35 McGrath, R. G., & MacMillan, I. C. (2000). *The entrepreneurial mindset: Strategies for continuously creating opportunity in an age of uncertainty* (Vol. 284, p. xv). Boston: Harvard Business Review Press.

36 Gielnik, M. M., Spitzmuller, M., Schmitt, A., Klemann, D. K., & Frese, M. (2015). "I put in effort, therefore I am passionate": Investigating the path from effort to passion in entrepreneurship. *Academy of Management Journal, 58*(4), 1012–1031.

37 Miller, D. (2015). A downside to the entrepreneurial personality? *Entrepreneurship Theory and Practice, 39*(1), 1–8.

38 Kahneman, D., & Tversky, A. (1979). Prospect theory: An analysis of decision under risk. *Econometrica: Journal of the Econometric Society, 47*(2), 263–291; Kahneman, D. (2011). *Thinking, Fast and Slow.* London: Macmillan.

39 Gompers, P., Kovner, A., Lerner, J., & Scharfstein, D. (2010). Performance persistence in entrepreneurship. *Journal of Financial Economics, 96*(1), 18–32.

40 Greene, F. J., Han, L., & Marlow, S. (2013). Like mother, like daughter? Analyzing maternal influences upon women's entrepreneurial propensity. *Entrepreneurship Theory and Practice, 37*(4), 687–711.

41 Kahneman (2011), ibid.

42 Cassar, G., & Craig, J. (2009). An investigation of hindsight bias in nascent venture activity. *Journal of Business Venturing, 24*(2), 149–164.

43 Ucbasaran, D., Westhead, P., Wright, M., & Flores, M. (2010). The nature of entrepreneurial experience, business failure and comparative optimism. *Journal of Business Venturing, 25*(6), 541–555.

44 Baker, L. A., & Emery, R. E. (1993). When every relationship is above average. *Law and Human Behavior, 17*(4), 439–450.

45 Cooper, A. C., Woo, C. Y., & Dunkelberg, W. C. (1988). Entrepreneurs' perceived chances for success. *Journal of Business Venturing, 3*(2), 97–108.

46 Busenitz, L. W., & Barney, J. B. (1997). Differences between entrepreneurs and managers in large organizations: Biases and heuristics in strategic decision-making. *Journal of Business Venturing, 12*(1), 9–30; Puri, M., & Robinson, D. T. (2007). Optimism and economic choice. *Journal of Financial Economics, 86*(1), 71–99; Cassar, G. (2010). Are individuals entering self-employment overly optimistic? An empirical test of plans and projections on nascent entrepreneur expectations. *Strategic Management Journal, 31*(8), 822–840; Townsend, D. M., Busenitz, L. W., Arthurs, J. D. (2010). To start or not to start: Outcome and ability expectations in the decision to start a new venture. *Journal of Business Venturing, 25*(2), 192–20; Dawson, C., & Henley, A. (2013). Over-optimism and entry and exit from self-employment. *International Small Business Journal, 31*(8), 938–954.

47 Koellinger, P., Minniti, M., & Schade, C. (2007). "I think I can, I think I can": Overconfidence and entrepreneurial behavior. *Journal of Economic Psychology, 28*(4), 502–527.

48 Moore, D. A., & Healy, P. J. (2008). The trouble with overconfidence. *Psychological Review, 115*(2), 502.

49 Camerer, C., & Lovallo, D. (1999). Overconfidence and excess entry: An experimental approach. *The American Economic Review, 89*(1), 306–318.

50 Herz, H., Schunk, D., & Zehnder, C. (2014). How do judgmental overconfidence and over-optimism shape innovative activity? *Games and Economic Behavior, 83*, 1–23.

51 Hayward, M. L. A., Shepherd, D. A., & Griffin, D. (2006). A hubris theory of entrepreneurship. *Management Science, 52*(2), 160–172.

52 Landier, A., & Thesmar, D. (2009). Financial contracting with optimistic entrepreneurs. *Review of Financial Studies, 22*(1), 117–150.

53 de Meza, D., Dawson, C., Henley, A., & Arabsheibani, G. R. (2019). Curb your enthusiasm: Optimistic entrepreneurs earn less. *European Economic Review,*

111, 53–69; Moore, D. A., & Cain, D. M. (2007). Overconfidence and underconfidence: When and why people underestimate (and overestimate) the competition. *Organizational Behavior and Human Decision Processes, 103*(2), 197–213.

54 de Meza, D. (2002). Overlending? *Economic Journal, 112*(477), F17–F31.

55 de Meza, D., & Southey C. (1996). The borrower's curse: Optimism, finance and entrepreneurship. *The Economic Journal, 106*(435), 375–386.

56 Bernardo, A. E., & Welch, I. (2001). On the evolution of overconfidence and entrepreneurs. *Journal of Economics & Management Strategy, 10*(3), 301–330.

57 Kahneman (2011), ibid.

CHAPTER 3

Entrepreneurial Characteristics and Contexts

Learning Outcomes

In this chapter, you will learn:

- How to use the occupational choice framework to understand start-up decisions.
- What motivates entrepreneurs and how their experiences and background influence the entrepreneurial choice.
- Why entrepreneurial contexts are important.

Mini Contents List

3.1 INTRODUCTION

Is having a business idea at university a good reason to drop out?[1] Bill Gates and Mark Zuckerberg did, and they went on to become two of the world's wealthiest people.[2] Or is staying at university better because most self-made billionaires have a university degree?[3]

Should you stay in a boring job with punishing hours or quit and start your own business? Is the lure of following your dream and the chance of making it big enough to sacrifice financial security in the short term?

Economists answer these questions by comparing the expected relative returns of one choice against another. They suggest people will choose one occupation over another if they believe the return is *relatively* greater. So they say that you will give up your job or studies for venture creation if you think that you will gain greater benefits from running your own business.

Known as the occupational choice framework, this simple economic model has developed over time to show why some individuals choose to become entrepreneurs. At its core is the concept of *utility*, which is either measured as a monetary benefit or in terms of nonmonetary benefits, such as freedom and autonomy. Entrepreneurial motivations and choices matter at start up because they influence the future development of the new venture (Chapter. 10, pp. 253–254).

In this chapter, you will learn how this framework can include how risk, ability and personal characteristics influence the start-up decision. You will see how factors such as a person's age, education or gender influence start-up outcomes, helping you to make more informed judgements about a start-up's feasibility.

You will also consider the importance of entrepreneurial contexts. Partly, this relates to how family circumstances, social networks and access to financial capital influence venture creation. However, a focus on contexts also brings into the foreground the external environment. If entrepreneurship is a play in which the spotlight is on what the actors do and say, then it is also important to consider the play's setting. You will see that entrepreneurship does not happen in a vacuum and that it is influenced by societal incentives.

3.2 UTILITY: WHAT MOTIVATES START UP

In the occupation choice framework, an understanding of utility is pivotal. If you believe you can earn more money as an entrepreneur, you may choose to give up a stable job. But you may also be aware that entrepreneurial incomes are more uncertain. An employee can be fairly certain of receiving a wage unless they are dismissed or made redundant. Most entrepreneurs, though, are uncertain about what their income levels will be. They buy inputs such as raw materials for their business at a *certain* price but can only sell their outputs for an *uncertain* price determined by the market. Suppose an entrepreneur buys 100 umbrellas at price X. This is a certain cost. However, they cannot be certain that they will be able to sell all of the umbrellas or at what price. Their income is the *uncertain* revenue minus the *certain* costs.

Economists also measure utility in terms of nonmonetary benefits. Some jobs are terrible because even if you are well paid you might have to put up with a manager who cannot manage or an organisation that cannot organise. This might cause you to believe that you will have greater utility in entrepreneurship because it gives you the independence and freedom to be your own boss. A focus on expected utility leads to a number of insights. First, nonmonetary motivations are important. Table 3.1 shows that in the European Union (EU), Russia, the United States (US), Japan and India people are attracted to self-employment because they believe it will give them independence and self-fulfilment. Another common nonmonetary reason – particularly in Brazil and South Korea – is the desire for autonomy and flexibility.

Case Study: Utility beyond money?

The usual story is that Steve Jobs and Steve Wozniak set up Apple. But there was a third founder, Ronald Wayne. Apple's ownership initially split three ways: 45 per cent each for Jobs and Wozniak, and 10 per cent for Wayne. Wayne said of Steve Jobs: 'Jobs had this focus. Once he got an idea in his head, that was it and you never wanted to be between him and where he wanted to go or you would end up with footprints on your forehead.' Wayne had a different set of beliefs: 'find something you enjoy doing so much that you'd be willing to do it for nothing ... and you'll never work a day in your life'.

Wayne's concern was that Apple was not the right opportunity for him. If Apple failed, he would be personally liable for its debts, whereas Jobs and Wozniak did not have 'two beans'. So he swapped his 10 per cent stock in Apple for a cheque for $1500. This 10 per cent would now be worth around $100 billion. Wayne had few regrets about leaving Apple: 'I would've wound up heading a very large documentation department at the back of the building, shuffling papers for the next 20 years of my life. That was not the future that I saw for myself.'[4]

Table 3.1 also shows that monetary motivations (better income prospects) play a role, particularly in India. This suggests that very many people are opportunity-based entrepreneurs who are pulled towards self-employment because they see it as a way of meeting their personal or financial goals. Far fewer people appear to be necessity-based entrepreneurs, pushed towards self-employment

Table 3.1 Motivations for self-employment in the EU and selected countries[5]

	EU 27	Russia	USA	Brazil	Japan	South Korea	India
Personal independence/ self-fulfilment	62%	60%	54%	37%	45%	42%	76%
Freedom to choose place and time of working	30%	14%	33%	42%	34%	48%	38%
Better income prospects	16%	21%	9%	19%	5%	28%	66%
Exploiting a business opportunity	4%	10%	2%	7%	2%	1%	30%
Lack of attractive employment opportunities	2%	1%	1%	2%	4%	1%	19%
Members of family/friends are self-employed	1%	0%	1%	3%	4%	1%	15%
Favourable economic climate	2%	3%	2%	4%	0%	0%	19%
To avoid uncertainties related to paid employment	3%	1%	2%	5%	1%	3%	8%
To contribute to society	2%	2%	1%	4%	1%	0%	4%

Source: Data compiled from the European Commission

because they lack opportunities in paid work. However, Table 3.1 also shows that people often have a mix of goals, indicating that start-up motivations come in bundles.[6]

A second insight is that differences in entrepreneurial motivations influence start-up development.[7] Californian wine producers who set up a winery for love focused on producing high-quality wines. But those who set up wineries for money focused on lower quality wines in the hope of making money.[8] Different motivations also influence outcomes: necessity-based entrepreneurs are less likely to survive in business while a prerequisite of growing a business is the desire to want to grow the business.[9]

○ *Go to Exercise W 1.2: What are your motivations towards entrepreneurship?*

Case Study: Mathieu Flamini, footballer and entrepreneur

© Getty Images/Miemo Penttinen - miemo.net

Mathieu Flamini is a professional footballer with a difference. Besides having played for clubs such as Marseille, AC Milan and Arsenal, he is also concerned about the effects of climate change. This led him, in partnership with his friend, Pasquale Granata, to set up GF Biotechnology. Working with experts from the University of Pisa in Italy, GF Biotechnology has tried to develop the commercial potential of levulinic acid as an alternative fuel source. He said: 'when you start something like that and you spend so much money, and where there is risk there is stress. To me, it was an escape. A football career is made of ups and downs. It cleared my mind and helped me to think about something different. And it was something intellectually challenging too.'[10]

A third insight is that the self-employed have higher levels of job satisfaction than employees.[11] This is because they have greater flexibility and choice about how, when or what work they do than employees.

The fact that entrepreneurs are happier in their work is puzzling. If entrepreneurs swapped business ownership for paid employment, they would earn on average anything from 9 to 35 per cent more in employment.[12]

Being in business has other downsides. Although some of the self-employed enjoy better physical and mental health than employees, they can work longer and more unsocial hours, suffer more from stress and experience health-related problems.[13] Figure 3.1 also shows that for some of the self-employed, their work may be intermittent and they may struggle to get paid. Their work environments also tend to offer their workers less formal training, be less safe and have greater rates of work-based accidents and injuries.[14]

- *Go to Exercise W 1.3: What do you think about the trade-offs involved in entrepreneurship?*

From a utility perspective, this makes little sense: even if a job provided variety and discretion, it is unlikely that very many people would choose an occupational status that left them relatively poorer and with a poor work–life balance. The answer may be that entrepreneurs under-report their true income. However, this is difficult to prove because people are reluctant to share how much money they make.

Figure 3.1 Difficulties faced by the self-employed (ec.europa.eu/eurostat/statistics-explained/index.php/Self-employment_statistics, Eurostat (lfso_sediff), author's own calculations

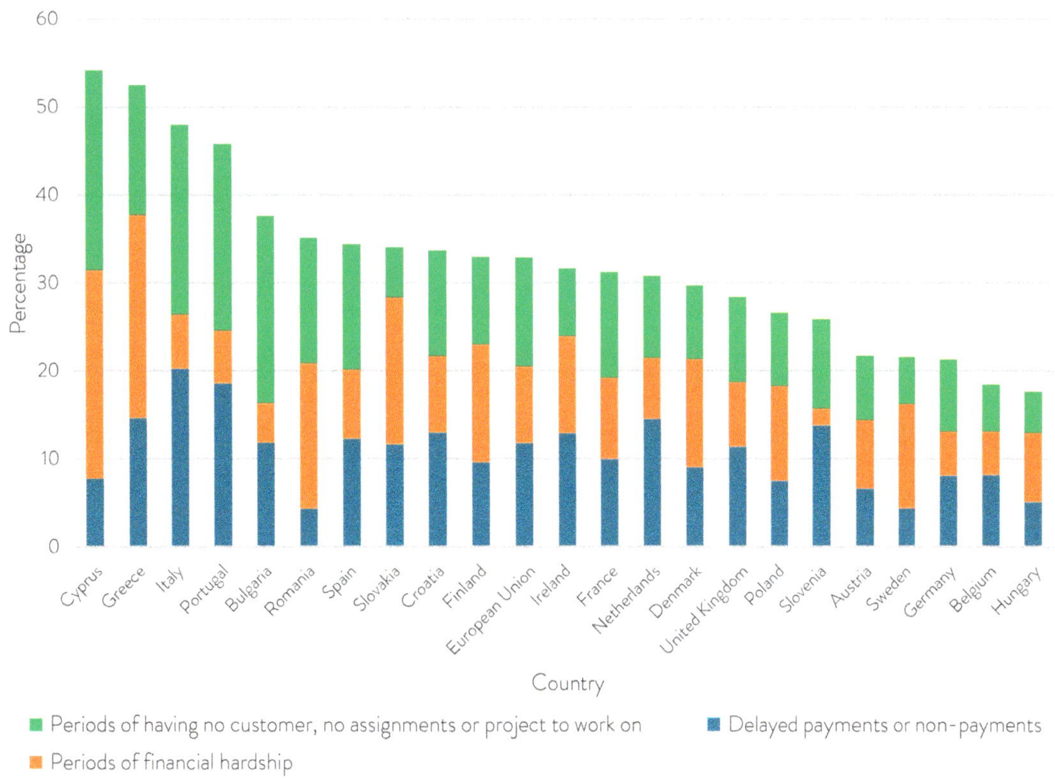

Source: Data compiled from the European Commission

Researchers get around this problem by asking people what they spend on food and other things such as cars. This is much less sensitive information, and it tends to be the case that the more money someone makes, the more they spend on discretionary items. Consequently, a useful comparison is between what employees and entrepreneurs spend on food and other goods. If entrepreneurs spend about the same money on these items as employees but report lower income levels, this would imply that they are under-reporting their actual income.

Such tests reveal that entrepreneurs in a range of countries consistently under-report their income (Table 3.2). By looking at food expenditure, a study found that American entrepreneurs under-reported their actual income by 30 per cent.[15] After correcting for under-reporting, another study found an average financial gain from entrepreneurship of 42 per cent.[16] The failure to declare income implies that some entrepreneurs are evading tax. This hurts society because lower tax incomes mean fewer resources are available for public services.

Table 3.2 Percentage of income under-reporting by the self-employed

Country	Percentage of income under-reported
UK[19]	51–64 'blue collared' self-employed; 28–54 'white collared'
Canada[20]	11–23
Finland[21]	10–24 (one person in household self-employed) 37–47 (two persons in household self-employed)
Korea and Russia[22]	38 (Korea), 47 (Russia)
Denmark[23]	42
Italy[24]	Average is 46 (varies between regions from 37 (Aosta) to 68 (Apulia))
USA[25]	30
Estonia[26]	62
USA[27]	42
Russia[28]	80

Examining the utility derived from entrepreneurship reveals that nonmonetary benefits are important. But it is misleading to assume that entrepreneurs do not also prize the monetary gains from entrepreneurship.

Discussion questions:

- Aside from monetary considerations, what other factors might motivate self-employment?
- Why might the self-employed express higher job satisfaction in spite of drawbacks such as longer working hours, stress and health-related problems?

Case Study: Why so many Porsche Cayennes in Greece?

© Getty Images/d3sign

Greece was a significant causality of the 2008 financial crisis. In the years that followed, it became a 'problem' for international financiers such as the International Monetary Fund, the World Bank and the EU. But despite relying on financial bailouts, it still had one of the highest ownership rates of luxury Porsche Cayenne cars in Europe.

The reason for this was that many Greeks – particularly Greek doctors, engineers, accountants and lawyers – were under-reporting their income, allowing them to evade their taxes. This was on a massive scale: 30 per cent (€28 billion) of the budget deficit for 2009 was due to tax evasion.[17] Subsequently, the Greek government sought to reduce these activities through sanctions, incentives and tax reforms.[18]

3.3 ABILITY, RISK AND PERSONAL CHARACTERISTICS

Simple static utility models assume all individuals are the same. Their value is limited because they fail to account for differences in ability and risk propensities between individuals.

The study of risk-taking in entrepreneurship can trace its history to the Irish economist Richard Cantillon in the eighteenth century. Later, Knight argued that different risk propensities explained why some individuals choose entrepreneurship (Chapter 1, p. 5). Richard Kihlstrom and Jean-Jacques Laffont's model also formalised the importance of risk-taking propensity. They found that risk-tolerant individuals are more likely to be entrepreneurs than either risk-neutral or risk-averse individuals.[29]

American economist Robert Lucas proposed that entrepreneurial ability was heterogeneous, varying between individuals with low and high ability.[30] Ability determines the likelihood of becoming an entrepreneur: those with greater ability than the marginal individual (who is indifferent between being an employee and an entrepreneur) become entrepreneurs while the less able become employees. Lucas's model implies that entrepreneurial ability also explains an entrepreneur's ability to grow a business: able entrepreneurs scale-up their firm because their talents can spread over a wide span of business activities.

However, Lucas's model does not define exactly what entrepreneurial ability is. Edward Lazear later extended Lucas's model by suggesting that skills (a proxy for ability) are either specialist or general.[31] Those with specialist skills such as marketing or finance tend to become employees because they can earn higher returns from these skills. Meanwhile, those with general skills ('jack of all trades') become entrepreneurs because they have the broad skills necessary to cope with the different pressures they face in entrepreneurship. Other studies confirm these findings.[32] Another standard presumption is that relevant experience predicts start-up because, for example, those who ran a business previously are more likely to develop a 'taste' for entrepreneurship.[33]

- *Go to Exercise W 1.4: Do you need to be a jack of all trades to be an entrepreneur?*

Table 3.3 shows that prior entrepreneurial, managerial and relevant industry experience all increase someone's chances of starting their own business.

For the unemployed, entrepreneurship is often an option, although this is likely to vary with how well or badly the economy is doing. In general, start-up may be a poor choice for many previously unemployed people. If the unemployed struggle to find a job, they are likely to struggle with starting and successfully running a business, since it requires a much wider range of skills than needed for employment.

Table 3.3 shows that education has an unclear impact on start-up. This sits comfortably with the occupational choice framework: it predicts that graduates have the cognitive ability to cope with start-up but, at the same time, are attractive (compared with the less well-educated) to employers.

- *Go to Exercise W 1.5: What roles does your background play in start up?*

Personal characteristics also determine start-up choices: women, the young (under 30 years old), seniors (over 55 years old) and ethnic minorities/immigrants are less likely to start up (Table 3.4). Such patterns fit, for example, with Murray Frank's model: a person close to retirement will devote less effort to their business than a younger person.[34]

However, focusing on personal characteristics in isolation hides complex associations between individual factors. The prime age for being self-employed is around 35–50 years old. This group is more likely to be self-employed than younger or older individuals. But they also have higher levels of social and financial capital than younger people and are perhaps better motivated to create a sustainable business than older people.

Assessment tip: Finding academic sources

The general preference in academic writing is to use academic sources to inform your arguments. However, finding relevant sources in the literature can be challenging.

A good place to start is to examine the literature review section of academic papers. These help to work out the important papers in a topic area. You can use these to build your own argument.

To complement this, and to make your argument up to date, you can use dedicated academic search engines such as the Web of Science (https://www.webofknowledge.com). This provides lists of other papers that cite a particular source. You can then read these to build your argument. One other great advantage of these search engines is that you can integrate sources into bibliographic software packages. This makes it easier to reference in a consistent style.

Google Scholar (https://scholar.google.com) is another helpful tool. It tells you how many times a paper has been cited. If a paper has too many citations, you can refine the list by restricting citations by date and by using 'search within citations'.

Table 3.3 Start-up determinants: Experience and education

Factor	Explanations for starting up	Evidence
Entrepreneurial experience	• Prior experience erodes employment skills and incurs opportunity costs such as having to retrain, which can discourage from re-entering employment • More likely to spot opportunities and have greater social and financial capital, thus making it easier to access and leverage resources • Experienced entrepreneurs acquire a taste for entrepreneurship	Former entrepreneurs return to entrepreneurship[35]
Management experience	• Less likely because they can earn more money in paid employment • More likely because they have fewer credit constraints, understand how to manage a business, are better able to enact entrepreneurial opportunities and have higher levels of social capital	Those with greater management experience are more likely to be entrepreneurs[36]
Industrial experience	• Provides information that can lead to spotting business opportunities	Those with greater relevant industrial experience are more likely to be entrepreneurs. However, some sectors have higher rates of self-employment, such as construction. The size of a person's former employer is also important: sectors where small businesses predominate are more likely to spawn start-ups
Unemployment experience	• Unemployment lowers the opportunity cost of entrepreneurship, making it more attractive • If unemployed during a recession, this increases the availability and affordability of second-hand equipment, lowering start-up costs • In recessions, entrepreneurs are likely to have lower incomes because demand is lower. This deters start-up since the unemployed perceive that start-up is riskier • Unemployed people are less likely to start a business if they recognise that they lack relevant skills and abilities	Unemployed are more likely to be pushed into entrepreneurship[37]. This 'refugee effect' suggests the unemployed are forced to work for themselves because they lack outside alternatives

Table 3.3 continued

Factor	Explanations for starting up	Evidence
University education	• Less likely if they believe they can earn more money in employment • More likely because they have fewer credit constraints, greater ability to spot and enact entrepreneurial opportunities[38]	No clear impact,[39] but higher education is clearly important in some skilled sectors such as biotechnology

Simplistic and blunt binary categories such as male or female, and immigrant or nonimmigrant also fail to examine how the intersectionality of sex, gender, class and education all combine to impact on entrepreneurial choices.[40] Mixed embeddedness is also poorly treated in traditional economic analyses of start-ups because they often only focus on the individual or the business, rather than the wider ways in which societal structures and institutions influence the decision to be an entrepreneur.[41]

© Getty Images/Veerasak Piyawatanakul / EyeEm

Discussion questions:

- What role does prior experience play in determining start-up? Do they matter more than personality dispositions?
- What role does gender play in start-up? Is it important? Examine this in light of the developing literature on gay and lesbian entrepreneurs.[42]
- Why are young people less likely to set up in business?
- If you were unemployed, is it a good idea to set up a business?
- Would you advise someone to follow their passion or the money?

Table 3.4 Start-up determinants: Personal characteristics

Factor	Explanations for starting up	Evidence
Gender	**Men:** • Greater risk propensities,[43] greater experience in sectors with high self-employment rates such as construction[44] • More likely to be educated in science and technology[45] • Have greater levels of experience, higher social capital such as 'old boys' networks; find it easier to access finance[46] **Women:** • Entrepreneurial stereotypes are male dominated[47] • Face labour market discrimination[48] • Greater family commitments, desire for a better work–life balance[49]	Men are more likely to start up.[50] However, some studies have suggested the gender gap is closing in line with women's increased participation in the labour market[51]
Ethnicity/ immigrants	• A culture that promotes entrepreneurship helps start-ups[52] • Having access to ethnic resources such as in-kind financial support, mentors, role models, cheap family labour makes it easier to start up[53] • Viable ethnic-specific markets – ethnic enclaves where there are distinctive communities that share a particular ethnic background[54] • Face perceived or actual discrimination in accessing finance makes it harder to start up,[55] while employment discrimination makes self-employment more appealing[56]	Ethnicity and immigrant status can increase chances of start-up but this differs between groups[57]
Age	**Younger people** (under 30): • Have more energy; higher risk propensities, more time to recover investments Prime age (30–50 year olds): • Greater levels of social, human and financial capital • Greater family commitments • A greater desire for increased financial returns **Seniors** (over 50): • Greater levels of social, human and financial capital • Greater desire for the autonomy and flexibility provided by entrepreneurship[58]	Clear inverted U-shape age effect[59] Note: Senior self-employment rates are for those who are active in the labour market. However, older people still have lower labour participation rates

Table 3.4 continued

Factor	Explanations for starting up	Evidence
Disability/ health	• More likely because it provides flexibility around health/disability • More likely to suffer discrimination in the labour market • Entrepreneurship can be stressful and often means long hours. This might limit its attractiveness to people with physical and mental disabilities or health concerns	**No clear impact**[60] because of difficulties in defining what is meant by 'disability'. Some evidence that disability has a negative impact on business entry[61]

3.4 THE IMPORTANCE OF CONTEXT

Context is the 'circumstances, conditions, situations, or environments that are external to the respective phenomenon and enable or constrain it'.[62] It both positively (assets) and negatively (liabilities) shapes the decision to start up. Table 3.5 shows household contexts are critical determinants in starting up. Couples, those with children and those having entrepreneurial parents all increase the chances of start-up.[63]

Social and financial capital also have a positive impact on their decision to become an entrepreneur (Table 3.5). Social capital is 'the sum of the actual and potential resources embedded within, available through, and derived from the network of relationships possessed by an individual or social unit. Social capital thus comprises both the network and the assets that may be mobilized through that network.'[64]

Social networks provide credibility, information and support. They build trust and reciprocity, making it easier and 'cheaper' to do business.[65] Entrepreneurs rely on family and friends ('strong' ties) but also draw on a range of support from business contacts and acquaintances ('weak' ties).[66] Similarly, access to financial resources increases the likelihood of starting up. As the economic model of occupational choice predicts, an individual may be more likely to become an entrepreneur if they face fewer financial constraints.[67]

Examining entrepreneurial contexts brings into focus how institutions, geography and time all influence entrepreneurial choices.[68] For example, today it is common to see entrepreneurs in heroic terms, even if they have some unsavoury characteristics. But in the past, entrepreneurs were often at the margins of society and associated with either fraudulent or corrupt practices.[69]

3.4.1 Baumol's entrepreneurial typology

One typology for understanding the importance of context is William Baumol's distinction between productive, unproductive and destructive entrepreneurship.[70] For Baumol, productive entrepreneurship provides benefits both for the individual and for society. The Cistercian monks of the Middle Ages developed new products and services, which benefited both themselves and society. These innovations – Belgian 'Trappist' beers and Dom Perignon champagne – are still with us today.

Unproductive entrepreneurship is some form of bureaucracy that typically benefits an individual or a group but has costs to wider society, such as rent-seeking. One example of this type of behaviour is vexatious compensation claims brought by a sacked employee who wants to cause as much discomfort to their employer as possible. Baumol also notes that, relative to the USA, Japan has fewer lawyers and has fewer lawsuits that seek out economic returns for mistakes or problems in markets. Consequently, there are fewer opportunities for rent-seeking lawyers in Japan.

Baumol's destructive entrepreneurship suggests that benefits go to the individual or the group but damages society. In ancient Rome and medieval China, one of the acceptable ways of gaining wealth was through political payments. Bribery and corruption are still common today.[71] Around the world, on average 17 per cent of businesses expect to pay a bribe and 29 per cent expect to provide a gift to get a government contract.[72] This varies from country to country: in Cambodia, 65 per cent of businesses expect to pay a bribe, while in Israel the figure is just 0.1 per cent.

Table 3.5 Start-up determinants: Household characteristics, teams and social and financial capital

Factor	Explanations for starting up	Evidence
Relationship status	Being in a relationship allows a couple to pool start-up capital and allows one partner to specialise on one area such as caring for children;[73] couples receive cheap or unpaid sweat labour and emotional support;[74] relationships provide tax advantages through shared allowances and other mechanisms	Clear impact of marital status.[75] This ignores that people are choosing to partner in different ways.[76] If a partner or spouse is already an entrepreneur, they are more likely to be an entrepreneur because of knowledge transfers between spouses[77]
Children	Provides incentives to earn more money in entrepreneurship, provides a flexible solution to childcare issues, cheap or unpaid (sweat) labour and emotional support; negative effects if the entrepreneurial parents are less willing to take risks	Clear impact of having children[78]
Parents	Parents help develop human capital that helps provide specific tacit knowledge on how to set up and run a business; social and financial capital provides start-up capital and networks of support and business contacts; parents transfer risk attitudes to their children	Clear impact that entrepreneurship runs in families.[79] This is likely to be due to transfer of personality, social and human capital and role models,[80] rather than financial capital[81]
Entrepreneurial teams	Provides diversity, a range of experience, skills and knowledge and greater levels of social and financial capital	No clear evidence of team-based start-ups being more common than solo entrepreneurship[82]
Social capital	Offers support for identifying and exploiting an opportunity, provides information, support, finance and skills and role models	Social capital helps with setting up a business[83]
Financial capital	Those with greater financial resources are more likely to be entrepreneurs	Access to finance promotes start-up[84]

Baumol's entrepreneurial typology suggests we should not focus on what increases or decreases the absolute supply of entrepreneurs. Attempts to improve the 'entrepreneurial mindset' are ineffective because there is no shortage of people inclined towards entrepreneurship. If a society appears to lack entrepreneurs, it is because those people are using their skills in an unproductive or destructive way.

Instead, Baumol suggests societies should focus on ensuring a switch to productive entrepreneurship, by changing the 'rules of the game'. Stronger competition, more transparent tax policy and other changes to the institutional and regulatory framework can encourage productive entrepreneurship. Increasing access to markets by improving demand conditions can also help. Ensuring resources such as skills and finance are easily available should be encouraged. The wrong incentives can have negative effects.

For example, in 1950, around 25 per cent of East Germans were self-employed. After more than 30 years of communist rule, the rate had fallen to less than 5 per cent by the 1980s.[85] A talented entrepreneur was better off becoming a Communist Party bureaucrat, given the rules of the game. After the communist regime collapsed and the Berlin wall fell in 1989, the unified Germany government introduced favourable entrepreneurial incentives, helping former communist areas to increase their self-employment rates.

It is easier to increase the numbers of self-made billionaires if property rights are strong and there are 'market enhancing' incentives, such as robust competition policy. Weak property rights and 'market-limiting' incentives such as bribery and corruption lead to high rates of relatively poor self-employed individuals.[86]

Academic insight: The extra-legal economy

Most of the entrepreneurs who run businesses in the world live in poorer countries. Peruvian economist Hernando de Soto showed that these people often have few ownership rights over their own businesses. They exist in the informal or what he called the 'extra-legal economy', placing them outside the mainstream legal system and often without property and business rights. This creates real problems for many entrepreneurs. No legal title makes it difficult to raise finance. Getting insurance to protect against fire, damage or theft is nearly impossible if an entrepreneur cannot legally own their building or farmland. Other basic business hopes such as growing their business are difficult if an entrepreneur cannot access the judicial system, gain intellectual property rights or issue shares in their business.[87]

De Soto encouraged the Peruvian government to shift people out of the extra-legal economy and into the legal economy by introducing practical administrative changes to the legal system that made it easier to own and trade assets. Although these changes have helped, many entrepreneurs still feel obliged to offer bribes to get access to electricity and water, to obtain construction licences and to get import or export permits.[88] However, de Soto argues that it took Europe and North America 250 years to become mature capitalist countries. By comparison, countries as diverse as Egypt or Indonesia have had far less time to institute market reforms that allow their entrepreneurs to prosper.[89]

Discussion questions:

- Do you think that Baumol's typology is useful for understanding entrepreneurial activities? Is there anything that can be done to improve productive entrepreneurship?
- Do you think that governments have a positive role to play in supporting entrepreneurship? Or do you think that entrepreneurship is more likely to prosper if governments stop interfering in markets?
- Do you agree with Baumol that the supply of entrepreneurs is fixed? What are the implications for training people to be entrepreneurs?

Entrepreneurship in Action

- Write up a case study of a group of ethnic or immigrant entrepreneurs. What motivated them to become entrepreneurs? How did their personal characteristics, social networks, family and financial circumstances influence their entrepreneurial activities?
- You have received a commission by your government to investigate how vibrant start-ups are in your country relative to another country. Provide a presentation/report that contextualises start-up activity in these two countries. Give recommendations on how your chosen country could improve the vibrancy of its start-ups.

3.5 WHAT YOU HAVE LEARNED IN THIS CHAPTER

You have learned how economists use an occupational choice framework to explain the start-up decision. This framework is based on:

1. An individual has a choice between becoming an entrepreneur or an employee and is able to switch between them.
2. This choice depends on the relative utility of each state.
3. Entrepreneurial income (profits) is more uncertain than unemployment benefits or waged income.

Using this framework provides insights into the types of people who choose entrepreneurship. Entrepreneurs tend to be male, of 'prime age', have prior relevant experience and be motivated by nonmonetary benefits.

However, you can make three main criticisms of the occupational choice approach.

1. Much of the evidence for the model is based on self-employment, if only because economists use a quantitative approach and because much of the publicly available data on entrepreneurship relates to self-employment. Self-employment, however, is a crude measure of entrepreneurial activity since it covers a broad spectrum, from part-time entrepreneurs through to those who run very successful businesses.

2. A core assumption of the framework is that people make rational decisions. As Chapter 2 (pp. 32–37) showed, this is unrealistic. We are bounded rationalists: we do sometimes make rational decisions, but we also often make decisions with incomplete information and rely on heuristics to make judgements.
3. The framework focuses on who is more likely to start up but it does not tell us how they got there or what processes they use to build a start-up. This limits the framework's ability to predict entrepreneurial outcomes.

You have also learned that the 'rules of the game' are pivotal, placing boundary conditions on the assets and liabilities available to entrepreneurs.

ASSESSMENT QUESTIONS

1. Explain the occupational choice model. What influence do utility, ability and risk play in the decision to become an entrepreneur?
2. In occupational choice models, there are a number of individual determinants of the decision to set up a business. Identify four of these. Of these four, what do you think is the most likely determinant of the decision to set up a new business?
3. There are groups in society that do not appear to set up businesses at the same rate as other groups in society. Identify examples of these groups. Pick one group and explain why they are less likely to be entrepreneurs.
4. Does the occupational choice model provide a good explanation of the reasons why some individuals set up a business?
5. Explain Baumol's typology. How might governments make productive entrepreneurship more appealing?
6. Are contexts more important than personality factors in explaining why some people choose entrepreneurship?

FURTHER READING

Åstebro, T., & Chen, J. (2014). The entrepreneurial earnings puzzle: Mismeasurement or real? *Journal of Business Venturing, 29*(1), 88–105.

Baumol, W. J. (1990). Entrepreneurship: Productive, unproductive, and destructive. *Journal of Political Economy, 98*, 893–921.

Benz, M., & Frey, B. S. (2008). The value of doing what you like: Evidence from the self-employed in 23 countries. *Journal of Economic Behavior & Organization, 68*(3–4), 445–455.

Notes

1 Buenstorf, G., Nielsen, K., & Timmermans, B. (2017). Steve Jobs or no jobs? Entrepreneurial activity and performance among Danish college dropouts and graduates. *Small Business Economics, 48*(1), 179–197.

2 content.time.com/time/specials/packages/article/0,28804,1988080_1988093_1988082,00.htm.

3 Wai, J., & Rindermann, H. (2017). What goes into high educational and occupational achievement? Education, brains, hard work, networks, and other factors. *High Ability Studies, 28*(1), 127–145.

4 www.bbc.co.uk/news/technology-35940300.

5 European Commission (2012). *Entrepreneurship in the EU and Beyond*, Flash Eurobarometer 354, European Commission: Brussels, Question 6: author's own calculations.

6 Jayawarna, D., Rouse, J., & Kitching, J. (2013). Entrepreneur motivations and life course. *International Small Business Journal, 31*(1), 34–56; Birley, S., & Westhead, P. (1994). A taxonomy of business start-up reasons and their impact on firm growth and size. *Journal of Business Venturing, 9*(1), 7–31.

7 El Shoubaki, A., Laguir, I., & den Besten, M. (2019). Human capital and SME growth: The mediating role of reasons to start a business. *Small Business Economics*, 1–15, https://doi.org/10.1007/s11187-018-0129-y.

8 Scott-Morton, F. M., & Podolny, J. M. (2002). Love or money? The effects of owner motivation in the California wine industry. *The Journal of Industrial Economics, 50*(4), 431–456.

9 Furdas, M., & Kohn, K. (2011). *Why is start-up survival lower among necessity entrepreneurs? A decomposition approach*. 2nd IZA Workshop on Entrepreneurship Research, Bonn, Germany; Rauch, A., Wiklund, J., Lumpkin, G. T., & Frese, M. (2009). Entrepreneurial orientation and business performance: An assessment of past research and suggestions for the future. *Entrepreneurship Theory and Practice, 33*(3), 761–787.

10 www.thesun.co.uk/sol/homepage/sport/football/6742052/Mathieu-Flaminis-no-fuel.html.

11 Benz, M., & Frey, B. S. (2008). The value of doing what you like: Evidence from the self-employed in 23 countries. *Journal of Economic Behavior & Organization, 68*(3–4), 445–455; Warr, P., & Inceoglu, I. (2018). Work orientations, well-being and job content of self-employed and employed professionals. *Work, Employment and Society, 32*(2), 292–311; Álvarez, G., & Sinde-Cantorna, A. I. (2014). Self-employment and job satisfaction: An empirical analysis. *International Journal of Manpower, 35*(5), 688–702; Tchinda, J. L., & Bing, H. R. (2017). Job satisfaction of self-employed workers: Empirical evidence from Cameroon data. *International Journal of Management Science and Business Administration, 3*(6), 43–58; Millán, J. M., Hessels, J., Thurik, R., & Aguado, R. (2013). Determinants of job satisfaction: A European comparison of self-employed and paid employees. *Small Business Economics, 40*(3), 651–670; Lange, T. (2012). Job satisfaction and self-employment: Autonomy or personality? *Small Business Economics, 38*(2), 165–177; Hessels, J., Arampatzi, E., van der Zwan, P., & Burger, M. (2018). Life satisfaction and self-employment in different types of occupations. *Applied Economics Letters, 25*(11), 734–740.

12 Hartog, J., Van Praag, M., & Van Der Sluis, J. (2010). If you are so smart, why aren't you an entrepreneur? Returns to cognitive and social ability: Entrepreneurs versus employees. *Journal of Economics & Management Strategy, 19*(4), 947–989; Hamilton, B. H. (2000). Does entrepreneurship pay? An empirical analysis of the returns to self-employment. *Journal of Political Economy, 108*(3), 604–631.

13 Eurofound. (2016). *Sixth European working conditions survey – Overview report*. Luxembourg, Luxembourg: Publications Office of the European Union; Hyytinen, A., & Ruuskanen, O. P. (2007). Time use of the self-employed. *Kyklos, 60*(1), 105–122; Cardon, M. S., & Patel, P. C. (2015). Is stress worth it? Stress-related health and wealth trade-offs for entrepreneurs. *Applied Psychology, 64*(2), 379–420; Hessels, J., Rietveld, C. A., & van der Zwan, P. (2017). Self-employment and work-related stress: The mediating role of job control and job demand. *Journal of Business Venturing, 32*(2), 178–196; Nikolova, M. (2018). Switching to self-employment can be good for your health. *Journal of Business Venturing, 34*(4), 664–691; Kollmann, T., Stöckmann, C., & Kensbock, J. M. (2018). I can't get no sleep – The differential impact of entrepreneurial stressors on work–home interference and insomnia among experienced versus novice entrepreneurs. *Journal of Business Venturing, 34*(4), 692–708.

14 Targoutzidis, A., Koukoulaki, T., Schmitz-Felten, E., Kuhl, K., Oude Hengel, K. M., Rijken, E., et al. (2014). *The business case for safety and health at work: Cost-benefit analyses of interventions in small and medium-sized enterprises*. Bilbao, Spain: European Agency for Safety and Health at Work.

15 Hurst, E., Li, G., & Pugsley, B. (2014). Are household surveys like tax forms? Evidence from income underreporting of the self-employed. *Review of Economics and Statistics, 96*(1), 19–33.

16 Åstebro, T., & Chen, J. (2014). The entrepreneurial earnings puzzle: Mismeasurement or real? *Journal of Business Venturing, 29*(1), 88–105.

17 Åstebro, N., Morse, A., & Tsoutsoura, M. (2016). Measuring income tax evasion using bank credit: Evidence from Greece. *The Quarterly Journal of Economics, 131*(2), 739–798.

18 Williams, C. C. (2016). *Diagnostic report on undeclared work in Greece*. Geneva, Switzerland: International Labour Office.
19 Pissarides, C. A. & Weber, G. (1989). An expenditure-based estimate of Britain's black economy. *Journal of Public Economics, 39*(1), 17–32.
20 Schuetze, H. J. (2002). Profiles of tax non-compliance among the self-employed in Canada: 1969 to 1992. *Canadian Public Policy/Analyse de Politiques, 28*(2), 219–238.
21 Johansson, E. (2005). An estimate of self-employment income underreporting in Finland. *Nordic Journal of Political Economy, 31*(1), 99–109.
22 Gibson, J., Bonggeun, K., & Chung, C. (2009). Using panel data to exactly estimate income under reporting of the self employed. *Labor Economics Working Papers*, 09-02, East Asian Bureau of Economic Research.
23 Kleven, H. J., Knudsen, M. B., Kreiner, C. T., Pedersen, S., & Saez, E. (2011). Unwilling or unable to cheat? Evidence from a tax audit experiment in Denmark. *Econometrica, 79*(3), 651–692.
24 Galbiati, R., & Zanella, G. (2012). The tax evasion social multiplier: Evidence from Italy. *Journal of Public Economics, 96*(5–6), 485–494.
25 Hurst et al. (2014), ibid.
26 Kukk, M., & Staehr, K. (2014). Income underreporting by households with business income: Evidence from Estonia. *Post-Communist Economies, 26*(2), 257–276.
27 Åstebro & Chen (2014), ibid.
28 Braguinsky, S., Mityakov, S., & Liscovich, A. (2014). Direct estimation of hidden earnings: evidence from Russian administrative data. *The Journal of Law and Economics, 57*(2), 281–319.
29 Kihlstrom, R. E., & Laffont, J. J. (1979). A general equilibrium entrepreneurial theory of firm formation based on risk aversion. *The Journal of Political Economy, 87*(4), 719–748.
30 Lucas Jr., R. E. (1978). On the size distribution of business firms. *The Bell Journal of Economics, 9*(2), 508–523.
31 Lazear, E. P. (2005). Entrepreneurship. *Journal of Labor Economics, 23*(4), 649–680.
32 Wagner, J. (2006). Are nascent entrepreneurs "Jacks-of-all-trades"? A test of Lazear's theory of entrepreneurship with German data. *Applied Economics, 38*(20), 2415–2419; Hartog et al. (2010), ibid.; Stuetzer, M., Obschonka, M., & Schmitt-Rodermund, E. (2013). Balanced skills among nascent entrepreneurs. *Small Business Economics, 41*(1), 93–114; Chen, L. W., & Thompson, P. (2016). Skill balance and entrepreneurship evidence from online career histories. *Entrepreneurship Theory and Practice, 40*(2), 289–305.
33 Henley, A. (2004). Self-employment status: The role of state dependence and initial circumstances. *Small Business Economics, 22*(1), 67–82.
34 Frank, M. Z. (1988). An intertemporal model of industrial exit. *The Quarterly Journal of Economics, 103*(2), 333–344.
35 Evans, D. S., & Jovanovic, B. (1989). An estimated model of entrepreneurial choice under liquidity constraints. *The Journal of Political Economy, 97*(4), 808–827; Henley (2004), ibid.; Westhead, P., Ucbasaran, D., Wright, M., & Binks, M. (2005). Novice, serial and portfolio entrepreneur behaviour and contributions. *Small Business Economics, 25*(2), 109–132; Poschke, M. (2013). Who becomes an entrepreneur? Labor market prospects and occupational choice. *Journal of Economic Dynamics and Control, 37*(3), 693–710; Millán, J. M., Congregado, E., & Román, C. (2014). Entrepreneurship persistence with and without personnel: The role of human capital and previous unemployment. *International Entrepreneurship and Management Journal, 10*(1), 187–206.
36 Henley (2004), ibid.; Lin, Z., Picot, G., & Compton, J. (2000). The entry and exit dynamics of self-employment in Canada. *Small Business Economics, 15*(2), 105–125.
37 Aubry, M., Bonnet, J., & Renou-Maissant, P. (2015). Entrepreneurship and the business cycle: The "Schumpeter" effect versus the "refugee" effect – A French appraisal based on regional data. *The Annals of Regional Science, 54(1)*, 23–55.
38 Davidsson, P., & Honig, B. (2003). The role of social and human capital among nascent entrepreneurs. *Journal of Business Venturing, 18*(3), 301–331.
39 Van der Sluis, J., Van Praag, M., & Vijverberg, W. (2008). Education and entrepreneurship selection and performance: A review of the empirical literature. *Journal of Economic Surveys, 22*(5), 795–841.
40 Martinez Dy, A., Martin, L., & Marlow, S. (2014). Developing a critical realist positional approach to intersectionality. *Journal of Critical Realism, 13*(5), 447–466; Barrett, R., & Vershinina, N. (2017). Intersectionality of ethnic and entrepreneurial identities: A study of post-war Polish entrepreneurs in an English city. *Journal of Small Business Management, 55*(3), 430–443.
41 Kloosterman, R., Van der Leun, J., & Rath, J. (1999). Mixed embeddedness: (In)formal economic activities and immigrant businesses in the Netherlands. *International Journal of Urban and Regional Research, 23*(2), 252–266.
42 Galloway, L. (2012). The experiences of male gay business owners in the UK. *International Small Business Journal, 30*(8), 890–906; Leppel, K. (2016). The incidence of self-employment by sexual orientation. *Small Business Economics, 46*(3), 347–363; Marlow, S., Greene, F. J., & Coad, A. (2018). Advancing gendered analyses of entrepreneurship: A critical exploration of entrepreneurial activity among gay men and lesbian women. *British Journal of Management, 29*(1), 118–135.
43 Langowitz, N., & Minniti, M. (2007). The entrepreneurial propensity of women. *Entrepreneurship Theory and Practice, 31*(3), 341–364; Dohmen, T., Falk, A., Huffman, D., Sunde, U., Schupp, J., & Wagner, G. G. (2011). Individual risk attitudes: Measurement, determinants, and behavioral consequences. *Journal of the European Economic Association, 9*(3), 522–550; Verheul, I., Thurik, R., Grilo, I., & Van der Zwan, P. (2012). Explaining preferences and actual involvement in

self-employment: Gender and the entrepreneurial personality. *Journal of Economic Psychology, 33*(2), 325–341; Koellinger, P., Minniti, M., & Schade, C. (2013). Gender differences in entrepreneurial propensity. *Oxford Bulletin of Economics and Statistics, 75*(2), 213–234.

44 Bates, T. (1995). Self-employment entry across industry groups. *Journal of Business Venturing*, 10(2), 143–156; Marlow, S., Henry, C., & Carter, S. L. (2009). Exploring the impact of gender upon women's business ownership. *International Small Business Journal, 27*(2), 139–148.

45 Charles, M., & Bradley, K. (2002). Equal but separate? A cross-national study of sex segregation in higher education. *American Sociological Review, 67*(4), 573–599; Leoni, T., & Falk, M. (2010). Gender and field of study as determinants of self-employment. *Small Business Economics, 34*(2), 167–185.

46 Koellinger et al. (2013), ibid.; Verheul, I., & Thurik, R. (2001). Start-up capital: "does gender matter?". *Small Business Economics, 16*(4), 329–346.

47 Eddleston, K. A., & Powell, G. N. (2008). The role of gender identity in explaining sex differences in business owners' career satisfier preferences. *Journal of Business Venturing, 23*(2), 244–256; Greene, F. J., Han, L., & Marlow, S. (2013). Like mother, like daughter? Analyzing maternal influences upon women's entrepreneurial propensity. *Entrepreneurship Theory and Practice, 37*(4), 687–711; Gupta, V. K., Goktan, A. B., & Gunay, G. (2014). Gender differences in evaluation of new business opportunity: A stereotype threat perspective. *Journal of Business Venturing, 29*(2), 273–288.

48 Clain, S. H. (2000). Gender differences in full-time self-employment. *Journal of Economics and Business, 52*(6), 499–513; Kuhn, P. J., & Schuetze, H. J. (2001). Self-employment dynamics and selfemployment trends: A study of Canadian men and women, 1982–1998. *Canadian Journal of Economics/Revue canadienne d'économique, 34*(3), 760–784; Marlow, S., & Patton, D. (2005). All credit to men? Entrepreneurship, finance, and gender. *Entrepreneurship Theory and Practice, 29*(6), 717–735.

49 Cowling, M., & Taylor, M. (2001). Entrepreneurial women and men: Two different species? *Small Business Economics, 16*(3), 167–175; Edwards, L. N., & Field-Hendrey, E. (2002). Home-based work and women's labor force decisions. *Journal of Labor Economics, 20*(1), 170–200; Wellington, A. J. (2006). Self-employment: The new solution for balancing family and career? *Labour Economics, 13*(3), 357–386.

50 Blanchflower, D. G. (2004). Self-employment: More may not be better (Working Paper 10286). Cambridge, MA: National Bureau of Economic Research; Georgellis, Y., Sessions, J. G., & Tsitsianis, N. (2005). Windfalls, wealth, and the transition to self-employment. *Small Business Economics, 25*(5), 407–428; Minniti, M., & Nardone, C. (2007). Being in someone else's shoes: the role of gender in nascent entrepreneurship. *Small Business Economics, 28*(2–3), 223–238.

51 Kelley, D. J., Brush, C., Greene, P., Herrington, M., Ali,. A., & Kew, P. (2015). *Global entrepreneurship monitor: 2014 women's report*. Babson Park, MA: Global Entrepreneurship Monitor.

52 Jones, T., & Ram, M. (2007). Re-embedding the ethnic business agenda. *Work, Employment & Society, 21*(3), 439–457.

53 Aldrich, H. E., & Waldinger, R. (1990). Ethnicity and entrepreneurship. *Annual Review of Sociology, 16*(1), 111–135.

54 Clark, K., & Drinkwater, S. (2000). Pushed out or pulled in? Self-employment among ethnic minorities in England and Wales. *Labour Economics, 7*(5), 603–628; Aldrich, H., Cater, J., Jones, T., McEvoy, D., & Velleman, P. (1985). Ethnic residential concentration and the protected market hypothesis. *Social Forces, 63*(4), 996–1009.

55 Asiedu, E., Freeman, J. A., & Nti-Addae, A. (2012). Access to credit by small businesses: How relevant are race, ethnicity, and gender?. *The American Economic Review, 102*(3), 532–537; Aldén, L., & Hammarstedt, M. (2016). Discrimination in the credit market? Access to financial capital among self-employed immigrants. *Kyklos, 69*(1), 3–31; Blanchard, L., Zhao, B., & Yinger, J. (2008). Do lenders discriminate against minority and woman entrepreneurs? *Journal of Urban Economics, 63*(2), 467–497; Blanchflower, D. G., Levine, P. B., & Zimmerman, D. J. (2003). Discrimination in the small-business credit market. *Review of Economics and Statistics, 85*(4), 930–943; Fraser, S. (2009). Is there ethnic discrimination in the UK market for small business credit? *International Small Business Journal, 27*(5), 583–607.

56 Clark & Drinkwater (2000), ibid.; Constant, A., & Zimmermann, K. F. (2006). The making of entrepreneurs in Germany: Are native men and immigrants alike?. *Small Business Economics, 26*(3), 279–300; Hammarstedt, M. (2006). The predicted earnings differential and immigrant self-employment in Sweden. *Applied Economics, 38*(6), 619–630.

57 Clark, K., & Drinkwater, S. (2010). Recent trends in minority ethnic entrepreneurship in Britain. *International Small Business Journal, 28*(2), 136–146; Fairlie, R. W., & Lofstrom, M. (2015). Immigration and entrepreneurship. In B. Chiswick & P. Miller (Eds.), *Handbook of the economics of international migration, 1* (pp. 877–911). Amsterdam: North-Holland; Clark, K., Drinkwater, S., & Robinson, C. (2017). Self-employment amongst migrant groups: New evidence from England and Wales. *Small Business Economics, 48*(4), 1047–1069.

58 Kautonen, T. (2013). *Senior entrepreneurship. Background Paper for the OECD Centre for Entrepreneurship. SMEs and Local Development* Paris: OECD.; Kautonen, T., Kibler, E., & Minniti, M. (2017). Late-career entrepreneurship, income and quality of life. *Journal of Business Venturing, 32*(3), 318–333.

59 Andersson, L., & Hammarstedt, M. (2010). Intergenerational transmissions in immigrant self-employment: Evidence from three generations. *Small Business Economics, 34*(3), 261–276; Caliendo,

M., Fossen, F., & Kritikos, A. S. (2014). Personality characteristics and the decisions to become and stay self-employed. *Small Business Economics, 42*(4), 787–814; Dunn, T., & Holtz-Eakin, D. (2000). Financial capital, human capital, and the transition to self-employment: Evidence from intergenerational links. *Journal of Labor Economics, 18*(2), 282–305; Nykvist, J. (2008). Entrepreneurship and liquidity constraints: Evidence from Sweden. *The Scandinavian Journal of Economics, 110*(1), 23–43.

60 Pagán, R. (2009). Self-employment among people with disabilities: Evidence for Europe. *Disability & Society, 24*(2), 217–229; Jones, M. K., & Latreille, P. L. (2011). Disability and self-employment: Evidence for the UK. *Applied Economics, 43*(27), 4161–4178; Renko, M., Parker Harris, S., & Caldwell, K. (2016). Entrepreneurial entry by people with disabilities. *International Small Business Journal, 34*(5), 555–578.

61 Renko et al. (2016), ibid.

62 Welter, F. (2011). Contextualizing entrepreneurship – Conceptual challenges and ways forward. *Entrepreneurship Theory and Practice, 35*(1), 165–184, 167.

63 Carter, S., Kuhl, A., Marlow, S., & Mwaura, S. (2017). Households as a site of entrepreneurial activity. *Foundations and Trends in Entrepreneurship, 13*(2), 81–190.

64 Nahapiet, J., & Ghoshal, S. (1998). Social capital, intellectual capital, and the organizational advantage. *The Academy of Management Review, 23*(2), 242–266.

65 Elfring, T., & Hulsink, W. (2003). Networks in entrepreneurship: The case of high-technology firms. *Small Business Economics, 21*(4), 409–422.

66 Granovetter, M. S. (1973). The strength of weak ties. *American Journal of Sociology, 78*(6), 1360–1380; Bosma, N., Hessels, J., Schutjens, V., Van Praag, M., & Verheul, I. (2012). Entrepreneurship and role models. *Journal of Economic Psychology, 33*(2), 410–424.

67 Evans & Jovanovic (1989), ibid.

68 Zahra, S. A., & Wright, M. (2011). Entrepreneurship's next act. *Academy of Management Perspectives, 25*(4), 67–83.

69 Stanworth, J., Stanworth, M. J. K., & Curran, J. (1973). *Management motivation in the smaller business.* Aldershot, UK: Gower.

70 Baumol, W. J. (1990). Entrepreneurship: Productive, unproductive, and destructive. *Journal of Political Economy, 98*, 893–921.

71 Dutta, N., & Sobel, R. (2016). Does corruption ever help entrepreneurship? *Small Business Economics, 47*(1), 179–199.

72 www.enterprisesurveys.org/data/exploreTopics/Corruption.

73 Hundley, G. (2001). Why women earn less than men in self-employment. *Journal of Labor Research, 22*(4), 817–829.

74 Baines, S., & Wheelock, J. (1998). Working for each other: Gender, the household and micro-business survival and growth. *International Small Business Journal, 17*(1), 16–35.

75 Taylor, M. P. (1996). Earnings, independence or unemployment: Why become self-employed?. *Oxford Bulletin of Economics and Statistics, 58*(2), 253–266; Ahn, T. (2010). Attitudes toward risk and self-employment of young workers. *Labour Economics, 17*(2), 434–442; Brown, S., Dietrich, M., Ortiz-Nuñez, A., & Taylor, K. (2011). Self-employment and attitudes towards risk: Timing and unobserved heterogeneity. *Journal of Economic Psychology, 32*(3), 425–433.

76 Özcan, B. (2011). Only the lonely? The influence of the spouse on the transition to self-employment. *Small Business Economics, 37*(4), 465.

77 Parker, S. C. (2008). Entrepreneurship among married couples in the United States: A simultaneous probit approach. *Labour Economics, 15*(3), 459–481.

78 Lin et al. (2000), ibid.; Henley (2004), ibid.; Wellington (2006), ibid.

79 Dunn & Holtz-Eakin (2000), ibid.; Hundley, G. (2006). Family background and the propensity for self-employment. *Industrial Relations, 45*(3), 377–392; Fairlie, R. W., & Robb, A. (2007). Families, human capital, and small business: Evidence from the characteristics of Business Owners Survey. *Industrial & Labor Relations Review, 60*(2), 225–245; Colombier, N., & Masclet, D. (2008). Intergenerational correlation in self employment: Some further evidence from French ECHP data. *Small Business Economics, 30*(4), 423–437; Lu, J., & Tao, Z. (2010). Determinants of entrepreneurial activities in China. *Journal of Business Venturing, 25*(3), 261–273; Mungai, E., & Velamuri, S. R. (2011). Parental entrepreneurial role model influence on male offspring: Is it always positive and when does it occur? *Entrepreneurship Theory and Practice, 35*(2), 337–357.

80 Chlosta, S., Patzelt, H., Klein, S. B., & Dormann, C. (2012). Parental role models and the decision to become self-employed: The moderating effect of personality. *Small Business Economics, 38*(1), 121–138; Dunn & Holtz-Eakin (2000), ibid.; Falck, O., Heblich, S., & Luedemann, E. (2012). Identity and entrepreneurship: Do school peers shape entrepreneurial intentions? *Small Business Economics, 39*(1), 39–59; Bosma et al. (2012), ibid.

81 Sørensen, J. B. (2007). Closure and exposure: Mechanisms in the intergenerational transmission of self-employment. In M. Ruef & M. Lounsbury (Eds.), *The Sociology of Entrepreneurship* (pp. 83–124). London: Emerald Group Publishing Limited; Lindquist, M. J., Sol, J., & Van Praag, M. (2015). Why do entrepreneurial parents have entrepreneurial children? *Journal of Labor Economics, 33*(2), 269–296.

82 Reynolds, P. D., Hechavarria, D., Tian, L. R., Samuelsson, M., & Davidsson, P. (2016). Panel study of entrepreneurial dynamics: A five cohort outcomes harmonized data set. *Res. Gate* (doi: 1.13140/RG.2.1.2561.7682).

83 Honig, B., & Karlsson, T. (2004). Institutional forces and the written business plan. *Journal of Management,*

30(1), 29–48; Kreiser, P. M., Patel, P. C., & Fiet, J. O. (2013). The influence of changes in social capital on firm-founding activities. *Entrepreneurship Theory and Practice, 37*(3), 539–567.

84 Blanchflower, D. G., & Oswald, A. J. (1998). What makes an entrepreneur?. *Journal of Labor Economics, 16*(1), 26–60; Fairlie, R. W., & Krashinsky, H. A. (2012). Liquidity constraints, household wealth, and entrepreneurship revisited. *Review of Income and Wealth, 58*(2), 279–306; Disney, R., & Gathergood, J. (2009). Housing wealth, liquidity constraints and self-employment. *Labour Economics, 16*(1), 79–88.

85 Fritsch, M., & Wyrwich, M. (2014). The long persistence of regional levels of entrepreneurship: Germany, 1925–2005. *Regional Studies, 48*(6), 955–973.

86 Sanandaji, T., & Leeson, P. T. (2013). Billionaires. *Industrial and Corporate Change, 22*(1), 313–337.

87 De Soto, H. (1989). *The other path: The informal revolution*. New York: Harper Collins.

88 www.enterprisesurveys.org/data/exploreTopics/Corruption.

89 de Soto, H. (2017). A tale of two civilizations in the era of Facebook and blockchain. *Small Business Economics, 49*(4), 729–739.

3

PART 2

Planning the Start-Up Journey

CHAPTER 4

From Idea to Start-Up Proposition

Learning Outcomes

In this chapter, you will learn:

- That entrepreneurs are problem solvers.
- Different techniques for generating ideas.
- How to assess if an idea provides a basis for a start-up.
- How an elevator pitch can help explain your start-up idea.

Mini Contents List

4.1 INTRODUCTION

The journey from an idea to a viable business opportunity can appear an instantaneous 'eureka' moment. The UK inventor James Dyson was frustrated by the poor suction of his bagged vacuum cleaner. This led to a 'eureka' moment when he saw a large industrial cyclone sucking 'bad air' up at a sawmill. Feeling inspired, he went back to his garden shed and developed a miniature version of the cyclone for a domestic vacuum cleaner.[1]

What this does not tell you is that it took Dyson 15 years and 5127 prototypes to get his bagless vacuum cleaner to market.

Dyson's journey is not unique. On average, it can take an entrepreneur about three years to set up a viable business, and even longer if it is a technology orientated business.[2]

In reality, the early stages or 'seed stage' of venture creation is a process- 'a sequence of individual or collective events, actions and activities unfolding over time in context'-[3] that identifies how entrepreneurs:

1. Come up with 'ideas' (creative solutions to problems).
2. Begin to develop a 'start-up proposition' (a plan in their head or a basic outline of the desirability and feasibility of a start-up).[4]
3. Turn their propositions into a viable business opportunity ('situations in which new goods, services, raw materials, and organizing processes can be introduced and sold at greater than their cost of production').[5]

In this chapter, you will learn how entrepreneurs solve problems and how they filter their resulting solution to see if they have a basis for a start-up proposition. To help you, Workbook 1 (pp. 329–344) has a number of practical exercises. These culminate in asking you to develop a short elevator pitch, which is a way of explaining to an external audience the customer problem that you are addressing and what your unique solution is.

Chapters 5, 6, 7, 8 and 9 show you how to further develop your emerging proposition. Supporting this are practical exercises in Workbook 2 (pp. 345–380).

The opening of this chapter, though, focuses on problems. A problem might be that there is a need in a market or, like Dyson, because someone is frustrated by how existing products or services work. Because entrepreneurial contexts are uncertain, these problems are likely to be ill defined, complex and take time and effort to uncover. Spending time on framing and reframing problems is important because 'a problem well put is half solved'.[6]

Generating ideas (solutions to problems) often relies on your prior knowledge, skills and experience. These ideas can emerge from spontaneous 'eureka' moments. However, they can also come from the application of divergent (generation of multiple novel ideas) and convergent (detection of applicable and useful ideas) thinking. This chapter shows you how to use three main idea generation techniques: brainstorming, SCAMPER and analogous thinking.

Not all ideas are the basis for a potential start-up. Ideas need to be filtered for their desirability and feasibility. This chapter shows you how the practical 'Me, Market and Money' model helps you to assess if your emerging idea is attractive and practical. 'Me' is the attractiveness of any match between 'me and the idea'. 'Market' is the belief that there is customer demand for your idea. 'Money' focuses on your assessment of the resources required to start up.

How long it takes to uncover a problem and create, discover or identify a solution depends on the person and the idea. Some people may make quick, almost unconscious, 'guesses' about how viable and desirable a proposed solution is. Others, meanwhile, will take time and effort to work out if their problem is a 'real' problem that they can genuinely solve.

4.2 PROBLEM FRAMING AND REFRAMING

In our everyday lives, problems occur because there is some discrepancy between where we are now and where we would like to be in the future. There is a gap, something is missing or something is wrong. Suppose you are working in a team whose goal is to deliver a project in six weeks' time. However, you are struggling to get in contact with one of your colleagues, they are not coming to meetings and they do not appear to be doing their part of the work. These are the typical symptoms of the 'free-rider' problem.

In entrepreneurial situations, problems are often much more complex and ill defined. It may take time to discover why customer service is poor, prices are high or why the needs of a disadvantaged community are not being met. What is wrong or missing may also be difficult to figure out because the problem is hidden. An entrepreneur can host a focus group with customers to work out if their new product solves the irritations faced by customers. However, all they might find out are current frustrations; it might not reveal future needs. As Steve Jobs suggested: 'It's really hard to design products by focus groups. A lot of times, people don't know what they want until you show it to them.'[7]

4.2.1 Formulating problems

A source for formulating a problem is your own experience. You might recognise a problem in a market or face an everyday frustration. In response, you can formulate 'how can I' problem questions such as:[8]

- How can I/we improve customer service in X industry?
- How can I/we make X service/product work better?
- How can I/we make better use of X?
- How can I/we better able to help disadvantaged people suffering from X?

Problem formulations might also come from:

- Interests, passions or ambitions: *how can I become an entrepreneur?*
- Wanting to use resources such as time, skills and knowledge: *how can I/we make better use of my/our time?*
- The challenges faced by friends and family: *how can I/we fix that for people close to me/us?*
- By actively searching for problems: *what is the biggest problem in X market?*

In focusing on goals, interests and resources, you might shift from stumbling into problem formulation to actively searching out problems to formulate. You can also talk to family and friends about the sorts of problems they face.

An entrepreneur may also apply existing ideas (solutions to problems) to their own context.[9] In the early days of the personal computer industry, Rank Xerox developed the mouse and the graphical user interface at their research facility in Palo Alto, California. Rank Xerox did not realise the potential of these new products, but Bill Gates and Steve Jobs did. This led to tensions. In developing their own personal computers, Jobs accused Gates: 'You're ripping us off! … I trusted you, and now you're stealing from us!' In reply, Gates replied: 'well, Steve … I think it's more like we both had this rich neighbor named Xerox and I broke into his house to steal the TV set and found out that you had already stolen it.'[10]

Problem formulations based on experience may be all an entrepreneur needs. However, this can leave them exposed to cognitive biases and personality dispositions (Chapter 2). Donald Trump objected to the building of a wind-farm close to one of his Scottish golf courses. He believed they would damage tourism. Asked by the Scottish Parliament what his evidence was for this, he replied: 'I am considered a world-class expert in tourism … So when you say, "where is the expert and where is the evidence" – I am the evidence!'[11]

Entrepreneurship in Action

- Write down as many problems as you can think of in ten minutes. Use Post-It notes or a piece of paper. Number and group the problems.
- Formulate the starting problem using 'how can I/we…'.
- Evaluate problems based on the perceived size of the problem, how attractive you find solving the problem, its importance to you or your group, your expertise and your knowledge.

4.2.2 Reframing the problem

Uncovering a problem is not necessarily the same as finding the real problem. A problem may be hidden. If someone is a free-rider in a group, we should not stop at the assumption free-riding is their problem. Instead, we could employ the 'five whys' method to understand the reasons for their behaviour:

1. **Why** is the team member not handing in their work for the project? Because they have been missing meetings.
2. **Why** have they been missing meetings? Because they have been off work for a month.
3. **Why** have they been off work for a month? Because they are stressed.
4. **Why** have they become stressed? Because they are being bullied at work.
5. **Why** are they being bullied at work? Because there are not systems in place to monitor and deal with workplace bullying.

Not all five whys may be needed. During a visit to one of Amazon's fulfilment centres, Chief Executive Officer Jeff Bezos used the technique to understand why one of his workers had damaged their thumb:

1. **Why** was the worker's thumb damaged? Because it was caught in a conveyor belt.
2. **Why** was it caught in a conveyor belt? Because the worker was chasing a bag that they had left on the conveyer belt.
3. **Why** was their bag on the conveyer belt? Because the worker had nowhere else to put their bag.

Amazon resolved this safety issue by introducing tables for their staff.[12]

An alternative way of uncovering the real problem is to ask six open-ended questions – Who, What, Where, When, How and Why.

1. **Why** is this a problem?
2. **Who** faces this problem most often?

3. **What** do they currently do to solve the problem?
4. **Where** does the problem most frequently occur?
5. **When** does the problem most frequently occur?
6. **How** do they feel about the problem?

Problems can also be reframed by paraphrasing them or reversing their focus. Altering the focus of problems to include or exclude additional information can also be useful. 'How can I use a pen to write in space?' is a problem because traditional pens do not work in zero gravity. Spending a large amount of money to develop an antigravity pen could be a solution. Reframing the problem as 'How can I write in space?' might lead someone to use a pencil instead.

In business, 'How can I improve sales?' might be restated as 'How can I increase customer satisfaction?' or 'How can I make the product/service at a cheaper price/higher quality?'

Problem formulations can be visualised using a mind map, in which the original problem is placed at the centre of a piece of paper, whiteboard or computer screen and related issues and new aspects are subsequently drawn. To show causality, arrows are drawn between the original idea and branch ideas.

Entrepreneurship in Action

- Use the five whys exercise to reframe the problem. Talk to users and customers to investigate what the root problem is.
- Use 'Who, What, Where, When, How and Why' to work out the problems facing a customer.
- Restate the problem by reframing using a mind map or 'how can I/we...'.

4.3 FACT-FINDING ABOUT THE PROBLEM

Even if a problem is framed and reframed, it still leaves entrepreneurs open to particular biases. They might assume that because the problem is a problem for them, it must be a problem for other people. One way to estimate if a problem is really a problem is to collect information on the problem context, who is most frustrated by the problem and who they currently use to solve this problem.

4.3.1 PEST analysis

A route towards understanding the business context for a problem is a PEST analysis. PEST is a strategic tool for examining the wider macro-environment. It stands for Political, Economic, Social and Technology:

- *Political* – how governments intervene in the economy such as through employment law, product regulations and by promoting intellectual property rights.
- *Economic* – how macro-economic conditions such as inflation, exchange rates and economic growth impact on business decisions.

- *Social* – how social trends and attitudes such as population size, structure and growth rates, buying patterns, consumer attitudes and lifestyle patterns influence business decisions.
- *Technology* – how new and improved technologies influence industry, consumer trends and business decisions.

4.3.1.1 Political

When the Indian government decided to fight corruption by withdrawing 500 and 1000 rupee notes overnight, it created frustrations for people trying to pay for goods and services. E-wallet companies such as Paytm and Instamojo were able to solve these problems and grew quickly. Governments can also support innovation. The Kenyan government decided to legislate in favour of e-payments, allowing M-Pesa (M for mobile, Pesa for money in Swahili) to become the dominant provider of e-wallet services in Africa.

4.3.1.2 Economic

The Zimbabwean government suspended its currency in 2008 after inflation rates of nearly 80 billion per cent and the introduction of a 100 trillion Zimbabwean dollar note.[13] The resulting economic uncertainties and the difficulties in accessing hard currency led to a return to the use of barter-based transactions. In some cases, goats were used as collateral for loans.[14]

4.3.1.3 Social

With a median population age of 47, Japan's aging population creates ripe conditions for new care homes. Niger's median age of 15 implies greater opportunities for workplace educational providers.[15]

4.3.1.4 Technological

Many major cities around the world have set up large bicycle lending schemes to promote cycling and reduce carbon emissions. These opportunities were traditionally only open to large businesses able to work with local governments and with enough resources to build city-wide docking stations in public areas. The development of apps that track and remotely lock bicycles without the need for docking stations has opened up the market for start-ups, particularly in China.[16]

PEST can be extended to include Legal and Environmental factors (PESTLE) or Ethical issues (STEEPLE: Social Technological Economic Environmental Political Legal and Ethical).

Entrepreneurship in Action

- Conduct a PEST analysis of a problem area. Identify key trends and relate these to the problem.
- Take part in an ideas challenge. Many governments, universities, private sector organisations, charities and non-governmental agencies across the world have open competitions where they ask for new ideas about how to solve societal, environmental and economic problems. These problems can be large-scale, open-ended and complex 'wicked problems'.[17] For example, climate change responses require changes to how consumers, regulators, researchers and

entrepreneurs act together to reduce greenhouse gas emissions. In response, organisations periodically offer idea challenges – sometimes with a cash prize – for ideas that provide ways to improve our planet's sustainability. Other idea challenges or 'hackathons' (short, intensive sessions where individuals and groups come together to discuss, design and develop solutions to problems) focus on 'tamer' problems that seek ways of solving particular issues.

- Find an ideas challenge running in your country or internationally for a problem that you want to solve. Get together a team to discuss, design and develop a solution to the problem. Alternatively, create your own ideas challenge or hackathon to solve a particular problem.

4

Assessment tip: Finding the gap

A good literature review maps out a topic. You can see where the evidence is strong and where there are gaps. Take the question 'Are women less likely to become entrepreneurs?'. The standard answer is yes because women have lower self-employment rates than men across the world. Standard reasons for this include sexism, discrimination and stereotyping.

Yet there are problems. One gap is that in some countries women are more likely to be self-employed than men (Chapter 1, p. 13). What explains this gap?

Spotting what is wrong or what is missing presents opportunities to develop insights in your academic writing. A major problem with the entrepreneurship literature is its focus on the experiences of entrepreneurs in richer countries. What is often missing is evidence about entrepreneurs in poorer countries.

4.3.2 Customer journeys

Another way of deliberately searching for problems is to create a model customer – a customer vignette – and consider how they might use a good or service (see Workbook Exercise W 1.13 and Chapter 6, p. 133 for more information). This customer vignette (or persona) should include demographic information such as their age, gender and income. It should also consider what they like and dislike about the product or service.

The next stage is to chart out their customer journey. This involves working out what the customer does before, during and after using a good or service.

For example, people with disabilities may encounter issues using train services. To find out if they face problems in their customer journey, a train company might work out if they face challenges *before* they start their journey, such as planning the journey, payment and ticketing, and arriving at the station. Next, they might examine how issues such as seating or on-board services affect disabled people *during* their train journey. Finally, they can look at what happens *after* the train journey, such as how easy is it for customers to get a refund. To make sure that their data is robust, the train company can collect information from relevant secondary sources and talk to train users about their frustrations and problems.

Case Study: Rome2rio

© Getty Images/iStockphoto

Australian entrepreneurs Bernhard Tschirren and Michael Cameron set up Rome2rio as a result of their frustrations with independently travelling from one place to another place. Travel search engines only present options for flying from one place to another and fail to identify how the traveller is going to get from the airport to their destination. This is particularly difficult in Europe and Asia where there are various ways of getting from place to place. Rome2rio offers an anywhere-to-anywhere search engine to help independent travellers work out the best way to reach their destination.

4.3.3 Jobs to be hired

Another approach is to focus on how people use existing products to solve problems. To increase sales of their milkshakes, McDonalds in the United States (US) ran focus groups on the key groups that bought milkshakes (a customer journey-style approach). These focus groups highlighted ways they could improve their milkshake recipe. This guidance did not lead to an increase in sales, so they tried a different approach.

This time the research focused on what 'job' milkshakes were 'hired' to do. By closely observing buying habits and interviewing customers, the McDonalds' researchers discovered men in the USA 'hired' milkshakes because they were easy to drink, were clean and kept hunger at bay on their long daily drive to work. Milkshakes did a better job than bagels because they were less messy. They were also better than bananas at preventing hunger before lunchtime.

Framing the milkshake as a 'job to be hired' led McDonald's to generate solutions such as thicker milkshakes, which made people feel fuller for longer, and the use of electronic payments to make it quicker to buy them.[18]

Entrepreneurship in Action

- Choose a product/service (a job) for 'hire'.
- Explore its use and the problems customers face with this 'job'.

Many entrepreneurial problems stem from personal experiences. Systematic approaches that search for additional information, frame and reframe problems can be useful in formulating a problem statement. These problem statements identify facts about the problem, such as who faces the problem and what is wrong or missing. An example of a problem statement is:

> Unfortunately, workplace bullying is a serious problem. Last year, 14 per cent of the European workforce experienced some form of bullying at work, and it was more of a problem for younger people.[19]

Go to Exercise W 1.6: What is your problem statement?

Discussion questions:

- Do you think it is worthwhile framing and reframing problems to solve? Is it better to rely on 'eureka' moments?
- Do you think it is better to start problem identification by focusing on unmet needs and problems, or is it better to focus first on how products or services are 'hired' for a job?

4.4 GENERATING SOLUTIONS

Some people do stumble on entrepreneurial solutions.[20] Alexander Fleming accidentally discovered Penicillin. He had gone on holiday, leaving a pile of Petri dishes smeared with the Staphylococcus bacteria in his sink. When he returned, he discovered that the bacteria Penicillium notatum had killed the Staphylococcus.

Post-It notes, Velcro and 'cat's eyes' on roads also came from 'eureka' moments. Accidental discoveries suggest there is something special about those that find solutions to problems. Kirzner (Chapter 1, pp. 6–7) argued that these people are 'entrepreneurially alert', leading to the idea that being able to spot solutions is innate.[21]

This is not the only mechanism for uncovering solutions. Entrepreneurs rely on their expertise, gained from their experiences and knowledge. They also rely on their social capital.

Academic Insight: Teresa Amabile's model of creativity

Teresa Amabile suggests that there are three influential factors in the emergence of creativity (Figure 4.1).[22]

1. Expertise – gained from knowledge, background or experience. Expertise frames the 'network of possible wanderings'.[23] It is difficult to be a creative accountant if you have no idea about how financial statements work. Solutions therefore often come from 'inside the box' rather than thinking 'outside the box'.[24]
   Entrepreneurs also use their experience to 'connect the dots'.[25] These mental models come from 'prototype' modelling, which compares existing knowledge with new information, and 'exemplar' modelling, which relies on learned best practice examples to identify potential business opportunities.[26]
   Having access to prior knowledge is a fertile route for discovering solutions.[27] About seven out of ten start-ups develop from prior work experience, reflecting Richard Branson's suggestion that 'the best businesses come from people's bad personal experiences ... if you keep your eyes open, you are going to find something that frustrates you and you think that maybe you can do it better than it has been done ... and if you can improve people's lives you have a business'.[28]

Figure 4.1 Amabile's model of creativity

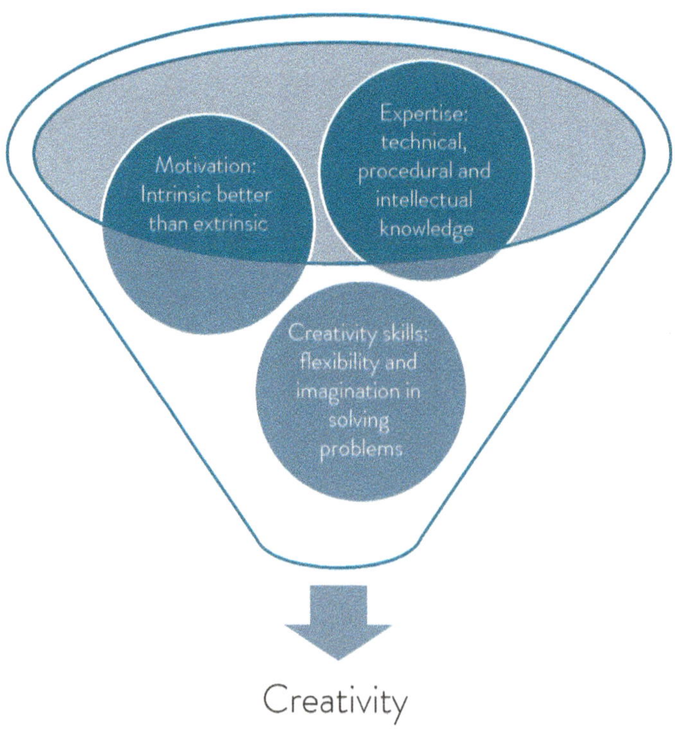

Social networks are also important for developing solutions.[29] If you have a wide portfolio of contacts, you might be able to 'bridge' between these different networks to identify solutions.[30] For example, the energy drink Red Bull only came to the European market after Dietrich Mateschitz had drunk a Thai drink called Krating Daeng to recover from the jet lag he got after his flight to Thailand. Sufficiently intrigued, Mateschitz used his contacts to set up a meeting with Krating Daeng's developer, Chaleo Yoovidhya. This resulted in a joint venture to modify Krating Daeng for the European market.

2. Motivation levels – entrepreneurs who are intrinsically motivated and passionate are more likely to be creative than those who are solely motivated by external factors, such as making sure employees work or paying the bills.

3. Creative skills – Amabile sees these as abilities to 'break mental set during problem solving'.[31] These skills might be innate and relate to 'eureka' moments. Relying on inspiration is only one way of getting to solutions; it might provide poor returns because spontaneity relies on luck.[32] Instead, deliberative and systematic search procedures to purposively scan and search the environment for solutions can develop creative skills.

There also exist a range of creative techniques for identifying solutions. These often rely on divergent thinking. Where convergent thinking often leads people to believe a problem has only one answer (e.g. 5 + 5 = 10), divergent thinking suggests there could be many potential solutions.

For example, ? +? = 10 can be solved by adding 5 + 5, but it can also be answered using fractions (e.g. 7¼ + 2¾) or negative numbers (25–15).

Divergent thinking allows for the identification of potential solutions. Below there are three key techniques: brainstorming, SCAMPER and analogous thinking. All of them involve stretching, expanding or changing solutions.

4.4.1 Brainstorming

This technique uses free association to come up with a wide range of solutions. A good initial brainstorm is one that first frames and reframes a problem to focus on the underlying issue. Brainstorming is suitable for a specific problem that has no single obvious answer, such as how to solve an aspect of global warming, improve people's health or provide better ways to use a good or service.[33]

Once the problem is set, brainstorming has four simple rules:

1. The larger the number of solutions, the better.
2. Wild solutions are welcomed.
3. Combining and improving ideas is good.
4. There should be no criticism of any idea generated.

Brainstorming can be done individually or as part of a group. One good way is for individuals to do brainstorming on their own first and do further brainstorming later in a group.[34] In another version – brainwriting – people write down as many solutions as they can think of and then pass their paper to a team member, who adds to these solutions.

4.4.2 SCAMPER

Checklists can also be useful in generating solutions. SCAMPER is a popular method:

- **S**_ubstitute_ a part of a process, product or service with another.
- **C**_ombine_ with other functions, materials or objects.
- **A**_dapt_ the product, service or design to another use.
- **M**_odify_ by either magnifying or minimising the product, service or design.
- **P**_ut to other uses_ by changing the original product, service or design to meet the needs of another type of consumer.
- **E**_liminate or elaborate_ the product, service or design.
- **R**_earrange or move sections_ of the product, service or design.

SCAMPER helped designers redesign the children's toothbrush. They identified that young children found it difficult to use a normal length toothbrush, so they shortened the toothbrush and made it fatter so that it fit more easily into the hands of young children.[35]

Case Study: Baubax Travel Jacket

© Getty Images/EyeEm

An Indian couple, Hiral Sanghavi and Yoganshi Shah, often forgot to bring a travel pillow with them on their flights between India and the USA. Having to buy a new pillow each time was irritating. They designed the Baubax Travel Jacket as a 'Swiss Army knife' jacket that combined, rearranged and modified a travel jacket to incorporate a built-in neck pillow, eye mask and gloves. Their jacket, which also features earphone holders, a drink holder and pockets of different sizes, subsequently raised $9 million on Kickstarter, a crowdfunding platform.

4.4.3 Analogical thinking

Bringing heterogeneous (diverse) ideas together can be another way of thinking 'outside the box'. Using analogies such as 'organisations can be compared to bee colonies' can stretch and extend ideas. Imaginatively applying metaphors such as 'he had a wooden heart' can bring contrasting or irrelevant elements together to create new solutions.

This can have practical benefits. It might involve translating a restaurant concept or style of food from one country to another or translating ideas from nature into a business.[36] The inspiration behind Velcro was that George de Mestral went for a walk with his dog and found that burrs had stuck to his clothes and to the hair of his dog. This gave him the idea of a hook and loop fastening system.

Entrepreneurship in Action

- Use brainstorming, SCAMPER or analogical thinking to generate ideas to solve a specific problem that you have framed and reframed.
- Start a creativity journal that records ten ideas each day for solving problems.

4.4.4 Evaluating ideas

Creativity techniques such as brainstorming emphasise the importance of coming up with a large number of solutions to a specific problem. At some point, these ideas have to be evaluated. One way of teasing out which is the 'best' is to work out if the idea is creative. There are two main criteria for judging the creativity of an idea:

1. If the idea is novel, original or rare relative to other ideas.
2. If the idea is useful – relative to other ideas.

Unfortunately, unless people are prompted to choose original ideas over useful ideas, they tend to favour practical ideas over ingenious or imaginative ideas.[37]

Entrepreneurship in Action

- Rate your ideas in terms of originality (1=completely unoriginal, 10=completely original).
- Rate your ideas in terms of usefulness (1=completely unuseful, 10= completely useful).

Ideas can come from 'eureka' moments inspired by chance discovery, but it is more likely they are rooted in someone's expertise and background. Rather than being found, they are often made. Entrepreneurs can build on problem statements such as:

> Unfortunately, workplace bullying is a serious problem. Last year, 14 per cent of the European workforce experienced some form of bullying at work, and it was more of a problem for younger people.

They can do so by using divergent thinking exercises such as brainstorming to help turn a problem into a solution. However, there are advantages in carefully and systematically scanning and researching solutions to problems. Both these approaches could lead to idea statements such as:

> Our solution is an app in which people record and document instances of bullying and inappropriate actions and behaviours.

- *Go to Exercise W 1.7: What is your idea statement?*

4.5 'ME, MARKET AND MONEY'

It is unlikely that most people have heard of Murray Spangler, Harvey Ball or Alexey Pajitnov. But Spangler came up with the vacuum cleaner, Ball with the 'smiley' icon and Pajitnov built the game Tetris. Each had an idea (a solution to a problem) but failed to make the most of it.

These examples also illustrate a basic difference between an inventor and an innovator. Inventors come up with new ideas. Entrepreneurs are innovators because they *commercialise* ideas: 'generating good ideas or adopting a new one, in and of itself, is only the start. To be an innovation, an idea must be converted into a product or service that customers want.'[38]

One other crude difference is that the inventor might just be interested in the idea because they like inventing: the idea is an end in itself. Nearly three-quarters of a group of Canadian inventors were told that there was no commercial basis to their invention. This did not stop them: they carried on developing the invention.[39]

For the entrepreneur, at some point the focus has to turn away from the idea to assessing its desirability and feasibility. Figure 4.2 suggests filtering ideas through an early sifting process ('Me, Market and Money') to establish if the idea is a start-up proposition. 'Me' relates principally to the attractiveness of the idea, whilst 'Market' and 'Money' focuses more on the practicality of the idea.

Figure 4.2 Idea to start-up proposition: 'Me, Market and Money'

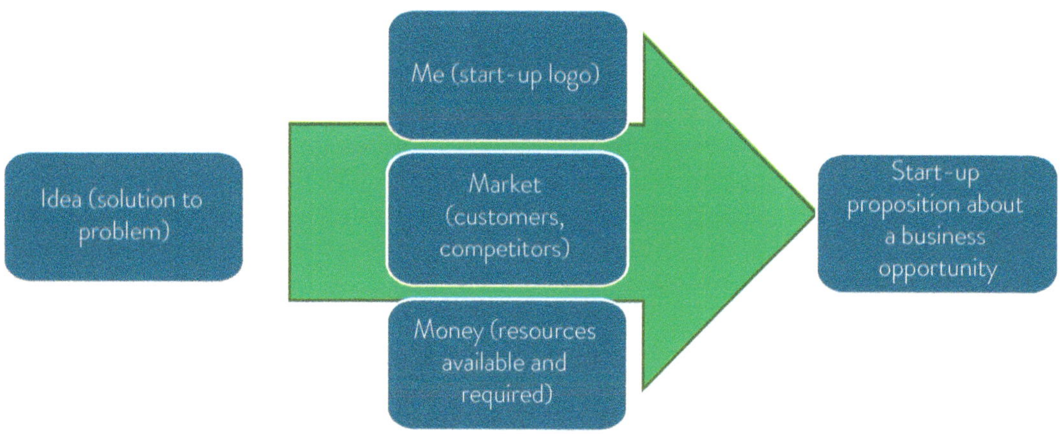

4.5.1 'Me'

'Me' relates to an entrepreneur's assessment of how attractive the match between themselves and any idea is. Richard Branson passed on an opportunity to invest in the board game Trivial Pursuit because it did not fit in with his existing portfolio of businesses.[40] Ideas have to be desirable and fit with an entrepreneur's goals to make them worth pursuing. This involves assessing four features:

1. Does an idea match the entrepreneur's goals? Can entrepreneurs picture how it will help them achieve goals such as making money, having more freedom or helping disadvantaged people? These goals may be fuzzy because the idea – like the entrepreneur's goals – is likely to change over time.[41]
2. Does the idea fit with the entrepreneur's skills, experience, interests and dispositions?[42]
3. Is the idea attractive to the entrepreneur's friends, family and colleagues?[43] If it is not, this may limit the idea's attractiveness for an entrepreneur.
4. Is it the 'right' time? An idea might be attractive and have a high degree of fit with the entrepreneur but still be rejected because it is not the most opportune time for them.[44]

These questions are important, particularly when the potential entrepreneur has developed a range of business ideas and is seeking to decide which one is the most promising.

○ *Go to Exercise W 1.8: How desirable is starting up?*

4.5.2 'Market'

'Market' is the belief that there is customer demand for an idea. This confidence can stem from different sources. The entrepreneur might presume that there *ought* to be people willing to pay for the idea. They may also have spoken to family and friends who believe in the idea. They may also have a few early customers. FedEx founder Fred Smith came up with the idea for FedEx in an undergraduate essay. He saw the potential of a fully integrated air-shipping next-day delivery service for the whole of the USA. However, to turn his 'just-in-time' logistics idea into a start-up required a customer. He began FedEx by setting-up a small operation to target medical service businesses that urgently needed to receive their products on a next-day basis.[45]

Not all customers are found. Some show up unexpectedly. About a quarter of start-ups emerge from hobbies because customers come along wanting to purchase what the hobbyist has to offer.[46]

Case Study: Caught in a mousetrap?

One of the most patented ideas is the mousetrap. Just in the USA, more than 4400 patents have been granted for mousetrap ideas. American writer Waldo Emerson supposedly said: 'a man need only build a better mousetrap and the world will beat a path to your door'. However, only 24 of these 4400 mousetraps ever made a return.[47] This led the advertising executive O. B. Winters to say: 'the manufacturer who waits for the world to beat a path to his door is a great optimist. But the manufacturer who shows his 'mousetrap' to the world keeps the smoke coming out his chimney.'[48]

○ *Go to Exercise W 1.9: Who is your target customer?*

Market feasibility is also determined by competition. An idea can meet consumer needs and have early customers but be impractical if the competition is too strong and there are regulatory or ethical barriers. Entrepreneurs might be further concerned if their idea is too easy for competitors to 'reverse engineer' and copy or because they are worried about being bullied out of the market by the competition.

- *Go to Exercise W 1.10: Who are your competitors?*

Ideas can also have a finite 'window of opportunity'.[49] Robert Thomson invented the pneumatic tyre in 1845. It was a radical advance on solid rubber tyres. Unfortunately, in 1845 there was no market for his tyres because cars and bicycles were only starting to emerge as a mode of transport. In 1887, John Dunlop rediscovered how to make pneumatic tyres just as cars and bicycle manufacturing was beginning to take off. He subsequently became one of the world's largest manufacturers of car and bicycle tyres. Twitter founder Jack Dorsey first had the idea for Twitter in the early 2000s. He could send micro-blog messages but this required that others had the same mobile phone. None of them did. As Dorsey said 'wrong time, good idea, put it [the idea] on the shelf'.[50]

- *Go to Exercise W 1.11: What is happening in your market?*

4.5.3 'Money'

Whether it is because market research is necessary or there is a need to build a product or sell a service, nearly all entrepreneurs have unavoidable start-up expenses.

- *Go to Exercise W 1.12: What financial resources do you have for a start-up?*

There are, however, instances of entrepreneurs who start up with no up-front financial resources. A fashion designer can take their design collection to a client who is so impressed that they draw up a contract there and then to buy their collection. With the security provided by this contract, the designer could next go to a manufacturer who agrees to make the collection. After the clothes are made and delivered, the designer could collect the payment from the client, pay the manufacturer and still have enough profit to fund their next collection.

Such a scenario is uncommon. Most start-ups have limited resources and have to economise on these resources. This is called 'bootstrapping' the business. To make their resources go further, entrepreneurs might choose to use a 'combination of methods that reduce overall capital requirements, improve cash flow, and take advantage of personal sources of financing'.[51] Rather than buy a brand-new piece of capital equipment, a bootstrapping start-up might choose to lease it or purchase it second-hand.

Case Study: The beginnings of Silicon Valley

Silicon Valley was born in a 12 by 18 foot (3.5 × 5.5 metre) garage at 367 Addison Avenue in Palo Alto, California. From its concrete floor and workbench, Bill Hewlett and Dave Packard began building prototype electrical equipment. While Lucile Packard supported her husband by working as a secretary, his and Hewlett's makeshift factory laid the foundations for Hewlett-Packard to become one of the world's leading information technology (IT) companies.[52]

© Getty Images/Bloomberg

○ *Go to Exercise W 1.13: How can you bootstrap your start-up?*

Also integral to the resources available to an entrepreneur is their social capital. This is their network of family, friends and acquaintances. These people might provide emotional support, act as a mentor, provide financial support or signpost a new entrepreneur to others who might be able to help them. These are often critical because if a prospective entrepreneur cannot find the right people to work with, they might decide that the idea is unworkable.

○ *Go to Exercise W 1.14: How can your social networks help you start up?*

Entrepreneurship in Action

One of the challenges facing potential entrepreneurs is deciding on which of their ideas is the most likely to meet their goals. This is difficult because entrepreneurs may have a hazy understanding of what they want from a business idea. Even if they have a clear goal, another problem is working out which one of their potential ideas is most likely to achieve their goal. Worse still, even if they have a goal and a clear idea, their idea may have applications in multiple markets.

Low-cost frameworks such as 'Me, Market and Money' can help entrepreneurs make initial choices about their goals, what idea to pursue, which market to focus on and if the idea can feasibly come to fruition.

Another way of identifying and classifying business ideas is to think through if an idea is a 'dream' business idea. The characteristics of this 'dream' winning business idea will vary but often contain these key features:

- **Idea solves a 'real' problem – it is a 'must-have' rather than a 'nice-to-have' solution.** Marcin Kleczynski set up his antivirus software business Malwarebytes when he was at university. He knew that this was a 'must-have' solution when he asked his university's IT service to send an IT technician to fix a virus on his university computer. The technician came along, logged onto Kleczynski's Malwarebytes website and downloaded Kleczynski's antivirus programme. Kleczynski's said: 'I didn't say anything, I stood behind him and watched him fix my computer with my software to get me back online. He left never knowing who I was, but to this day I love that moment.'[53]

- **The market is large and growing rapidly.** Developments in artificial intelligence, blockchain, machine learning and natural language processing have developed new and fast growing markets in areas such as 'fintech' (technological applications to financial services), 'regtech' (regulation) and 'pubtech' (public services), which can offer new disruptive entrepreneurial opportunities.
- **Barriers to entry exist.** One way of guarding and developing a competitive advantage is to have access to intellectual property (Chapter 7, pp.157–162). Another is to develop a business method or a strong customer relationship that makes it difficult for competitors to replicate or reverse engineer a business idea.
- **It is easy to overcome customer habits.** Although a competitor may be slow or inept, the idea still has to overcome prior buying habits and the risks inherent in a new product or service. Easing this process is a sales and marketing strategy that allows customers to easily find, evaluate and buy a new product or service (Chapter 6, pp. 142–144).
- **There are strong early positive cashflows.** Cash is king in a start-up (Chapter 8, 202–207) because a start-up needs money to fund and develop a business idea. A start-up that is under-capitalised is more likely to close (Chapter 11, p. 284). Strong early cashflows are also likely to attract investors willing to support and develop the business.

Although these key characteristics of a 'dream' business idea can be expanded to include other characteristics such as a capable team (Chapter 7, 162–170), it is unlikely at the very start that all of the benefits and challenges of a business idea will be known. For that reason, it is often important to keep an open mind about different ideas and markets until you are clearer about the opportunity.

- Use the 'Me, Market and Money' framework to evaluate your business ideas. Rank your ideas in terms of their feasibility and desirability.
- Assess your ideas against the characteristics of a dream business idea. Rank them.
- It is likely that your initial assessment of your ideas against the 'dream' characteristics will produce significant 'unknowns'. For example, it may be difficult at this preliminary stage to know what the best way of reaching customers is or how much money you will need to develop a business idea. Categorise your business ideas into three: your 'best for now' idea, your 'back-up' idea and your 'cold storage' idea.

These issues are considered further in Chapter 5 (p. 102).

4.6 IS STARTING UP RIGHT FOR THE IDEA?

Although the 'Me, Market and Money' model provides a way of beginning to evaluate if an idea is a practical and attractive start-up proposition, entrepreneurs still face risks and uncertainties. Setting up might eat up all of their savings, be stressful and involve long hours during which they see little of their family and friends.

Before embarking on a start-up, founders ought to consider alternative ways of developing their business idea. There are three main options:

1. Licensing or selling an idea.
2. Buying an existing business.
3. Franchising.

Some ideas can be protected by intellectual property rights (Chapter 7, pp. 157–162). If so, this opens up the option of selling or licensing the idea to an existing business. Licensing the idea (an up-front licence payment followed by regular royalty payments on each sale) is attractive if an inventor does not want to become an entrepreneur. Alternatively, licensing is common in some industries because it is costly and difficult to commercialise an idea. For example, to develop a new drug involves lab, animal and human testing. Beyond these expenses, there are the costs of producing and marketing the drug. Subsequently, an inventor might license a drug to a large company that has the capability to commercialise, manufacture and sell the drug. In doing so, inventors often draw up a licensing agreement that specifies if the licence can be only used by the company or is available to other companies (exclusive, non-exclusive), how long the licence lasts and in which countries or sectors can it be used.

Case Study: Left with a poor taste in the mouth?

Having developed the original formula for Listerine mouthwash in the 1880s, Dr Joseph Lawrence licensed it to Warner-Lambert Pharmaceuticals. The company dutifully paid Lawrence and his heirs royalties for the next 70 years. However, when other companies began to reverse engineer and copy the formula, Warner-Lambert took the Lawrence family to court to try and get out of its obligations. The judge dismissed the case, pointing out there was no stipulation in the licence agreement that royalty payments would ever end.

Another option is to buy an existing business. This can save the entrepreneur the expense, time and effort of venture creation. Existing businesses also often have a 'brand' and pre-existing ways of doing business. An entrepreneur may take their idea and seek to develop it within an existing organisation.

But buying a going concern can be expensive, and it can be difficult to find out why the business is being sold. Although it is often possible to examine the accounts, there may be hidden problems such as low staff morale and a hostile set of customers, suppliers and financiers. There is also no guarantee that the idea can be easily transplanted into an existing organisation.

The final option for business ownership is franchising. This can be an attractive alternative to starting a business from scratch, particularly if someone is more interested in being a business owner than further developing their own business idea. It involves two main parties: a franchisor and a franchisee. A franchisor is a company that provides a range of benefits for a regular fee or a mark-up on sales. These include the use of its brand, the ability to sell its products and services, a method for doing business and expert support. Famous franchisors include Domino's Pizza, McDonald's, Subway and convenience stores such as 7-Eleven.

A franchisee is a separate independent company that agrees to pay for the franchisor's services and accept its terms and conditions. Having met these commitments, the franchisee keeps the remaining income and is free to run their business in a way that suits them.

Franchising can be attractive to both parties. For franchisors, it has these advantages:

- **Lower costs** – franchisees usually have to fund the setting up of their own franchise outlet; the more franchisees there are, the greater the purchasing power of the franchisor to drive down their own costs.
- **Lower management costs** – franchisees are responsible for employing and managing their own staff.
- **A viable exit route** – if the franchisee fails to uphold their terms and conditions, the franchisor can cancel their contract; if the franchisor has a 'brand', it may be possible to sell the franchise.
- **Better growth incentives** – independent franchisees may be better motivated towards business growth than directly owned outlets run by managers who have a secure salary.
- **Cost effective business growth** – because franchisees fund their own set up costs and may have to pay for the right to set up an outlet, growth funding may be easier and cheaper than going to a bank or investors.

For the start-up franchisee, there are also benefits:

- **Limits uncertainty** – they are given a brand, a proven formula for doing business and opportunities for economies of scale such as bulk buying and shared marketing costs.
- **Support** – start-up can be lonely, so being part of a franchise gives the start-up access to training and assistance that helps to grow the business.
- **Exclusivity** – franchisees often have exclusive rights to sell the product or service in an area, potentially making it easier to establish and grow the business.
- **Eases entry costs** – if the franchise has a proven well-known brand, there is less need to test market the product or service and develop relationships with suppliers.
- **Lower costs** – it may be cheaper to buy a franchise than set up a new business; external financiers may be more willing to invest knowing that the franchisee is part of a wider established franchise network.

Case Study: The Subway franchise model

Fred DeLuca started Subway to fund his future career as a medical doctor. With backing from a family friend, Peter Buck, DeLuca set up Doctor's Associates to manage the sandwich chain's business operations. The company now has more than 43,000 stores worldwide in 110 countries. As a franchisor, Doctor's Associates Inc. provides a range of support for new franchisees, such as training through the University of Subway, support with restaurant design, site selection and equipment ordering. After opening, franchisees get ongoing support from field consultants, advertising and from Subway's economies of scale in bulk food purchasing. Franchisees pay 8 per cent of their net sales to Doctor's Associates plus 4.5 per cent for advertising and marketing activity. Franchisors also source their own restaurant location and fund their own restaurant set up costs.[54]

Discussion questions:

- Franchising ought to provide better performance benefits such as better growth or an increased chance of business survival. However, the evidence suggests that franchised businesses do not survive for any longer than independent businesses, and even when they do they only perform better for a short time.[55] Why do you think this is the case?

Entrepreneurship in Action

- Find and examine a franchise business in the same industry as your business idea. Is becoming a franchise a better way for you to achieve your goals?
- Being a franchisee is a balance between lower uncertainty and having to share profits and control in your business. Would you be happy with this balance?

Go to Exercise W 1.15: Is starting up the right choice?

4.7 THE ELEVATOR PITCH

The 'Me, Market and Money' model can be used to begin to develop a mental model of what a start-up might look like. Entrepreneurs can use it to self-assess if their idea is both feasible and desirable. If it meets these conditions, it provides confidence in pursuing the idea. If not, it suggests that the idea either needs to be abandoned or changed before further resources and effort are spent on developing the idea.

Go to Exercise W 1.16: Is the idea really a start-up proposition?

Often, though, start-up entrepreneurs have to convince others. If they want support and assistance from friends and family, they usually need some explanation of why they are embarking on starting up.

Sometimes they also have to convince external audiences or financiers about their start-up proposition. One way of achieving this is to develop a short 'elevator' pitch. The basis for this is the idea that a prospective entrepreneur happens to meet a potential mentor or funder in an elevator. In the short time available, the entrepreneur takes up the opportunity to pitch their business idea hoping that it will lead to a concrete action such as having a full meeting later on, at which the entrepreneur can explain more fully their idea through a presentation or a plan.

There is no one format for an elevator pitch. It may be as short as ten seconds or last a few minutes. Nonetheless, a basic format is to first identify a problem (problem statement) and propose a solution (idea statement). The entrepreneur might then explain how the idea will help improve the lives of people (the customer) and why it is better than what is currently on offer (the competition). They may also identify why they or their team can deliver on the idea (motivations and expertise) and what support they need (call to action with stakeholder).

For example, the elevator pitch of an entrepreneur interested in developing driverless cars for blind people in China could be:

- Hi, I am Liang Han. Did you know 17 million blind people in China do not have an easy way to get to work?[56]
- This means that they have to rely on others to get them to work and often have to accept unsuitable work.[57]
- So I came up with a driverless car. This is better than what is currently on offer because there are no driverless cars that are specifically adapted to help blind people drive and can use as their mobile office.

- As an engineer with ten years' experience in the automotive industry, I have the expertise and passion to push this start-up forward so that blind people will have greater opportunities to work and be productive.
- I am looking for your help to give blind people the freedom to live a fuller life. Are you interested in talking further?

Entrepreneurship in Action

Another way of structuring an elevator pitch is to use the pitching method developed by animation studio Pixar. It has this logic[58]:

- Once upon a time there was ... Every day ... One day ... Because of that ... Because of that ... Until finally...

Pixar uses this logic to summarise its film Finding Nemo:

- Once upon a time there was ... Marlin who was over-protective towards his only son Nemo
- Every day ... Marlin warned Nemo of swimming away
- One day ... Nemo got annoyed and swam away
- Because of that ... Nemo got caught by a diver who put him in his fish tank in Sydney
- Because of that ... Marlin sets off to find Nemo
- Until finally ... Marlin and Nemo find each other and learn love depends on trust.

This structure can be adapted to business elevator pitches:

- Once upon a time there was ... a problem (specify who faces the problem)
- Every day ... this is a big problem (how many and what type of people face the problem)
- One day ... we came up with a solution (who we are and what our idea is)
- Because of that ... (what we are going to do)
- Because of that ... (how our solution will impact on the problem)
- Until finally ... what is the wider impact of the solution to the problem?

- *Go to Exercise W 1.17: Assessing and pitching your idea.*

4.8 WHAT YOU HAVE LEARNED IN THIS CHAPTER

You have charted the early fuzzy entrepreneurial journey from ideas (solutions to problems) to start-up propositions (a mental model or early sketch of the desirability and feasibility of a start-up). And you have learned that framing and reframing problems is critical. Entrepreneurs are seen sometimes as 'inventors' of ideas but it is often better to see them as problem-solvers.

Solving problems can stem from 'eureka' moments where you spontaneously find an idea. More likely, though, is that ideas come from your personal experiences, motivations and creative skills. The chapter has shown you a range of creative techniques like brainstorming for generating ideas.

You should now also understand that filtering an idea's desirability and feasibility is a core step in making the transition towards start-up viability. You have seen how the 'Me, Market and Money' model allows you to initially self-assess if an idea is a start-up proposition. The idea has to resonate with you, give you confidence that it is feasible and allow you to judge if the right vehicle for the idea is a start-up. Workbook 1 provides a range of practical exercises to help you develop your start-up idea. It also gives you the chance to create a brief elevator pitch for an external audience.

Chapters 5, 6, 7 and 8 and Workbook 2 suggest ways that you can further sketch and detail your start-up planning.

ASSESSMENT QUESTIONS

1. Kirzner suggests that entrepreneurs have to be 'alert' to opportunities. Do you think that this is an innate ability?
2. Is the entrepreneur an inventor or innovator?
3. Explain Amabile's model. What implications does it have for understanding creativity?
4. Are entrepreneurial solutions to problems more likely to be found by systematically searching for opportunities?
5. In assessing an idea, should entrepreneurs give more weight to its desirability or its feasibility?

FURTHER READING

Amabile, T. M. (1998, September–October). How to kill creativity, *Harvard Business Review*, pp. 77–87.

Baron, R. A. (2006). Opportunity recognition as pattern recognition: How entrepreneurs "connect the dots" to identify new business opportunities. *The Academy of Management Perspectives*, *20*(1), 104–119.

Fiet, J. O. (2007). A prescriptive analysis of search and discovery. *Journal of Management Studies*, *44*(4), 592–611.

Shane, S. (2000). Prior knowledge and the discovery of entrepreneurial opportunities. *Organization Science*, *11*(4), 448–469.

Notes

1 www.telegraph.co.uk/finance/newsbysector/supportservices/2795244/James-Dyson-the-vacuum-dreamer.html.

2 Hechavarría, D. M., Tian, L. R., & Reynolds, P. D. (2017, October). To plan or not to plan: The effects of business planning on start-up speed and outcomes. researchgate.net; Liao, J. J., & Welsch, H. (2008). Patterns of venture gestation process: Exploring the differences between tech and non-tech nascent entrepreneurs. *The Journal of High Technology Management Research, 19*(2), 103–113; Hopp, C., & Greene, F. J. (2018). In pursuit of time: Business plan sequencing, duration and intraentrainment effects on new venture viability. *Journal of Management Studies, 55*(2), 320–351.

3 Pettigrew, A. M. (1997). What is a processual analysis. *Scandinavian Journal of Management, 13*(4), 337–348, 338.

4 Bhave, M. P. (1994). A process model of entrepreneurial venture creation. *Journal of Business Venturing, 9*(3), 223–242; Hsieh, C., Nickerson, J. A., & Zenger, T. R. (2007). Opportunity discovery, problem solving and a theory of the entrepreneurial firm. *Journal of Management Studies, 44*(7), 1255–1277; Murphy, P. J. (2011). A 2 × 2 conceptual foundation for entrepreneurial discovery theory. *Entrepreneurship Theory and Practice, 35*(2), 359–374; Wood, M. S., & Williams, D. W. (2014). Opportunity evaluation as rule-based decision making. *Journal of Management Studies, 51*(4), 573–602; Vogel, P. (2017). From venture idea to venture opportunity. *Entrepreneurship Theory and Practice, 41*(6), 943–971.

5 Shane, S., & Venkataraman, S. (2000). The promise of entrepreneurship as a field of research. *Academy of Management Review, 25*(1), 217–226.

6 Quote from the philosopher John Dewey: quotefancy.com/quote/1162051/John-Dewey-It-is-a-familiar-and-significant-saying-that-a-problem-well-put-is-half-solved.

7 www.forbes.com/sites/davidsturt/2014/01/03/delight-your-customers-by-giving-them-what-they-didnt-ask-for/#343654e41e48.

8 Baer, J. M. (1988). Long-term effects of creativity training with middle school students. *The Journal of Early Adolescence, 8*(2), 183–193.

9 Von Hippel, E., & Von Krogh, G. (2015). Crossroads—Identifying viable "need–solution pairs": Problem solving without problem formulation. *Organization Science, 27*(1), 207–221.

10 mspoweruser.com/bill-gates-response-to-steve-jobs-on-windows-rip-off-claim.

11 www.bbc.co.uk/news/resources/idt-sh/Trump_and_Scotland.

12 www.shmula.com/jeff-bezos-5-why-exercise-root-cause-analysis-cause-and-effect-ishikawa-lean-thinking-six-sigma/987/.

13 Hanke, S. H., & Kwok, A. K. (2009). On the measurement of Zimbabwe's hyperinflation. *Cato Journal, 29*(2), 353–364.

14 www.theindependent.co.zw/2017/04/21/zim-regresses-barter-trade/.

15 https://www.cia.gov/library/publications/resources/the-world-factbook/geos/ng.html

16 www.thenational.ae/business/technology/china-rides-into-a-bike-sharing-future-1.700338.

17 Rittel, H. W., & Webber, M. M. (1973). Dilemmas in a general theory of planning. *Policy Sciences, 4*(2), 155–169.

18 https://store.hbr.org/product/finding-the-right-job-for-your-product/smr240?sku=SMR240-PDF-ENG.

19 www.eurofound.europa.eu/publications/report/2015/violence-and-harassment-in-european-workplaces-extent-impacts-and-policies.

20 Dew, N. (2009). Serendipity in entrepreneurship. *Organization Studies, 30*(7), 735–753.

21 Nicolaou, N., Shane, S., Cherkas, L., & Spector, T. D. (2009). Opportunity recognition and the tendency to be an entrepreneur: A bivariate genetics perspective. *Organizational Behavior and Human Decision Processes, 110*(2), 108–117.

22 Amabile, T. M. (1983). The social psychology of creativity: A componential conceptualization. *Journal of Personality and Social Psychology, 45*(2), 357; Amabile, T. M. (1988). A model of creativity and innovation in organizations. *Research in Organizational Behavior, 10*(1), 123–167.

23 Newell, A., & Simon, H. A. (1972). *Human problem solving* (p. 82). Englewood Cliffs, NJ: Prentice-Hall.

24 Hill, S. A., & Birkinshaw, J. M. (2010). Idea sets: Conceptualizing and measuring a new unit of analysis in entrepreneurship research. *Organizational Research Methods, 13*(1), 85–113; Cliff, J. E., Jennings, P. D., & Greenwood, R. (2006). New to the game and questioning the rules: The experiences and beliefs of founders who start imitative versus innovative firms. *Journal of Business Venturing, 21*(5), 633–663.

25 Nicolaou et al. (2009), ibid.

26 Baron, R. A., & Ensley, M. D. (2006) Opportunity recognition as the detection of meaningful patterns: Evidence from comparisons of novice and experienced entrepreneurs. *Management Science, 52*(9), 1331–1344.

27 Shane, S. (2000). Prior knowledge and the discovery of entrepreneurial opportunities. *Organization Science, 11*(4), 448–469.

28 Bhide, A. V. (2000) *The origin and evolution of new businesses*. Oxford: Oxford University Press; www.forbes.com/sites/ryanrobinson/2016/05/10/richard-branson-on-finding-a-business-idea-listen-to-your-frustrations/#7d0ce6b85907.

29 Ozgen, E., & Baron, R. A. (2007). Social sources of information in opportunity recognition: Effects of

mentors, industry networks, and professional forums. *Journal of Business Venturing, 22*(2), 174–192; Shaw, E., & Carter, S. (2007). Social entrepreneurship: Theoretical antecedents and empirical analysis of entrepreneurial processes and outcomes. *Journal of Small Business and Enterprise Development, 14*(3), 418–434.

30 Hills, G., Lumpkin, G., & Singh, R. (1997). Opportunity recognition: Perceptions and behaviors of entrepreneurs. *Frontiers of Entrepreneurship Research, 17*(4), 168–182.

31 Amabile (1988), ibid., p. 133.

32 Fiet, J. O. (2007). A prescriptive analysis of search and discovery. *Journal of Management Studies, 44*(4), 592–611.

33 Rietzschel, E. F., Nijstad, B. A., & Stroebe, W. (2014). Effects of problem scope and creativity instructions on idea generation and selection. *Creativity Research Journal, 26*(2), 185–191.

34 Putman, V. L., & Paulus, P. B. (2009). Brainstorming, brainstorming rules and decision making. *The Journal of Creative Behavior, 43*(1), 29–40.

35 Kelley, T. (2001). *The art of innovation: Lessons in creativity from IDEO, America's leading design firm.* London: Profile Books.

36 Vandor, P., & Franke, N. (2016). See Paris and … found a business? The impact of cross-cultural experience on opportunity recognition capabilities. *Journal of Business Venturing, 31*(4), 388–407.

37 Rietzschel et al. (2014), ibid.

38 Afuah, A. (2003). *Innovation management* (2nd ed.). New York: Oxford University Press, p. 13.

39 Åstebro, T. (2003). The return to independent invention: Evidence of unrealistic optimism, risk seeking or skewness loving? *The Economic Journal, 113*(484), 226–239.

40 www.virgin.com/richard-branson/the-business-idea-that-got-away.

41 Eckhardt, J. T., & Shane, S. A. (2003). Opportunities and entrepreneurship. *Journal of Management, 29*(3), 333–349; Dimov, D. (2007). From opportunity insight to opportunity intention: The importance of person-situation learning match. *Entrepreneurship Theory and Practice, 31*(4), 561–583; Dimov, D. (2011). Grappling with the unbearable elusiveness of entrepreneurial opportunities. *Entrepreneurship Theory and Practice, 35*(1), 57–81; Ramoglou, S., & Tsang, E. W. (2016). A realist perspective of entrepreneurship: Opportunities as propensities. *Academy of Management Review, 41*(3), 410–434; Carsrud, A., & Brännback, M. (2011). Entrepreneurial motivations: What do we still need to know? *Journal of Small Business Management, 49*(1), 9–26.

42 Grégoire, D. A., Barr, P. S., & Shepherd, D. A. (2010). Cognitive processes of opportunity recognition: The role of structural alignment. *Organization Science, 21*(2), 413–431; Haynie, J. M., Shepherd, D. A., & McMullen, J. S. (2009). An opportunity for me? The role of resources in opportunity evaluation decisions. *Journal of Management Studies, 46*(3), 337–361.

43 Wood, M. S., & McKinley, W. (2010). The production of entrepreneurial opportunity: A constructivist perspective. *Strategic Entrepreneurship Journal, 4*(1), 66–84.

44 Mitchell, J. R., Shepherd, D. A. (2010). To thine own self be true: Images of self, images of opportunity, and entrepreneurial action. *Journal of Business Venturing, 25*(1), 138–154.

45 https://about.van.fedex.com/our-story/history-timeline/history/; www.pbs.org/wgbh/theymadeamerica/whomade/fsmith_hi.html; www.bloomberg.com/news/articles/2004-09-19/online-extra-fred-smith-on-the-birth-of-fedex.

46 Kim, P. H., Longest, K. C., & Lippmann, S. (2015). The tortoise versus the hare: Progress and business viability differences between conventional and leisure-based founders. *Journal of Business Venturing, 30*(2), 185–204.

47 https://www.theatlantic.com/technology/archive/2011/03/mousetraps-a-symbol-of-the-american-entrepreneurial-spirit/70573/.

48 www.thebusinesslaunchpad.com/the-great-mousetrap-fallacy/.

49 Short, J. C., Ketchen Jr., D. J., Shook, C. L., & Ireland, R. D. (2010). The concept of "opportunity" in entrepreneurship research: Past accomplishments and future challenges. *Journal of Management, 36*(1), 40–65; Tumasjan, A., Welpe, I., & Spörrle, M. (2013). Easy now, desirable later: The moderating role of temporal distance in opportunity evaluation and exploitation. *Entrepreneurship Theory and Practice, 37*(4), 859–888.

50 https://www.youtube.com/watch?v=xZ8vdyGUft4.

51 Ebben, J., & Johnson, A. (2006). Bootstrapping in small firms: An empirical analysis of change over time. *Journal of Business Venturing, 21*(6), 851–865, 853.

52 https://www8.hp.com/us/en/hp-information/about-hp/history/hp-garage/partner-in-greatness.html.

53 www.bbc.co.uk/news/business-49015609.

54 www.subway.com.au/About/Franchisee.

55 Bates, T. (1995). Analysis of survival rates among franchise and independent small business startups. *Journal of Small Business Management, 33*(2), 26–36; Lafontaine, F., Zapletal, M., & Zhang, X. (2019). Brighter prospects? Assessing the franchise advantage using census data. *Journal of Economics & Management Strategy, 28*(2), 175–197.

56 https://www2.ohchr.org/english/bodies/crc/docs/ngos/Association.

57 www.dinf.ne.jp/doc/english/asia/resource/z00ap/003/z00ap00308.html.

58 www.danpink.com/wp-content/uploads/2013/01/sixpitches.pdf.

CHAPTER 5

Start-Up Planning Pathways

Learning Outcomes

In this chapter, you will learn:

- Why writing a business plan first is a bad idea.
- What business models and the 12 fundamental start-up questions are.
- How the Business Model Canvas, feasibility studies and a business plan all aid start-up planning.
- How alternative approaches such as effectuation, bricolage and lean start-up can help with start-up planning.

Mini Contents List

5.1 INTRODUCTION

Mike Tyson, the former world heavyweight boxing champion, was once asked what his next opponent would do in their impending fight. Would he dance around, counter-punch or seek to tire him out? Tyson replied: 'Everybody has a plan until they get punched in the mouth.'

This is an important lesson for entrepreneurs. Business plans are valuable, but writing them first is a bad idea. This is not because a 40-page plan can take more than two months to write.[1] Nor is it because some successful entrepreneurs such as Steve Jobs, Jack Ma and Bill Gates started up without a formal written plan.

Instead, the main reason for not writing a formal plan first is that it is unlikely to survive initial contact with customers.[2] Ideas about who the customers are, what the opportunity may look like, who the competitors are, what the risks are and what the likely returns are all remain provisional at the outset of a start-up.[3] A plan written first can lock an entrepreneur into a course of action that leads nowhere, wastes time or gives them a story that turns out to be a fable.[4]

A quick and low-cost approach to start-up planning such as the 'Me, Market and Money' model (Chapter 4, pp. 80–84) is often a better place to start. If an entrepreneur works out that they have relevant experience and motivation (Me), willing customers (Market) and sufficient resources (Money), this might be all the planning they need.[5]

However, entrepreneurs often have to convince others such as cautious investors, hesitant potential employees or sceptical mentors. To better sketch out their start-up, entrepreneurs need to describe, clarify and potentially justify their start-up business model.

A business model is a narrative that demonstrates how the entrepreneur will create, deliver and capture value.[6] It is the story of how a founder uncovers a real problem, what actions they take to resolve this problem and how they relate to key characters such as customers, suppliers and competitors along their start-up journey.

This chapter provides a route map highlighting the different ways you can approach your start-up planning. It shows you that there are 12 fundamental start-up questions that entrepreneurs need to answer to build a full and coherent business model for their start-up. These 12 questions range from who the start-up's target customer is through to its plans for growth.

One method of beginning to answer these questions is to use a simple one-page business planning tool called the Business Model Canvas (BMC). This allows founders to 'storyboard' some of the core features of their business model.

A potential next step is to write a feasibility plan or presentation. This chapter shows you each of the sections in a feasibility plan and presentation, where detailed information on these sections appears in subsequent chapters and what the supporting practical exercises are in Workbook 2.

Key outputs such as the BMC or feasibility planning may be all that an entrepreneur needs to conclude their start-up planning. But one reason why entrepreneurs *eventually* write formal plans is because feasibility studies only contain limited financial information. Without this information it is difficult to judge if projected financial rewards outweigh risks. Having detailed financial plans and targeting them at the right investor helps explain why entrepreneurs who eventually write a formal plan are more likely to create a viable start-up.[7]

Moving from a start-up idea through to outlining the business model and then detailing your answers to the 12 start-up questions presumes that there is a logical sequence to planning. It also seems to privilege planning over start-up activities such as getting finance or assembling resources. However, this chapter shows you that three alternative planning logics – effectuation, bricolage and 'lean start-up' – may also be fruitful ways of approaching start-up planning.

5.2 WHY WRITING A BUSINESS PLAN FIRST IS A BAD IDEA

5.2.1 *The benefits of plans*

Writing a business plan first seems a good idea. A business plan scripts the 'markets to be served, proposed products/services, required resources and the anticipated growth and profitability of the new venture'.[8]

Writing a good plan answers essential questions such as where is the business concept now, where does it want to get to and how is it going to get there.

When writing a plan, entrepreneurs should aim to create a document that:

- Profiles the opportunity – what product or service is to be sold, to whom, how the start-up will grow, how fast it will grow and what the economics of the business are.
- Highlights the big picture – how changes in the economy and society are likely to impact on the start-up.
- Details the start-up team or individual and key advisors.
- Specifies the nature of risks and rewards – a discussion of what is likely to go right and wrong with the start-up and how it will respond.[9]

In return, a good plan gives entrepreneurs:

- A way to learn more about if a potential business opportunity is desirable and feasible.
- Ways to select, evaluate and fine-tune their start-up activities.[10]
- Opportunities to anticipate and avoid demand and supply issues such as supply bottlenecks arising from a mismatch between resource and customer demand.[11]
- Give confidence and improve perceptions of control, which can also promote task persistence and goal commitment.[12]
- A reality check that helps avoid inbuilt cognitive biases (Chapter 2, pp. 32–37).
- Credibility among external stakeholders, making it easier to access external finance.[13]

There are also theoretical reasons for writing a plan first. Those who support formal 'purposive' planning argue that it takes time and effort to start up a viable venture. It is also complex and uncertain. Because a start-up is a 'stretch' goal, a plan could help to avoid the old saying that 'failing to plan, is planning to fail'.[14]

Jerome Katz and William Gartner further imply that writing a plan first is a good idea.[15] In their model of how start-ups emerge, they suggest four essential activities – or properties – that a start-up has to complete if it is to come into existence. New business creation is an 'entrepreneurial journey' that starts with the formation of a start-up motive (Intention), goes through collecting Resources and forming Boundaries and ends when the start-up has more money coming in than going out (Exchange).[16] An acronym for Katz and Gartner's four properties is BRIE (Figure 5.1). BRIE suggests a causal logic to start-up.

Figure 5.1 The 'BRIE' causal model

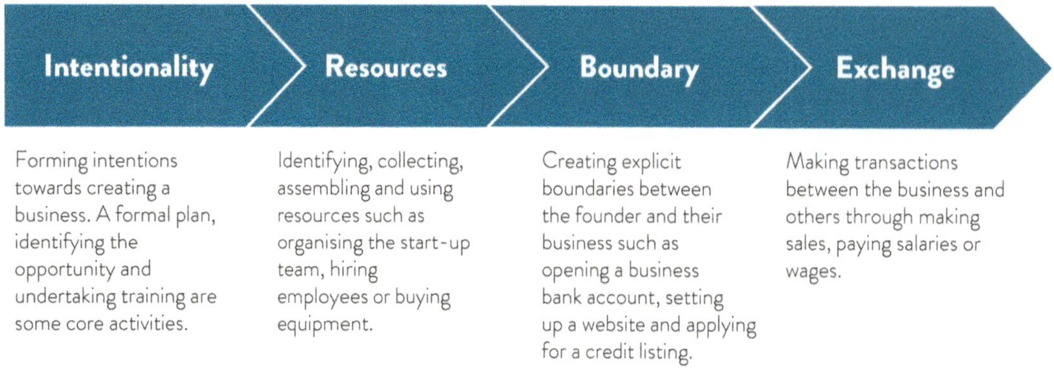

Entrepreneurship in Action

- Write down what you think are the most important activities that a start-up has to complete in order to reach viability. Katz and Gartner suggest that there is a particular order to pursuing the start-up.[17] Do you agree?
- How would you sequence your start-up activities?

5.2.2 *The trouble with plans*

An entrepreneur who writes a formal business plan first is no more likely than a non-planner to create a viable start-up. This is because projections about who customers are, how much competition there is and the likely risks and rewards are just ideas until someone actually starts up.[18]

Founders must navigate a number of twists and turns along the start-up journey to turn their hazy business outline into something more tangible. They might start by focusing on one customer, only to later find out another has a more pressing need for their offer.[19] Early activities such as collecting customer information and defining the market opportunity are much more likely to lead to success.[20]

Start-ups do not follow the BRIE model's logical causal sequence. Intentionality does not necessarily precede Resources, Boundary or Exchange.[21] Some start-ups begin with an exchange (a sale) and then form an intention to start up. In the United States 'organizing a new venture is not a patterned or linear process but rather is simultaneous, messy and iterative'.[22] In Australia, although 'discovery' such as product development and defining market opportunities generally precedes 'exploitation' activities such as purchasing liability insurance or hiring an accountant, it is still the case that '97 per cent of the venture creation sequences sampled follow their own trajectory'.[23]

Writing a plan too early has unintended consequences. It might present a poor picture of reality if market assumptions are unreliable or unproven.[24] New business founders might subsequently end up inflexibly following a start-up trajectory that wastes time and money.[25] Even if an early plan does help secure external funding, it may become inadequate for future needs if it is too early to know how much finance is needed. Perhaps, though, the biggest weakness of writing a plan first is that it implies planning is a one-off activity. This is misguided. Start-up planning is a process that involves the entrepreneur having to come back – often repeatedly – to reassess earlier assumptions and hopes.

Discussion questions:

- List the benefits and drawbacks of a business plan. Do you think that the advantages outweigh the disadvantages?

Assessment tip: Planning your writing

One of the first things to do with an assessment question is to underline its key words. These are often instructions such as describe, discuss, analyse and critically evaluate. Working out what is being asked is vital because a fundamental feature of your answer is that it **must** answer the question. Underline and refer back to these key words throughout the writing process to ensure you keep on track.

Few people set up a business with no clue of what they are going into. Similarly, in planning your answer you should focus on understanding a topic and its main debates. Potentially, you can mind map connections and areas of disagreement between sources.

You can capture your understanding of the question and knowledge of the research by structuring your answer around an introduction, a main body and a conclusion.

Introductions tell the reader what is coming up: it is your way of saying what you are going to say. It is also your first chance to be clear and specific on how your answer contributes to understanding the question.

The main body is your opportunity to say it. A challenge in this section is to organise your points in a logical way. This can be done by making sure that each paragraph has a core topic sentence. These summarise your paragraph, in the same way newspaper headlines summarise stories. Your conclusion is an opportunity not just to summarise but for you to reflect, weigh, evaluate and propose implications.

Planning and writing an answer – like building a business – is an organic iterative process with many frustrations. Fundamental to writing is rewriting, so it is always good to have enough time to edit and refine an answer.

5.3 UNDERSTANDING THE THEORY OF A BUSINESS MODEL

A business model is a theory of a business that explains how a business intends to create, deliver and capture value.

It is a narrative that 'articulates the logic and provides data and other evidence that demonstrates how a business creates and delivers value to customers. It also outlines the architecture of revenues, costs and profits associated with the business enterprise developing that value.'[26]

Practically, business models are often seen as revenue models that show how a business makes money. Having a wider business model perspective on the start-up's operations and strategy, though, allows a start-up to focus on the sum rather than the individual parts of the business.

Business models can also help entrepreneurs critically reflect on their start-up and identify new ways of meeting customer needs and wants. Creating a coherent narrative can further convince external audiences and, in particular, mentors or funders to become involved in the start-up.

Academic Insight: What is in a business model?

There is no agreed definition of what a business model is.[27] However, Morris and his colleagues suggest that entrepreneurs need to use their business model to look beyond how their venture makes money and consider the start-up's strategy and operations.[28] They suggest that entrepreneurs should ask themselves six questions:

1. How do we create value? Is it by offering a product or service, customising this product or service or bundling it up with other products or services? Or is it via how the product or service is sold or distributed?
2. Who do we create value for? Is it other businesses? Is it for a niche? Where are they?
3. What is the source of our competence? Is it production, selling, technology, networking or supply chain management?
4. How do we competitively position ourselves? Is it operational or service excellence? Being cheaper or closer to the customer?
5. How do we make money? Is it through selling more or having better profit margins?
6. What are our time, scope and size ambitions? How do we intend to survive and grow?

5.3.1 *The 12 key business model questions*

There is no one way of developing a business model for a start-up. Individual founders are likely to have idiosyncratic ways of distinguishing their start-up's cast of characters and their storyline of likely events and timelines. Nonetheless, there are 12 key questions that a potential founder has to answer:

Q.1. **Who are we?** What is the identity and purpose of the start-up?
Q.2. **Is there a market out there?** Is the start-up focused on a problem worth solving? How large is the potential market? How fast is it growing?

Q.3. **Is the business idea worthwhile?** What is the idea? How does it benefit customers?
Q.4. **Who is the customer?** Who *specifically* is the target customer? Why them?
Q.5. **How does the business reach its customers?** What is its sales and marketing strategy?
Q.6. **How is the offer different in the market?** Does it have an advantage over competitors?
Q.7. **How does the business source, make and distribute its products and services?**
Q.8. **How does it make money? What is the revenue model?** How does the business get paid, and who does it have to pay?
Q.9. **Why is this the right team?** What skills and attributes do the people involved have to exploit the opportunity?
Q.10. **What is the plan for growth?** How does the business intend to scale the business in subsequent years?
Q.11. **What does the start-up lack?** Does the business need money to fund its development, operations or growth? Does it need mentors to bring expertise to the business? What is its exit strategy?
Q.12. **Is the start-up viable?** What are the likely risks and rewards? Do the rewards outweigh the risks?

5.3.2 *The Business Model Canvas*

One of the most common and popular ways of starting to 'storyboard' a new venture's business model and answer some of these questions is to use the Business Model Canvas (BMC). It is a simple one-page template that graphically sketches out key start-up activities (Figure 5.2). It enables entrepreneurs to brainstorm and imaginatively change the internal logic of their business model. In alphabetical order, its nine key building blocks are:

1. **Channels** – How will it reach its customers? Is it through selling door to door, via the web, through its own or another partner store or through a wholesaler? How will the business raise awareness, help customers evaluate the product and make a purchase, and how will it deliver and provide aftersales services to them?
2. **Cost structure** – What are the costs in the business? Does it focus on providing cost advantages or quality advantages to customers?
3. **Customer Relationships** – What relationship will the start-up have with its customers? Will it provide personal assistance or self-service? Will it build communities?
4. **Customer Segments** – Who is the start-up creating value for? The mass market or a niche?
5. **Key Activities** – What are the start-up's core business activities? Will the start-up make products? How does it manage its supply chain?
6. **Key Partners** – What help will the business receive from suppliers and partners? Can they help to reduce risks or optimise the allocation of resources?
7. **Key Resources** – Does the start-up need physical assets such as manufacturing facilities or vehicles? What sorts of staff are needed and does it require access to intellectual property?
8. **Revenue Streams** – What value are the customers willing to pay for? What is the revenue model?
9. **Value Propositions** – What value does the business deliver to customers? What problems does it solve?

Figure 5.2 Business Model Canvas, Business Model Canvas template © Strategyzer AG; strategyzer.com/canvas

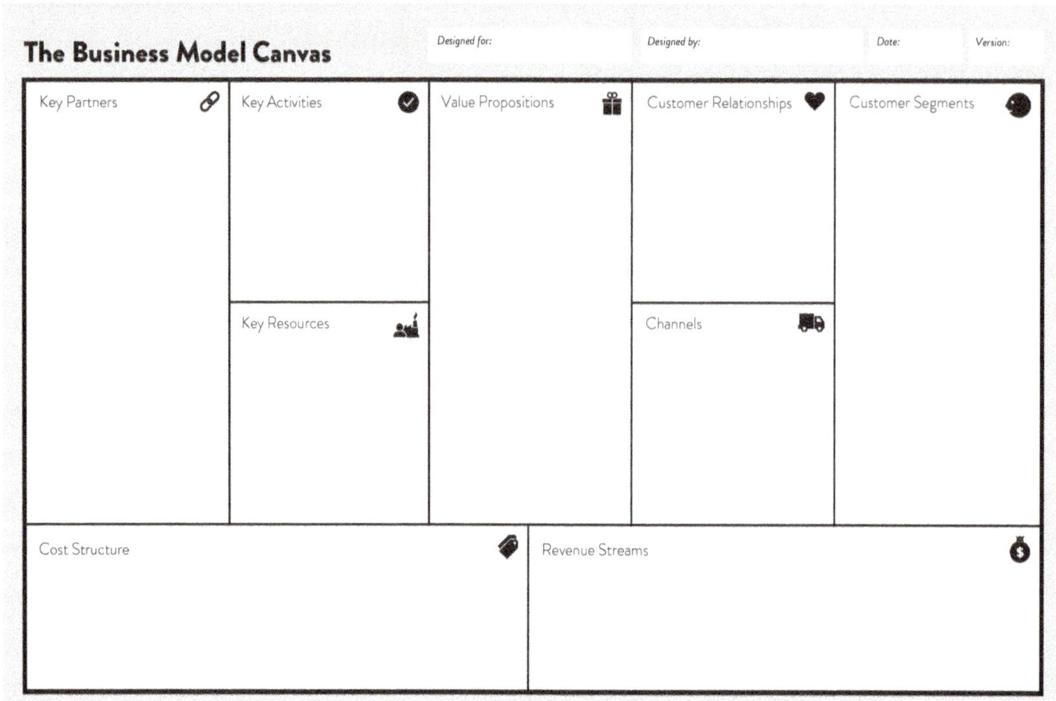

Case Study: Using the BMC to chart a smoothie business model

Figure 5.3 shows a BMC for a smoothie business. Its value proposition is to provide fresh, natural drinks on the go. Its customer segment is festivalgoers, who are typically younger people. Relationships are managed by personal selling, and selling is done through a stall at the festival.

Key activities are making the smoothies, marketing them and selling them. Key resources are the smoothie ingredients, the stall, smoothie-making equipment and people to sell them. Key partners are the festival organisers, who provide a pitch and electricity, and the local authority, which provides food permits. Revenues come from sales. Costs include ingredients, the festival's fee for the stall, wages and the cost of marketing flyers.

This is how the three founders of Innocent drinks set up their business. They went along to a summer festival, set up a stall and sold their smoothies. They also put up a sign saying 'Should we give up our jobs to set up a business making smoothies?'. If customers thought yes, they put their empty cup in a bin saying yes; if no, they put their cup in a bin marked no. At the end of the festival, they had more positive responses, and this was enough to convince them that their business idea was feasible.

Figure 5.3 A smoothie BMC Business Model Canvas template © Strategyzer AG; strategyzer.com/canvas

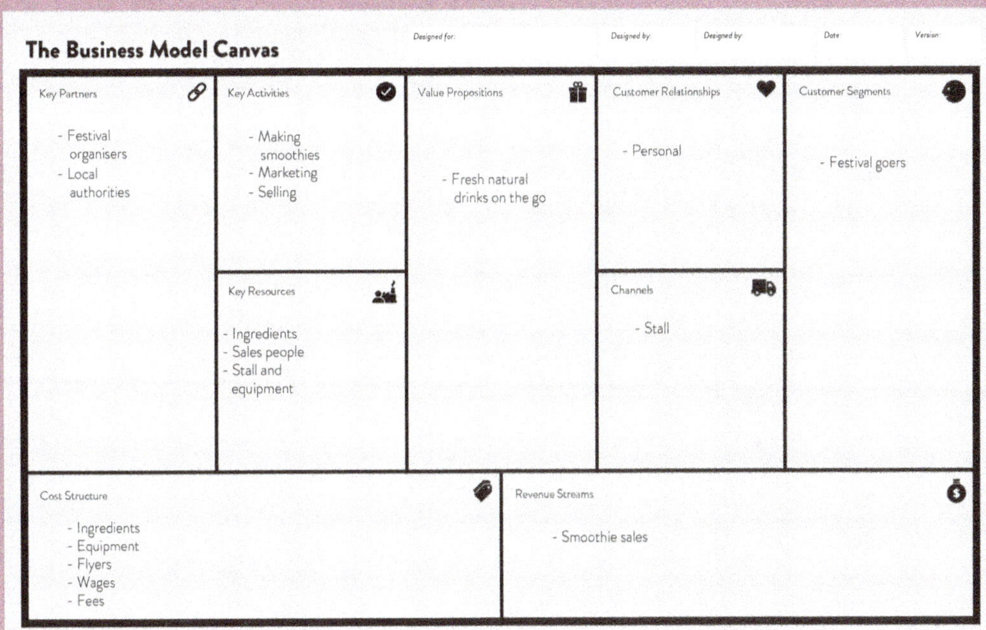

The BMC is a visual storyboarding tool that structures an intuitive initial understanding of start-up feasibility. It answers key start-up questions such as:

- Is there a market out there? **(Q.2.)** and Who is the customer? **(Q.4.)** (customer segments);
- Is the business idea worthwhile? **(Q.3.)** (value proposition);
- How does the business reach its customers? **(Q.5.)** (customer relationships and channels);
- How does the business source, make and distribute its products and services? **(Q.7.)** (key activities, resources and partners); and
- How does it make money? **(Q.8.)** (revenue and cost streams).

For founders with few financial concerns, prior start-up experience and an obvious opportunity, the BMC might be all that is needed to complete start-up planning. Completing the nine building blocks is a relatively quick, low-cost activity, and start-ups can include and change each section as new information emerges.

Entrepreneurship in Action

One of the dangers that potential entrepreneurs face is that they can decide too quickly on a business idea, market and business model. One way of avoiding this is to use the Me, Market and Money framework to assess different business ideas (Chapter 4, pp. 80–84). Another route is to assess individual competing ideas against the 12 start-up questions (pp. 98–99) or to draw separate BMCs for each idea.

- An alternative early stage approach is to answer the questions below. These questions ask you to evaluate up to three business ideas: your 'best for now' idea, your 'back-up' idea and your 'cold storage' idea. One advantage of these questions is that they provide a quick and low cost 'back-of-an-envelope' understanding of the potential of different business ideas before you launch into a given idea. Another benefit is that these questions ask you to identify what you do not currently know. If these are significant, it suggests that you should pause and investigate further before committing to one idea.

	'Best for now' idea	'Back-up' idea	'Cold storage' idea
What is the idea?			
What am I selling?			
Who is my customer?			
How do I make money from them?			
How do they pay me?			
How do they hear about my business?			
What does success look like for me?			
What is innovative about my business model?			
Why would an employee come and work for my start-up?			
What do I not know yet?			

The BMC does have disadvantages. Table 5.1 shows it misses out key parts of start-up planning. The founder and their team's motivations are missing. What roles they assume, how they relate to each other and how they intend to split the rewards are all pivotal issues the BMC fails to examine. Its focus on market attractiveness fails to account for industry attractiveness: a market may have rich customers who are easily parted from their money, but they may be found in an industry dominated by a possessive and vindictive competitor. Crucially, the BMC also does not consider why the entrepreneur is embarking on a start-up. It offers little insight into what the purpose is behind the business, what its social or environmental mission might be or what its future growth plans are. However, although there are other versions of a one-page template that focus on the environment (the triple-layered canvas) or on social enterprises (social BMC), the basic challenge is that no one page template is likely to itemise all of the start-up risks and rewards.[29]

Table 5.1 Answering the 12 start-up questions

	Business Model Canvas	Feasibility planning	Business planning
Who are we?	✗	✓	✓
Is there a market out there?	✓	✓	✓
Is the business idea worthwhile?	✓	✓	✓
Who is the customer?	✓	✓	✓
How does the business reach its customers?	✓	✓	✓
How is the offer different in the market?	✓	✓	✓
How does the business source, make and distribute its products and services?	✓	✓	✓
How does it make money?	✓	✓	✓
Why is this the right team?	✗	✓	✓
What is the plan for growth?	✗	?	✓
What does the start-up lack?	✗	?	✓
Is the start-up viable?	✗	?	✓

5.3.3 *Feasibility planning*

A fuller sketch of a start-up's business model can come from feasibility planning. Feasibility planning sits between early start-up planning activities such as having a back-of-an-envelope plan or using the BMC and writing a full detailed business plan. A written feasibility plan or a presentation – what is called a pitch deck – gives an assessment of the viability of an idea. Founders might use it to self-assess their start-up's strategy, operations and financial vitality. More likely, though, is that founders use a feasibility plan or pitch deck to encourage and convince outside audiences to back their idea.

This is often important if there is a funding shortfall. This is implied in one of the practical definitions of entrepreneurship: 'the process by which individuals – either on their own or inside organizations – pursue opportunities without regard to the resources they currently control'.[30] Indeed, one of the main impetuses for start-up planning is to acquire external resources.[31]

Table 5.2 shows how to translate each of the 12 start-up questions into a feasibility plan or pitch deck. For example, 'How is the offer different in the market?' equates to the 'Competition' section of a plan and pitch. Founders can demonstrate their competitive advantage through a mix of primary and secondary research and by using a competitor positioning mapping and benchmarking. Table 5.2 also shows that using the BMC (Chapter 6, Workbook exercises 2.1–2.12) can help with some start-up questions but that Chapters 7 and 8 and Workbook exercises 2.13–14, 2.16–20 help with answers to the other start-up questions.

Working out answers to all 12 questions is important because there is often a structure to feasibility plans and pitches. They usually start with a summary of the opportunity and then provide information on the product and market, competition, sales and marketing and growth plans before ending with an assessment of likely risks and rewards.

Table 5.2 Key elements of feasibility plans and pitches

Start-up question	Business model canvas	Feasibility plan sections	Feasibility pitch deck slides	Chapter	Exercises
Q.1. Who are we?	• *Not included in BMC*	*Cover page* • Business name, logo, contact details *Executive summary of the opportunity* • Who we are, what we do and what value we create • Financial request (the ask – see Q. 11 below)	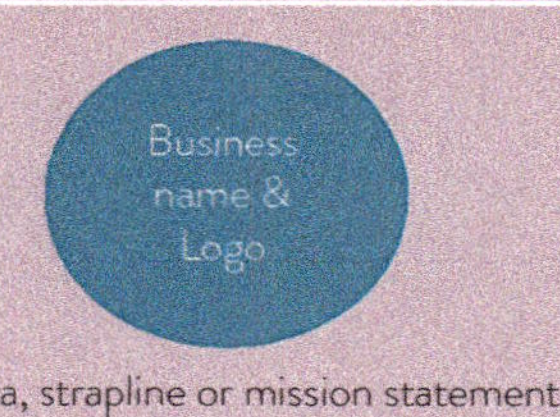	7	W 2.13 W 2.14
Q.2. Is there a market out there? *Q.3. Is the business idea worthwhile?* *Q.4. Who is the customer?*	• *Customer segments* • *Value proposition*	*Product & market* • How the solution works; features and benefits; product positioning statement; intellectual property • Market analysis: primary and secondary information on market size, patterns and dynamics; PEST analysis • Customer profiling (TAM, SAM, SOM (Chapter 6, p. 132); customer vignette; testimonials)	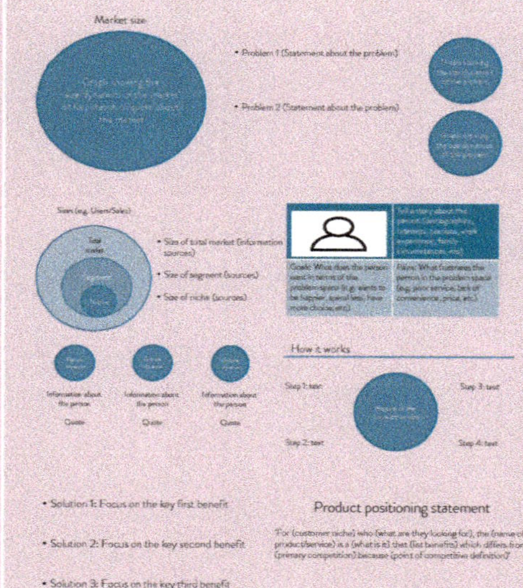	6 6 6	W 2.1, W 2.2, W 2.3 W 2.4, W 2.5, W 2.6, W 2.7, W 2.8, W 2.15

Table 5.2 continued

Start-up question	Business model canvas	Feasibility plan sections	Feasibility pitch deck slides	Chapter	Exercises
Q.5. How does the business reach its customers?	○ *Customer relationships/ channels*	*Marketing & Sales* ○ Routes to market; sales and marketing strategy	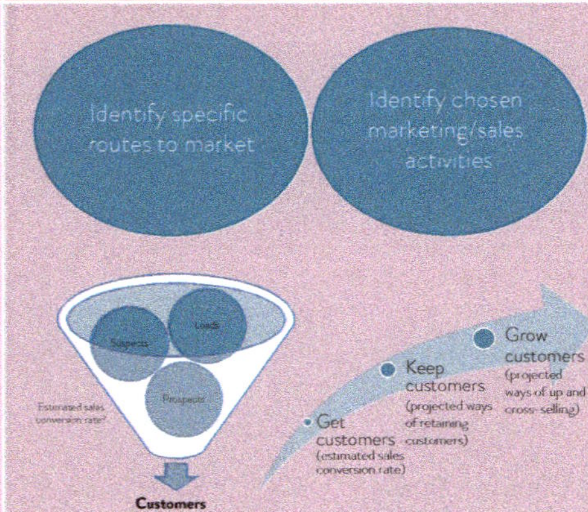	6	W 2.9, W 2.10
Q.6. How is the offer different in the market?	○ *Not included in BMC*	*Competition* ○ Primary and secondary research on competitors (direct and indirect); competitor analysis and benchmarking; product positioning mapping and statement	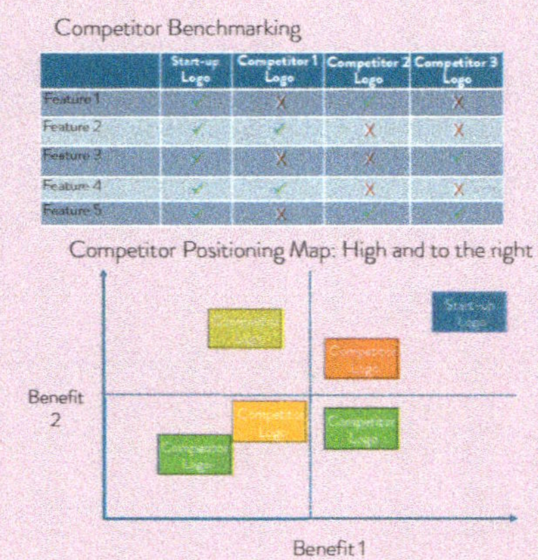	7	W 2.17

5

Table 5.2 continued

Start-up question	Business model canvas	Feasibility plan sections	Feasibility pitch deck slides	Chapter	Exercises
Q.7. How does the business source, make and distribute its products and services?	◦ *Key activities* ◦ *Key resources* ◦ *Key partners*	*Business operations and logistics* ◦ Key business resources, activities and partners and timelines (Gantt chart, roadmap)	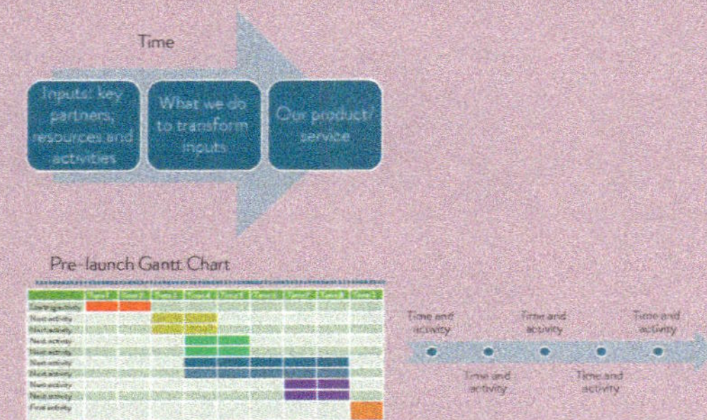	6	W 2.12
Q.8. How does it make money?	◦ *Revenue streams* ◦ *Cost structure*	*Revenue model* ◦ How the start-up gets paid		6	W 2.11
Q.9. Why is this the right team?	◦ *Not included in BMC*	*Team* ◦ Ownership team, managers and employees, advisors	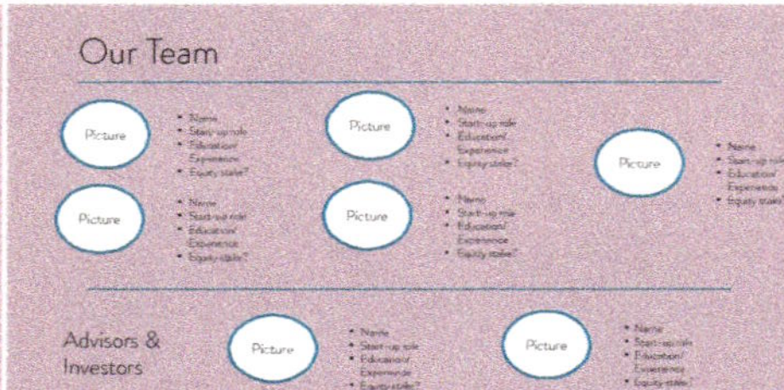	7	W 2.16

Table 5.2 continued

Start-up question	Business model canvas	Feasibility plan sections	Feasibility pitch deck slides	Chapter	Exercises
Q.10. What is the plan for growth?	○ Not included in BMC	*Scaling the start-up* ○ Plans for getting, keeping and growing customers; routes to growth (growth by acquisition, organic growth or franchising)	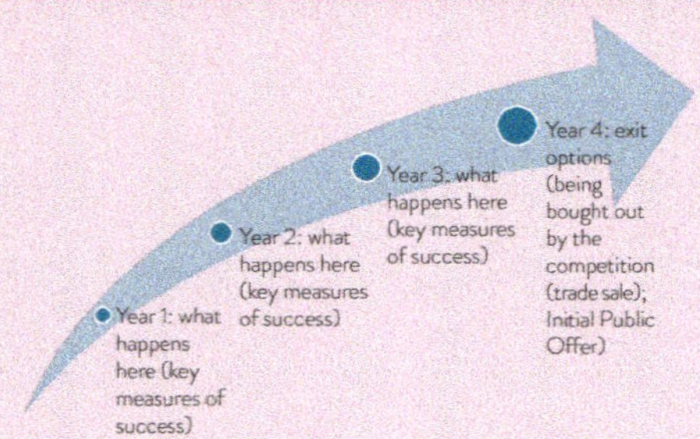	8	W 2.18
Q.11. What does the start-up lack?	○ *Not included in BMC*	*The 'ask'* ○ Investment required, purpose, return for the investor, exit strategy	The 'ask' • Investment amount here • Reasons for this 'ask' • What the investor gets in return (e.g. trade sale, IPO)	8	W 2.19
Q.12. Is the start-up viable?	○ *Not included in BMC*	*Feasibility assessment* ○ SWOT analysis, financial information such as break-even point, revenue, cashflow and profitability	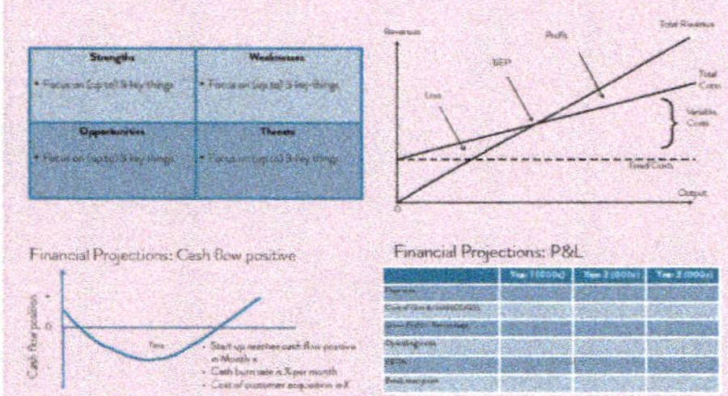	8	W 2.20

This assessment of viability can include financial information such as a break-even point, information on the revenue model and cashflow and profitability information. It may also include a Strengths, Weaknesses, Opportunities and Threats (SWOT) analysis.

Strengths and weaknesses are a business's internal capabilities and where it has an advantage or problem relative to the competition. Opportunities and threats relate to the external environment: whether or not others can cause the business either trouble and where the venture can exploit competitors' weaknesses.

Some plans or pitch decks may have appendices that outline supplementary information such as market research results or product specification details.

However, there is no one way of developing a feasibility plan or pitch. Nor should there be. An entrepreneur may start a pitch by explaining their personal start-up journey. Alternatively, early on they might want to indicate what the purpose or 'the ask' is behind a pitch or plan. This involves identifying the investment amount required, what it is for and how the investors get their return (see Chapter 9 for more information on finance providers).

The 12 start-up questions may not always be required. Some external audiences may only require a narrative or pitch around the bare bones of a business model or a focus on parts of a founder's business model such as their financial plan or the attractiveness of the idea.

Table 5.2 shows that the information in a plan and a pitch is easily transferable. Much of the necessary information to assess competition such as a product positioning statement or competitor benchmarking can be adapted from a plan to a pitch and vice-versa. However, there are two main differences between a pitch and a plan:

1. A pitch can conclude with a 'call to action' such as a request to speak to interested parties or an invitation to take questions. In a feasibility plan, any call to action usually occurs in a cover letter.
2. It is harder to be objective in a pitch about a start-up's prospects. Pitching is a 'contact sport' and it is more difficult to admit frailties in a pitch than in a written plan.

5.3.4 Business planning

A more detailed, refined and financially literate version of feasibility planning is a written business plan. Table 5.3 shows that a business plan broadly has a similar format to a feasibility plan and draws on similar material. For example, to answer the start-up question 'Why is this the right team?' equates to the 'Management Structure' section in a business plan. Like a feasibility study, this section and other sections draw on prior data collection, diagrams such as a product positioning map that demonstrate the ways in which the start-up has a distinctive competitive advantage.

A business plan differs, though, in three main ways from feasibility plans:

1. A full plan is likely to include detailed information on costs, revenues and financial ratios. It will also typically take in cashflow, profit and loss and balance sheet projections. These forecasts might cover a number of years and consist of 'worst', 'likely' and 'best' case financial plans for the start-up (Chapter 8, pp. 195–197).
2. It may provide a cover letter or email that introduces the plan, summarises key benefits and encourages the recipient to make contact with the founder.
3. Appendices are likely to be more detailed information on the curricula vitae of the team and advisors and supporting information such as patent application, survey results and findings, letters of intent and contracts. Financial scenarios and balance sheet information may also be included here.

Table 5.3 Key elements of a business plan

Start-up question	Business plan	Chapter	Exercises
Q.1. Who are we? *Q.11. What does the start-up lack?*	*Cover page:* Business name, logo, contact details (address, email, social media and website); *Table of contents; Start-up overview:* a (one page) executive summary that summarises the opportunity and explains what the 'ask' is	7	W 2.13, W 2.14, W 2.19
Q.1. Who are we? *Q.3. Is the business idea worthwhile?*	*Business objectives:* introduces the problem and solution; how the solution works; features and benefits; product positioning statement; intellectual property	6	W 2.6, W 2.7, W 2.8, W 2.15
Q.2. Is there a market out there? *Q.4. Who is the customer?*	*The Market and customers:* market size and potential; customer segmentation approach; primary and secondary market research, PEST analysis	6	W 2.1, W 2.2, W 2.3, W 2.4, W 2.5
Q.6. How is the offer different in the market?	*The competition:* identification of in/direct competitors; five forces/blue ocean analysis; competitor analysis and benchmarking (competitor positioning map, product positioning statement)	7	W 2.17
Q.5. How does the business reach its customers?	*Sales and marketing:* routes to market; sales and marketing strategy and customer acquisition process	6	W 2.9, W 2.10
Q.7. How does the business source, make and distribute its products and services?	*Operations:* timings of key activities (Gantt chart) and key partners, relevant regulatory requirements	6	W 2.12
Q.9. Why is this the right team?	*Management structure:* team, advisors, managers and employees	7	W 2.16
Q.10. What is the plan for growth?	*Future plans:* indication of likely future customer traction (plans for getting, keeping and growing customers); and for routes to growth (growth by acquisition, organic growth or franchising)	8	W 2.18
Q.8. How does it make money? *Q.12. Is the start-up viable?*	*Financial projections:* key revenues and costs; key ratios (gross profit margin) and measures (break-even point, cash burn rate); cashflow, profit and loss projections; estimation of risk and rewards (SWOT analysis)	6/8	W 2.11, W 2.20

Assessment tip: Plans and pitches

There is no one way of writing a plan or presenting a pitch. Although they have basic formats, these can be changed and adapted to suit. This might be welcome if the intention is to stand out from other pitches or plans. Nonetheless, following good practices can improve your plan and pitch. For a plan:

- **Stick to the required format**. If asked for a plan of a certain length, deliver on that. If asked to format it in a particular way, stay with that. Usually, plans are written in the third person.
- **Start strongly**. Financiers such as venture capitalists and business angels see lots of plans (Chapter 9, 225–233). If the plan cannot quickly explain who you are, what you do, who it is for and what the opportunity is, the risk is that the plan will be put in the 'No' pile.
- **Shows not just tells**. Graphs and numbers are shortcuts for explaining your story. Pitch deck slides can be adapted for use in a plan.
- **Identify your sources**. Use footnotes, endnotes or a list of references in your plan.
- **Target the plan**. Who is the recipient of the plan? Why would they be interested in your plan? Adapt the sections of the plan to their interests. Remember, a plan is also a 'call to action': what is your strategy for gauging their interest once they have received the plan?

In pitching your start-up, there are a number of good practices to follow:

- **Tailoring your number of slides to the allotted time**. If there are too many slides, the tendency is to go over them too quickly, so be selective.
- **Be visual**.[32] Use pictures and diagrams because they convey meaning much more quickly than words. Identify your sources. Consider using videos. If you have a prototype of the product bring it along.
- **If you use text, none of the text on a slide should be smaller than a 30 point font.**[33] Having a larger font forces you to concentrate on distilling down to your key messages.
- **PowerPoint is not the only way of presenting**. There are also different packages available for developing slides and non-face-to-face ways of delivering your information such as using video animation software or filming your own videos.
- **Dress as well as you can**. Even if the dress code is very casual, there is nothing wrong with using an iron.
- **Introduce yourself at the start**. Make and keep eye contact with your audience.
- **Try to avoid using notes**. If you must, use little cards that fit in one of your hands. Do not read from the pitch deck: the panel can read the words quicker than you can say them. Do not memorise your talk: you can come across as a robot.
- **Keep to time**. Use a timer on your phone.
- **Start strongly and make sure that you explain how the product or service works.**
- **Make sure you know your audience**. If you have an 'ask' of a funder, they will want to know what it is for, how much is required and what their return is (Chapter 10, pp. 224–234).
- **Be prepared**. Pitch audiences are more impressed by presenters that are plausible and well-prepared than those that are just passionate.[34] Go to the venue and make sure the technology works. Have a back-up plan if the technology fails.

- **If possible, have extra slides in an appendix to your pitch deck.** You can use these slides to show extra information such as financial information, sources and information on assumptions.
- **What are the next steps?** Like plans, pitches are often 'calls to action'. One way of ending a pitch is to invite questions. However, the main aim is often to arrange follow up meetings, either before or after showing the interested party your plan.
- **Anticipate the questions.** Typical questions focus on your market, customer, competitors and how you are going to market and sell your offer and the feasibility of your start-up. If asked questions, respond as best you can. Do not make stuff up. This can destroy your credibility. Promise instead to find out the information.
- **Practise, practise and practise.** And then practise again.

© Getty Images

This 'propose' (Chapter 4: Me, Market and Money), 'sketch' (BMC, feasibility plan and pitch deck) and 'detail' (business plan) approach to business model development asks entrepreneurs to take a logical, incremental and ordered approach to start-up planning. Using early-stage activities such as the Me, Market and Money model and tools such as the BMC requires few resources and can help entrepreneurs decide if an idea is worth pursuing. This is better than writing a plan first because it promotes flexibility and improvisation. It may also be all the planning needed by a start-up founder. However, as entrepreneurs begin to convert uncertainties about the start-up into measurable risks, they often have to return and iterate their planning by investing more resources to further sketch out and detail their proposition. External audiences may ask for them to outline their business model in a feasibility study or pitch or require further financial information as part of a full business plan.

Nonetheless, given the diversity of start-ups, it is unlikely that this or any other approach will fit all start-ups.

As you will see in Section 5.4, supporters of improvisational logics such as effectuation, bricolage and lean start-up also argue this emphasis on incremental sequential start-up development is based on an unrealistic expectation that entrepreneurs follow a causal linear process in developing a start-up.[35] This potentially misrepresents entrepreneurial behaviours because it emphasises 'learning by planning' over 'learning by doing'.

Discussion questions:

- What sorts of founders are least likely to use a BMC, feasibility study or a business plan?
- Do you think that entrepreneurs just write business plans and feasibility studies because they are expected to? Is there any intrinsic value in learning by planning?

5.4 ALTERNATIVE APPROACHES TO STARTING UP

5.4.1 *Effectuation*

If setting up a business was similar to cooking, the presumption behind a 'propose, sketch and detail' start-up planning approach is that the best way forward is for the cook (founder) to follow a recipe (feasibility study, business plan) to make a meal (start-up).

Effectuation theory argues this only describes how some start-ups begin. Instead, it is more often for the cook (entrepreneur) to find themselves creating a meal in an unfamiliar kitchen, using new utensils and unexpected ingredients.[36] Setting up a new business is not a linear causal process that can be sequentially planned. Rather, it is a creative process through which entrepreneurs have to use their imagination and be resourceful in how they use limited resources. Effectuation theory also suggests opportunities are created rather than found, and starting-up is not a solitary activity but requires other people to shape and support its development.

Effectuation theory argues founders use five principles in creating a start-up.

1. **Pilot in the plane.** This is a different logic of control from causality: 'effectual rationality lies in exercising control over what can be done with resources at hand, rather than optimizing decisions about what ought to be done given a set of predictions about what happens next'.[37]
2. **Bird in the hand.** Entrepreneurs improvise using three of their key resources: who they are (traits, abilities and preferences), what they know (experiences, training, education and expertise), and who they know (social and professional networks).
3. **Affordable loss.** Causal logic suggests entrepreneurs focus on maximising the financial upsides from any opportunity ('I am going to make a million from this business'). Effectuation argues that founders evaluate options based on what they can afford to lose ('I am only willing to risk some portion of my savings on this opportunity'). If the loss – in time or resources – is likely to be more than they can afford or are willing to pay, an entrepreneur will abandon the start-up.
4. **Crazy quilt.** Effectuation downplays the formal analysis of competition or markets. It argues that founders do not assume that there is a predetermined market but instead stitch together markets and opportunities by leveraging strategic partnerships with others. By focusing on whom they can work with rather than on worrying unduly about competitors, entrepreneurs can develop commitments to the opportunity. Co-creation through these partnerships also helps to increase the resources available to the start-up.
5. **Lemons into lemonade.** Effectuation argues entrepreneurs embrace contingencies, believing that unexpected events are opportunities to turn 'lemons into lemonade'.

Table 5.4 shows effectuation appears distinct from causal logic. In seeking to control what is around them (pilot in the plane), entrepreneurs utilise their means (bird in the hand), co-create with stakeholders (crazy quilt) to embrace changes in means and contingencies (lemons into lemonade) and to dynamically shape their means and their goals. Guided by these commitments and the affordable loss principle, entrepreneurs may decide to pursue the opportunity to create a new product, business or market.

Table 5.4 Differences between effectuation and causal logics

Effectuation	Causality
Entrepreneurs use means at their disposal (bird in the hand)	Entrepreneurs begin with a given goal
Focus on affordable losses	Focus on expected returns
Develop strategic alliances (crazy quilt)	Develop a competitive analysis
Exploit contingencies (lemons into lemonade)	Exploit pre-existing knowledge
Seek to *control* an unpredictable future (pilot in the plane)	Seek to *predict* an uncertain future

5.4.2 Are entrepreneurs really effectual?

Although effectuation and causal logics are not mutually exclusive, implicit in an effectuation logic is that it ought to provide better business performance.[38] One study of biotech entrepreneurs found that effectuation did not always lead to better outcomes: entrepreneurs flipped between causation and effectuation, with effectuation being important in pre-clinical stages but, as external constraints such as external funders and regulatory bodies bit, they switched to using causation.[39] Another study showed that 'flexible decision-making is more prominent in the earlier stages of venture creation, with a transition to more planning-based decision-making over time as the new venture and its market mature'.[40]

Case Study: The Ice-Hotel

Much of the evidence for effectuation relies on a small number of case studies of 'expert' entrepreneurs.[41] One example is the IceHotel, set up by the Swede Nils Bergqvist. Bergqvist had a summer canoeing and rafting business in Northern Sweden. He also wanted to operate a winter business. Meeting up with Japanese entrepreneur Sakata San and going to Japanese ice festivals gave Bergqvist the idea of running an ice sculpture festival back in Sweden. When rain destroyed the sculptures, he embraced contingency (turning lemons into lemonade) and worked with others to develop a transient ice hotel (crazy quilt) that existed only in winter months. Working also with his available means, this later led to a partnership with a vodka producer to develop 'ice-bars' in Northern Sweden, Stockholm and London.[42]

© Getty Images/iStockphoto

5.4.3 Is effectuation ineffectual?

There are doubts about the practical worth of effectuation. It suggests that entrepreneurs should downplay their competitors and focus only on available means rather than having a vision or goal. It also seems to imply that entrepreneurs should rely on 'groping along' to create their start-up.[43] If so, this ignores that 'specific, high (hard) goals lead to a higher level of task performance than do easy goals or vague, abstract goals such as the exhortation to 'do one's best'.[44] Equally, those who rely upon a 'mental plan' and improvisation are also less likely to create a viable start-up than those that eventually write a start-up business plan.[45]

Theoretically, there are also substantive challenges. It does not provide a robust explanation of how the vast majority of start-ups are set up.[46] This is for four main reasons:

1. It fails to specify its shared intellectual roots with other improvisational logics.
2. It fails to explain why founders would choose effectuation.
3. It downplays that founders have a goal or a vision.
4. It makes unreasonable assumptions about how founders act.

5.4.4 Bricolage

Like effectuation, bricolage argues when resources are scarce, founders improvise by using their available resources, their expertise, the labour of others and their network of contacts to overcome barriers and create opportunities. It is defined as 'making do by applying combinations of resources at hand to new problems and opportunities'.[47] An engineer might apply their expertise to drawing up detailed plans and gathering the necessary resources to build a table. However, given the same task, a bricoleur is more likely to use the 'resources on hand to solve the problem in a new way or combine existing resources to potentially unlock a new source of value'.[48]

Bricolage also points to the socially constructed nature of start-ups (opportunities are created rather than discovered) and suggests founders are action orientated.[49] One illustration is a farmer whose land contained a number of abandoned coal mines. These mines had large quantities of methane gas. By making do and creatively combining resources, the farmer adapted a generator to harness the methane to supply the power grid, to grow tomatoes, to warm a large pond for tropical fish and to use the fish waste as fertiliser for his tomatoes.[50]

Bricolage differs from effectuation because it involves the creative application of resources. If the founder is independently wealthy, the application of these resources is only an example of bricolage if the use of their wealth is novel. This differs from effectuation, which argues that just having resources at hand is important. Unlike effectuation, it also argues there are goals (volition) in creatively designing solutions to resource scarcity. This means that 'Bricolage can also occur as part of even carefully pre-planned processes'.[51]

5

5.4.5 Problems with bricolage

Bricolage shares a belief with effectuation that founders can easily develop start-up 'expertise'. The trouble is that developing expertise is difficult in start-up contexts. Expertise relies on 'an environment that is sufficiently regular to be predictable' and 'an opportunity to learn these regularities through prolonged practice'.[52] However, no two start-up situations are likely to be the same, making it hard to apply past experiential learning to the current situation.[53] Similarly, most founders do not run more than two businesses in their lifetime.[54]

Entrepreneurship in Action

- Interview someone who started a successful business about the process they followed and how they sequenced activities when they started up. Evaluate whether they used a causal or improvisational logic.
- Investigate how far – if at all – they followed a bricolage or effectual planning approach.
- If they did use effectuation or bricolage, were they more likely to do so in the early stages of their start-up planning?

Discussion questions:

- List the similarities and differences between effectuation and bricolage. What is the better improvisational approach to starting up? Why?
- Is the Nike school of planning ('just do it') better than a logical and incremental approach to planning?

5.4.6 Lean start-up

More than 35 per cent of new products fail.[55] Globally, only half of those who want to start up actually become business owners.[56] Lean start-up advocates argue that start-ups fail to reach viability because they are too product-focused. Entrepreneurs spend too long and invest too much time in developing a product and testing it with their team or with outside experts (alpha testing). Consequently, too little time is spent on customer (beta) testing. The net result is a product launched and shipped that does not meet customer requirements.

Lean start-up suggests there is a middle way between causality and improvisation, through 'smart experimentation'. 'Lean' does not mean starting-up cheaply (bootstrapping) but relates to Japanese lean manufacturing ideas such as just in time and quicker product development iteration. The approach argues that if less time and fewer resources are wasted on developing unnecessary product features, this will speed up business creation.

It also seeks to balance improvisation with the need for 'a true north, a destination in mind: creating a thriving and world-changing business'.[57] This vision is unlikely to change even if the strategy ('a business model, product roadmap, a point of view about partners and competitors, and ideas about who the customer will be') for realising this vision changes.[58]

New founders should aim to apply a scientific methodology of build, test and learn in order to develop a start-up (Figure 5.4). Core is that the founder has a vision (its 'true north') translated into testable guesses or hypotheses (its strategy) about the viability of the start-up. The aim is to assess if the core value hypothesis is correct: are there actual customers out there who are willing to pay for the idea?

Individual hypotheses have to be both credible and falsifiable. A start-up may use social media to market its product. In doing so, one hypothesis might be that 'our product will spread out through social media'. This is likely to be irrefutable. A more credible and falsifiable hypothesis might be that 'we will reach 10,000 'likes' on Facebook in the first three months' or 'using social media will deliver 10,000 customers in the first year'.

To test particular hypotheses, lean start-up argues that developing a Minimum Viable Product (MVP) is important. MVPs are products and services pared down to their basic components. They allow the founders to test if their hypotheses are correct by uncovering if there is a 'product-market' fit between what the start-up offers (the product) and what customers want (the market). Central to the approach is 'getting out of the building' by testing the MVP and associated hypotheses with 'early adopters': target customers who are likely to need or want the product.[59]

Figure 5.4 Lean start-up approach

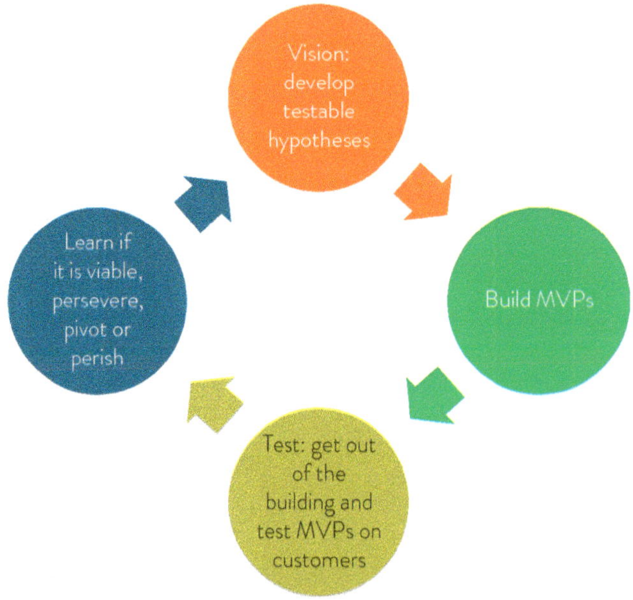

Lean start-up claims to reduce waste and speed up start-up viability. Being quicker has first-mover advantages and can help in fast-paced environments where there are gains from being first into the market.[60] Iterating quickly also promises cost savings (shorter development cycles cheapens labour costs), product improvements (including more recent technology/customer feedback in product/service design) and opportunities for learning.[61]

Case Study: Dropbox

Dropbox's co-founder, Drew Houston, posted a three-minute video explaining Dropbox's MVP online and asked potential users and customers to provide feedback (beta testing). The reaction exceeded Houston's expectations: 'our beta waiting list went from 5000 people to 75,000 people literally overnight. It totally blew us away.'[62]

Analysing the results from experiments with their MVP allows the founder to make one of three decisions:

1. *Persevere* – the results from the tests suggest that the business model is appropriate and the founder should scale the business.
2. *Pivot* – results show the need to reshape the business model.
3. *Perish* – the feedback suggests that the business is non-viable.

Lean start-up emphasises pivoting or perishing are likely outcomes. This allows new founders to 'fail cheaply' and to preserve their resources for another business opportunity.

If the decision is to pivot, lean start-up advocates further iteration of the business model, more testing of customer data and further analysis of this data to assess viability.

Entrepreneurship in Action

- Interview a lean start-up founder or examine a case study of a lean start-up business. What was their value hypothesis and how did it translate into their MVP? Explore how the 'build, test and learn' lean start-up model led them to decide an outcome (persevere, pivot or perish).

Once the business model is validated, lean start-up suggests that start-ups are faced with the 'growth hypothesis': can the business optimise its business model to scale it for the average customer?

Building a scalable 'repeatable' business model requires further learning, iteration and development. In the end, the start-up has to decide if scaling up is possible. If so, it should persevere, but if not, it should decide to pivot to a new customer or close the business.

Case Study: Scaling long hair

© Getty Images/Caiaimage

Consultancy can be a viable and lucrative business. Consultants have expertise gained from their experience and insights they can turn to their advantage. Their challenge is to make this expertise into a repeatable business model. The New Zealand hair stylist, Patrick Cameron is an expert hair styling consultant for women with long hair. To grow his business, he used videos, demonstrations, hairdressing schools and books to build his brand and deliver value to customers he could not reach directly.

5.4.7 Problems with lean start-up

Evidence to support a link between lean start-up and the speed of business creation is thin. It rests on a tiny sample of start-ups.[63] The model's focus on web- and app-based businesses ignores the fact that not all start-ups operate in fast-paced and turbulent industries. More haste can also lead to poorer outcomes such as slower growth or business failure.[64] It may be better to build the start-up slowly.[65]

Building an MVP with a bare number of features may appear sensible, but it can lead to misleading customer data, particularly if there are false positives (the hypothesis is confirmed when in reality it is not valid) or false negatives (hypothesis is disproved but is actually valid).

A 'ship then test' mantra might also provide initial sales but may also damage the start-up's fragile reputation if the product has too many defects.

Developing an MVP is likely to be costly. It opens up the prospects of 'sunk cost' bias. Founders who have spent a lot of time and money on developing an MVP can find it emotionally difficult to pivot away. Creating a narrative about how the start-up will create, deliver and capture value may be cheaper and more effective in the long term.

Finally, a lean start-up approach might be just a new way of expressing an old truism: the founder needs to 'test pilot' the idea by first testing it with consumers and then map out its viability prior to investing (scaling) the business.

5.5 WHAT YOU HAVE LEARNED IN THIS CHAPTER

Writing a formal business plan first is a bad idea. You have learned how it can lead founders to waste scant resources on unproven ideas that may not go anywhere. Instead, developing a business model that provides a coherent narrative of a start-up's cast of characters, ideas and actions is a better way of beginning start-up planning.

This chapter has also shown you that one way of first sketching out and then detailing your business model is to focus on 12 start-up questions. These range from your motivations for starting up through to your plans for growth.

You have seen a route map of different methodologies and approaches you can take to answer these 12 start-up questions. One method is to use the BMC. This is a simple one-page template for understanding the core aspects of a business model. Although this is not the only way of sketching out a start-up, it may be all that a founder needs to conclude start-up planning. Chapter 6 shows you how to use the BMC.

However, external audiences often require further information. This chapter has demonstrated that one further avenue for showing viability is through a written feasibility plan. A related document is a pitch deck. Greater financial information can also lead to the development of a detailed business plan, which itemises the start-up's risks and rewards.

Start-up populations are large and diverse, and entrepreneurs have different ways of achieving start-up viability. They also learn in different ways, with some likely to prefer learning by doing rather than learning by planning. You should now understand why improvisational approaches such as effectuation, bricolage and the lean start-up approach may be appealing start-up alternative methodologies.

ASSESSMENT QUESTIONS

1. Write down the five principles of effectuation. Explain and critically discuss how 'effectual' entrepreneurship differs from 'causal' entrepreneurship.
2. Should founders follow a casual or improvisational logic in starting a business? Critically discuss and evaluate.
3. Explain bricolage and effectuation. How does bricolage differ from effectuation?
4. Is there a need for speed in starting up a business?
5. Explain the lean start-up approach. What are its advantages and disadvantages?
6. Are entrepreneurs more likely to set up a new venture if they rely only on learning by doing?

FURTHER READING

Baker, T., & Nelson, R. E. (2005). Creating something from nothing: Resource construction through entrepreneurial bricolage. *Administrative Science Quarterly, 50*(3), 329–366.

Blank, S. (2013). Why the lean start-up changes everything. *Harvard Business Review, 91*(5), 63–72.

Delmar, F., & Shane, S. (2003). Does business planning facilitate the development of new ventures? Strategic *Management Journal, 24*(12), 1165–1185.

Honig, B., & Karlsson, T. (2004). Institutional forces and the written business plan. *Journal of Management, 30*(1), 29–48.

Hopp, C., & Greene, F. J. (2018). In pursuit of time: Business plan sequencing, duration and intraentrainment effects on new venture viability. *Journal of Management Studies, 55*(2), 320–351.

Morris, M., Schindehutte, M., & Allen, J. (2005). The entrepreneur's business model: Toward a unified perspective. Journal of Business Research, 58(6), 726–735.

Ries, E. (2011). *The lean startup: How today's entrepreneurs use continuous innovation to create radically successful businesses.* New York: Random House.

Sarasvathy, S. D. (2001). Causation and effectuation: Toward a theoretical shift from economic inevitability to entrepreneurial contingency. *Academy of Management Review, 26*(2), 243–263.

Notes

1 Lange, J. E., Mollov, A., Pearlmutter, M., Singh, S., & Bygrave, W. D. (2007). Pre-start-up formal business plans and post-start-up performance: A study of 116 new ventures. *Venture Capital, 9*(4), 237–256; Hopp, C., & Greene, F. J. (2018). In pursuit of time: Business plan sequencing, duration and intraentrainment effects on new venture viability. *Journal of Management Studies, 55*(2), 320–351.

2 Blank, S. (2013). Why the lean start-up changes everything. *Harvard Business Review, 91*(5), 63–72.

3 Sahlman, W. A. (1997). How to write a great business plan. *Harvard Business Review, 75*, 98–109.

4 Dencker, J. C., Gruber, M., & Shah, S. K. (2009). Pre-entry knowledge, learning, and the survival of new firms. *Organization Science, 20*(3), 516–537.

5 Bhide, A. (2000). *The origin and evolution of new businesses.* Oxford, UK: Oxford University Press.

6 Hopp & Greene (2018), ibid.

7 Ibid.

8 Stevenson, H., & Van Slyke, J. (1985). *Pre-start analysis: A framework for thinking about business ventures.* Harvard Business School Case Study Product Number 9-386-075.

9 Sahlman (1997), ibid.

10 Delmar, F. & Shane, S. (2003). Does business planning facilitate the development of new ventures? *Strategic Management Journal, 24*(12), 1165–1185.

11 Gruber, M. (2007). Uncovering the value of planning in new venture creation: A process and contingency perspective. *Journal of Business Venturing, 22*(6), 782–807.

12 Greene, F. J., & Hopp, C. (2018). Are formal planners more likely to achieve new venture viability? A counterfactual model and analysis. *Strategic Entrepreneurship Journal, 11*(1), 36–60.

13 Burke, A., Fraser, S., & Greene, F. J. (2010). The multiple effects of business planning on new venture performance. *Journal of Management Studies, 47*(3), 391–415; Chwolka, A., & Raith, M. G. (2012). The value of business planning before start-up – A decision-theoretical perspective. *Journal of Business Venturing, 27*(3), 385–399; Honig, B. & Karlsson, T. (2004). Institutional forces and the written business plan. *Journal of Management, 30*(1), 29–48.

14 Ansoff, H. I. (1991). Critique of Henry Mintzberg's "The design school: Reconsidering the basic premises of strategic management". *Strategic Management Journal, 12*(6), 449–461.

15 Katz, J., & Gartner, W. B. (1988). Properties of emerging organizations. *Academy of Management Review, 13*(3), 429–441.

16 McMullen, J. S., & Dimov, D. (2013). Time and the entrepreneurial journey: The problems and promise of studying entrepreneurship as a process. *Journal of Management Studies, 50*(8), 1481–1512.

17 Katz & Gartner (1988), ibid.

18 Sahlman (1997), ibid.

19 Drucker, P. F. (1985). The discipline of innovation. *Harvard Business Review, 63*(3), 67–72.

20 Hopp & Greene (2018), ibid.

21 Brush, C. G., Manolova, T. S., & Edelman, L. F. (2008). Properties of emerging organizations: An empirical test. *Journal of Business Venturing, 23*(5), 547–566.

22 Ibid., p. 548.

23 Gordon, S. R., & Davidsson, P. (2013). *Unpacking the venture creation process* (p. 23). Business Creation in Australia, 07. Brisbane, Australia: Queensland University of Technology Business School.

24 Gruber (2007), ibid.

25 Bhide (2000), ibid.

26 Teece, D. J. (2010). Business models, business strategy and innovation. *Long Range Planning, 43*(2), 172–194, 173.

27 Zott, C., Amit, R., & Massa, L. (2011). The business model: Recent developments and future research. *Journal of Management, 37*(4), 1019–1042; George, G.,

& Bock, A. J. (2011). The business model in practice and its implications for entrepreneurship research. *Entrepreneurship Theory and Practice, 35*(1), 83–111; DaSilva, C. M., & Trkman, P. (2014). Business model: What it is and what it is not. Long Range Planning, 47(6), 379–389; Massa, L., Tucci, C. L., & Afuah, A. (2017). A critical assessment of business model research. *Academy of Management Annals, 11*(1), 73–104.

28 Morris, M., Schindehutte, M., & Allen, J. (2005). The entrepreneur's business model: Toward a unified perspective. *Journal of Business Research, 58*(6), 726–735.

29 Joyce, A., & Paquin, R. L. (2016). The triple layered business model canvas: A tool to design more sustainable business models. *Journal of Cleaner Production, 135*, 1474–1486; www.socialbusinessmodelcanvas.com; socialenterpriseinstitute.co/wp-content/.../Social-Business-Model-Canvas.pdf.

30 Stevenson, H. H., & Jarillo, J. C. (1990). A paradigm of entrepreneurship: Entrepreneurial management. *Strategic Management Journal, 11*(5), 17–27, 23.

31 Honig & Karlsson (2004), ibid.

32 Clarke, J. (2011). Revitalizing entrepreneurship: How visual symbols are used in entrepreneurial performances. Journal of Management Studies, 48(6), 1365–1391; Clarke, J. S., Cornelissen, J. P., & Healey, M. (2018). Actions speak louder than words: How figurative language and gesturing in entrepreneurial pitches influences investment judgments. Academy of *Management Journal, 62*(2), 335–360.

33 https://guykawasaki.com/the-only-10-slides-you-need-in-your-pitch/.

34 Chen, X. P., Yao, X., & Kotha, S. (2009). Entrepreneur passion and preparedness in business plan presentations: A persuasion analysis of venture capitalists' funding decisions. *Academy of Management Journal, 52*(1), 199–214.

35 Mintzberg, H., & Waters, J. A. (1985). Of strategies, deliberate and emergent. *Strategic Management Journal, 6*(3), 257–272.

36 Sarasvathy, S. D. (2001). Causation and effectuation: Toward a theoretical shift from economic inevitability to entrepreneurial contingency. *Academy of Management Review, 26*(2), 243–263.

37 Dew, N., & Sarasvathy, S. D. (2002). What effectuation iis not: *Further development of an alternative to rational choice*. Paper presented at the Academy of Management Conference, Denver, August, p. 7.

38 Sarasvathy, S. D. (2009). *Effectuation: Elements of entrepreneurial expertise*. Cheltenham, UK: Edward Elgar.

39 Maine, E., Soh, P. H., & Dos Santos, N. (2012). Decision-making processes in biotech commercialization: Constraints to effectuation. *Technology Management for Emerging Technologies (PICMET), 2012 Proceedings of PICMET'*. IEEE, 12, 611–616.

40 Reymen, I. M., Andries, P., Berends, H., Mauer, R., Stephan, U., & Burg, E. (2015). Understanding dynamics of strategic decision making in venture creation: A process study of effectuation and causation. *Strategic Entrepreneurship Journal*, 9(4), 351–379, 374.

41 Sarasvathy (2009), ibid.

42 www.effectuation.org/?page_id=15; www.icehotel.com/about-icehotel/; www.icehotel.com/about-icehotel/icebar/.

43 Dimov, D. (2010). Nascent entrepreneurs and venture emergence: Opportunity confidence, human capital, and early planning. *Journal of Management Studies, 47*(6), 1123–1153.

44 Locke, E. A., & Latham, G. P. (2006). New directions in goal-setting theory. *Current Directions in Psychological Science, 15*(5), 265–268, 265.

45 Greene and Hopp, 'Are formal planners more likely to achieve new venture viability?'

46 Arend, R. J., Sarooghi, H., & Burkemper, A. (2015). Effectuation as ineffectual? Applying the 3E theory-assessment framework to a proposed new theory of entrepreneurship. *Academy of Management Review, 40*(4), 630–651.

47 Baker, T., & Nelson, R. E. (2005). Creating something from nothing: Resource construction through entrepreneurial bricolage. *Administrative Science Quarterly, 50*(3), 329–366, 330.

48 Welter, C., Mauer, R., & Wuebker, R. J. (2016). Bridging behavioral models and theoretical concepts: effectuation and bricolage in the opportunity creation framework. *Strategic Entrepreneurship Journal, 10*(1), 5–20, p. 8.

49 Baker and Nelson (2005), ibid.

50 Ibid.

51 Ibid., p. 360.

52 Kahneman, D. (2011). *Thinking, fast and slow* (p. 240). London: Macmillan.

53 Gottschalk, S., Greene, F. J., & Müller, B. (2017). The impact of habitual entrepreneurial experience on firm closure outcomes. *Small Business Economics*, 48, 303.

54 Greene, F., Mole, K., & Storey, D. (2008). *Three decades of enterprise culture? Entrepreneurship, economic regeneration and public policy*. London: Springer; Lafontaine, F., & Shaw, K. (2016). Serial entrepreneurship: Learning by doing? *Journal of Labor Economics, 34*(S2), S217–S254.

55 Castellion, G., & Markham, S. K. (2013). Perspective: New product failure rates: Influence of argumentum ad populum and self-interest. *Journal of Product Innovation Management, 30*(5), 976–979.

56 Bergmann, H., & Stephan, U. (2012). Moving on from nascent entrepreneurship: Measuring cross-national differences in the transition to new business ownership. *Small Business Economics, 41*(4), 945–959.

57 Ries, E. (2011). *The lean startup: How today's entrepreneurs use continuous innovation to create radically successful businesses* (p. 22). New York: Random House.

58 Ries (2011), ibid., p. 22.

59 Blank, S., & Dorf, B. (2012). *The startup owner's manual: The step-by-step guide for building a great company*. Pescadero, CA: K & S Ranch.

60 Chen, J., Reilly, R. R., & Lynn, G. S. (2012). New product development speed: Too much of a good

thing? *Journal of Product Innovation Management, 29*(2), 288–303.

61 Langerak, F., & Hultink, E. J. (2005). The impact of new product development acceleration approaches on speed and profitability: Lessons for pioneers and fast followers. *IEEE Transactions on Engineering Management, 52*(1), 30–42; Kessler, E. H., & Chakrabarti, A. K. (1996). Innovation speed: A conceptual model of context, antecedents, and outcomes. *Academy of Management Review, 21*(4), 1143–1191; Menon, A., Chowdhury, J., & Lukas, B. A. (2002). Antecedents and outcomes of new product development speed: An interdisciplinary conceptual framework. *Industrial Marketing Management, 31*(4), 317–328.

62 techcrunch.com/2011/10/19/dropbox-minimal-viable-product/.

63 www.theleanstartup.com/casestudies.

64 Capelleras, J., Greene, F. J., Kantis, H., & Rabetino, R. (2010). Venture creation speed and subsequent growth: Evidence from South America. *Journal of Small Business Management, 48*(3), 302–324; Perlow, L. A., Okhuysen, G. A., & Repenning, N. P. (2002). The speed trap: Exploring the relationship between decision making and temporal context. *Academy of Management Journal, 45*(5), 931–955; Forbes, D. P. (2005). Managerial determinants of decision speed in new ventures. *Strategic Management Journal, 26*(4), 355–366.

65 Brush et al. (2008), ibid.; Kim, P. H., Longest, K. C., & Lippmann, S. (2015). The tortoise versus the hare: Progress and business viability differences between conventional and leisure-based founders. *Journal of Business Venturing, 30*(2), 185–204.

CHAPTER 6

Start-Up Feasibility Planning I: Using the Business Model Canvas

Learning Outcomes

In this chapter, you will learn:

- The importance of working out your 'product–market' fit.
- How to reach your customers.
- How to work out your revenue model.
- What you need to do to deliver value to your customers.

Mini Contents List

6.1 INTRODUCTION

The Business Model Canvas (BMC) is one of the most common ways for start-up founders to sketch out their initial business model. It helps because it uses a simple one-page template that has nine fundamental building blocks for creating, delivering and capturing value.[1]

This chapter shows you that the BMC has a hierarchical approach to business model development. It proposes that entrepreneurs will develop a viable business model if they can align their customer (the market) with their value proposition (the product).

Once this 'product–market fit' is developed, the BMC suggests that the founder needs to scope out their marketing and sales, how they intend to make money and what key activities and key partners they have to use to produce and deliver their product or service. It is particularly valuable for answering these key start-up questions (Chapter 5, pp. 98–99):

- Is there a market out there?
- Who is the customer?
- Is the business idea worthwhile?
- How does the business reach its customers?
- How does the business source, make and distribute its products and services?
- How does it make money?

Using the BMC to 'storyboard' a start-up proposition may be the only start-up planning tool you need. To support the use of the BMC, this chapter points you to a series of practical exercises in Workbook 2. The advantage of these exercises is that they also help with developing other start-up planning activities such as writing a feasibility plan or developing a pitch deck.

Chapter 7 provides further valuable information on further developing your feasibility planning while Chapters 8 and 9 complete the picture by providing ways of understanding financial information and key audiences for a start-up seeking resources to develop the business.

6.2 THE BUSINESS MODEL CANVAS

Chapter 5 introduced the fundamentals of the BMC. As Figure 6.1 shows, the BMC is a graphical tool that enables entrepreneurs to brainstorm and imaginatively change the internal logic of their business model.

However, it is a mistake to see the BMC as having multiple starting points. For example, a founder may be tempted to first work out what their key resources and activities are. This is not how the BMC is meant to be applied in entrepreneurial contexts.

The BMC takes a customer-led approach to start-up. It focuses first on target customers and asks entrepreneurs to align the benefits of their product or service (value proposition) with the needs and wants of these customers. Focusing first on the fit between a customer and a product (what is called the product–market fit) is vital because a start-up is only really a business if it has paying customers.

Identifying this product–market fit begs further questions about reaching and servicing customers (channels and customer relationships), how a start-up delivers value through its key activities, its resources and with its partners, what the costs of this business infrastructure are and how the start-up intends to make money from creating and delivering value to customers.

The BMC, therefore, is not a flat canvas but asks entrepreneurs to follow a hierarchy made up of[2]:

1. Customer segments.
2. Value propositions.
3. Channels.

4. Customer relationships.
5. Revenue streams.
6. Key resources.
7. Key activities.
8. Key partners.
9. Cost structure.

Figure 6.1 Business Model Canvas Business Model Canvas template © Strategyzer AG; strategyzer.com/canvas

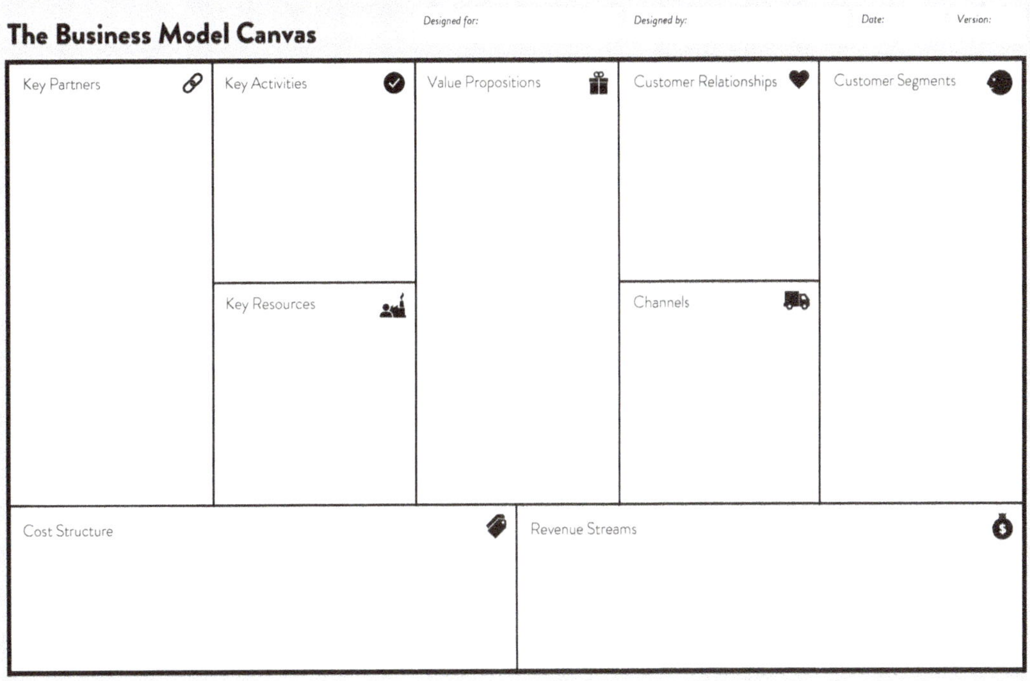

Entrepreneurship in Action

- Should you always focus first on customers and the value proposition? A start-up's source of competitive advantage – what gives it an unfair advantage – might be its ability to be innovative in how it reaches customers (channels) and/or how it charges customers (revenues), because it has particular key partners or because it has lower costs. Alibaba (retail), WeChat (social media), Uber (taxis) and Airbnb (accommodation) all have low costs: Alibaba has no stock, WeChat creates no content, Uber does not own its taxis and Airbnb has no rooms of its own.
- What happens if you brainstorm how to disrupt the hierarchy proposed by the BMC? Are there ways that you can innovate your business model?
- The BMC is not the only template available to entrepreneurs. Another popular tool is the one page Lean Canvas developed by Ash Maurya (Figure 6.2).[3] This also has nine building blocks. Like the BMC, this canvas also has a suggested order.
- Do you think that the lean canvas is more suited for a start-up?

Figure 6.2 The Lean Canvas

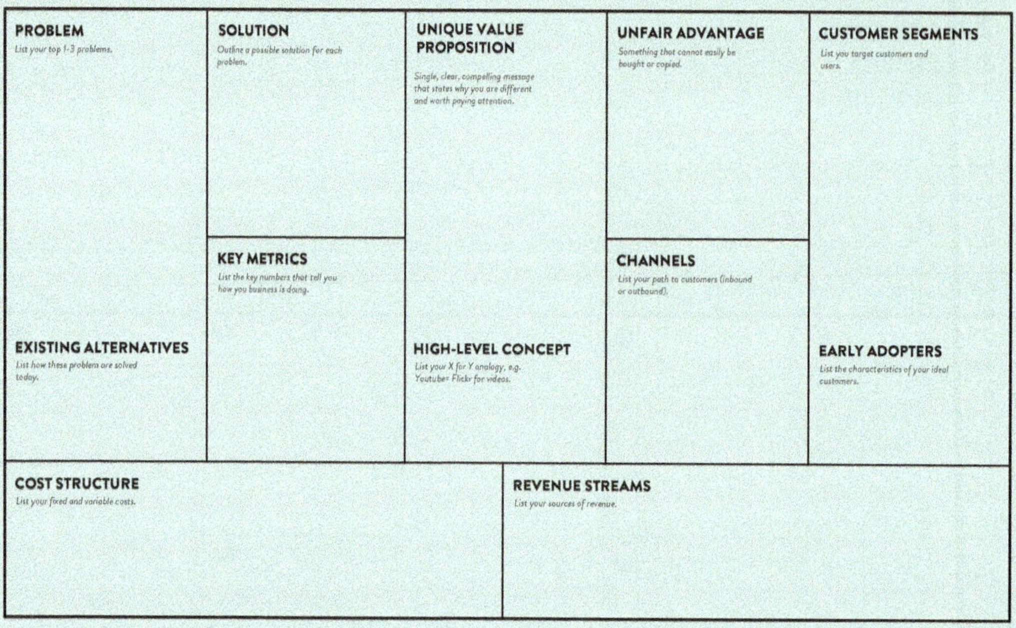

1. The problem (top three problems).
2. Customer segments (who are the early adopters of the programme?).
3. Unique value proposition (simple concise explanation of central benefits of product or service).
4. Solution (what are the three top features of your solution to the problem?).
5. Channels (routes to market).
6. Revenue streams (revenue model, gross margin).
7. Cost structure (costs of acquiring customers, distribution costs, employee costs).
8. Key metrics (key measures of performance).
9. Unfair advantage (what is the source of your competitive advantage?).

6.3 FOCUSING ON THE CUSTOMER

Surprisingly, entrepreneurship shares some characteristics with murder.[4] Like homicide, setting up a business requires a motive, a means of doing it and an opportunity. But where murder is an act of force on an unwilling person, there is 'no entrepreneurial opportunity without customer demand. The founder can be in the right place at the right time, but what makes this place and time "right" is the presence of a customer who is willing and able to pay the entrepreneur's asking price. Without this demand, no opportunity exists.'[5]

Popular depictions of entrepreneurs include someone quietly labouring away in a workshop on their latest invention. In 1955, Adolph Buckner patented a lock for a toilet seat lid.[6] Why he thought this was a good idea remains a mystery because – like ear muffs for dogs – it is hard to see why anyone would want to purchase a lock for a toilet lid.[7]

A better way of understanding the role of entrepreneurs is to see them as problem solvers for a large and growing market. To estimate how big the problem is, how fast it is growing and what the current alternative solutions are, founders can use secondary desk research. National statistic agencies can provide a wealth of information such as demographic, census, economic trends and regional data. News agencies, trade industry information, web search engines or dedicated providers of market intelligence such as Mintel and MarketLine Advantage can also be a source of valuable consumer intelligence.

For example, climate change is perhaps the greatest problem facing society today. An increase in global temperatures of just 1.5 degrees centigrade will have a significant environmental impact and dramatic effects on all that live on our planet.[8] One way consumers have sought to solve this huge problem is by turning vegetarian because reducing meat consumption has a positive effect on limiting greenhouse gases from agriculture.[9] Entrepreneurs can use statistics to show the size and changing nature of this market. In Europe, the market is large (about 33 million people are vegetarians) and growing (up by 3 million in five years).[10]

However, although this is a tempting market, a potentially naïve assumption is that a new founder could easily serve 10 per cent or 3.3 million vegetarian customers at start-up. This is likely to be wildly optimistic because start-ups suffer from what is called the 'liability of smallness'.[11] In practice, their available financial resources are just too limited to reach all the customers in a large market. They also suffer from the 'liability of newness'.[12] This is a challenge because they are an unknown quantity to suppliers and financiers who are worried about if the start-up will deliver what they promise and pay what they owe. Even if they could find the money and gain trust, new businesses are often preoccupied in the early stages with working out how to do business and what resources, such as plants, people and machinery, they need to build their infrastructure.

Faced with these challenges, many start-ups embark on a market research journey to decide who conceivably could buy their solution (the total market), which groups from within this total market might feasibly buy their products or services (customer segments) and which group from these customer segments the start-up can profitably target (target customer or customer niche). Finding a niche is crucial because start-ups have limited resources and have to concentrate their sales and marketing efforts on whoever their first target customer is.

6.3.1 The mass market

Assessing the ideal total market involves judging how many customers there are in theory and what they are likely to spend on average for a particular product or service. This measure of the mass market might be calculated using secondary data sources such as industry reports. This idealised number may be for the whole planet if the start-up aims to open up from the very beginning in multiple markets. These 'born globals', though, are relatively rare (Chapter 10, p. 264). A more common mass or total market is a block of countries (Europe, Latin America or Asia) or an individual country or province.

Choosing the market – or what is sometimes called the beachhead market – is rarely done based solely on the attractiveness, growth or size of a total market. Market attractiveness is not the same as industry attractiveness (Chapter 7, pp. 170–178). The soft drinks industry appears attractive to a new entrant. But in Indonesia, Coca-Cola has a 72 per cent share of the market by value.[13]

Equally, geography matters: potential entrepreneurs often locate their start-up where they live rather than choosing where the market may be most favourable (Chapter 10, p. 264). For example, India is a very attractive place to start-up a business for vegetarians because it has more vegetarians than any other country in the world.[14] Italy is also attractive because it has one of the fastest-growing vegetarian populations in Europe.[15] Despite this, entrepreneurs with no connection to India or Italy are unlikely to see these as places to set up a new vegetarian business.

Case Study: Have a heart

Swedish entrepreneurs Jakob Gelber and Robert Sabelström wanted to help charities gain extra income. They realised a large and growing number of phone users wanted to donate from their handset but found it difficult to do so. Their response, Big Heart, is an app that connects phone users with advertisers. In return for reading advertisements on their lock screen, phone users earn money to donate to worthy causes.

Entrepreneurship in Action

- Use a library's electronic resources and an internet search engine to provide key statistics about the chosen market. How big is the total market for your product or service? Is the market growing? How does this break down geographically?

- *Go to Exercise W 2.1: How big is the problem?*

6.3.2 Segmenting customers

A total market or mass market consists of subsets of different customers, each with different aims, aspirations and problems. One main challenge is to distinguish these different customers into segments and evaluate which of these is the target customer. Customer segments are *potential* customers who share similar characteristics. They might use similar products or services to the start-up's offer or buy these products and services in a similar way.

It can be difficult to distinguish which customer segments to focus on. One approach is to rely solely on a hunch or gut feeling. A potential entrepreneur may believe that their market is people like them. A group of Chinese student entrepreneurs studying in Australia or Germany might, for example, find 'Western' teas unpalatable and decide to set up a tea shop for other Chinese students. This ignores their own cognitive bias (Chapter 2, pp. 32–37). It also downplays that undergraduate students tend to be extremely price-conscious and only attend university for particular parts of a calendar year. It may also miss other customer segments, such as professional people or the retired, who may be interested in drinking more authentic teas.

Another option is to brainstorm which customer segments are most likely to buy a product or service. Someone who wants to start a residential cleaning business could quickly segment different customers that might be interested, such as students, single older people, professionals, millennials or the disabled. Subsequently, a qualitative evaluation of these segments can be undertaken to see which of them appears the most promising.

A more formal approach for businesses selling to customers (B2C businesses) is to segment potential customers in four ways:

- **Demography** – dividing individuals by their personal attributes, such as age, gender, sexuality, education, occupation or income.
- **Geography** – focusing on particular towns and cities, regions or countries, and perhaps dividing these into rural and urban.
- **Psychology** – dividing people by their personality attributes, values or preferences.

- **Behaviour** – focusing on how people use existing products, what they want from them and how loyal they are to the existing offering. Do they favour socially conscious or environmentally friendly products and services?

For start-ups selling to other businesses (B2B businesses), there are similar ways of segmenting:

- **Business characteristics** – dividing businesses by sector, size, organisational structure, the technology they use and their location.
- **Purchasing characteristics** – focusing on why and how the key decision-making unit, such as the purchasing department, business owner or information technology department, buys products. Large purchases are more likely to involve a long sales and marketing process.
- **Attitudes** – a business customer's willingness to take risks, the similarities buyers and sellers have and the strength of customer loyalty.

6.3.3 Talking to customers

Desk research can offer 'top-down' insights about the mass market, potential customer segments and eventual target customers. However, it is no substitute for speaking to people to find out what they buy and why.

A 'bottom-up' approach to market research is often better because it is practical. Entrepreneurs do not always have the time and money to investigate the shape, size and dynamics of a market. There are trade-offs: spending too long evaluating may detract from actually building the business. Information published on the web or in industry reports is historical rather than what is happening or might happen.

Talking directly to customers can be defined as 'entrepreneurial marketing', which is 'the proactive identification and exploitation of opportunities for acquiring and retaining profitable customers through innovative approaches to risk management, resource leveraging and value creation'.[16] An active customer focus relies on potential customers to validate an offer and to provide customer intelligence and ideas for further product development.[17] This builds the start-up's reputation and helps overcome its liability of newness.[18]

Case Study: Crushing bugs

Omar Gabr and Moataz Soliman started AStarApps after finishing their degrees at Cairo University. Their business idea was a platform that allowed app developers to beta test their applications. To assess this business idea they saw 60 app developers in Egypt. The feedback was that the AStarApps was a terrible product. Its design was awful and its functionality was dreadful. However, they also found out that developers really liked that instead of having to send separate emails or using screenshots, their platform gave the developer the ability to directly report bugs. Based on this, Omar Gabr and Moataz Soliman abandoned AStarApps and set up Instabugs. Subsequently, they were able to raise $1.7 million in venture capital funding.[19]

Consequently, entrepreneurs tend to rely on haphazard, informal networking to learn about potential customers.[20] This often leverages the social capital of family, friends and contacts and might involve contacting 10, 20, 50 or 100 people they know. If these contacts are positive, this may form their evidence base for affirming the presence of customers. Richa Bhalla used her network to validate her bicycle-based courier service, Pedals. Conversations with her contacts suggested her customers were other start-ups who, like her, wanted an environmentally conscious solution for delivering parcels in London.

Entrepreneurship in Action

- Do some mystery shopping. There are strict data protection rules about how to do this.[21] If you can get informed consent, observe and talk to different customers who use a product or service. Which of these has the greatest need for the product? Who is willing to pay?
- Talk to potential customers outside a competitor's store. Find out more about their demographics, behaviours and attitudes in relation to the product. For example, what would make them change from the competitor to a new product? How did they find out about the competitor's product?
- Talk to your family and friends to see who has used and bought a similar product or service. Ask them to recommend someone to talk to about the product or service.
- Visit a trade show or go to a conference. Talk to existing suppliers and customers to find out more about different customer segments and which of these are the most promising.

Too much, though, is made of the distinction between formal (desk research) and informal (networking with customers) approaches to customer segmentation.[22] Many start-ups rely on both and how much one, compared to another, is used varies depending on the business. It is not worth 'getting out of the building' as the lean start-up approach implies if a founder does not know where they are going. Doing secondary research is also important if external finance is required because funders often need concrete market information.

Evaluating customer segments is done based on a gut feeling, brainstorming different segments, observing or interviewing different types of customers, using secondary desk research or using a mix of or more than one of these approaches. Speaking to customers often gives a better idea of who the most promising target customer is, particularly if it is validated by secondary desk research.

Entrepreneurship in Action

Table 6.1 shows some common factors a business can use to score the attractiveness of different segments. It asks you to evaluate the different segments in your market and decide which is the most promising customer niche.

Table 6.1 Evaluating customer segments

	Segment A (rate 1–5, 5 is high)	Segment B (rate 1–5, 5 is high)	Segment C (rate 1–5, 5 is high)
What is the size and growth rate of the customer segment?			
Does the segment have a real itch (currently uses a 'workaround' to solve their problem)?			

Is the customer segment willing to pay for the offer?			
Is the customer segment able to pay for the offer?			
Is the customer segment easy to market and sell to?			
Is the customer segment guarded by a major competitor?			
Total score			

- *Go to Exercise W 2.2: Who are your likely customer segments?*

Case Study: Rêve En Vert

Cora Hilts and Natasha Tucker set up Rêve En Vert to sell fashionable but sustainable designer wear. They worked out that their segment was 'up-market' women who were interested in well-being and purchasing conscientiously sourced products. As Figure 6.3 shows, after drilling down to uncover these women's characteristics they discovered two niches that were likely to buy their designer clothes.

Figure 6.3 Target niches

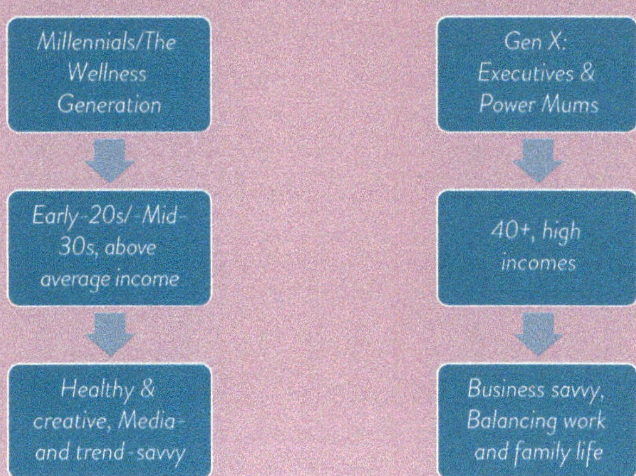

6.3.4 TAM, SAM and SOM

The TAM, SAM and SOM approach is another popular way of arriving at a niche or target customer (Figure 6.4). It starts by calculating the TAM. TAM stands for the Total Addressable Market. It is the theoretical total sales that a business could reach if it had the capacity and capability to reach all of its customers and was the only solution in the market. This mass market might be all the people who purchase home security or deodorants. One potential way of estimating TAM is to use secondary market research to count up the revenue share of existing companies. For example, in Egypt consumers spend around 1.4 billion Egyptian pounds on deodorants. Three companies (Unilever, Henkel and Beiersdorf) make up around half of this market, with the other half consisting of a range of smaller players.[23]

A subset of the TAM is the SAM. This stands for the Serviceable Available Market. It is the proportion or customer segment of the TAM a company could feasibly reach over time. For example, young men are most likely to be online gamblers, while home security systems are largely bought by families. The 'smart' home security business Cocoon arrived at their SAM by calculating the overall home security market and what proportion of it was made up of family households that were not on welfare.

Figure 6.4 TAM, SAM and SOM

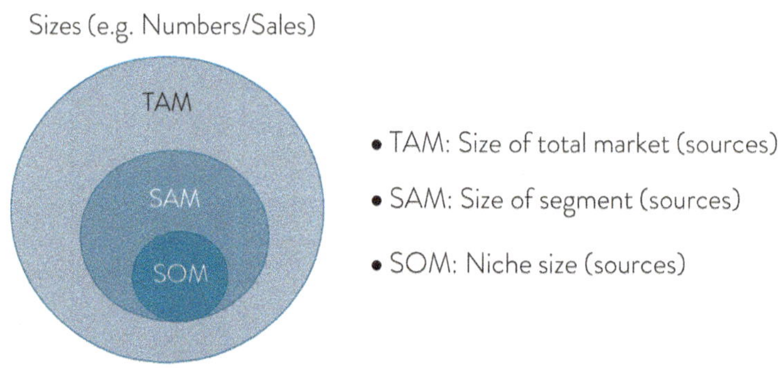

The final subset is the SOM, which stands for Serviceable Obtainable Market. For the founder, this is the target customer or niche that is most likely to buy their product or service. One way of arriving at the SOM is to better detail a customer segment. For example, if an Egyptian entrepreneur wants to develop a new deodorant that uses natural fresh ingredients, they might use secondary desk research to identify that out of the total market (TAM) they are more likely to gain traction with women (SAM). However, they may conjecture that their first customer is professional women, living in Cairo who can afford to pay for a more environmentally friendly deodorant (SOM).

Relying just on secondary data to conduct a 'top-down' TAM, SAM and SOM analysis is limited. It usefully validates primary market research but a more 'bottom-up' approach to estimating the market, evaluating segments and choosing a niche often provides a more detailed picture of the target customer.

- *Go to Exercise W 2.3: What's your TAM, SAM and SOM?*

6.3.5 Profiling and validating the target customer

Primary and secondary research into different customer segments may help identify if a chosen target customer is promising. Of the two, spending time talking to target customers is most likely to be helpful because:

- It validates if the target customer is, in fact, the target customer.
- If done early, it helps avoid later costly mistakes that stem from targeting marketing and sales at the 'wrong' customer.[24]
- It helps with developing a more fine-grained and up-to-date 'bottom-up' TAM, SAM and SOM. Customer interviews can reveal actual spending preferences and help with developing revenue estimates (Chapter 8, pp. 187–188).

One way of assessing the promise of a target customer is to develop a detailed customer 'vignette'. This is a short portrait of a customer and is also called a customer 'persona'. Figure 6.5 shows this includes a picture of the target customer, a description of their lifestyle and their problems, or 'pains', and what they are looking for, or their 'gains'. It should be as detailed as possible and include key demographics, experiences and family circumstances. Pains should detail such areas as what the customer lacks or has too much of, what they dislike and their fears. Gains include what delights them, what they enjoy doing and their hopes.

Figure 6.5 Customer vignette

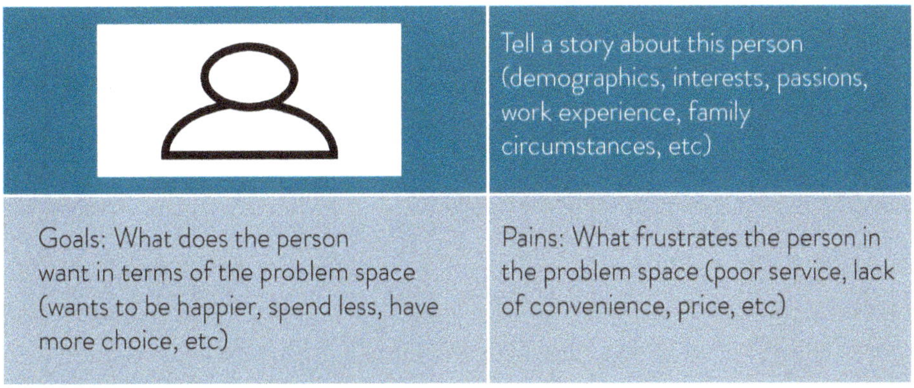

Case study: Rachel

Up-market frozen meals business The Cook Kitchen segmented a range of customers based on their age: young professionals, empty nesters, working mothers and the elderly. After researching their market, they developed a vignette for their target customer, Rachel. She is 'a thirtysomething mum who's a good cook but doesn't always have time to do it herself. Serving her family and friends fabulous food makes Rachel feel good about herself.'[25]

Entrepreneurship in Action

In talking to your target customers, there are a number of golden rules worth following:

- Write down your goals for the interview and tell the target customer why you need their time.
- Write down the questions that you want to ask. Pilot test your questions on family and friends.
- Think about what you are hoping to get out of these questions. Usually, if you are seeking to write up a feasibility plan, collect information to go into your pitch deck, or have primary research for your business plan, the key question you are asking is about the viability and feasibility of the start-up. Although this might be your central research question, within this you are often attempting to test key assumptions about your business model. This usually involves finding out about the market (Chapter 5, p. 98: Q.2. Is there a market out there?), customer perceptions about your offer (Q.3. Is the business idea worthwhile?), the competition (Q.6. How is the offer different in the market?), marketing and sales (Q.5. How does the business reach its customers?), how you intend to deliver value (Q.7. How does the business source, make and distribute its products and services?) and your revenue model (Q.8. How does it make money?).
- Take notes and ask open-ended questions such as 'Could you tell me about the [problem, itch or irritation] you face?' It is better to avoid questions that end in yes, no or don't know. To get better quality information it is often useful to give a range of options that may be ranked or scored. For example, you could list out all the potential benefits of your offer and ask customers to rank these in order. You can subsequently ask them or 'prompt' them by asking them further questions (see the 'Five Whys' or 'Who, What, Where, When, How and Why questions in Chapter 4, p. 70).
- In the actual interview with the customer, focus on three question types:
  - *Situation questions* – the aim of these questions is to establish if the customer fits your customer profile (Chapter 5, p. 99: Q.4. Who is the customer?). You can do this by asking them questions that establish if the customer is similar to your customer vignette. If they do not, you should abandon the interview. It is also not a good idea to ask personal facts about a person. Respondents are unlikely to tell you their exact age or give you precise details on their income.
  - *Problem questions* – the aim is to work out how the respondent currently solves the problem. This involves asking if, how, why and what they use to solve a problem. For example, is the problem a real irritant to the customer? How good is the current solution they use? Does a competitor's solution solve the problem or do its 'pains' outweigh its 'gains'? In an ideal world, what would they like a product or service solution to this problem to achieve?
  - *Opportunity questions* – the aim is often to explain your business model and then seek to test key elements. For example, after you have explained how your business intends to work, one focus in these set of questions may be on your revenue model, and a 'freemium model' is better than a subscription model (Q.8. How does it make money?). Asking potential customers gives you customer-based reviews of what

might work. It can also can tell you about the feasibility of your operations (Q.7. How does the business source, make and distribute its products and services?), sense check if customers also see benefits in your product or service relative to the competition (Q.3. Is the business idea worthwhile?, Q.6. How is the offer different in the market?) and if your route to market is viable (Q.5. How does the business reach its customers?).

- Listen. Don't sell and avoid talking about your product or service – your aim is to validate that the 'problem' is real, if there is a product–market fit and if you can deliver and capture value.
- After the interview, reflect on what you have learned. Iterate your questions and prompts.
- If the first interview is a friend, family member or personal business contact, subsequently interview strangers. As a rule, see family and friend as pilot interviews as they tend to give you positive reviews of your business idea.
- Interview as many people as you can. Alternatively, run a focus group of target customers and walk them through their pains and gains, how they use existing products or services and if your business model assumptions are robust.

Entrepreneurs can also develop an empathy map to define their target customer. Figure 6.6 demonstrates how this places the customer at the centre and asks a business to work out how they see, feel, act and think. It also links to the customer's pains and gains. Seeing involves understanding their environment, where the person lives and who their family, friends and colleagues are. Saying and doing involves understanding their attitudes, what they tell others and how they use outside information – and where from – to inform what they say. Thinking is influenced by emotions, aspirations and hopes, both now and in the future. Pains can be assessed by investigating irritations, obstacles and fears, while gains focus on what the person wishes to achieve and how they measure success.

Figure 6.6 Empathy map

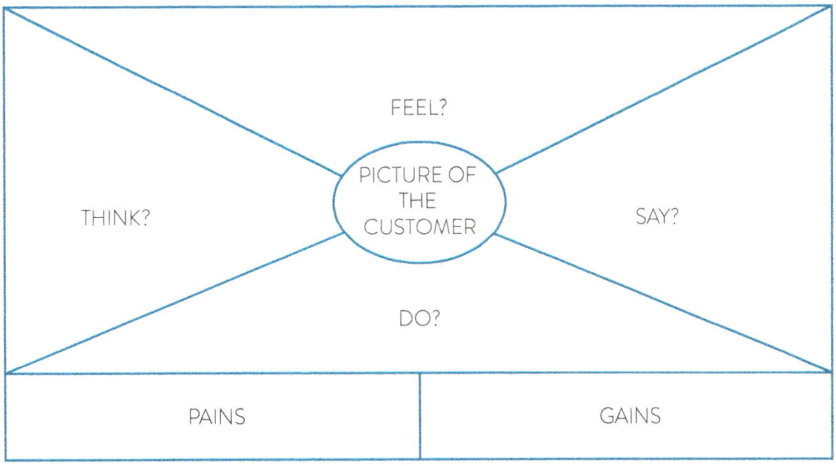

Charting the customer journey before, during and after a purchase can expand the insights from a customer vignette or empathy map. Someone who develops a new algorithm that matches potential partners might see potential in the dating market. After identifying their target customer, they could complete a customer vignette or empathy map for the customer, and then chart how they go about meeting people, what happens during the date and what happens later on (Table 6.2).

Table 6.2 Customer journey and empathy map for a new dating platform

	Before	During	Afterwards
Think			
Feel			
Do			
Say			
Pains			
Gains			

○ *Go to Exercise W 2.4: What is your target customer's profile?*

A crucial aspect of developing a viable business model is to understand the customer. Without a customer, it is difficult to describe a start-up as a business.[26] Entrepreneurs can profile their target customer using desk research and by talking to potential customers. It is unlikely that there is a one-size-fits-all approach. But by going through a process of customer segmentation and identification, businesses can find, profile and validate their target customer. They can subsequently use this information to complete the 'Customer Segments' section of the BMC. They may also develop a graph that explains their TAM, SAM and SOM approach for a pitch or a plan. Data (appendices) and information from customer testimonials can complement this information.

○ *Go to Exercise W 2.5: How have you validated your targeted customer?*

6.4 THE VALUE PROPOSITION

Identifying how a product or service is valuable to the target customer is integral to finding a product–market fit. Businesses must demonstrate their offer gives customers pain relief or provides customer delight to be sustainable. A starting point is an explanation of how the product or service works. This outlines its features. Features are what a product or service *is to the customer*.

Case Study: Pitching Kar-Go

Pitches and plans often come undone if they fail to describe how the product or service works. If the audience does not get how the offer works, they will quickly lose interest and can become critical.

Prototypes or drawings of how the product are useful. A food business might show a menu or bring along some of its dishes to the pitch. Another way is having figures either in a plan or a pitch deck slide that shows how the service or product works. For their pitch to funders, the start-up Kar-Go explained that they had set up to solve the 'last mile' problem: this is important because the last mile represents the bulk of total delivery costs. Kar-Go's autonomous driverless vehicle worked by (1) the sender putting their package in the Kar-Go, (2) informing the recipient they are sending the package, (3) the Kar-Go delivering the product and (4) the recipient picking up the package from a predesignated site.

6

- *Go to Exercise W 2.6: How does your product or service work?*

This understanding is the basis of turning features into benefits. Benefits are what a product or service *does for the customer*. Developing a distinction between tells and sells (features and benefits) is vital because it helps identify the value of the proposition. Table 6.3 shows that a humble water bottle might have particular features and benefits.

Table 6.3 Features and benefits of a water bottle

Features	Benefits
Made of BPA free plastic	No chance of plastic contaminating your water
Comes in a variety of colours	Choose a colour that suits you
Has a lid	The bottle will not leak in your bag
Filters water to remove bacteria, metals and waterborne pathogens	You can take it anywhere in the world
Folds up	Fits neatly in your bag when you are not using it

The features side of Table 6.3 fails to make a connection between the water bottle and the customer. Benefits identify core Unique Selling Propositions (USPs) that are at the heart of the competitive advantage of the business. They help distinguish why your offer is like a flower in a field of weeds. Inventor James Longford started Ch$_2$oose to tackle the problem of single-use and non-biodegradable water bottles. His water bottle is fully biodegradable and 100 per cent plastic-free. The benefits of these features are that the water bottle will not pollute the environment. Additionally, 100 per cent of Ch$_2$oose's profits go to charity.[27]

Businesses can provide a range of USPs to customers:

- Saves them time, money, energy or space.
- Reduces their worries and limits their risks.
- Increases their satisfaction levels.
- Brings them convenience.
- Improves their status or image.
- Makes it easier for them to earn more money.

Assessment tip: Features and benefits in academic writing

One of the potential problems with just 'describing' in academic writing is that it becomes a long list of features about a particular topic. Not only is this flat and boring, but also the reader probably already knows the main elements on this 'shopping' list.

A good way of engaging the reader is to convert features into benefits that add value to the reading experience. In academic writing, these benefits are often called 'contributions'. In your introduction, you might say that you are going to offer one, two or three main contributions. These might be providing insights into an overlooked area of the topic, explaining how you are going to link theories and evidence together or successfully weigh up competing claims.

It is a good idea to return to these contributions in your discussion section or conclusion, again explaining why they are important and what potential implications they have for entrepreneurial practice, policy or for further research in the topic.

This need to identify contributions becomes particularly important in postgraduate studies and in writing academic articles. A good rule of thumb for a poor piece of academic writing is that it fails to explain its contribution.

6.4.1 Aligning the value proposition with the customer niche

Making the connection between the value proposition and the customer niche is important because the start-up will only be sustainable if there is a fit between what the customer wants and what it offers.

A popular way of showing product-market fit is to use the Value Proposition Canvas (Figure 6.7). On the right-hand side (customer segment), it identifies three customer discovery activities:

Figure 6.7 The Value Proposition Canvas template © Strategyzer AG; strategyzer.com/canvas/value_proposition canvas

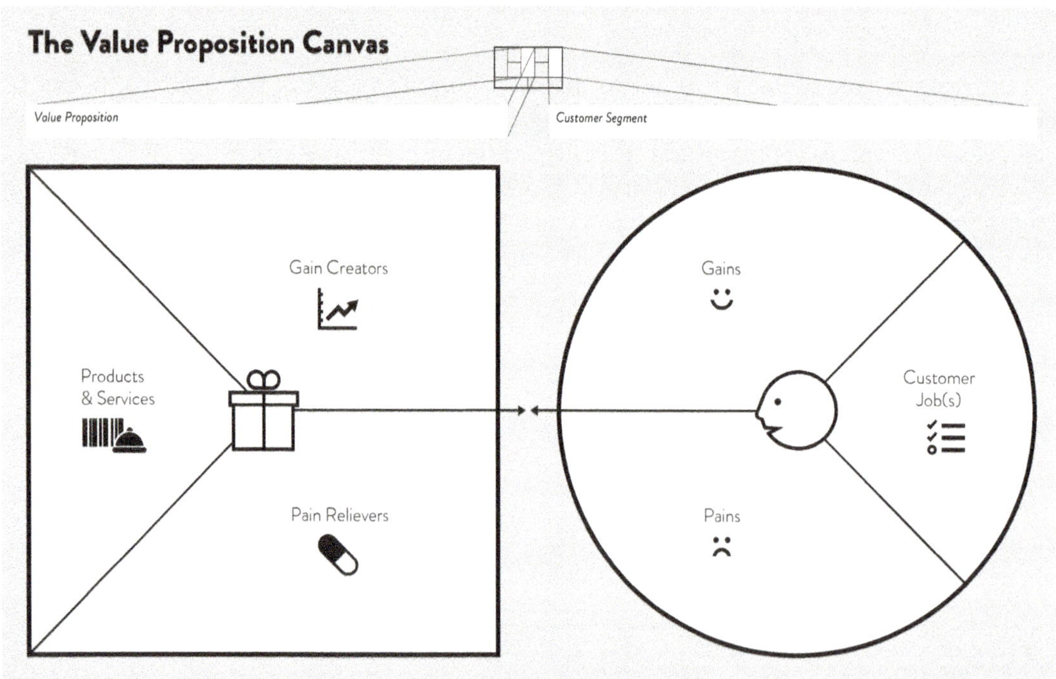

- Jobs (Chapter 4, pp. 74–75 on 'jobs to be hired') that a customer wants to do such as getting from A to B, or meeting their social, physical and emotional needs.
- What pains the customer, such as what frustrates them about their daily commute.
- What their gains are, or what they are looking to achieve from buying a good.

On the left, the canvas lists products and services and how these either alleviate the pain the customer experiences or will add value. It then maps out the ways in which the gain creators or pain relievers solve problems or provide benefits for a customer.

Swiss business Punkt, set up by Norwegian Petter Neby, designs stylish 'dumb' mobile phones that are not hooked up to the internet. The 'job to be done' is that Punkt allows users to communicate with others either by text or calls. This relieves customer pains for people who value privacy because they are not distracted by social media or the internet. It creates gains because these customers are also seeking phones that are intentionally designed to be distinctive, high quality and built to last.

Another way of capturing the product–market alignment is to use a product (or service) positioning statement. It has the following generic form:

- 'For (customer niche) who (what are they looking for), the (name of product/service) is a (what is it) that (list benefits)'.

Punkt's product positioning statement might be:

- 'For (busy individuals) who (value their privacy), the (Punkt) is a (mobile phone) that (provides stylish, carefully designed and elegantly crafted technology for those people who want to be in charge of technology).

- *Go to Exercise W 2.7: What's your value proposition?*

A product positioning statement also gives a sense of the start-up's strategic position. In basic terms, the benefits offered to a customer can lead to a cost, differentiation or a focus-based strategy. A cost strategy focuses on low costs and or low prices. Airline French Bee extended the low-cost airline model to long haul international flights, forcing it to pay close attention to costs, improve efficiency by reducing turnaround speed at airports and achieve high sales volumes.

A differentiation strategy involves being creative and innovative. This can be based on access to intellectual property (Chapter 7, pp. 157–162) and creates a barrier to entry to competitors. Innovation may also be attractive to some customers. When Kourosh Mohadjeri's motorcyclist son was nearly involved in an accident with a car at night, he developed his start-up 4Light to provide portable innovative LED lighting systems to help cyclists and motorcyclists stand out in the dark.

A focus strategy involves maintaining close customer relationships. Johnny Wang and Wen-Chih Chen started Taiwanese social enterprise, iHealth, to help elderly and disabled people who struggled to visit their pharmacy. iHealth solved this problem by developing a mobile home delivery prescription service run by dispensing pharmacists. They built customer loyalty by offering counselling and health education advice to the elderly and disabled.

Because start-ups are resource-constrained, a core part of a start-up's initial strategy is to focus on a niche that gives a product–market fit. Complementing a focus on a niche is to have a focused cost strategy that recognises customers are price sensitive. Alternatively, a start-up might have a focused differentiation strategy that aligns innovation with the target customer.

Entrepreneurship in Action

- Write down the features of your product or service. Convert these into benefits. Separate benefits into plusses and minuses. List the ways it gives them more satisfaction, money, time or status. List the ways it takes away their worries, hassle, uncertainties or stress. Again, how does this fit in with your brand?
- How would you describe the key benefits of your product or service? What would be your business strapline?
- How would you characterise the strategic positioning of your business?

- *Exercise W 2.8: Do you have product-market fit?*

6.5 GETTING TO THE CUSTOMER

6.5.1 Channels

Although identifying the product-market fit is pivotal, a start-up will fail if it cannot reach out to, communicate with and sell to its customers. A core strategic choice is a founder's route to market (how a business reaches its customers). There are two basic choices. One is direct contact with customers. This means the start-up *itself* promoting and selling direct to customers through social media, flyers, launch parties, hosting or attending networking events, cold calling or public relations. Other options to promote and sell to a customer include opening a shop, employing a salesperson or building a website.

Indirect channels are an alternative way to reach customers. These rely on *others,* such as agents, resellers, retailers or wholesalers, to promote and sell on the business's behalf. Hotels can use direct channels such as websites or passing trade to generate traffic. However, they increasingly rely on online intermediaries, such as Expedia and Booking.com, and metasearch engines, such as Kayak and Trivago, to act as their 'billboard' or shop window.

Table 6.4 shows the advantages and disadvantages of using direct, indirect or a mixture of both channels. There is also a need to consider a range of practical issues:

- Likely profits from a channel.
- Ability to deliver products and services successfully in a channel.
- Ability to market and sell into a channel.

Table 6.4 Advantages and disadvantages of direct sales

Advantages	Disadvantages
Maintains greater control of the process and is more responsive to customers	Intermediaries tend to be better at reaching large numbers of customer, making it easier to scale the start-up
Without intermediaries, the business has higher margins	Costly to train and develop a sales team
If the product or service is complex and or sales lead times are long, direct sales might be required	Finding sufficiently qualified sales force; may be easier to use intermediaries

Case Study: Fancy a golfing holiday?

Golf4you.com is a German business set up by an Irishman, Paul Smyth, who noticed many German-speaking golfers independently organised their own golf trips by booking their own flights, hotel and golf sessions. Paul's market research showed that this was a frustrating and time-consuming process. His solution was a one-stop shop for booking all these activities together. Paul recognised that to make Golf4you.com a success he required money to educate and convert customers. He needed to hire relevant marketing and website developers, phase the development of the website and spend extensively on increasing customer awareness and take up.

6.5.2 Customer relationships

How a start-up intends to form and maintain customer relationships is also integral to its ability to sell to its chosen customer niche. The BMC suggests a number of ways to acquire, retain and develop a customer base:

- Personal assistance, such as interacting with a shop assistant or someone on a telephone hotline.
- Dedicated personal assistance, such as interacting with a personal shopper or having a named telephone contact.
- Self-service.
- Automation, such as automated robo-financial advisors that provide advice on financial products.
- User communities. Businesses such as the Dutch non-food discounter, Action, use social media to invite customers to identify products that they want and to comment on their existing products.
- Co-creation. A start-up that aims to be 'Trip Advisor for local lawyers' relies on co-creation by individuals willing to review and rate lawyers.

The choice of the kind of customer relationship used should match what customers want. Some customers prefer self-service if it reduces their final costs and speeds up the delivery of a product or service. Others prefer more dedicated assistance because they want help to navigate their way through the available choices.

Greater levels of human interaction may require a sales team. This can add to a start-up's cost base and may mean increased costs to customers.

Case Study: Having a mojo

A source of innovation can be how a business chooses to relate to its customers. The German start-up Modomojo identified that although some professional men wanted to be well dressed, they lacked the time and inclination to go shopping. The company's solution was to offer a web-based dedicated personal shopping service that selected and shipped suitable clothes for cash-rich but time-poor men.

- *Go to Exercise W 2.9: How does the business reach its customers?*

6.5.3 Marketing and sales

BMC's focus on channels and customer relationships points to the importance of sketching out the customer acquisition process. The AIDA model is a simple and helpful way of understanding what it will take to acquire customers. It stands for:

1. Awareness/Attention – customers become aware of the offer.
2. Interest – customers learn more about the offer.
3. Desire – customers have a favourable view of the offer.
4. Action – customer buys the offer.

Figure 6.8 shows how the sales funnel that turns prospective leads into suspects, prospects and eventually into customers can expand this model.

Figure 6.8 AIDA and the sales funnel

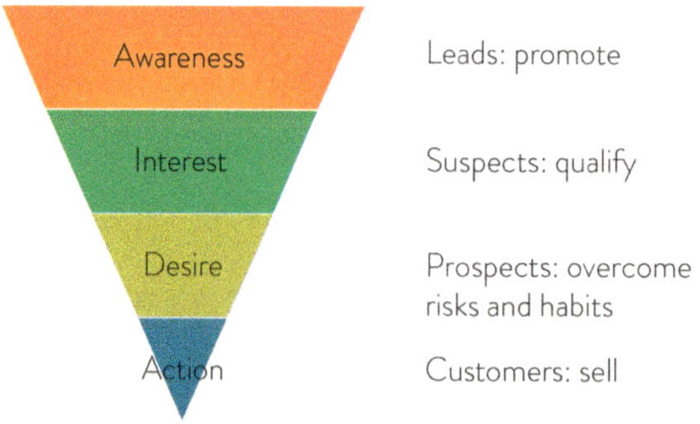

Leads are target customers who are unaware of the offer. A business can use a variety of methods to get their attention. A tour operator offering adventure holidays may use a website and blog to highlight its expertise in this market. Search engine optimisation, emails, personalised or customised social media postings can also build customer awareness. More traditional ways of generating leads include cold calling, getting referrals from a social network, going to trade fairs or exhibitions or engaging a professional marketing business to help.

Once customers are aware of a start-up's offer, converting leads into suspects involves developing their interest. At this stage, they are often still learning about the available options for solving their problem and often are just looking, not buying. To raise their interest, a business might have to spend time and money increasing their knowledge about its offer by highlighting its benefits (USPs).

Interest and desire can be stimulated through vlogs, blogs, promotions, networking, emails or using a sales force to turn suspects into prospects. Other signals that individuals are suspects include visits to webpages, agreeing to share their details, discussions with a sales team and meetings at a conference or trade show. Part of this process is overcoming risks and habits. Potential customers usually buy from other suppliers and are used to buying in a particular way. Because a start-up is new, they may also have concerns about whether the new offer will provide poorer, similar or better benefits than those from competitors.

Guarantees, positive customer reviews, sales promotions and discounts for first-time customers can help reduce these risks and change customer habits. Discounting, though, can bite into profit margins (Chapter 8, p. 189).

Another way is to sell: demonstrating and guiding potential customers to the benefits of a start-up's offer and how this meets customer needs. Start-ups might choose to sell via, for example, trade shows, or by having brand ambassadors. Brick and mortar physical retailers can have an advantage over internet-based retailers because they offer a space for customers to try products out. Freemium models are also effective. Making a limited number of a product's features or benefits free at the point of use allows prospects to try for themselves – perhaps supported by online information, chat-bots that allow businesses to virtually interact with customers and peer-to-peer community forums – to see if they want to purchase the premium part of the offer.

At the end of AIDA and the sales funnel is a customer willing to act, hopefully by signing a contract or walking away with the offer there and then. However, businesses are likely to have to deal with a number of objections or barriers to closing a sale along the way, such as:

- 'It's too expensive.' Responses can include offering finance to spread the payments or restating why the benefits outweigh the costs.
- 'I am too busy and need more information.' This could prompt a business to follow up with targeted information via email.
- 'We are not in a position right now.' This could be overcome by teaching the customer more about the offer or providing a free or discounted trial.

The AIDA/sales funnel process varies over time from start-up to start-up. Selling a new innovative medical device can take years, whereas selling a water bottle can be much quicker. Suspects are only a proportion of leads. Prospects and eventual customers are an even smaller proportion of leads. The ratio between sales and leads can vary. Dropbox has an estimated 2–4 per cent sales conversion rate, while Spotify's is 45 per cent and Slack's more than 30 per cent.[28] The costs of acquiring customers (marketing spend/number of new customers) also varies.

Case Study: Struggles in craft beer

In an ideal world, the Australian start-up craft beer brewer Black Hops would like to sell its beers in national and regional supermarkets, pubs and restaurant chains. Profit margins would be low but this would be offset by high sales volumes. Realistically, this is challenging because the company lacks the resources to scale production to the levels required by these chains. Even if it could, selling through chains is difficult because the industry is dominated by a few large brewers who tie pubs and restaurants to exclusive contracts. To reach its customers, Black Hops employ a salesperson to sell to independent beer and wine shops, pubs and restaurants. While this is viable, profits are thin and the salesperson can only serve a regional market. Black Hops can make healthier profits via its website and through a sales room, but it is a challenge to drive customers to visit the website and sales room.

If a business struggles to convert leads into sales or the cost of customer acquisition is too high, the chances are it will fail. Having tactics in place to keep target customers going through a sales funnel can avoid this. Spotify does this through its advertisements, personalising content, having family and student plans and by making it easy to use across different platforms.

Customer acquisition is not the end of the sales process. A business must also devise a way to get paid. Acquiring customers is also relatively more expensive than retaining customers. Keeping existing customers by maintaining regular contact and through customer loyalty programmes allows a start-up to either cross-sell complementary products or 'up-sell' additional features.

Entrepreneurship in Action

- Outline your customer acquisition process. Explain how you are going to convert leads into customers: how will you raise awareness, interest, desire and action?
- What is the cost of customer acquisition? What is your sales conversion rate?
- How long will it take you to get to your first sale?
- How are you going to keep and grow your customer base?

- *Go to Exercise W 2.10: What is your sales strategy?*

6.5.4 Revenue streams

Working out how to make money is central to a start-up. Because of this, the BMC asks questions such as 'Are customers willing to pay?', 'How do they pay?', 'What are they prepared to pay for?' and 'How much does each type of customer contribute to the revenue?'

These 'how much' questions relate to other aspects of the BMC such as customer segments, value proposition and channels. If the customer niche is too specific, a business might struggle to find and sell in sufficient quantities to be viable. This can be compensated by high prices, but only if the customer is willing to pay.

There are a number of ways in which a business can get paid:

- **A direct sales model.** This is selling your product or service directly to customers. A basic example is making a fruit smoothie and selling it directly to customers.

Case Study: Banking on an app

Banks used to offer services through physical branches. In recent years, they have become more likely to follow a 'bricks and clicks' business model that supplements branches with internet banking services. New business models continue to disrupt banking. Paytm, run by the Indian entrepreneur Vijay Shekhar Sharma, has moved from providing an 'e-wallet' marketplace for customers to pay for services such as electricity, gas and transport to giving them an app-based payments bank for storing, sending and receiving money on their smartphones. A payment bank is a valuable service for many poorer people in India who cannot access formal banks.

- **The 'bait and hook' model.** Men's razors are often sold at cost price (the bait), but the manufacturer recoups the costs through replacement blades (the hook). This also applies to cheap or free mobile phones that have expensive calling plans and cheap video game consoles with expensive games. This model works because customers tend to focus on up-front prices rather than long-term costs.
- **A freemium model.** Cloud storage businesses such as Dropbox provide free storage for basic users but charge a premium to those who want more space. Game apps such as Boom Beach, Candy Crush or Clash of Clans are all free but offer in-game purchases to ease progress in the game. A more traditional example is Singapore's *Today* newspaper, which is freely available at travel interchanges for commuters. Its customers are the advertisers willing to pay to get their message in front of large numbers of people on their way to work.

- **Fining models.** This involves paying a surcharge for being late in returning or paying for a good or service. Going overdrawn with a bank or failing to pay off a credit card can mean paying charges. The DVD business Blockbuster used this model, charging low rates for renting films but fining customers who returned them late. However, over time this eroded customer satisfaction and contributed to Blockbuster's bankruptcy.
- **Subscription models.** This is the payment of a regular fee for the use of a service or good. Netflix has used a three-tiered pricing subscription model that offers customers a basic, standard or premium service. Subscription models can offer the first month free, be open-ended or use standard 12- or 18-month contracts. They can also be 'topped up' to include access to additional services.
- **Brokerage models.** This involves the business acting as a market maker. Real estate agents act as market makers to bring home buyers and sellers together and often charge them a percentage fee for their services. Amazon and eBay also use their platforms as marketplaces that broker deals between buyers and sellers.
- **Advertising-based models.** Although its news and 'social experience' is free to users, Facebook's sheer size has attracted third-party advertisers interested in targeting Facebook users. The more users there are, the more likely advertisers will pay. This is a network effect. Google also benefits from network effects. Because it is the standard default search browser among users, it gets the majority of its income from advertisers keen to pay per click every time a user clicks a sponsored link or banner advert in the search results. Another version is an affiliate-based model. The UK site MoneySavingExpert.com (MSE) provides guidance on how consumers can save money. Its revenue comes from the affiliated third parties, services or goods the website has independently verified as good deals for customers. These parties pay MSE each time a user clicks through to their website from MSEs.
- **Peer-to-peer models.** In the past, sharing of resources was typically between family and friends. If a family member owned a resource such as a specialist DIY tool and was not currently using it, they might lend it to another family member who needed it. Because of the internet, it is now possible to extend this sharing of under-utilised resources with strangers. Instead of having to rely on buying or renting a specialist resource from a store, one peer can connect with another peer through the internet to make use of the resource, either in exchange for a fee or for agreeing to offer a service in return. This collaborative consumption, sharing economy or peer-to-peer economy has led to the development of platform business models such as Airbnb, which connects people looking to rent out spare space in their property with others looking for a cheap place to stay. Ride-sharing apps such as Lyft and Uber also use a peer-to-peer business model because they connect car owners with people who need a ride.
- **Circular economy models**. Most human consumption follows a linear 'make, take and dispose' approach. For example, car manufacturers, mobile phone companies and supermarkets all sell goods that people use for a limited period and then dispose of, usually as waste. The aim behind circular economy business models is to change this and make consumption ethically, socially and environmentally sustainable. These models can prolong the life of materials or goods, or design-out waste and pollution.[29] Niaga ('again' spelt backwards) redesigned the humble carpet so that it was made of only one material that could be recycled into new carpets. This helps cut down on waste because 95 per cent of carpets end up either being burnt or going to landfills.[30]

Discussion questions:

- Some 'sharing economy' business models suggest that they provide new ways of doing business that benefit society. The ride-sharing app Uber has claimed to reduce 'congestion in cities by getting more people into fewer cars'. It also provides ways for workers to work flexible hours and is often cheaper than taxi firms. Others say that it is a taxi firm that uses an internet platform, exploits its workers and is only cheaper because it does not have to pay for the purchase or maintenance of its taxi fleet. Do you think that the sharing economy can benefit consumers and workers?[31]
- Do you think that circular economy business models will become even more popular in the future in response to climate change?
- Do you think that entrepreneurship should be defined in terms of how it can support and sustain social change?

A start-up's revenue model can sometimes be regarded as its business model even though a revenue model is how a business captures value, while a business model is a framework for understanding how a business creates, delivers and captures value. Nonetheless, the importance of a revenue model is often lost, and with dramatic effects.

Case Study: Who forgot about the money?

At the turn of the millennium, dotcom start-ups raised huge amounts of money. Many had strong assumptions about how they could create and deliver value to customers. There was less clarity about capturing value. The dotcoms did not pay sufficient attention to what potential customers wanted, if they were willing to pay for the dotcom's goods or services, or how customers preferred to pay. The dotcom's business model often failed to capture their revenue model: how they were going to make money from their customers.

Pets.com had a clear business model for creating and delivering value. It spent $61 million on marketing to raise awareness and interest in buying pet products online. It built an enormous warehouse to collect, store and ship pet products. But it never did any market research and misunderstood how consumers bought pet food. Despite selling products for around 25 per cent below cost, it was only able to make revenues of $620,000. After two years in which it chewed through $300 million, the company went bust.[32] This lack of a viable revenue model often stalks other internet based businesses: from 2006, it took Twitter 11 years until late 2017 before it posted its first quarter of profitability.[33] This is despite being valued at $24 billion at its Initial Public Offer (where its shares are sold on a stock market) and having more than 330 million users.[34]

In many revenue models, there is a close alignment between a customer and a user. However, start-ups face wasting valuable resources if there are differences between a customer and a user. One of the frustrations faced by students who start studying in a new place is finding out where there are good clubs, bars, meeting places and restaurants. One solution is a free app that details for students local up-to-date real-time information. This app can be promoted on social media. But students are unlikely to be the paying customers. The app's revenues are likely to come from commissions or advertising paid for by local businesses. If so, it is questionable if the app's developers should spend their limited marketing budget only targeting students. Because local businesses are the ones providing future revenues, there is tangible value in selling the app to them.

Case Study: School Notices

School Notices is a digital marketplace that connects independent schools, parents and outside businesses. Founded by Clare Reid and Gordon Dawson, the service is free for parents to use. The large number of users is attractive to outside businesses, particularly as many of the parents are relatively wealthy. It sells them advertising space in direct emails and banner adverts and then hands back 25 per cent of its revenues to independent schools, which helps them cover the annual subscription for membership and funds school activities.

Entrepreneurship in Action

- What is your revenue model? Is it, for example, a freemium, peer-to-peer or direct sales model?
- What are its strengths and weaknesses?
- Is there a clear distinction between users and customers?

Go to Exercise W 2.11: How do you make money?

6.6. START-UP INFRASTRUCTURE

Creating and capturing value relies on businesses having the infrastructure they need to deliver value. It involves making decisions about how to configure and manage resources to deliver products and services to the customer. In the BMC, there are three core elements of business infrastructure:

1. Key resources, such as specialist workers, physical assets including machinery and vehicles, available finance and access to intellectual property.
2. Key activities, such as producing a good or service, acting as a knowledge source that provides know-how such as consultancy services or managing a supply chain to minimise risks or increase efficiency.
3. Key partners to provide key resources or conduct key activities for the business.

There is often a trade-off at the heart of these operational issues: ownership of activities gives start-ups control, but it also inhibits growth as many lack the resources needed to scale the business quickly. Some shortcut this by either buying an existing business or entering into a franchise relationship (Chapter 4, pp. 85–87).

New businesses must work out how to transform key inputs such as labour and materials into outputs for customers. Key partners are also required: even a simple lemonade stand in a park requires a permit from the local council. Understanding the motivations for collaborating is important.

Universities that own their own sites and already have quite sophisticated retail operations are unlikely to want to partner with any new start-up that offers competition to their retail offer.

Developing a business infrastructure comes with a price tag. These include fixed costs that do not change such as salaries and rent as well as variable costs that change as the business scales such as production expenses (Chapter 8, pp. 194–195).

At a strategic level, it is important to establish how the costs of delivering value integrates with other start-up activities. Operational issues vary depending on the business type. In a physical retail start-up 'location, location, location' is pivotal because it determines customer 'footfall', which is the number of people who pass by that area. A new shop can gauge footfall patterns through desk research, surveys of car or pedestrian numbers and by talking to nearby businesses. However, these patterns may only indicate potential leads, which can be difficult to convert into sales.

A key factor is property availability and is the length of the rental period. Fit-out costs for adapting the building and signage can also be expensive. Operating the store also involves getting supplies, storing them and selling them. This often requires hiring staff, identifying good suppliers and understanding how stock moves through the business.

Food-based businesses also often have to think through where to locate their business. Launch events, menus and other promotional events cost money. So does hiring staff including waiters and chefs, sourcing ingredients from local producers and controlling and storing stock. They often need to subscribe to payment merchant accounts to process card transactions so they can be paid, and pay for licences, such as food hygiene certificates, so they can operate.

For services such as constancy businesses, location may be less pivotal. However, there are still costs for training staff, obtaining licences and meeting regulations. Staff also need equipment such as computers to do their jobs. Meanwhile, manufacturers need premises to transform raw materials into their products. Sourcing international raw materials means paying import taxes and transportation costs. These businesses also face delivery costs, may have fit out a factory, require capital equipment, such as machines, and need a warehouse to store their goods.

Web-and app-based businesses have their own concerns. Key is the development and design of the website or app. This can require software developers. Another issue is driving traffic to the site through understanding how to use the internet to 'get, keep and grow' customers. Holding customer data securely and processing payment is important. If the aim is to use the internet to sell physical products, there is a need to source, transport, store and ship goods. All of these key inputs to the start-up require it to consider the cost of doing key activities itself, relative to the costs of outsourcing to other providers.

Entrepreneurship in Action

- A useful analogy for developing your product or service is to see it as being similar to cooking a meal. One way to create your dish is to write down a recipe. This recipe needs to list all the ingredients, activities, help and timings that you need to produce and make your product or service. For example, to make spaghetti bolognese for 100 people you will need some pans, key ingredients such as pasta and tomatoes, help to peel and chop, a preparation method and an estimate of how long it will take you to make the dish. Once you have done that, you have to deliver it to the waiting customers and collect payment.
- Adapt Table 6.5 for your own needs.

Table 6.5 A recipe for preparing your product or service 'dish'

Type of dish being served (type of start-up e.g. gaming app, fashion retailer); number catered for?	
List of ingredients and utensils needed (e.g. premises, vehicles, workforce) (key resources)	
List of helpers (e.g. business mentor, suppliers) (key partners)	
List out the steps and timings for preparing the 'meal' (e.g. when are resources to be assembled, when is the product launch, when is marketing and sales to be conducted) (key activities)	

- *Go to Exercise W 2.12: How does the business source, make and distribute its products and services?*

6.7 WHAT YOU HAVE LEARNED IN THIS CHAPTER

The BMC is a visual storyboarding tool that structures an intuitive initial understanding of start-up feasibility. You have seen how it answers key start-up questions that revolve around the 'who' (customer segments, customer relationships and channels), the 'what' (value proposition), the 'how' (key activities, resources and partners) and the 'how much' (revenue).

For founders with few financial concerns or high levels of expertise, the BMC might be all that is needed. As you have learned, completing the nine building blocks is a relatively quick activity, and start-ups can repeat each section as new information emerges. It is less painful and faster than developing or altering a prototype. Nonetheless, lean start-ups can use the nine BMC building blocks to develop hypotheses, or guesses, about how to create and capture value (right side) and how to deliver value (left side). A Minimum Viable Product may emerge from the canvas, which allows the new business to assess with the product–market fit.[35]

A great advantage of the BMC is that it focuses on the customer. This helps because too many start-ups are products and services looking for a problem rather than meeting actual needs and wants in the market. The BMC, therefore, usefully informs other ways of developing a start-up story, including a pitch or a plan, and helps with core questions such as:

- Is there a market out there?
- Is the business idea worthwhile?
- Who is the customer?
- How does the business reach its customers?
- How does the business source, make and distribute its products and services?
- How does it make money?

The BMC does have disadvantages. It may be a one-time-only activity that runs the risk of ending up – like a formal plan written at the very start of planning – lurking forgotten somewhere on a computer. Because of the heterogeneity of start-ups, the BMC (or any model) will not fit all circumstances or provide a universal blueprint for every type of start-up. There is also little evidence to show if it provides better start-up outcomes, reflecting the lack of knowledge about how specific business models relate to subsequent entrepreneurial performance.[36]

By mostly focusing on the internal logic for a business model logic, the BMC does not fully detail the opportunity. This might not matter if the BMC is used solely for internal planning purposes. However, the lack of consideration for competitors and team strengths will be telling if they ever need help or money for outsiders. Chapter 7 considers these missing start-up planning issues.

ASSESSMENT QUESTIONS

1. Do you agree with the hierarchy proposed in the BMC?
2. Are effectuation and bricolage logics better ways of developing a start-up than using the BMC's hierarchy?
3. Are entrepreneurs first and foremost problem solvers?
4. Is entrepreneurial marketing a better way of achieving start-up viability than formal market analysis?
5. Very many start-ups fail quickly. Is this because they fail to develop robust and coherent revenue models?
6. Identify a platform-based business model. Explain how it works. Critically evaluate if it provides benefits to customers and society.

FURTHER READING

Osterwalder, A., & Pigneur, Y. (2010). *Business model generation: A handbook for visionaries, game changers, and challengers*. Hoboken, NJ: Wiley.

McMullen, J. S., & Dimov, D. (2013). Time and the entrepreneurial journey: The problems and promise of studying entrepreneurship as a process. *Journal of Management Studies, 50*(8), 1481–1512.

Stokes, D. (2000). Entrepreneurial marketing: A conceptualisation from qualitative research. *Qualitative Market Research, 3*(1), 47–54.

Notes

1 www.strategyzer.com/canvas/business-model-canvas.

2 Osterwalder, A., & Pigneur, Y. (2010). *Business model generation: A handbook for visionaries, game changers, and challengers*. Hoboken, NJ: John Wiley & Sons.

3 Maurya, A. (2012). *Running lean: Iterate from plan a to a plan that works*. Sebastopol, CA: O'Reilly Media.

4 McMullen, J. S., & Dimov, D. (2013). Time and the entrepreneurial journey: The problems and promise of studying entrepreneurship as a process. *Journal of Management Studies, 50*(8), 1481–1512.

5 Ibid., p. 1494.

6 https://patents.google.com/patent/US2698439.

7 www.freepatentsonline.com/crazy.html.

8 www.ipcc.ch/report/sr15/.

9 www.greenpeace.org/international/press-release/15111/greenpeace-calls-for-decrease-in-meat-and-dairy-production-and-consumption-for-a-healthier-planet/.

10 www.portal.euromonitor.com/portal/statisticsevolution/index.

11 Stokes, D. (2000). Entrepreneurial marketing: A conceptualisation from qualitative research. *Qualitative Market Research, 3*(1), 47–54.

12 Stinchcombe, A. L. (1965) Organizations and social structure. *Handbook of Organizations, 44*(2), 142–193.

13 MarketLine. (2018). MarketLine Industry Profile, Carbonated Soft Drinks in Indonesia, October.
14 Euromonitor. (2018). Top 5 countries with the largest vegetarian populations, April. www.portal.euromonitor.com/portal/Analysis/Tab#.
15 www.portal.euromonitor.com/portal/statisticsevolution/index.
16 Morris, M. H., Schindehutte, M., & LaForge, R. W. (2002). Entrepreneurial marketing: A construct for integrating emerging entrepreneurship and marketing perspectives. *Journal of Marketing Theory and Practice, 10*(4), 1–19, p. 5.
17 O'Donnell, A. (2011). Small firm marketing: Synthesising and supporting received wisdom. *Journal of Small Business and Enterprise Development, 18*(4), 781–805.
18 Phua, S., & Jones, O. (2010). Marketing in new business ventures: Examining the myth of informality. *International Journal of Entrepreneurship and Innovation Management, 11*(1), 35–55.
19 Hegazi, A. (2018). *Startup Arabia*, Transforma Publishing: Santa Monica; www.naharnet.com/stories/en/71132; https://innovative.jo/instabug-dramatic-journey-behind-egypts-booming-startup/.
20 Stokes (2000), ibid.
21 www.mrs.org.uk/pdf/2014-09-01%20Mystery%20Shopping%20Research%20Guidelines.pdf.
22 Jayawarna, D., Jones, O., Lam, W., & Phua, S. (2014). The performance of entrepreneurial ventures: Examining the role of marketing practices. *Journal of Small Business and Enterprise Development, 21*(4), 565–587.
23 Euromonitor. (2018). 'Deodorants in Egypt', May. www.portal.euromonitor.com/portal/Analysis/Tab#.
24 Hopp, C., & Greene, F. J. (2018). In pursuit of time: Business plan sequencing, duration and intraentrainment effects on new venture viability. *Journal of Management Studies, 55*(2), 320–351.
25 The Cook Kitchen. (2014). 'Annual report'. www.cookfood.net/info/jobs/essential-ingredients/reports-downloads/.
26 McMullen & Dimov (2013), ibid.
27 www.ch2oose.co.uk/.
28 Spotify IPO offer. www.sec.gov/Archives/edgar/data/1639920/000119312518063434/d494294df1.htm#rom494294_4; process.st/freemium-conversion-rate/.
29 www.ellenmacarthurfoundation.org/circular-economy/overview/concept.
30 www.dsm-niaga.com/carpet.html.
31 Ravenelle, A. J. (2017). Sharing economy workers: Selling, not sharing. *Cambridge Journal of Regions, Economy and Society, 10*(2), 281–295; Friedman, G. (2014). Workers without employers: Shadow corporations and the rise of the gig economy. *Review of Keynesian Economics, 2*(2), 171–188; Burtch, G., Carnahan, S., & Greenwood, B. N. (2018). Can you gig it? An empirical examination of the gig economy and entrepreneurial activity. *Management Science, 64*(12), 5497–5520.
32 Cheyfitz, K. (2003). *Thinking Inside the Box: The 12 Timeless Rules for Managing a Successful Business* (New York: Simon and Schuster).
33 https://www.theguardian.com/technology/2018/feb/08/twitter-makes-first-quarterly-profit-history.
34 www.valuewalk.com/2017/02/snapchat-ipo-vs-facebook-ipo-twitter-ipo/; twitter (2018) Annual report, https://investor.twitterinc.com/financial-information/annual-reports.
35 Blank, S., & Dorf, B. (2012). *The startup owner's manual: The step-by-step guide for building a great company*. Pescadero, CA: K & S Ranch.
36 Demil, B., Lecocq, X., Ricart, J. E., & Zott, C. (2015). Introduction to the SEJ special issue on business models: Business models within the domain of strategic entrepreneurship. *Strategic Entrepreneurship Journal, 9*(1), 1–11.

CHAPTER 7

Start-Up Feasibility Planning II: Identity, Ideas, Teams and the Competition

Learning Outcomes

In this chapter, you will learn:

- How to form an identity for your start-up.
- How to assess your responsibilities, roles and rewards.
- How attractive your chosen industry is.
- Ways you can protect your business idea.

Mini Contents List

7.1 INTRODUCTION

In this chapter, you will learn about areas of start-up planning often overlooked by the Business Model Canvas (BMC).

One missing piece in the jigsaw is why entrepreneurs do it. You have seen that motivations (Chapter 3, pp. 44–46) are important predictors of the future development of a business. What the business is called, what it stands for and how it is organised all clearly matter.

A start-up's name and logo identifies the central character in a start-up story. However, at the same time, founders have to consider if they can claim naming rights over who they are and what they do. This chapter introduces you to the different types of intellectual property rights and what entrepreneurs can do to safeguard these rights.

Another aspect of identity is the founding team. As Apple's founder Steve Jobs suggested, great start-ups are not just done by one person; they are done by a team of people. In the early days, the start-up team is the business: it sets the start-up's goals, develops its revenues and gets investors. But it is not just team roles that matter, such as who is the boss or who is responsible for a functional business area of the start-up. Potential investors are often interested in the relationships in a team, whether this is a husband and wife team, a family or colleagues. They also pay close attention to how a team splits the ownership of the start-up. Decisions about team relationships, roles and rewards are pivotal because they have long-lasting effects on start-up development.[1]

The BMC is also guilty of downplaying the role of competitors. Competition is a good thing. A lack of competitors can signal there is little demand for a new product or service. On the other hand, a market dominated by an unforgiving 'bully' may prove too competitive to enter. This chapter shows you how models such as Porter's Five Forces and the Blue Ocean approach can help entrepreneurs to identify competitive advantages that can help start-ups overcome these challenges.

This chapter, therefore, helps with these core start-up planning questions:

- Who are we? What is the identity and purpose of the start-up?
- Why is this the right team? What skills and attributes do the people involved have to exploit the opportunity?
- How is the offer different in the market? Does it have an advantage over competitors?

7.2 FORMING A START-UP IDENTITY

7.2.1 What is in a name?

One of the early ways of starting to develop a business model is to come up with a name for the business. Much like a logo, a name can capture the essence of an enterprise. Having an identity for their start-up is important because it expresses who the founders are and what they stand for.[2] Some founders use a pun or a joke – 'lawn order', 'tree wise men' and 'ground control by major tom' – are just a few of the many used by gardening businesses. Describing what the business does is another branding option. Middle Eastern entrepreneur Loulou Khazen Baz named her freelance job search site nabbesh.com because nabbesh means search in Arabic. Some businesses make up a new word. Chocolate manufacturer Mondelez's name combines the Latin word for world, Monde, with delez, a slang version of delicious. Meanwhile, some entrepreneurs such as Ben & Jerry, Ford and Chanel named their company after themselves.[3]

- *Go to Exercise W 2.13: What are your start-up's name and logo?*

Another important part of developing the start-up's identity or brand is how the entrepreneur chooses to structure the ownership of their business. A business name can signal to external audiences and potential investors the purpose behind a start-up and how it is owned and organised.[4] There are five basic types of business ownership structure:

1. **Sole traders or proprietors** – these are businesses owned and controlled by one individual. This is a common ownership structure in many countries, found in sectors such as gardening services, small-scale retailing and construction. One reason why it is a popular choice is that it is administratively simple and it is still possible to employ workers (Table 7.1).
2. **Partnerships** – two or more people who come together to agree to own, control and profit from their shared endeavours. This is a general partnership. One variant is a limited partnership. This is owned and managed by general partners but has limited partners who are not involved in running the business and may be only liable to debts up to how much they have invested in the business. Another variant is a limited liability partnership. This partnership is a legal entity that is separate from the partners. Partners usually share profits equally and their liability is only usually for the amount of money they have invested in the business. Partnerships are common in professional services such as accountancy, law and architecture.
3. **Limited liability companies** – these are separate legal entities with their own property and contracts with other businesses. Its finances and tax arrangements are also separate. This advantages its owners – the shareholders – because if the company falls into debt, they are theoretically only liable up to the amount they have invested in the company and personal assets such as their house are not at risk. A common feature of limited companies is that ownership can be separate from day-to-day management control. Often, though, owners also manage the company. Most companies are private limited companies (Ltd in the United Kingdom (UK), LTDA in Chile, GmbH in Germany and LLC in the United Arab Emirates (UAE)). If a company decides to sell (or 'float') its shares on the public stock market, it becomes a public limited company (plc (UK), S.p.a. (Italy) or PT Tbk (Indonesia)). Table 7.1 shows that the trade-off for limited liability is increased accountability. Both types of limited company are common in all sectors of an economy.
4. **Co-operatives** – these are defined as 'people-centred enterprises jointly owned and democratically controlled by and for their members to realise their common socio-economic needs and aspirations'. They can be set up, owned and run for and by consumers, workers, businesses or a mix of these communities. Like limited companies, co-operatives have a separate legal personality. In some co-operatives, the members are only liable up to their investments into the co-operative. Generally, each member has an equal vote, but the co-operative usually appoints officers or directors who run it on a day-to-day basis. Co-operatives are common in farming (India's IFFCO co-operative, Denmark's Arla group, Ireland's Kerry group and New Zealand's Fonterra Co-operative group). Large co-operatives are also common in financial services (Groupe Crédit Agricole, Rabobank Group), insurance (Vienna Insurance Group, MAPFRE) and in retail (John Lewis Partnership, REWE group) as well as in health (Confederação Nacional das Cooperativas Médicas Unimed do Brasil) and manufacturing (Mondragon Corporacion).[6]
5. **Social enterprises** – these are trading organisations that are specifically set up to use their profits to primarily meet social and community objectives rather than for private gain. Social enterprises can achieve this by structuring their business as a sole trader, a partnership, a limited company or a co-operative. For example, a sole trader can decide to give away all or a part of their profits to the local community. Nonetheless, in the UK, a business can set up as a Community Interest Company. This type of company explicitly identifies how it will use its surpluses to benefit its community (Table 7.1). In other countries, there exist associations and foundations that are designed to meet community needs.

Table 7.1 Advantages and disadvantages of different legal forms

Legal Form					
	Sole trader	**Partnership**	**Limited company**	**Co-operative**	**Community interest company**
Control	Complete	Shared between partners	One vote per share	One member, one vote	One vote per share
Governance	Owner's discretion	Partnership agreement	Articles – the contract between the company and its shareholders	Rules on governance and sharing	The same as a limited company but has to register a community interest statement
Set up requirements	Simple	Less simple	More complex	More complex	More complex
Tax filing and payments	Easy	Easy	More difficult	More difficult	More difficult
Tax rate	Personal	Personal	Corporate	Corporate	Corporate
Tax deductions on losses	Yes	Yes	On business income	On business income	On business income
Need to publish accounts	No	No	Yes	Yes	Yes: annual community interest report
Meetings	Not required	Minimal	Periodic and necessary	Periodic and necessary	Periodic and necessary
Management	Owner	Partners	Board of directors	Members or directors	Board of directors
Initial investment levels	Small: owner's capital	Modest: partner's capital	Larger: shareholder's capital	Larger: member's capital	Larger: shareholder's capital
Liability for losses and debts	Personal	Personal	Limited to business	Limited to business	Limited to business
Ability to raise external funding	More difficult	More difficult	Easier: can sell shares	More difficult: limited distribution of profits	More difficult: can only out dividends by resolution of members
Ability to sell the business	More difficult	More difficult	Easier	More difficult: focus on member's interests rather than investment returns	More difficult: has an 'asset lock' to ensure assets and profits are used in the community interest

Entrepreneurship in Action

- Although start-ups can and do delay deciding on their legal form, what is your favoured legal form? If your ambition is to grow the business, it is better to be a limited company than a sole trader or partnership (Chapter 10, p. 246).
- Are you more comfortable with the light touch regulation given to sole traders and partnerships or the potential for limited liability in a company?

7.2.2 *Missions and mantras*

All start-ups have a purpose. These are rooted in the founder's own motivations to, for example, make money and meet a social or community objective (Chapter 3, p. 000; Workbook 1, Exercises W1.2–1.5). At some point, though, entrepreneurs need to tell others about who they are, what they do and why they are doing it. One shortcut for defining a start-up's purpose is a mission statement. Mission statements are short aspirational statements that aim to show where the business is going, how it is going to get there and why this is important. It typically has three main components:

1. **A vision** – what are the start-up's long-term aspirations? Slack, the organisation communication platform founded in 2013, suggests that it is there to 'Make work life simpler, more pleasant and more productive'.[8]
2. **A mission** – what are the start-up's main tasks, who are these tasks for and how does it deliver on these tasks? Slack describes itself as: 'Slack is the collaboration hub that brings the right people, information, and tools together to get work done. From Fortune 100 companies to corner markets, millions of people around the world use Slack to connect their teams, unify their systems, and drive their business forward.'[9]
3. **Values** – what is the start-up's philosophy and values that guide how and why it does business? Slack suggests that: 'We live by our mission, and improving people's working life starts with our own company. We're building a platform and products we believe in – as well as a strong, diverse team of curious, creative people who want to do the best work of their lives and support each other in the process.'[10]

An alternative way of capturing the essence of a business model is for entrepreneurs to develop a 'mantra' or strapline that succinctly evokes the aims and values of the venture.[11] If a coffee store intends to source its coffee beans direct from a local community, pay a fair price, and roast and grind its beans, its 'mantra' might be 'quality, freshness and fair trade'.

○ *Go to Exercise W 2.14: What are your start-up's mission, mantra and summary pitch?*

7.3 PROTECTING IDENTITIES AND IDEAS

Legally, business names, logos and straplines can be protected from others who might be interested in copying or improving them. So too can expressions of ideas, how products look and products and processes themselves. These are all forms of intellectual property, which is 'the creation, use, and exploitation of mental and creative labour'.[12]

Protecting an identity or an idea is difficult because these are intangible, non-physical assets. For example, if a business idea is posted on social media, it can be difficult to stop others from imitating or adapting the idea.

To help entrepreneurs, governments offer them a deal: they can claim ownership rights so long as at the end of a specified period others can also use the idea. This is a negative right. It gives entrepreneurs the right to prevent others from using the idea or their identity. To enforce these rights, they can go to the courts and be granted compensation and an injunction that prevents idea infringers from using their idea or identity. Marvin Gaye's family successfully argued that Pharrell Williams and Robin Thicke's song 'Blurred Lines' relied on Gaye's song 'Got to Give It Up'. The Gaye family subsequently won compensation of nearly $5 million.[13]

Owning intellectual property acts as a barrier to entry. It helps entrepreneurs in three ways:

1. **In markets where there is a number of ways of solving a particular need, it protects a brand.** One popular mint product is Polo. It is distinctive because it has a hole in the middle. *Nestlé*, the owners of the Polo brand, wanted to trademark their mint. However, Mars – a rival confectionery company – objected, fearing that if the trademark was given, all mints with holes in them would be guilty of trademark infringement. Mars won, with the judge saying that there was a 'hole in the middle' of *Nestlé's* argument.
2. **It attracts a premium.** Mondelez paid £11.9 billion for Cadbury's. This is not because they were after Cadbury's ability to manufacture chocolate-based products. Instead, they paid a premium because Cadbury has brands that are well known and trusted. Motorola and Nokia were bought for high premiums because each had access to intellectual property that stopped others from innovating and provided access to superior dynamic knowledge. Having ownership of ideas is big business: in 1975, only 17 per cent of the value of top US companies was due to their ownership of intellectual property but 40 years later this was up to 84 per cent.[14]
3. **It is attractive to equity financiers.** Equity financiers (see Chapter 9, pp. 225–233 for more information) are keen on early-stage businesses with access to intellectual property because it can make it easier to defend and develop a sustainable competitive advantage.

There are four main types of intellectual property:

- Patents – protection for how inventions and innovations work, how they are made or what they are made of.
- Designs – how something looks.
- Trademarks – the quality and identity (brand) of an idea (business).
- Copyright – an expression of an idea, such as literary works or computer programmes.

It is possible to protect an idea in multiple ways: a patent, trademark and copyright covers the baby bottle Dr. Brown's 'Natural Flow'.

7.3.1 Patents

Patents are a monopoly right given by a government to an inventor. If granted, it offers a window of time (usually 20 years) in which entrepreneurs can stop others from exploiting a new product or process without their permission. A nation's intellectual property office usually grants patents. These can cover more geographic areas on a country-by-country basis, across countries (such as the European Patent Office) or for the world (World Intellectual Property Organization).

For a venture to get a patent, it is advisable to have a patent attorney draft the application to the intellectual property office. The patent has to show three things:

1. That the product or process is novel.
2. It involves an inventive step.
3. It is capable of industrial application.

In Europe, patents are only granted for products or processes. They do not cover methods of doing business, scientific theories, mathematical models, playing games or computer software unless it makes a technical improvement to the running of a computer device.

There are still ambiguities about patents. The Australian John Keogh decided to test the patent system by applying for an innovation patent for a circular transportation facilitation device in Australia.[15] If this patent was defendable, this would have made him extremely rich because another name for a circular transportation facilitation device is the wheel.

Case Study: Who invented the windsurf?

One of the problems faced by inventors is showing that their idea is novel and has not been done or made beforehand. Failing to show this 'prior art' led two Americans, Hoyle Schweitzer and Jim Drake, into difficulties over their claim to have invented the windsurf. In the United States (USA), they got a patent and subsequently set up a business, Windsurfing International, to manufacture and license their windsurf worldwide. One of the businesses that licensed it was Tabur Marine. Tabur Marine subsequently decided that they wished to reduce their royalty payments (licence fees) to Windsurfing International, so they sought to find someone who had invented a windsurf prior to Windsurfing International. Peter Chilvers showed that he had indeed done this. Tabur Marine went to court and showed this 'prior art', and no longer had to pay royalty fees to Windsurfing International.

Another difficulty is that patent rules tend to be different in different countries. In the USA, the decision on who owns a patent is decided by who is first to file for a patent. In Europe, the test is who was the first to invent. Hence, because Windsurf International was the first to apply they got a US patent, whereas in Europe they could not show they were the first to invent.

7.3.2 Design rights

These cover the outward appearance of an article. To obtain a registered design from a country's intellectual property office, entrepreneurs have to show that it is new and materially different. Design rights mainly cover fashion clothing, jewellery and furniture design but can include white goods. Designs do not have to be formally registered. If they are not, entrepreneurs have to show that they came up with the design. This indicates the importance of keeping records showing the evolution of the design. Another issue arises if someone is working for a product design company: it is likely that any designs they produce will remain the property of the business (unless stipulated in the employment contract). However, a freelancer might be able to claim the design is their property.

Case Study: The Trunki

Rob Law identified that children struggled with their suitcase when they were travelling. This was also a problem for parents. Parents had to struggle with their own luggage and look after both their children and their luggage. To solve these problems, Law designed a range of colourful child-friendly suitcase with wheels that allowed children to ride on their suitcase. For these 'Trunki' suitcases, Law successfully applied for and got design rights. His success attracted competitors. One competitor, Kiddee, imported from Hong Kong similar ride-on suitcases for children but used different animal designs. Law decided to take Kiddee to court for infringing their his animal designs. Law lost his case. The judge ruled that Kiddee's designs were different and that Law had to pay his own legal costs and he could not prevent Kiddee from selling their suitcases.

7.3.3 Trademarks

Trademarks cover the graphical representation of a good or service that distinguishes it from other goods or services. Out of the different types of intellectual property, trademarks are the most easily recognised: trademarks are common on clothes that advertise the logo or the strapline of a particular brand. These include the polo player for Ralph Lauren, the wings for Emporio Armani or the strapline 'Because you're worth it' for L'Oreal. It is not only logos and straplines that trademarks apply to; almost anything used to distinguish one good or service from another is capable of being a trademark–the shape of the Coca-Cola bottle, Christian Louboutin's red coloured shoe soles and the turquoise colour on Heinz baked beans. Trademarked sounds include the 'D'Oh' by Homer Simpson or the sound of a lightsabre from *Star Wars*. A Dutch company trademarked the smell of 'fresh cut grass' for their tennis balls while the sprinter Usain Bolt trademarked his distinctive lightning victory pose.

Applying for a registered trademark involves applying to a government's intellectual property office. If it is granted, the business can put the sign ® alongside the graphical representation of their brand (the symbol™ is the sign for an unregistered trademark and might as well stand for Totally Meaningless). Although there is no formal requirement for gaining a trademark, businesses do so to prevent others from using their reputation (brand). This is obviously important in stopping counterfeiters of fashion goods 'passing off' their fake goods as those of the actual company. Nike is likely to object to another company calling itself Nyke. However, other examples are less clear: the Danish company Lego failed to trademark the shape and dimensions of its Lego bricks.[16] This led to a host of competitors offering cheaper alternatives.

Case Study: Right to copy?

Textilis offers the highest quality fabrics and uses classic designs. It believes that using classic designs does not lead to design right issues: 'our products all went into mass production more than 25 years ago, and our reproductions are therefore in full compliance with UK law. We believe that copyright protection periods longer than 25 years only serve to create monopolies and maintain artificially high prices, without generating anything for the original designer.' The Swedish design house Svenskt Tenn Aktiebolag (Svenskt Tenn), took exception to Textilis selling its famous 'Manhatten' design. This was a design created in the 1920s. Svenskt Tenn argued that Textilis had infringed their Manhatten design. The Swedish court ruled that Textilis had infringed on the design rights of Svenskt Tenn and prohibited Textilis from selling the Manhatten design in Sweden. Subsequently, Textilis closed down, blaming copyright laws for its demise.[17]

7.3.4 Copyright

Copyright usually protects artistic or creative works such as literature, books, articles, instruction manuals, computer programmes, song lyrics, website content and databases. It also applies to drama, music, art maps, diagrams, technical drawings and architecture, recordings and broadcastings of works such as sound and film recordings. Copyrighted materials are usually given by the symbol ©, but there is no need to use this mark since copyright automatically comes into existence when a work is created.

Copyrights last a long time: an author of a book is able to exploit their work by selling, reproducing, or letting others use it for all of their lifetime plus 70 years. Like design rights, if they produce copyright material as part of their paid employment, the likelihood is that the material belongs to their employer. Copyright protection is fundamental to academia's concerns about plagiarism. This can range from major disputes about who came up with calculus in mathematics (Isaac Newton or Gottfried Leibniz) to worries about citing and referencing the words and ideas of others.

Assessment tip: Avoiding plagiarism

Plagiarism involves 'the practice of taking someone else's work or ideas and passing them off as one's own'.[18] This can be difficult because in answering a question such as 'Define entrepreneurship' you are often required to build on and credit the words and ideas of others while at the same time trying to bring alive in your own words an argument that might perhaps disagree with what has been said previously. An obvious example of plagiarism is someone who copies word for word a quote without referencing where it came from. So too is simply paraphrasing a piece, cutting and pasting from the internet or buying essays via the internet.

One way of avoiding plagiarism is to fully cite and acknowledge where your ideas come from. Indeed, if in doubt cite. This is also useful because it shows that you are part of a 'conversation' about a particular topic.

7.3.5 *Guarding and leveraging ideas*

Once an idea has been disclosed, often the only defending of it is in court. This is difficult for many start-ups because going to court is an expensive business. One other way of protecting an idea is to keep it a 'trade secret', an example being the recipe for Coca-Cola. This may offer some protection, but someone who stole this secret would still not be able to call their product Coca-Cola® because this would infringe their trademark. Another way of guarding intellectual property is by using a non-disclosure agreement. These legal documents detail guidelines about sharing, storing and restricting information concerning a business idea.

Entrepreneurship in Action

- Go to google.com/patents to see if your idea has been patented. If you are interested in design rights or a trademark, go to your national intellectual property office to see if a name, logo or strapline is taken.
- If you believe that you could have intellectual property, how are you going to manage the protection of your idea?

Go to Exercise W 2.15: What is 'curve-jumping, paradigm-shifting, patent-pending' about your start-up?[19]

7.4 TEAM START-UPS

It is tempting to believe that the drive behind a business idea and the identity of a business is a 'superhuman' single individual. Carlos Slim Helu was the child of Lebanese immigrant parents who went on to build a Mexican business empire (Grupo Carso). Richard Branson began with a student magazine, went on to found Virgin Records and subsequently set up more than 400 businesses.[20]

But it is a mistake to believe that entrepreneurship is a solo activity: Richard Branson has said that there are almost no entrepreneurs who ever successfully achieved anything of any scale without connecting, collaborating and delegating to a team.[21]

Team members might not be formally involved in the start-up. Outside helpers such as family members often provide emotional or financial support, business advice and cheap labour.[22] Carlos Slim Helu's holding company (Groupo Carso) owes its name to his first three letters of his name and the first two letters of his wife's name (Soumaya). These sources of close familial or friendship support are 'strong ties'.[23] Outside these, founders might rely on non-family sources of support such as accountants, lawyers or their business contacts. These looser links are 'weak ties'.

There are clear advantages in founders developing their start-up social capital (Chapter 3, p. 55). Social capital promotes start-up performance if entrepreneurs can leverage their weak ties.[24] As they develop their start-up, it also helps if they can develop both their strong and weak ties.[25] This often requires the use of bonding (the links within an existing group) and bridging social capital (the links between different groups). Bonding social capital promotes trust while bridging social capital helps to share and exchange information.[26]

Teams are more common amongst high growth-orientated or technology-based start-ups, lead to more commercialisations of products and tend to perform better than solo start-ups.[27]

Teams – which can be defined as 'two or more individuals who have a significant financial interest and participate actively in the development of the enterprise' – are more likely to perform better if they have access to superior human, social and financial capital.[28] Stronger capital provides greater breadth and depth of relevant expertise, wider business contacts and deeper pools of financial capital, helps with identifying better opportunities, provides greater operational efficiency and aids the leveraging of outside finance.[29]

Case Study: Importance of a team to Dropbox

Dropbox's founder, Drew Houston, was promised equity finance but only if he could find a business partner in two weeks. Houston asked his friends. None of them was willing to commit to Dropbox. Houston went back to his old university, met up with a complete stranger, Arash Ferdowsi, and asked him to be his business partner. Ferdowsi agreed. He dropped out of university and Dropbox got their funding.[30]

Three core issues influence a team start-up's chances of success:[31]

- Relationships.
- Roles.
- Rewards.

Relationships are what binds members of the start-up team together. Roles reflect the diversity of start-up activities such as operations, human resources and marketing. Both are important because the experiences, values and personalities of a start-up team all influence the choices that are made at start-up and the start-up's long-run chances of success.[32] This is because start-up teams have a great deal of discretion about how to combine and allocate resources.[33]

Every team also has to decide how to split ownership. Reward allocation is a key decision and again has long-term effects on a new venture.[34]

Case Study: The Social Network

© Getty Images/Drew Angerer

The subtitle of the film The Social Network is 'you don't get to make 500 million friends without making a few enemies'. It tells of the evolution of Facebook and suggests that Mark Zuckerberg originally worked on an idea for a social network – called HarvardConnection – developed by Divya Narendra and twin brothers Cameron and Tyler Winklevoss. At around the same time Zuckerberg was developing thefacebook.com, and subsequently launched it. The Winklevoss brothers believed that Zuckerberg had stolen their idea. They complained to the principal of Harvard, but he dismissed their complaint. As thefacebook.com grew and morphed into facebook.com, the brothers decided to sue Zuckerberg for stealing their idea. The film ends with the brothers receiving a settlement for $65 million at around the time Facebook was worth £23 billion.

7.4.1 Team relationships

Many founders prefer working on their own.[35] If they believe that they have the skills and experience to start-up, there might be no need to 'compensate' by partnering.[36] Sharing may also impede control, dilute creativity and lead to partners stealing intellectual property.[37]

One way of partnering is for entrepreneurs to rationally evaluate their bundle of resources and seek to fill gaps.[38] This 'resource dependency' approach occurs rarely: fewer than 10 per cent of start-up teams involve 'strangers' who are picked because they have skills and experiences that complement the team.[39]

A second approach is to rely on interpersonal relations.[40] This approach predicts that start-up teams consist of people who are similar to each other. This is the tendency towards homophily ('birds of a feather flock together'). Team formation draws on strong ties: about half of all teams are made of spousal partners, while around one-in-five start-ups come from kinship teams (family members).[41] A minority of teams consist of friends. These often share similar occupational backgrounds and ethnicities.

Family- and friendship-based teams save on the search costs associated with finding team members and may have shared goals and high levels of trust that, in turn, diminish the chances of a team member being work-shy.[42] A downside is the likelihood of having similar skills and experiences. This restricts resources and choices, making it harder to access relevant contacts and sources of finance. Being similar does not mean less conflict, particularly in family businesses.[43]

A spousal team is more likely than family or non-family business teams to achieve first sales.[44] This hides sexism: in spousal teams, women are much less likely to be the 'boss'.[45]

One way of avoiding relationship difficulties is to separate personal and business relationships, to discuss issues and develop a disaster plan in the event of relationships turning sour.[46]

Case Study: Pretty Young Professional

Four work colleagues who worked for McKinsey, a global consultancy business, set up Pretty Young Professional. Each shared a vision for providing career support for young professional women. After a year developing the business and investing her life savings, one of the founders, Kathryn Minshew, was forced out of the business. She lost her life savings. Minshew said: 'At a very basic level, the core thing that was wrong was the team. We had a team that had all come together, not necessarily initially saying, let's be co-founders. Let's start a business. Let's structure the world like this, but rather, we are all passionate about something. So let's just work on it and worry about the rest of that stuff later. When it came time to figure out who was in charge, and who made what decisions, and who got what equity, we really struggled with those decisions. It came down to some pretty fundamental differences of opinion around where the business should be heading. I think, naively, we assumed that if we kicked the can down the road on some of those things, we'd be able to sort them out.'[47]

This outcome typifies the comment of Peter Theil, the co-founder of PayPal and an initial investor in Facebook: 'When you start something, the first and most crucial decision you make is whom to start with. Choosing a founder is like getting married, and founder conflict is just as ugly as divorce.'[48]

Entrepreneurship in Action

One way to start the process of team building is to look at what you bring to a team in terms of your values, ambitions, strengths and weaknesses. Below is a 'coat of arms' (Figure 7.1), split into four quarters. For each one, draw a logo or logos (perhaps based on emojis) that best describes your values, ambitions, strengths and weaknesses. Beneath it is space for you to write out your personal motto (your slogan or strapline).

Figure 7.1 Your 'coat of arms'

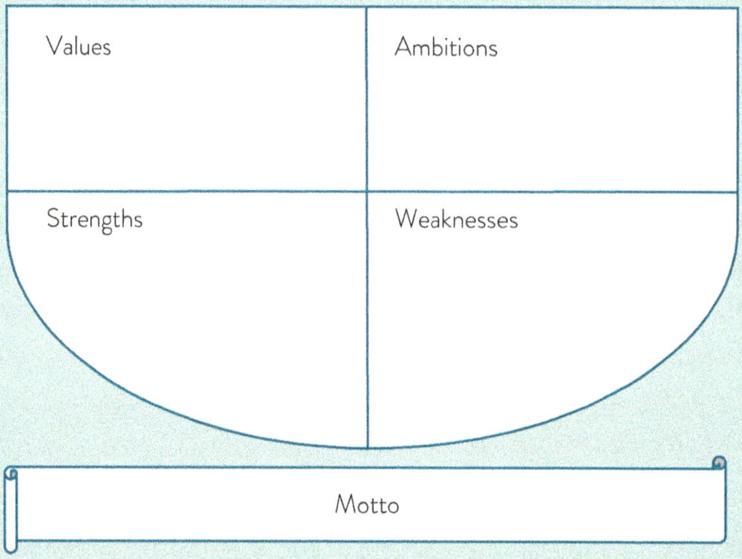

There are five main types of founder relationship options:

- Solo founder.
- Spousal team.
- Family team.
- Friendship/colleague team.
- Stranger team.

For your team relationship detail its advantages and disadvantages as well as methods to mitigate any disadvantages. For example, a colleague-based start-up team is likely to have a wide range of different experiences. But they may have limited financial resources or different values and ambitions. One way forward is to use outside business advisers.

Advantages	Disadvantages	Ways forward
•	•	•
•	•	•
•	•	•

7.4.2 Team roles

Setting up a business involves allocating different functional roles such as operations and sales.[49] One prediction is that it is important to have the right balance of skills and experience to achieve better performance outcomes.[50] Team skill diversity can lead to a team performing better than more homogeneous teams.[51] And if teams lack skills and experience at inception, they will struggle to add role expertise later on, have trouble developing fully-fledged functional structures and, ultimately, fail to grow quickly.[52]

Few start-ups have fully developed teams at start-up. Most teams are set up with just two people and very few (less than 1 per cent) have a start-up team of five people.[53] Role allocation is biased. Those who come up with the idea, have prior start-up experience and are an earlier investor are all more likely to become the start-up's chief executive officer (CEO).[54] Team members with particular expertise such as in finance are more likely to occupy a similar role in the start-up.[55] These decisions are often not 'rational': males, whites and those with higher levels of occupational or educational prestige are more likely to occupy higher-ranked roles in a USA start-up.

Just because role allocation repeats unequal societal outcomes does not mean that decision-making also has to be unequal. Some social enterprises deliberately use collective decision-making. In 'for-profits', consensual decision-making can build cohesion and trust. The counter-argument against is that given the complexity and uncertainty that founders face it is better for one individual to make the decisions to move the start-up forward.

Case Study: Snapchat – How much is an idea worth?

At its Initial Public Offer (IPO), Snapchat was worth $28 billion.[56] This made its co-founders – Evan Spiegel and Bobby Murphy – billionaires. Both had met at Stanford University. Both had been part of the same fraternity society. Both were friends and had worked on a previous business idea together. Each of their roles in Snapchat reflected their experiences. Murphy did a degree in Mathematics and Computational Science and had extensive coding experience. He became Snapchat's Chief Technology Officer. Spiegel was doing a degree in product design. He became its CEO.

There was a third founder, Frank 'Reggie' Brown. Like Spiegel and Murphy, Brown was at Stanford and was a member of the same fraternity society. Brown claimed that he came up with the idea for Snapchat and its 'ghost' logo. To develop Snapchat, both Brown and Spiegel realised that they needed a programmer to develop the app, and because they knew Murphy, they asked him to join the team.

The founders developed Snapchat in a shared house. Murphy did the coding and app development, Spiegel was responsible for strategy while Brown's role was to patent the app. Brown believed that they were all equal partners in Snapchat. As it turned out, Spiegel and Murphy disagreed. Murphy and Spiegel changed the passwords on the Snapchat server and locked Brown out. Brown got no equity in Snapchat.

He sued. The questions were how much the idea, the logo and his initial work were worth. Brown claimed that the equity split should be 40 (Spiegel), 40 (Murphy) and 20 (Brown) per cent. But Spiegel and Murphy brought Snapchat to market and raised external funding. Prior to the IPO in 2016, Brown received a compensation of $157.5 million: this was less than 1% of Snapchat's IPO valuation.

Entrepreneurship in Action

Here is a list of the main functional roles for any business: Human Relations, Strategy, Finance, Operations and Sales and Marketing.

Discuss these factors in determining the allocation of roles in a start-up team:

- Educational background.
- Prior experience in a functional role.
- Prior entrepreneurial experience.
- Gender.
- Coming up with the idea.
- Providing finance.

- If you did not use these criteria because, for example, you lack industrial experience or start-up experience, how did you allocate team roles?
- What criteria did you use?
- Are there still gaps in the team? What outside resources can the team draw on to compensate for gaps?
- How are decisions made? Is this participative or more directed? What are the advantages and disadvantages of this leadership style?
- Has the team discussed what culture they want to foster in the start-up?

7.4.3 Team rewards

The third and final main issue is splitting the shares (equity) in the start-up. This is deciding who gets what, why they should get a share and when to take these decisions. These decisions are crucial because few founders will get a decent initial salary from their start-up and often find themselves with lower salaries than a specialist employee such as an engineer or information technology developer at start-up. Indeed, many start-up founders only realise a financial benefit when they sell their share of the start-up.

About 70 per cent of start-ups allocate equity equally.[57] This can promote team cohesion and commitment.[58]

Another logic to follow is that of self-interest. One of the team may have developed the idea, made a larger capital contribution, given up a high-paid job or have invaluable experience and contacts. In particular, those with entrepreneurial experience retain greater levels of equity.[59] There also may be downsides to equal equity splits: if founders had not agreed to an equal split, one study found that they would have been about $500,000 better off.[60]

In general, it may be inadvisable to conclude the discussion about the equity split too quickly or by a simple handshake.[61] One or more of the team might simply coast along in the business. Without a plan for sharing equity, it may be difficult to offer equity to new team members who bring valuable skills and experiences to the start-up.

Case Study: Allen & Gates

Paul Allen, the other co-founder of Microsoft, originally thought a better name for his partnership with Bill Gates was Allen & Gates. They settled on Microsoft. Gates was responsible for writing most of the early programming and had dropped out of university. Allen, meanwhile, had a degree and a job. Gates argued that rather than the usual 50–50 partnership deal it should be 60–40 to reflect Gates's risks and efforts. As Gates continued to develop the business, he suggested that 'I've done most of the work on BASIC [an early programming code] and I gave up a lot to leave Harvard, he said. I deserve more than 50 percent.'[62] The equity split became 64–36.

Following its incorporation, this partnership deal ended but Allen and Gates still had the same equity share. Enter Steve Ballmer. His job was to run the business for which he got a salary and, crucially, 10 per cent of Microsoft's profits. As Microsoft boomed, the Microsoft board suggested that Ballmer's deal was unsustainable and that Ballmer needed to swap his profit share for equity. According to Allen, he agreed to a 5 per cent equity share for Ballmer, but nonetheless Gates went behind his back and offered him 8 per cent.[63]

Allen subsequently became ill with cancer. This led to Ballmer and Gates discussing how they might dilute his equity share.[64] Subsequently, Allen felt that his illness meant that he had to resign. Gates offered $5 a share; Allen wanted $10. They failed to agree; and Allen kept his shares.

At its IPO, Microsoft shares were worth $21 per share. Over time, both Gates and Allen diluted their equity shares. Steve Ballmer, the former employee, kept his and ended up with more Microsoft stock than either Gates or Allen.

One way of deciding on equity splits is to delay these until roles, individual contributions and commitments to the start-up become clearer. This means using dynamic equity splits to account for the composition and balance of the start-up team evolving over time.[65] One way of achieving this is to use 'vesting': the process by which founder's earn equity shares by achieving milestones such as reaching the first sale.

Entrepreneurship in Action

- What criteria did you use to decide on the equity shares in your start-up?
- Was this based on who came up with the idea, who put the money in, prior experience or team roles in the start-up? If you are in a mixed team, did the women get less? If so, why?
- Develop a 'pre-nup' for your team.

One way of doing this is to first allocate your shares among the team. Say that there are four in your start-up team, and you split ownership equally so that out of 100,000 shares each has 25,000 shares. Each share is worth a nominal 0.001 cents at start-up (total of €25 share capital) and is just for the purposes of recording the start-up's ownership structure.

Suppose that the business grows and sells for €100 million after four years. Each founder is now due €25 million. This is because the founders had non-fungible rights over the stock. This might be fair if each co-founder invested equal amounts of time, money and effort into the start-up. But in this case, one of the founders left the start-up for personal reasons after six months and another left after two years owing to 'irreconcilable differences' with the other founders. Understandably, the two founders that drove the business forward might feel that they should have got more from the sale.

One solution to this is a 'vesting' (share buy-back) agreement. This is an agreed schedule that itemises when the shareholder can claim rights over their shares and when the start-up can buy back these shares from shareholders. It generally lasts four years and works on the linear principle that for every year that a founder is in the business, they are entitled to a quarter of their share allocation. The hope is that a vesting agreement better aligns the effort and contribution of the start-up team.

In this example, this means that the founder who left after two years is entitled to 12.5 per cent of the shares, with the remaining shares being bought back at their nominal value (€0.001).

Vesting agreements also have a 'cliff' in the first year. If a founder works for 364 days in a start-up, they get no shares in the start-up, but if they are there for 365 days, they get a quarter of the shares due in a four-year vesting deal.

This vesting agreement means that the payout for the founders in the example is: zero for the founder who left after six months, €12.5m for the founder who left after two years and €43.75 for each of the two other founders.

This 'straight-line' approach to vesting is only one way of aligning incentives between founders. Four years may be too long or too short. Measuring time in the business may also be a poor proxy: alternative incentive milestones might be achieving first sale or profitability.

Few people set up a business on their own. Even if they lack equity partners, they rely on informal support. The issues of the 3 Rs – relationships, roles and rewards – are pivotal in setting the start-up's future direction.

- *Go to Exercise W 2.16: Why is this the right team?*

7.5 INDUSTRY ATTRACTIVENESS

The BMC identifies how attractive a market is. Used in isolation, it shows setting up a new bank is an attractive proposition. The average net profit margins in banking are 24 per cent. This is much higher than the 5 per cent average net profits in food retailing.[66]

But the BMC underweights the importance of industry attractiveness. Banking is a deeply unattractive industry for most start-ups. It involves drowning in several metres of regulation, having very deep pockets and a willingness by the owner to undergo painful investigations into their background. Unsurprisingly, despite the profits potentially on offer, few new banks ever get off the ground: over a century (1910–2010), there were no new banks in the UK.[67]

Understanding the attractiveness of an industry means conducting preparatory competitor analysis, through conducting desk research and talking to customers and competitors. This competitor assessment involves deciding on the breadth of the industry, taking a snapshot of the industry and understanding where the industry is in its life cycle.

Case Study: Careem and competition from Uber

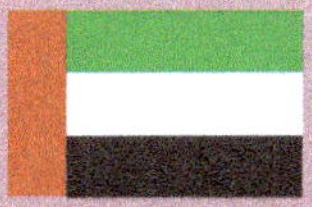

Careem is a taxi ride-sharing platform that works in a similar way to Uber. It was set up in Dubai in the UAE by the Pakistani Mudassir Sheikha and the Swede Magnus Olsson. Their first step was to investigate systematically the attractiveness of a range of Middle East markets. They settled on an Uber style business. Based on their experience and their research, they found that it was difficult to book a reliable taxi. They were also pleased that there were no existing ride-sharing businesses in the UAE.

However, nine months after starting up, they found out that Uber was coming to the UAE. Matters looked bleak for Careem. As Mudassir Sheikha explained, 'Uber had already raised a lot of money by then. They had an app, and it was undeniably very slick. We had no app. We had no on-demand service. We didn't even have our first round of funding closed.'[68]

But competition is a good thing as Mudassir explained: 'it was frankly a very high-stress time for us, but there's nothing like competition to get you running really, really fast. Instead of sleeping six hours a day, we started sleeping three hours a day. We said, we have to launch an app, and we have to have it up and running before they come to the market. And we did just that.'[69]

Careem went on to outperform Uber in terms of its customer service and rapidly expanded across the Middle East. In March 2019, it was sold to Uber for US $3.1 billion.[70]

© Getty Images/Bloomberg

7.5.1 Segmenting the industry

One way of segmenting other sellers is to divide them into direct and indirect competitors. Direct competitors sell similar products such as a new bank offering financial services. Indirect competitors are other sellers selling into the same market, such as Google or Apple offering financial services.

The advantage of just focusing on direct competitors is that it helps distinguish sources of competitive advantage. A new hotel may work out what is distinctive about its offer relative to other hotels in its area by mapping out the geographical location of its competitors and assessing the travel times for consumers to their projected location.

However, a broader approach may be beneficial. A new hotel might consider bed and breakfasts as indirect forms of competition. If so, these substitutes may make it easier for the new hotel to work out its offer in the wider industry. Focusing on indirect competitors can also lead to fewer surprises. If hotels had undertaken a broader analysis of industry trends, they could have prepared for disruptive new entrants such as Airbnb.

Entrepreneurship in Action

- Use research to identify potential competitors. Segment these into direct and indirect competitors. Figure out what the three top customer benefits of competitors are. Brainstorm how you can improve on their offer.

Appropriately segmenting an industry makes it easier to conduct a competitor analysis using Michael Porter's Five Forces (Figure 7.2).

These five forces are:

1. **The threat of new entrants/entry barriers.** Barriers exist to new entrants owing to regulation, intellectual property rights, having highly specialised assets and if a business is only viable when it operates at a high minimum efficient scale (the lowest point at which economies of scale can efficiently are realised). Many entrants push up competition and are likely to reduce profits. In an ideal world, start-ups prefer industries that have low entry barriers but that these barriers become higher once they have established themselves.
2. **Buyer (customer) power.** This is high in some industries. Food retailing is a monopsonic industry with lots of suppliers (food manufacturers) but few buyers (supermarket chains). The power of buyers is weaker if switching costs make it difficult for buyers to change suppliers. If customer power is high, it is likely to reduce profitability. Start-ups, ideally, prefer weak buyer power.
3. **Supplier power.** This is strong if there are only a few suppliers, if they can produce the buyer's product themselves (integrate forward) and if it is costly to switch to an alternative supplier or the buyer is ignorant of alternatives. Again, because supplier power can reduce profitability, start-ups tend to prefer weak supplier power.
4. **The threat of substitutes.** In the energy industry, the threat to oil and gas suppliers has grown with the growth of substitute renewable sources of energy such as wind or solar. This creates opportunities for new entrants. A start-up wants an industry with few substitutes as this can reduce profitability.
5. **Intensity of rivalry (competition).** Shaping this are a range of factors such as the number of competitors, how high the minimum efficient scale is, what the switching costs are and what the market growth is. Ideally, for the start-up, competition in an industry should be low and profits high.

Figure 7.2 Porter's Five Forces

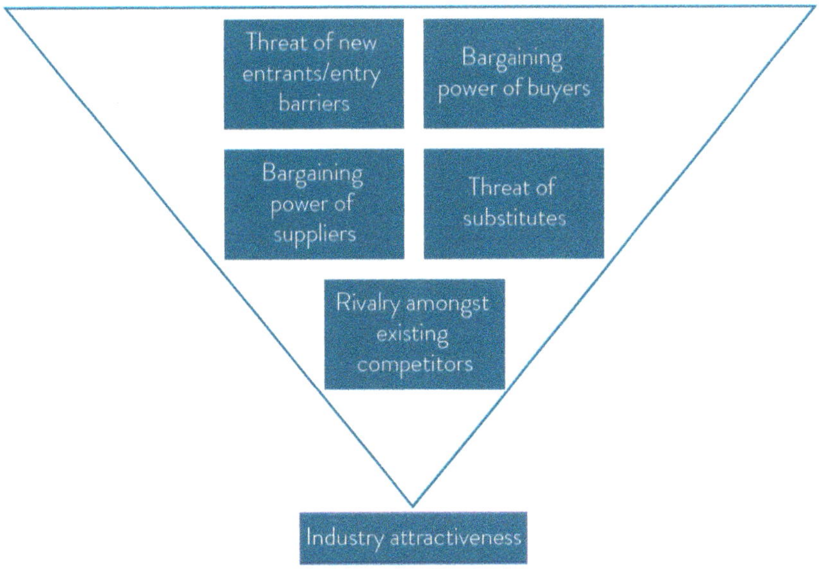

Porter's Five Forces help to evaluate industry attractiveness in terms of potential profits. It poses questions such as whether the competition is savage or gentle, who has the power in the industry to set terms and conditions and what are the opportunities for new entrants. The framework also raises questions about the source of competitive advantage (profitability) in an industry and a start-up's likely place in this industry. Chapter 6 (p. 139) showed that start-ups have three potential sources of competitive advantage: cost-based advantages stemming from lower costs or prices, differentiation benefits owing to offering an innovative product or service or focus-based advantages derived from, for example, having close customer relationships. Because most start-ups enter with a narrow set of products or services, the reality is that they have to adopt a cost-focused or differentiation focused strategy. If the source of competitive advantage is difficult to identify, then the industry can be very ugly, and can make it worthwhile to re-evaluate the viability of a start-up.

Entrepreneurship in Action

There are a number of ways to find out how attractive an industry is: industry reports, internet- and library-based keyword searches, analysis of social media activity, trade shows talking to customers and competitors and mystery shopping (Chapter 6, p. pp. 129–131). Based on this, you can use the grid in Table 7.2 to create a five forces start-up matrix.

Table 7.2 Five Forces grid for a start-up

	1	2	3	4	5
The threat of new entrants (1=Low to High=5)					
Buyer power (1=Weak to Strong=5)					
Supplier power (1=Weak to Strong=5)					
The threat of substitutes (1=Few to Many=5)					
Competitive rivalry (1=Weak to Intense=5)					

7.5.2 Heading towards the Blue Ocean

A different way of scanning the competitive landscape is Blue Ocean thinking. One of the problems with a five forces analysis is that it is static: it focuses on *existing* markets and competitors.[71] It also assumes that industries have clear and accepted norms about how to compete. This can lead to trading off differentiation (quality advantages) against price (low cost) advantages. In essence, in competing for profits and market share, the presumption is that the 'ocean' (industry) will turn 'red' because of competitive rivalries. One example of this is the strategic choices faced by someone setting up a new hair salon. In many locations, there are already too many competitors offering similar pricing and service levels. Such hyper-competition promotes low price entry strategies and pushes those already in the industry to lower their prices.

An alternative approach is to focus on a Blue Ocean strategy (Table 7.3).[72] This involves creating new uncontested markets that make the competition irrelevant and provide new ways of meeting untapped demand. It also claims to break the value–cost trade-off and focus on ways of eliminating or reducing costs by providing new goods or services that buyers want.

Table 7.3 Red Ocean versus Blue Ocean strategies

Red Ocean strategy	Blue Ocean strategy
Compete in existing markets	Create uncontested markets
Beat the competition	Make the competition irrelevant
Focus on exploiting existing demand	Create and capture new demand
Make the value–cost trade-off	Break the value–cost trade-off
Align the business model to either focus on differentiation or low cost	Focus both on differentiation and low costs

Case Study: Mr. Cesar dog food

There is perhaps nothing duller than dog food. It is a commodity made up of animal grade meat, dairy products, cereals, vegetables and vitamins and minerals, and comes in wet (canned) or dry formats. A few key players dominate this market. Illustrative of this is Table 7.4.

Table 7.4 Brazil – pet food: company retail market share by volume (%)[23]

Market player	Percentage of market
Mars Inc.	36.3
Nestlé S.A.	15.2
Lupus Desenvolvimento em Alimentos Ltda	12.9
Mogiana Alimentos S.A.	7.8
Total Alimentos S.A.	7.4
Grand Food Indústria e Comércio Ltda	5.4
Others	15

Dog food has clear customer segments, depending on if the dog is treated as a guard dog, as a companion or as a family member. Price points reflect these different relationships between the owner and their dog, with dogs that are part of the family being more likely to attract higher priced dog food. Dog food producers have limited opportunities to discriminate on price and typically compete by cutting costs or moving into new markets. Further competition damages profit margins.

An alternative path is to focus on the four Blue Ocean questions:

Q1. Eliminating taken for granted industry factors.
Q2. Reducing factors below industry standards.
Q3. Raising factors well above industry standards.
Q4. Creating new factors.

Focusing on Q1 and Q2 could give cost advantages while Q3 and Q4 offer differentiation.

A new dog food, Mr. Cesar, reduced portion size, increased packaging quality and, above all, created a new underserved market segment that treated a dog as a substitute child. This fitted in with changing demographic tastes for smaller pedigree dogs such as pugs and chihuahuas. Mr. Cesar could deliver higher value to customers but at a higher price and lower costs for producers.

Entrepreneurship in Action

- Apply the Blue Ocean questions to your own industry.
- Can you eliminate, reduce, raise and create new factors that will give you a competitive advantage?

7.5.3 The industry life-cycle

Any competitor analysis should also examine where a venture sits on its industry life cycle. New industries have greater rates of business entry and can see radical disruptive innovations come forward to meet unmet customer needs. Being an early entrant can lead to sustained first-mover advantages.[74] One downside of early entry is that a start-up may enter before there are enough customers to build a profitable business. Time lags between inventing a product and it taking off commercially are important: the time lag for the commercialisation of radio was 11 years, but it took 57 years for the dishwasher to take off commercially.[75]

Another common feature of an industry is that at some point it develops an accepted way of doing business. This is a dominant design. The QWERTY keyboard is a dominant design. Although initially designed to prevent mechanical typewriters jamming, it became the standard way of designing a keyboard because typists became trained using this layout.

As Figure 7.3 shows, once a design becomes dominant this leads to there being fewer product innovations and more process innovations.[76] The emphasis also shifts from disruptive to incremental innovations that improve cost savings, lead to better product and service integration and greater standardisation. The emergence of economies of scale and scope mean that the number of incumbents in an industry fall (an industry shakeout). This results in fewer opportunities for start-ups if the industry is mature.

Figure 7.3 A stylised view of an industry life cycle

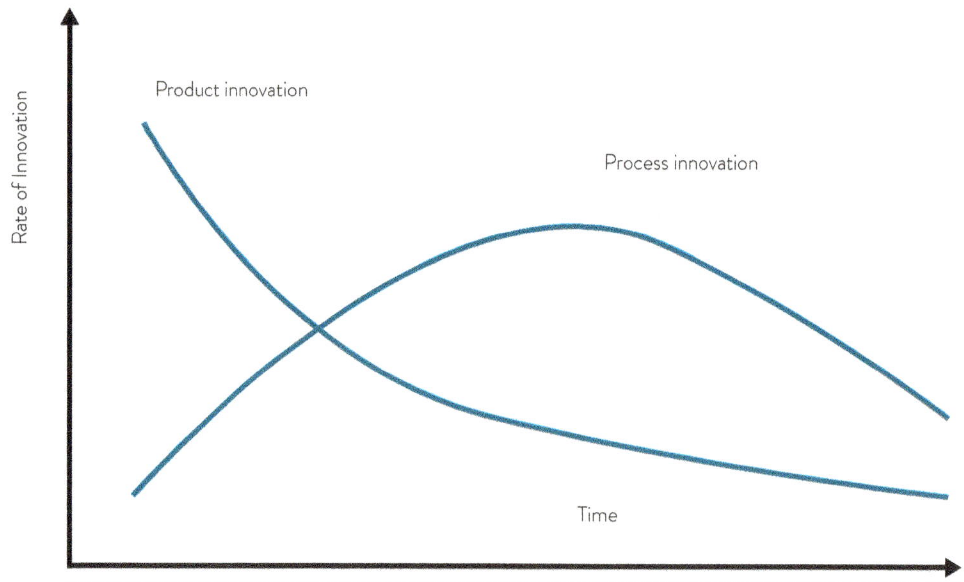

Stage 1: Fluid	**Stage 2: Transitional**	**Stage 3: Specific**
Focus on exploration and flexibility; lots of start-ups competing to bring radical designs	The emergence of dominant design; industry 'shakeout' with the emergence of industry oligopoly, more process innovation but fewer product innovations; switch to incremental innovation	Economies of scale and scope (cost saving, standardisation, integration); evident industry oligopoly; start-ups in niche markets

These patterns occur in many industries. When the automobile industry began, there was an explosion in the number of new car manufacturers competing to bring radical new car designs to the market.[77] However, once the petrol engine became common, this crowded out electric and steam-powered cars. The resulting industry shakeout left only a few large car manufacturers that were able to exploit economies of scale and scope. The focus also shifted to fine-tuning car designs, such as front-wheel drive, disc brakes, five-speed transmissions, improving passenger comfort by having air conditioning, power steering and cruise control and making higher build quality and cost-effective cars through the introduction of Japanese lean production systems. At this stage, new start-ups became niche players offering particular forms of expertise.

Entrepreneurship in Action

- Redraw Figure 7.3 for your start-up: is your industry new, growing or mature?
- Is there a dominant design?
- Has a shake-out occurred?
- Is the innovation focus of the industry on radical or incremental innovation?
- Is the industry still bringing new product innovations to the market or has it switched towards process innovations?

Academic insight: Changing your mind – Schumpeter Mark I and Mark II

The role of entrants in stimulating innovation and societal change is one of the fundamental reasons for studying entrepreneurship. The economist Robert Solow argued that where innovation occurred was due to chance. Some places were lucky because they had favourable resources. Europe had the horse, South America the llama while Africa had the zebra. The zebra cannot be tamed. This stymied innovation in Africa because there were no horses or llamas to carry and transport goods. In other words, innovation was primarily exogenously determined.

Another view is that it is not what resources you are given but what you do with these resources (innovation is endogenously determined). In the 1930s, California was a fruit growing area. Now, if it were a country, California would be the fifth biggest economy in the world.[78] So, rather than resources being pivotal, the argument is that what explains innovation is how humans use their ingenuity to create opportunities.

Josef Schumpeter's work focuses both on how resources and behavioural advantages support innovation. In Schumpeter Mark I, he took an entrepreneurship-centred view of innovation.[79] He showed that in the nineteenth century entrepreneurs drove the radical shift from relying on horses to using trains. This was due to a swarm of innovations by railway entrepreneurs who came together to creatively destroy the old routine of horse travel. Entrepreneurs were able to revolutionise travel because they had behavioural advantages such as being flexible, risk-takers and opportunity seekers. Their radical innovations had enormous societal effects: travel became faster, helped unify such countries as the USA and Germany, spurred on the development of tourism and standardised time zones across and within countries. Alongside this creativity, there was the wholesale destruction of 'horse-based' occupations such as ostlers, smiths and coachmen.

Later on, Schumpeter changed his mind. He argued that in the twentieth century innovation itself became routinised.[80] Large businesses managed to invent a method for inventing. Individual inventors such as Kia Silverbrook (Australia), Shunpei Yamazaki (Japan) or Thomas Edison (USA) who have thousands of patents to their name stand out because they are unusual. A more likely source of innovation was well-resourced research and development (R&D) facilities by large businesses. This resource-based view of innovation is called Schumpeter Mark II.

If innovation is measured in terms of R&D spend or in terms of intellectual property ownership, large businesses are much more innovative than small or new businesses. This does not take account of industrial structure, competition and geography. Innovation fertility (the number of innovations/number of employees) of large or small businesses depends on the sector.[81] It also varies by how innovation is measured. So, although large businesses spend more on innovation, smaller businesses still play an important innovative role, particularly when the industry is new.

- *Go to Exercise W 2.17: How is your offer different in the market?*

7.6 WHAT YOU HAVE LEARNED IN THIS CHAPTER

This chapter examined the key features of start-up planning that are overlooked by the BMC. It focused on three key start-up questions:

- Who are we?
- Why is this the right team?
- How is the offer different in the market?

It showed you that the identity of the business was important because it was integral to a start-up's core ambitions and values and how it chose to organise itself. Ideas could also be protected by applying for intellectual property rights.

It also showed you that better understanding a team is key, particularly at start-up when the team *is* the start-up. Entrepreneurs, therefore, have to consider the potentially thorny issues of team relationships, roles and rewards.

You also learned that industry attractiveness is not necessarily the same as market attractiveness. Finding and focusing on who competitors are and what they do allows entrepreneurs to sharpen their understanding of what is distinctive about their start-up.

Focusing on these areas of start-up planning builds on the questions examined in Chapter 6:

- Is there a market out there?
- Who is the customer?
- Is the business idea worthwhile?
- How does the business reach its customers?
- How does the business source, make and distribute its products and services?
- How does it make money?

Together they provide the basis for developing a feasibility plan or pitch. If you do not need outside funding, answering these questions may be all that is needed to make a decision about the feasibility of a start-up. However, if there is a need for external funding or greater assurances, Chapters 8 and 9 provide support on how you can develop your financial plan.

ASSESSMENT QUESTIONS

1. Audit the nature of 'strong' and 'weak' ties in a start-up. How does the social network of the team evolve, if it does at all?
2. Investigate a start-up team. What does this tell us about team relationships, roles and rewards?
3. How important is it for a founder start-up team to have a diverse set of skills and experiences? What influence does team heterogeneity or homogeneity have on start-up performance?
4. What factors are likely to be important in sharing equity among start-up founders?
5. Which are more innovative, large or small businesses? Discuss.

FURTHER READING

Beckman, C. M., & Burton, M. D. (2008). Founding the future: Path dependence in the evolution of top management teams from founding to IPO *Organization Science*, *19*(1), 3–24.

Hambrick, D. C. (2007). Upper echelons theory: An update. *Academy of Management Review*, *32*(2), 334–343.

Ruef, M., Aldrich, H. E., & Carter, N. M. (2003). The structure of founding teams: Homophily, strong ties, and isolation among US entrepreneurs. *American Sociological Review*, *68*(2), 195–222.

Yang, T., & Aldrich, H. E. (2014). Who's the boss? Explaining gender inequality in entrepreneurial teams. *American Sociological Review*, *79*(2), 303–327.

Notes

1 Beckman, C. M., & Burton, M. D. (2008). Founding the future: Path dependence in the evolution of top management teams from founding to IPO. *Organization Science*, *19*(1), 3–24.

2 Livengood, R. S., & Reger, R. K. (2010). That's our turf! Identity domains and competitive dynamics. *Academy of Management Review*, *35*(1), 48–66, 51.

3 Belenzon, S., Chatterji, A. K., & Daley, B. (2017). Eponymous entrepreneurs. American Economic Review, 107(6), 1638–1655.

4 Navis, C., & Glynn, M. A. (2011). Legitimate distinctiveness and the entrepreneurial identity: Influence on investor judgments of new venture plausibility. *Academy of Management Review*, *36*(3), 479–499.

5 www.ica.coop/en.

6 https://monitor.coop/sites/default/files/publication-files/wcm-int-dollars-2017-rankings2015-data-1013346240.pdf.

7 Defourny, J., & Nyssens, M. (2010). Conceptions of social enterprise and social entrepreneurship in Europe and the United States: convergences and divergences. *Journal of Social Entrepreneurship*, *1*(1), 32–53.

8 https://slack.com/about.

9 https://slack.com/about.

10 https://slack.com/about.

11 Kawasaki, G. (2004). *The art of the start: The time-tested, battle-hardened guide for anyone starting anything*. London: Penguin.

12 Bently, L., & Sherman, B. (2001). *Intellectual property law* (p. 1). Oxford: Oxford University Press.

13 www.bbc.co.uk/news/entertainment-arts-43497970.

14 www.oceantomo.com/2015/03/04/2015-intangible-asset-market-value-study/.

15 www.newscientist.com/article/dn965-wheel-patented-in-australia/.

16 www.bbc.co.uk/news/business-11302614.

17 http://www.textilis.com/
18 https://www.lexico.com/en/definition/plagiarism.
19 Kawasaki (2004), ibid.
20 www.theguardian.com/business/2012/jan/08/virgin-brands-richard-branson-owns.
21 www.virgin.com/entrepreneur/richard-branson-why-you-should-never-go-solo-business.
22 Kim, P. H., Longest, K. C., & Aldrich, H. E. (2013). Can you lend me a hand? Task-role alignment of social support for aspiring business owners. *Work and Occupations, 40*(3), 213–249.
23 Granovetter, M. S. (1973). The strength of weak ties., *American Journal of Sociology, 78*(6), 1360–1380.
24 Stam, W., Arzlanian, S., & Elfring, T. (2014). Social capital of entrepreneurs and small firm performance: a meta-analysis of contextual and methodological moderators. *Journal of Business Venturing, 29*(1), 152–173.
25 Newbert, S. L., Tornikoski, E. T., & Quigley, N. R. (2013). Exploring the evolution of supporter networks in the creation of new organizations. *Journal of Business Venturing*, 28(2), 281–298; Kreiser, P. M., Patel, P. C., & Fiet, J. O. (2013). The influence of changes in social capital on firm–founding activities. *Entrepreneurship Theory and Practice, 37*(3), 539–567.
26 Honig, B., & Karlsson, T. (2004). Institutional forces and the written business plan. *Journal of Management, 30*(1), 29–48.
27 Wasserman, N. (2012). *The founder's dilemmas: Anticipating and avoiding the pitfalls that can sink a start-up*. Princeton, NJ: Princeton University Press; Åstebro, T., & Serrano, C. J. (2015). Business partners: Complementary assets, financing, and invention commercialization. *Journal of Economics & Management Strategy, 24*(2), 228–252; Stam, E., & Schutjens, V. (2006). The fragile success of team start-ups. In R. Oakey, W. During, & S. Kauser (Eds.), *New technology-based firms in the new millennium* (Vol. V, pp. 219–233). Oxford: Elsevier Science.
28 Cooney, T. M. (2005). What is an entrepreneurial team? *International Small Business Journal, 23*(3), 226–235, 229.
29 Klotz, A. C., Hmieleski, K. M., Bradley, B. H., & Busenitz, L. W. (2014). New venture teams: A review of the literature and roadmap for future research. Journal of Management, 40(1), 226–255; Jin, L., Madison, K., Kraiczy, N. D., Kellermanns, F. W., Crook, T. R., & Xi, J. (2017). Entrepreneurial team composition characteristics and new venture performance: A meta-analysis. *Entrepreneurship Theory and Practice, 41*(5), 743–771.
30 www.bbc.co.uk/news/business-44766487.
31 Wasserman (2012), ibid.
32 Hambrick, D. C., & Mason, P. A. (1984). Upper echelons: The organization as a reflection of its top managers. *Academy of Management Review, 9*(2), 193–206.
33 Hambrick, D. C. (2007). Upper echelons theory: An update. *Academy of Management Review, 32*(2), 334–343.
34 Wasserman (2012), ibid.
35 Cooper, D. J., & Saral, K. J. (2013). Entrepreneurship and team participation: An experimental study. *European Economic Review, 59*, 126–140.
36 Witt, P. (2004) Entrepreneurs' networks and the success of start-ups. *Entrepreneurship & Regional Development, 16*(5), 391–412.
37 Deichmann, D., & Jensen, M. (2018). I can do that alone … or not? How idea generators juggle between the pros and cons of teamwork. *Strategic Management Journal, 39*(2), 458–475.
38 Forbes, D. P., Borchert, P. S., Zellmer-Bruhn, M. E., & Sapienza, H. J. (2006). Entrepreneurial team formation: An exploration of new member addition. *Entrepreneurship Theory and Practice, 30*(2), 225–248.
39 Ruef, M., Aldrich, H. E., & Carter, N. M. (2003). The structure of founding teams: Homophily, strong ties, and isolation among US entrepreneurs. *American Sociological Review, 68*(2), 195–222.
40 Aldrich, H. E., & Kim, P. H. (2007). Small worlds, infinite possibilities? How social networks affect entrepreneurial team formation and search. *Strategic Entrepreneurship Journal, 1*(1–2), 147–165.
41 Ruef et al. (2003), ibid.
42 Cruz, A., Howorth, C., & Hamilton, E. (2013). Intrafamily entrepreneurship: The formation and membership of family entrepreneurial teams. *Entrepreneurship Theory and Practice, 37*(1), 17–46.
43 Kellermanns, F. W., & Eddleston, K. A. (2004). Feuding families: When conflict does a family firm good. *Entrepreneurship Theory and Practice, 28*(3), 209–228.
44 Brannon, D. L., Wiklund, J., & Haynie, J. M. (2013). The varying effects of family relationships in entrepreneurial teams. *Entrepreneurship Theory and Practice, 37*(1), 107–132.
45 Yang, T., & Aldrich, H. E. (2014). Who's the boss? Explaining gender inequality in entrepreneurial teams. *American Sociological Review, 79*(2), 303–327.
46 Wasserman (2012), ibid.
47 https://mixergy.com/interviews/kathryn-minshew-the-muse-interview.
48 Thiel, P. A., & Masters, B. (2014). *Zero to one: Notes on startups, or how to build the future* (p. 108). New York: Broadway Business.
49 Mathias, B. D., & Williams, D. W. (2018). Giving up the hats? Entrepreneurs' role transitions and venture growth. *Journal of Business Venturing, 33*(3), 261–277.
50 Hambrick & Mason (1984), ibid.
51 Steffens, P., Terjesen, S., & Davidsson, P. (2012). Birds of a feather get lost together: New venture team composition and performance. *Small Business Economics, 39*(3), 727–743.
52 Beckman & Burton (2008), ibid.
53 Reynolds, P. D., Hechavarria, D., Tian, L. R., Samuelsson, M., & Davidsson, P. (2016). Panel study of entrepreneurial dynamics: A five cohort outcomes harmonized data set. *Research Gate*. doi: 1.13140/RG.2.1.2561.7682.
54 Wasserman (2012), ibid.
55 Jung, H., Vissa, B., & Pich, M. (2017). How do entrepreneurial founding teams allocate task

positions?. *Academy of Management Journal, 60*(1), 264–294.

56 www.theguardian.com/technology/2017/mar/02/snapchat-ipo-valuation-evan-spiegel-bobby-murphy-snap-inc.

57 Ruef, M. (2009). Economic inequality among entrepreneurs. In *Economic sociology of work*, pp. 57–87. London: Emerald Group.

58 Breugst, N., Rathgeber, P., & Kleinknecht, S. (2014). How should we divide the pie? Perceived justice of equity distribution and its impact on entrepreneurial team interactions and outcomes. *Frontiers of Entrepreneurship Research, 34*(9), 1.

59 Kotha, R., & George, G. (2012). Friends, family, or fools: Entrepreneur experience and its implications for equity distribution and resource mobilization. *Journal of Business Venturing, 27*(5), 525–543.

60 Hellmann, T., & Wasserman, N. (2016). The first deal: The division of founder equity in new ventures. *Management Science, 63*(8), 2647–2666.

61 Ibid.

62 Allen, P. (2012). *Idea man: A memoir by the cofounder of Microsoft* (p. 102). New York: Penguin.

63 Ibid.

64 Ibid.

65 Wasserman (2012), ibid.

66 www.investopedia.com/ask/answers/052515/what-average-profit-margin-company-banking-sector.asp; https://yourbusiness.azcentral.com/profit-margin-supermarket-17711.html.

67 www.telegraph.co.uk/finance/newsbysector/banksandfinance/11351625/How-to-set-up-a-new-bank-Itll-take-you-longer-than-you-think-and-cost-more-than-you-think.html.

68 Hegazi, A. (2018). *Startup Arabia* (p. 53). Santa Monica, CA: Transforma Publishing.

69 Ibid.

70 https://www.reuters.com/article/us-careem-m-a-uber/uber-buys-rival-careem-in-3-1-billion-deal-to-dominate-ride-hailing-in-middle-east-idUSKCN1R70IM.

71 Kim, W. C., & Mauborgne, R. A. (2014). *Blue ocean strategy, expanded edition: How to create uncontested market space and make the competition irrelevant.* Cambridge, MA: Harvard Business Review Press.

72 Ibid.

73 Mintel Pet Foods in Latin America (2016).

74 Chen, J., Reilly, R. R., & Lynn, G. S. (2012). New product development speed: Too much of a good thing?. *Journal of Product Innovation Management, 29*(2): 288–303.

75 Agarwal, R., & Bayus, B. L. (2002). The market evolution and sales take-off of product innovations. *Management Science, 48*(8), 1024–1041.

76 Utterback, J. M., & Abernathy, W. J. (1975). A dynamic model of process and product innovation. *Omega, 3*(6), 639–656.

77 Klepper, S. (2002). The capabilities of new firms and the evolution of the US automobile industry. *Industrial and Corporate Change, 11*(4), 645–666.

78 www.cbsnews.com/news/california-now-has-the-worlds-5th-largest-economy/.

79 Schumpeter, J. (1934). *The Theory of Economic Development: An Inquiry into Profits, Capital, Credit, Interest, and the Business Cycle* (trans. by Redvers Opie). Cambridge, MA: Harvard University Press.

80 Schumpeter, J. (1942). *Capitalism Socialism, and Democracy*. New York: Harper and Row.

81 Acs, Z. J., & Audretsch, D. B. (1988). Innovation in large and small firms: An empirical analysis. *The American Economic Review, 78*(4), 678–690.

PART 3

Financing the Venture

© Getty

CHAPTER 8

Start-Up Financial Information

Learning Outcomes

In this chapter, you will learn:

- The fundamentals of business' revenues and costs.
- How to construct and use profit and loss, cash flow and balance sheet. statements to assess a start-up's risks and rewards.
- How you can use financial forecasts in your business planning.

Mini Contents List

8.1 INTRODUCTION

Start-ups can fail for many reasons. Product entry might be too early or late into the market. A new business may fail to educate and inform customers about its product or service benefits. Entrepreneurs may be unable to sell, create dysfunctional working environments or badly organise product production and delivery. Competitors can also eat a new business for breakfast.

In this chapter, you will examine two other crucial reasons why businesses fail to become viable: they mess up their costs and/or they fail to get their revenues right.

Sound financial planning is important for three reasons:

1. If your revenues exceed your costs, the result is financial happiness. Happiness results in survival and prosperity. But if costs are greater than revenues, financial misery ensues, even for not-for-profit organisations. If a social enterprise night shelter for the homeless cannot raise the funds to pay its bills it will close, sending its users back to the streets and leaving its employees without jobs.
2. Financial forecasts hold up a mirror to a start-up's strategic assumptions about how it intends to create, deliver and capture value. This can lead to a feasibility study or a pitch deck (Chapters 6 and 7). One step further is to focus on your financials. Working out your revenues and costs and the 'holy trinity' of financial forecasts – the profit & loss (P&L), cash flow and the balance sheet statements – allows you to better assess start-up viability.
3. Financial plans allow you to access money from external financiers. The information helps bankers, business angels, crowdfunders and venture capitalists (Chapter 9, pp. 224–334) to evaluate a start-up's risks and rewards. It shows them how much it will cost to get a start-up off the ground, how they will benefit from supporting a new venture and how long it will take to get their money back.

Better understanding your financial planning allows you to answer these final three questions for your start-up planning and pitching (Workbook 2):

- What is the plan for growth?
- What does the start-up lack?
- Is the start-up viable?

Developing your revenue and cost models gives you a strong sense of what the options are for start-up growth and development. Your financial planning also allows you to estimate the extra funding you need to take your venture to the next level. Equally, it provides insights both for you and potential outside investors about the prospects for the business.

8.2 REVENUES AND COSTS

Chapter 6 (pp. 144–148) identifies a range of revenue models. Businesses can get paid by subscription (Netflix), through commissions (estate agents, eBay), by advertising (Google, Facebook) or via one-off payments (dentists, retailers and solicitors). Core to all revenue models is a simple relationship between what the customer pays and how much they buy. Both price and volume are pliable. Both reflect judgements and assumptions about the likely price and the number of people who are likely to buy a start-up's offer. Four basic factors affect these decisions:

8.2.1 What the customer is willing to pay

Value-based pricing reflects assumptions about the perceived or estimated value to a customer of a good or service. Not all cotton T-shirts are the same; some people will pay a premium to wear a branded one. A price discrimination strategy is an opportunity to charge different customers different prices for the same product. It also helps to manage excess demand. Uber uses 'surge' pricing to achieve a better equilibrium between the number of people booking rides at any one time and average wait times. This works for the company when there is extra demand because of poor weather but has reputational side-effects when surges have followed terrorist attacks and natural disasters.

Value-based pricing also plays on consumers' cognitive biases. A product appears more attractive priced at \$9.90 than \$10. Bundling offers such as 'buy one get one free' can also give customers the impression they are getting more for less. Social enterprises often reframe pricing decisions by comparing a donation to the price of a coffee. Similarly, coffee chains create a 'Goldilocks choice' between small, medium and large cups, to encourage people to buy medium. This works if medium makes them the biggest profit. They might also use a 'decoy' pricing strategy that offers an extra-large option if it encourages more customers to choose large.

Price skimming is another value-based pricing strategy for maximising profits. Companies such as Samsung and Apple use it to sell mobile phones, at first for a high price to a customer segment of 'early adopters', before lowering the price to attract other customers once demand from the first group is saturated. Hotel and flight operators use the same strategy in reverse, offering the best prices to early buyers before gradually increasing the cost as the date of travel grows closer.

Entrepreneurship in Action

Surveys are a common way to validate a start-up's offer. They consist of three types of question:

1. Closed questions (yes or no), such as have you purchased X in the past 12 months?
2. Attitudinal rating or ranking questions, such as on a scale of 1–5 when you purchase X, which of the following benefits is most/least important?
3. Open questions asking respondents for in-depth information through face-to-face, video or telephone interviews, email, paper or online questionnaires or feedback forms.

Survey questions tend to focus on:

- Customer demographics, such as age, gender, location and income levels.
- How a product or service's pricing compares with competitors.
- Whether customers tend to buy online or in store, how frequently and how much they spend.
- What customers think of a product or service's features and benefits, how they compare to competitors, what they value and what might make them switch to another provider.

Surveys can be relatively quick and simple to do. Survey responses can be analysed and turned into tables and charts. Therefore, survey results can help validate a start-up's strategy. However, surveys will fail to produce useful results if:

- **The survey focuses on the wrong people**. For the survey to be useful, it needs to target relevant customers not users. Freemium revenue models rely on paying customers, not users. A survey that fails to focus on paying customers provides few insights.
- **They ask the wrong questions**. Poorly drafted questions include:
  - Leading questions, such as 'isn't this product the best?'.
  - Asking two questions at once, such as 'how and why do you use X product?'.
  - Using jargon, such as 'how would you rate this minimum viable product?'.
- **The sample is biased**. Most surveys rely on 'snowball' convenience sampling. Typically, this involves entrepreneurs asking their friends to participate in their survey and then asking friends of friends. This can work if the group is a 'hard to reach' group such as the informally self-employed. But this approach can lead to confirmation bias (Chapter 2, p. 36). One simple way of attempting to avoid this is to survey complete strangers.

  An alternative approach to convenience sampling is probability sampling. This randomly selects individuals by, for example, surveying every fifth business from a business population. Stratified random sampling takes this further by dividing a population into similar but non-overlapping groups and using random sampling within each of these groups.
- **Sample sizes are too small**. Estonian start-up Weps wanted to help users build a website online in less than two minutes. To validate viability, Weps could focus on Estonian households because they are familiar and it is a relatively small European market. So, out of the 592,000 Estonian households, they might decide to survey 100 households. This is not enough to ensure the sample is representative of Estonian households. To get really robust results, Weps would need to survey 1066 Estonian households.

If done well, surveys can validate a chosen customer niche. Done badly, surveys can lead to inaccurate findings. Before conducting a survey, a start-up should first talk to its target customers to build a customer vignette or persona (Chapter 6, pp. 129–131).

Competitor pricing

Customers often use a competitor's price as an anchor. Supermarkets price everyday staple goods at about the same price as their competitors. This gives their customers the impression that their wider store offer is 'value for money'. The challenge for a start-up is that they are typically 'price takers' (Chapter 1, p. 18): so they often have to price in line with their competitors. When the UK's Innocent drinks started out, their market research showed that customers were only prepared to pay for their smoothie if it was at a similar price to their main competitor. They could not compete: their costs were too high for a standard 330 ml bottle. This forced them to compete in non-price ways and to size their smoothies to smaller 250 ml bottles.

Start-ups sometimes use penetration pricing to attract customers. The hope is that if prices start low they will lure customers away from competitors and increase their market share. Once they have customers, the start-up often aims either to increase their prices to these customers over time or to sell them other products or services. A new accountancy practice may use penetration pricing for its auditing services to gain market share. The strategy is that once it has built its client base, it can then seek to sell other, more profitable, services such as business succession planning to its audit customers.

There are dangers with pricing low. It is easier to reduce high prices than increase low ones. Customers quickly get used to low cost or free products such as apps. Pricing low is also a struggle because it might indicate that the product or service is cheap and disposable. Discounting high-quality items can cut into profits and wreck a company's finances. Jewellery gross margins are around 50 per cent in Australia. If a jeweller decides to offer a 20 per cent discount, they have to sell around two-thirds more stock.

Aggressive pricing can upset larger competitors. They usually have much deeper pockets and have lower costs because of their high output levels (economies of scale). If so, they can happily engage in a price war that can destroy a new business.

Prices can be above or below competitors' anchor pricing, but they must align with a start-up's overall competitive strategy. Otherwise, they can confuse and deter potential customers.

What the good or service costs to produce

'Cost-plus' pricing involves calculating the costs of a good or service and adding a profit on top. This is usually done in two ways:

- If it costs a Polish workshop 1000 zlotys to make a table and it sells it for 3000 zlotys, making a profit of 2000 zlotys, it will have a 67 per cent *profit margin* ((profit/price) × 100)= profit margin percentage).
- The *mark-up* on the table is 200 per cent ((profit/cost) × 100).

Cost-plus prices are easy to calculate and can be applied across different product ranges. Knowing how to establish them is important if a start-up's strategy is to offer cost leadership. However, focusing on costs does not account for what the offer is worth to customers. The start-up could actually charge more. Cost calculations are also often incomplete. Some start-up teams never factor their own living expenses into their financials and often forget sales and marketing costs and post-sales costs, such as returns and customer care.

The volume of customers

Alongside price, the size of the customer niche is important: generally the smaller the number, the greater the need to follow a differentiation rather than cost-based strategy (Chapter 7, p. 173).

Start-ups can estimate customer numbers by using a mix of a 'top-down' and bottom-up' approach (Chapter 6, pp. 126–136).

Working out the first year's revenue model

A number of factors influence how new entrepreneurs construct a first-year revenue model:

- **What price should they charge?** Entrepreneurs might use prior secondary and primary research to work out if they should follow value-based, cost-based or anchor-(competitor) based pricing.
- **Is their pricing aligned to their value proposition?** Offering a high-quality product or service for a low price might drive forward customer acquisition but is unlikely to be sustainable.
- **How do organisational capacity constraints limit customer volumes?** Start-ups need time to set up and organise their product or service offer. Even when they are fully operational, there are limits to how many customers they can serve in the short-term. This often inhibits revenue generation in the first year.
- **How long does it take to inform, educate and sell to customers?** For example, new to market products and services take time to gain customer acceptance and adoption. This, again, limits revenue generation.
- **Is the offer seasonal?** Many products and services experience fluctuations in customer demand over a year. Peaks and troughs in sales are evident in diverse areas such as garden maintenance, tourism and travel.

The aim of a first-year revenue model is to robustly estimate expected revenues. This rests on well-worked out assumptions. Suppose that a chef wanted to open a French restaurant in Athens, Greece. Their assumptions might include:

- Their chosen location serves a maximum of 50 covers.
- When they are fully operational, they will close on Mondays and Tuesdays and shut in January for four weeks (48 weeks × 5 days = 240 evenings).
- Potentially, the chef could serve 12,000 covers in the first year (50 covers × 240 evenings).
- But the chef estimates that in the first two months (8 weeks = 40 evenings) they will only be able to attract 25 covers per night as they build up their customer base. This is helpful because it gives them time and space to develop their capabilities to run the restaurant. This reduces the number of covers to 11,000 ((50 covers × 200 evenings) + (25 covers × 40 evenings)).
- Further, the chef's research shows her that for two months of the year trade will be slow. Again, the chef estimates that this will mean that they get 25 covers per evening for eight weeks. The total customer volume is 10,000 covers ((50 covers × 160 evenings) + (25 covers × 80 evenings)).
- Having done market research with customers, the chef estimates that the average cover will spend €45.
- The maximum forecast revenue is €450,000 (10,000 covers each paying €45).

Strong robust assumptions allow for the development of different revenue scenarios. Besides the 'expected case' scenario, entrepreneurs can show the worst-case or best-case scenarios. Ways of doing this include changing how quickly or slowly customers can be acquired, showing how speedily operational capabilities can be developed and by estimating the impact of changing prices charged on revenues. Entrepreneurs might develop these alternative scenarios to plan for eventualities and to demonstrate to investors that they have carefully thought through the implications of changing circumstances.

Entrepreneurship in Action

- How do you get paid? Does your start-up rely, for example, on subscriptions, one-off payments or commissions?
- How many target customers are there?
- What does your market research show about your pricing strategy?
- Why is your chosen pricing strategy (value-, anchor- or cost-based) the right one for your business?
- In your revenue model, do you account for how long it takes to set up and get your business fully operational?
- How long will it take you to sell to your customers? What impact does this have on your revenue projections?
- Is your business seasonal? What impact does this have on your revenue model?
- What are your expected revenues for the first year? What happens if you change one or more of your core assumptions?

8.2.2 Working out the revenue model for subsequent years

Funders are also usually keen to see future revenue performance. In doing so, they recognise that as time goes by, current information becomes more difficult to trust, assumptions become weaker and revenue forecasts more prone to error. Nonetheless, revenue projections for Year 2 and beyond are valuable in pointing to a start-up's growth strategy. One expansion path is to grow the business organically. A founder has four main options for organic growth (Chapter 10, pp. 255–256):

1. Sell more of their existing products or services to their existing customers – this requires building on *existing* information to model, for example, the rate of customer acquisition.
2. Sell their existing products to new customers – this requires a rationale for the choice of a new regional, national or international market and *new* information on customers in this target market.
3. Develop new products for their existing customers – this requires a justification and *new* information on when revenues for the new product will begin.
4. Develop new products for new customers – this requires a justification and *new* information on both customers and the product.

Option 1 is the least risky option for many start-ups. In contrast, option 4 is essentially a brand new start-up.

Another possible route for business growth is franchising the business (Chapter 4, pp. 85–87). Franchising is an agreement between a business (franchisor) to license its business model and sell its products and services to an independent business (franchisee). While franchising can occur quickly, there are a number of obstacles to its speedy adoption.

- It takes time to set up the agreement between the business (franchisor) and franchisee.
- Franchisees need time to set up their franchise.
- The franchisor has to demonstrate a track record of strong revenue growth. Usually, this means showing how their business has organically grown.
- It takes time to build a network of franchisees.

A start-up can also grow quickly by acquiring other businesses. What motivates this is the desire to access intellectual property, to build a strategic alliance or to dampen competition down in a marketplace. Acquisitive growth is unusual for start-ups. One exception is Facebook. Soon after it was founded, Zuckerberg started acquiring companies, and has subsequently acquired more than 70, partly to get access to intellectual property but also to bring entrepreneurial staff to Facebook.[3]

Developing future revenue projections usually involves focusing on how the business can grow organically. Because information for subsequent years is likely to be sketchy, founders often develop best, expected and worst-case revenue scenarios.

Entrepreneurship in Action

- How do you intend to scale your start-up?
- What are your justifications for your route to growth?
- Develop your revenue projections for subsequent years.
- What are your best, expected and worst-case revenue scenarios for these years?

- *Go to Exercise W 2.18: What's your plan for growth?*

8.2.3 Counting the cost of starting up

If working out Price × Volume = Revenues is important, so is understanding pre-launch costs. Some of these stem from key regulatory requirements such as insurance, health and safety liabilities, registering with the tax office and other government agencies. A start-up may also need to invest in capital equipment. If these costs are more than the start-up budget available, a founder may need to find more money or bootstrap (Chapter 4, p. 83) the business. Undercapitalised start-ups are more likely to fail (Chapter 11, p. 284), so if neither option is available, it may be better if the entrepreneur aborted the new venture and cut their losses.

Table 8.1 itemises three main types of specimen launch costs: regulatory costs, pre-launch operational costs incurred to get the product or service ready and personal costs. Founders need money to meet their living expenses. Depending on the sector, they may also need to pay for registration, permits or licences.

Some costs are recurring: a limited liability company has to use an accountant and a lawyer periodically to meet its reporting responsibilities. Sales and marketing costs are also likely to be ongoing. Other costs include stock, buying or leasing capital equipment, warehousing and logistics. Table 8.1 suggests that keeping some money spare (a contingency reserve) is prudent, because if there are delays, pre-launch cost estimates may be inaccurate.

Table 8.1 Pre-launch costs

	Amount
Regulatory costs	
Adviser fees (e.g. legal and accountancy)	
Registration fees (e.g. setting up as limited company)	
Insurance costs (e.g. public liability)	
Permit/licence fees (e.g. food hygiene certification)	
Membership/accreditation fees	
Staff costs (e.g. recruitment costs, such as advertising and recruiting personnel)	
Operational costs prior to launch	
Market research costs (e.g. visits to suppliers, customers, conducting a focus group)	
Premise costs (e.g. fit-out costs for interior and exterior design of premises)	
Staff costs (e.g. costs to get product/service ready, recruitment and training costs)	
Equipment costs (e.g. machines to manufacture product, tools, office equipment, vehicles)	
Office equipment (e.g. laptop/printer, initial consumables)	
Stock (inventory): stock needed to begin production or to offer a service	
Shipping costs (e.g. costs of getting raw materials transported)	
Product development costs (e.g. costs of developing an app)	
Personal costs	
Survival budget (money needed to pay for personal expenses such as housing costs and food)	
Contingency reserve	(20–30%)
Total pre-launch costs	

Entrepreneurship in Action

- Develop a budget for your pre-launch costs. Include an estimate of the money you need to pay your living expenses.
- List out your key assumptions. In practice, this means itemising those costs that are likely to eat significantly into your start-up budget. Sources of this information include industry reports for supplier prices and transportation costs, online marketplaces for sales costs, recruitment websites for wages and property agents for property costs.
- How do you intend to bootstrap the business or get extra funding if you run out of money to fund your pre-launch costs?

8.3 KEEPING SCORE: THE P&L STATEMENT

All businesses need to keep a financial score if they want to survive and grow. A P&L statement, also known as an income statement, is a summary of revenues, costs and profits for a given period.

At the top is revenues. Next, the P&L details costs that change, depending on how many goods or services are sold. The more sandwiches a shop sells, the more it has to pay for ingredients to make its sandwiches. These variable costs are known as Cost Of Goods Sold (COGS).

Not all businesses have significant variable costs. The costs to an e-book publisher, a digital music provider or an app developer of one extra customer for a book, song or game is close to zero, even if they have had to buy extra server space to host additional customers.

To estimate variable costs, founders have to have information on such things as their raw materials, shipping costs, credit card payments and commissions paid for sales. A hotelier, for example, has to pay a commission if a customer uses a third party or a platform to book a room. Their bank will also charge them a fee every time one of their customers uses a credit card to pay for their room.

If a business does have variable costs, these have to be subtracted from revenues to give a gross profit (**Revenues – COGS = gross profit**).

Gross profit is important. Fat profits signal where the opportunities for the business lie. Thin profits might mean that the founder may have no money to pay staff, keep the lights on, fund their marketing or look after their customers. This is because, the P&L shows that gross profits pays for fixed costs.

8.3.1 Fixed costs

Fixed costs – also known as operating expenses or overhead costs – do not change with revenues. An entrepreneur who sells nothing still has to pay their fixed costs. Fixed costs come in four forms:

1. Total sales and marketing costs: the costs involved in promoting and selling a product or service.
2. Total general and administrative costs: costs such as rent, insurance, utility payments and office expenditure.
3. Total personnel costs: such as founder and employee salaries.
4. Total product development costs: costs that relate to research and development such as patent costs, designing and testing prototypes.

Founders can distinguish between fixed and variable costs by asking themselves whether a cost is one they *must* pay no matter how much they sell. Paying the rent is a necessity regardless of the level of sales. If a cost will last for a year or more, it is also likely to be a fixed cost.

Entrepreneurship in Action

- Work out your variable and fixed costs. Where applicable, provide information to show how these costs are made up.

Gross profit – fixed costs = operating profit. Another name for operating profit is **EBITDA**, which is an abbreviation of **E**arnings **B**efore **I**nterest is charged, **T**axes are paid, or account taken for **D**epreciation or **A**mortisation.

EBITDA – Interest + Depreciation + Amortisation = Profit before tax

Normally, to get to profit before tax involves subtracting the following from EBITDA:

1. Interest expenses from any loans or other borrowing.
2. Depreciation: a financial adjustment for spreading the costs of tangible assets, such as vehicles, over their lifetime of use.
3. Amortisation: a financial adjustment for spreading the cost of intangible assets such as patents over their lifetime of use.

Figure 8.1 shows the sequence of steps needed to arrive at a pre-tax net profit on a P&L.

Subsequently, a founder might find themselves liable to a range of taxes on their profits, on their sales and on their premises.

Figure 8.1 The P&L formula

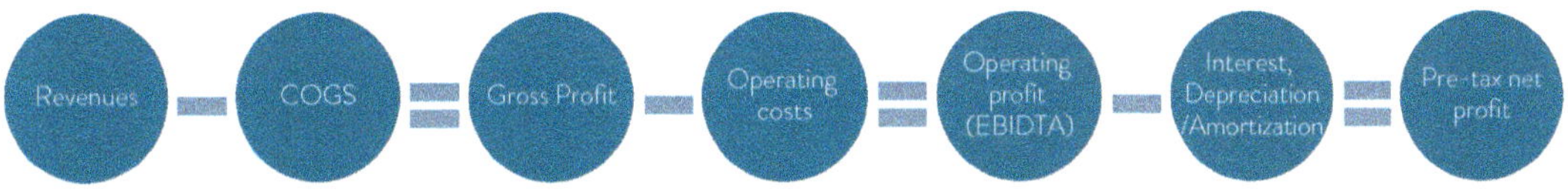

Entrepreneurship in Action

- Interest expenses are the amount of money that you have to pay to cover your borrowings. If you borrowed £10,000 from the bank and the interest rate was 8 per cent, this means that your interest expense is £800.
- There are a number of methods for accounting for depreciation and amortisation. One of the popular methods is the straight line approach. To use the straight-line method, you have to: (1) know how much the asset initially costs, (2) estimate what its salvage value is (what you can sell it for once you have finished using it) and (3) how long you estimate it will last. The formula for working this out is: (purchase price–salvage value)/estimated life-time of usage.
  If capital equipment costs £25,000, lasts ten years and you estimate it will sell for £2500 (salvage price), this means that you have to depreciate its 'book value' (what it is worth in accounting terms) by £2250 each year ((25,000/2500)/10= 2250 per year).
  Book value is what an asset is worth in accounting terms. It does not mean that the asset will sell for this amount.
- For your business, depreciate the value of your tangible assets.

8.3.2 P&L scenario planning

Entrepreneurs also build on their revenue modelling to develop three different P&L scenarios (Table 8.2): expected, worst and a best case for their first year of operations. Scenarios stress-test a founder's predictions and provide insights into a start-up's risk and reward profile.

Table 8.2 Sample P&L statement

	Expected case	Best case	Worst case
Revenues	100	200	50
Cost of Goods Sold (COGS)	50	100	25
Gross Profits (Revenues - Costs)	50	100	25
Fixed costs			
Total sales and marketing costs	10	10	10
Total general and administrative costs	10	10	10
Total personnel costs	10	10	10
Total product development costs	10	10	10
Total fixed costs	40	40	40
Earnings before Interest, Tax, Depreciation and Amortisation (EBITDA) (Gross Profit-fixed costs)	10	60	-15
Interest, Depreciation and Amortisation	2	2	2
Net pre-tax profit (loss)	8	58	-17

Entrepreneurs can also build on their revenue projections for the first and subsequent years by developing quarterly or yearly P&L forecasts. Table 8.3 shows three-year P&L projections for a sample manufacturing business. By segmenting their market carefully, the business - perhaps under their 'expected' scenario - makes projected sales of 15,000 in year 1. Production doubles in year 2. But fixed costs remain a worry. This start-up has large initial research and development costs and expects to have to re-engineer their product in years 2 and 3. Marketing costs are high, reflecting the challenge of educating and selling to their niche.

Table 8.3 Three-year P&L for a manufacturing business

	Year 1	Year 2	Year 3
Price	20	20	20
Volume	15,000	30,000	45,000
Revenues	300,000	600,000	900,000
Costs			
Buying in price	15	15	15
Cost of Goods Sold (COGS)	225,000	450,000	675,000
Gross Profits (Revenues -COGS)	75,000	150,000	225,000
Gross Profit Margin (Gross Profit/ Revenues × 100)	25%	25%	25%
Fixed costs			
Total sales and marketing costs	-33,500	-38,000	-40,000
Total general and administrative costs	-20,000	-20,000	-20,000

Total personnel costs	-36,000	-36,000	-36,000
Total product development costs	-40,500	-10,000	-30,000
Total fixed costs	-130,000	-104,000	-126,000
EBITDA	-55,000	46,000	99,000
Interest/Depreciation/Amortisation	-4000	-4000	-4000
Pre-tax profits (loss)	-59,000	42,000	95,000

8

Entrepreneurship in Action

- Develop best, expected and worst-case first-year P&L scenarios.
- What are you going to do if your worst case turns out to be the reality?
- Develop P&L projections for subsequent years.
- What do these projections show about the profitability of the business? If they show losses what are your options?

Assessment tip: Crossing the T's and dotting the I's

In all academic writing, there are constraints. Academics writing a journal paper must follow the journal's style guide and word limit. If they fail to, the academic's paper can be rejected.

You face similar constraints in your academic writing such as word limits, using particular font types and sizes, setting margins, providing page numbers and references. Follow these conventions. They matter because one of the ways of identifying poor academic practice is to look at a bibliography. If this is messy and inconsistent, it is a clue to a lack of care taken with the actual writing. To standardise your referencing use referencing software.

8.3.3 The break-even point

P&L statements help start-ups to work out their Break-Even Point (BEP). The BEP is a quick but informative calculation that shows the level of sales (how many units and at what price) a business needs to have to cover its costs and become profitable. As Figure 8.2 shows, if a business earns or produces nothing, it still has to pay its fixed costs. As it starts to make sales, it incurs variable costs (COGS), which add to its total costs (variable + fixed costs). The BEP is the tipping point at which losses turn into profits.

To calculate BEP, two formulas are used:

1. Number of *sales* to reach BEP = total fixed costs/gross profit percentage.
2. Number of *units* that have to be sold to reach BEP = total fixed costs/(price of product – contribution cost of product (variable costs)).

Figure 8.2 The break-even point (BEP)

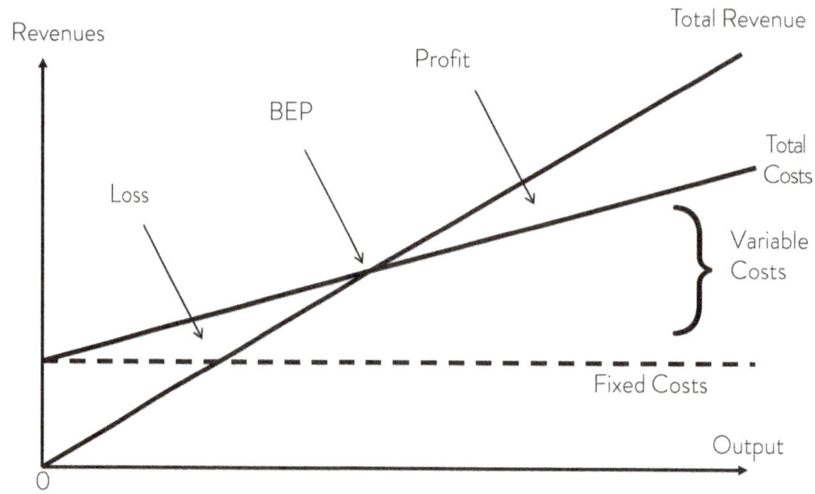

BEP analysis tells founders at what point financial misery or happiness occurs. Suppose someone has the idea of setting up an online floristry service to connect high-quality florists with customers. They do some research to test the idea and find a potential unmet demand among high earners for professionally designed and bespoke floral bouquets. Talking to this group reveals that the average customer spend is \$50 per bouquet. The founder plans to charge a transaction fee of 20 per cent (\$10). Their variable costs to fulfil each order is \$3. This is a gross profit margin of 70 per cent (gross profit/revenues × 100). They estimate fixed costs such as marketing and sales to be \$300,000 in the first year.

As Figure 8.3 shows, this potential entrepreneur would need to make sales of \$428,571 (300,000/70 per cent) or make 42,857 (300,000/(10–3)) transactions during the first year to reach BEP. This is 117 bouquets a day, 824 a week and 3571 a month.

Based on this simple BEP analysis, this leaves the founder with three main options:

1. Improve their gross profit margin, by either increasing their fee or reducing their COGS. However, having talked to the florists, the founder finds that the florists are already being charged at the top end of what they can afford. As a start-up, the founder also recognises that they do not have enough traction in the market to negotiate down their COGS.
2. Increase sales. This will help, but often requires further spending on marketing and sales. Without outside investment, this option looks difficult.
3. Reduce their fixed costs by bootstrapping existing resources. The founder could consider working from home rather than using an office. Another option is to outsource their online presence to a cheaper provider. However, this can lead to the founder losing control of their ordering process, which in turn results in falling rates of customer satisfaction and declining sales.

Figure 8.3 Break-even for an online floristry business

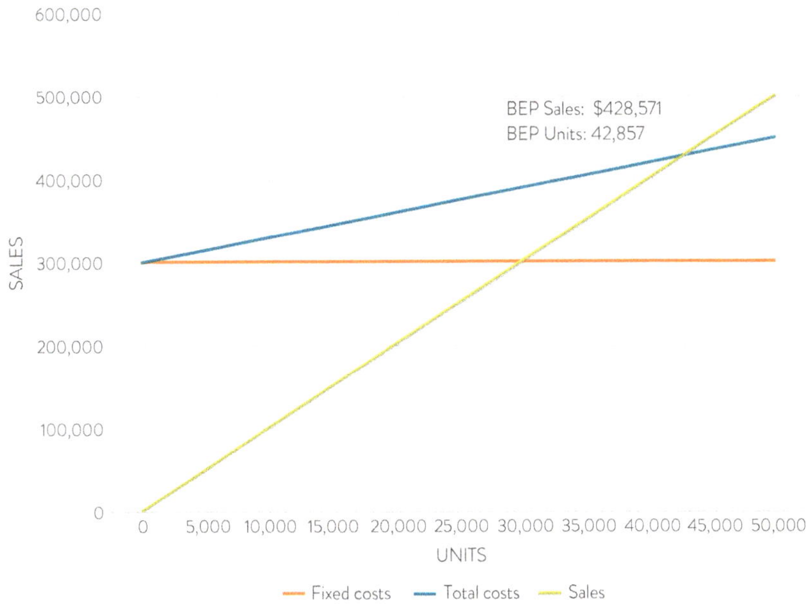

8

Case Study: Looking for love?

© Getty Images

In response to her mother's urgings to get married, Gong Haiyan (Rose Gong) joined an online dating service. She got ripped off: the prospective dates given to her were phoney. Bruised by this, she decided to set up her own website, Jiayuan.com, to help people who were serious about getting a partner. She studied the business models of other dating websites. They usually charged a membership fee. Her financial innovation was to charge nothing for joining but a small fee for the email traffic associated with setting up prospective dates. She set about developing her business by getting her friends to join her website. Money was tight, and she needed outside investors to help her develop the business.

As Table 8.4 shows, she grew the business to more than 12 million registered users. Actual paying customer numbers, though, remained low. The sales conversion rate (number of registered users/monthly paying customers) was 0.73 per cent. Gross profits were thin at only 23 per cent, requiring break-even sales of RMB 89,344k (operating costs of RMB 20,549k/gross profit of 23 per cent).

Knowing that her BEP was low forced Gong Haiyan to think strategically about how to make her business profitable. She could focus on increasing revenues but would require more spending on marketing and sales. Alternatively, Rose could improve her sales conversion rate. This would push up the volume part of the price × volume part of her revenue equation. However, she also needed to drive down her COGS.

She focused on increasing her sales conversion rate up from 0.73 (2008) to 1.58 (2010) and cutting her COGS (RMB 232 per customer (2008) to RMB 110 per customer (2010)). Her break-even point also fell for 2009, allowing her to market heavily and invest in research and development (R&D) in 2010.

Once profitable, Jiayuan.com subsequently floated on the NASDAQ stock market through an Initial Public Offering. Rose also met her husband through her website.

Table 8.4 Financial information on Jiayuan.com, 2008–2010[4]

	2008	2009	2010
Number of registered user accounts	12,702,855	19,243,134	35,090,025
Number of average monthly paying user accounts	92,102	203,317	552,930
Sales conversion rate (registered users/ monthly paying accounts)	0.73	1.06	1.58
Estimated average revenue per customer (revenues/registered monthly users)	300	314	303
Estimated average GOGS per customer (COGS/registered monthly users)	232	140	110
	RMB (000s)	*RMB (000s)*	*RMB (000s)*
Revenues	27,625	63,894	167,589
COGS	21,353	28,448	61,049
Gross profit	6272	35,446	106,540
Gross profit percentage	23	55	64
Fixed costs			
Selling and marketing expenses	14,677	16,574	57,867

General and admin expenses	5872	8631	24,338
Research and development expenses	–	8	381
Total fixed costs	20,549	25,213	82,586
Operating profit(loss)	(14,277)	10,233	23,954
Break-even (sales)	89,344	45,448	129,909
Break-even (units)	302,192	144,902	427,907

8

8.3.4 Leaving the 'valley of death'

Understanding its BEP also tells a business how long it will take to cross its 'valley of death'. This is the time it takes to reach the point at which business losses are zero. Figure 8.4 shows that at the start of this journey, a new venture incurs few initial costs. But as time goes on, and as they conduct start-up activities, costs mount up. Losses further increase at the point of product launch

Figure 8.4 Into the 'valley of death'

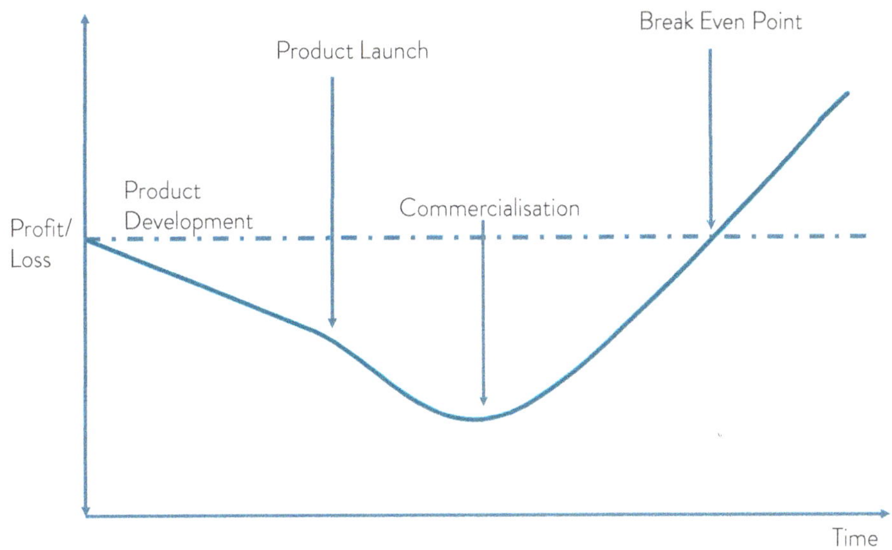

and become even greater when the start-up seeks to market and sell its products in the marketplace. Eventually, the new business hopes they will make enough sales to climb out of this 'U' shaped 'valley of death' and reach its BEP.

How long and how arid this journey is through the valley of death towards BEP varies. Independently wealthy founders might not even notice any difficulties. For others with limited financing needs, the journey is likely to be short. A new consultancy business is likely to break even quickly, particularly if its founder bootstraps the business; some can, for example, work from home. In contrast, a high technology R&D start-up that needs to use advanced manufacturing is likely to take much longer to reach the 'promised land' of positive profits.

Case Study: Belgian start-up's BEP is too big to swallow

Belgian business Take Eat Easy used couriers to deliver quality food from restaurants to people's doors. To prove the concept in Brussels, it raised €6 million. It raised another €10 million to sign up more couriers and restaurants, increase their marketing and promotional activities, improve their information technology systems and hire new workers to manage these changes. The business increased from a team of 10–160, scaled to 20 cities and grew from 30,000 to 350,000 customers. But this was still not enough to break even. To cover both their fixed and variable costs, the company needed to increase its customer base even more. Take Eat Easy went for further funding of around €30 million. Despite going to visit 114 venture capital funds, it did not raise this funding and subsequently went into administration.

© Getty Images/Pinkypills

Entrepreneurship in Action

- If your gross profits are low, what are your strategies for making it higher?
- Work out your BEP. How can you improve it?
- How long is your estimated journey through your 'valley of death'?

○ *Go to Exercise W 2.19: What does your start-up lack?*

8.4 CASH IS KING

Although profitability is core to business growth, it is not pivotal to survival. Many start-ups fail to reach break-even in their first years. Post-start-up, both Amazon and Tesla took quite a few years to make any sort of profit.[5] Similarly, profitable businesses often go out of business.

A main reason is that they simply run out of cash. If a start-up cannot pay its bills, it is likely to be heading towards the cemetery. Equally, if the start-up is undercapitalised, there might not be enough cash available to fund its activities through the 'valley of death'. All businesses face difficulties if there are timing differences between when cash comes in and when it goes out. If a company gives its customers 90-day payment terms, it can mean waiting three months for the money to come into the business. In the meantime, bills still have to be paid, and if these are not paid, it can mean going out of business.

Case Study: Growing but going bust?

A common business pitfall is overtrading. It occurs when a company has invoiced sales (money not yet paid into the business) but cannot fulfil them because they lack the cash to pay suppliers or workers.

Suppose a start-up wins a large contract to make and supply halal certified cosmetics to a store in Oman with payment terms of 90 days after delivery. It also agrees to have the first order ready to ship to the customer by the end of Month 2, with payment due at the end of Month 5 (90 days). It orders ingredients from its suppliers, who ship them immediately but require payment in 60 days (end of Month 3). This big order means now having to pay for extra staff, equipment and storage space. The start-up goes to the bank and arranges an overdraft.

By month 4, the start-up has reached its overdraft limit and has run out of cash to pay its workers and suppliers. At the start of Month 5, the customer tells the start-up they will be paying late. The start-up's bank refuses to pay the bills, the workers leave threatening to take the company to court and the suppliers stop shipping ingredients and begin legal action. The founders have no choice but to close the business. They blame the bank but ignore the fact they were unable to adequately manage their cash flow.

8.4.1 The cash flow statement

To assess cash flow issues, the solution is a cash flow statement. For a given period, it records when cash came in, when it went out and what is left over. Since cash is king, the common practice is to do a month-by-month cash flow statement for the first year. It is also advisable for later years and can be complemented by best, expected and worst-case cash flow scenarios.

A cash flow statement consists of the following simple equation (Figure 8.5): The cash flow statement differs from the P&L in a number of ways:

1. Depreciation/amortisation is not included in the cash flow. Both are non-cash items that simply account for the lifetime of an asset. These are accounted for in the P&L (pp. 194–197).
2. Capital introduced such as founder's own savings, bank loan and equity investment is included in the cash flow because it is money put into the business. It is not included in the P&L because the P&L measures revenue performance.

Figure 8.5 Cash flow statement equation

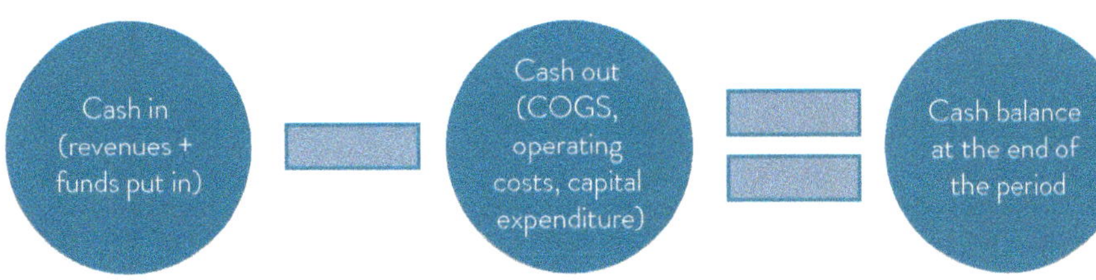

3. Both sales and costs in the cash flow are entered when they are paid. This differs from the P&L, where a sale may only be recorded when goods or services are delivered and money is collected. This accrual accounting ensures that the P&L accurately reflects the revenue flows in the business. It ties together the sale with the activities that lead to the sale (expenses). So a sale might be only recorded when goods are delivered and when the money is collected. To make sure revenues are tied together with their relevant costs, provisions are made in the P&L to account for expenses incurred but not yet paid for. The practical implication is that cash flow statements often appear more 'lumpy' than P&L statements. This reflects timing differences.

Case Study: Cooking the books

One way of abusing accrual accounting is to break the link between expenses and sales. A company called Sunbeam, which made kitchen appliances, did this by placing expenses occurring in one year into a different financial year. This reduced their cost base, making them look more profitable than they actually were. Sunbeam also operated a book and pay revenue system. This meant that customers could book a Sunbeam product and pay for it later. This is legal. What is illegal is treating these bookings as actual sales.[6]

To illustrate these differences, Table 8.5 shows an abbreviated P&L statement for the first year of a model start-up. It shows that from revenues of 160,000, gross profits were 100,000. Total fixed costs were 93,000, leaving an operating profit (EBIDTA) of 7000.

Out of this operating profit, there is no interest to be paid on any loans, and the start-up has no intangible assets such as patents or trademarks but has purchased capital equipment worth 25,000. This does not appear in the P&L because the P&L records revenues. Instead, because it is a cash expenditure, it appears in the cash flow statement (Table 8.6).

However, because this capital equipment has a finite use, the fact that it will lose value over time is accounted for in the P&L. Using the straight-line method of depreciation (p. 195), Table 8.5 shows that the annual depreciation is 2250 ((25,000(cost of capital equipment) – 2500 (salvage price))/10 years (lifespan of asset)).

The model start-up ends the year with a pre-tax profit of 4750.

Table 8.5 First-year model start-up P&L

	Amount
Revenues	160,000
Cost Of Goods Sold (COGS)	-60,000
Gross Profits	100,000
Total sales and marketing costs	-30,000
Total general and administrative costs	-28,000
Total personnel costs	-24,000
Total product development costs	-11,000
Total fixed costs	-93,000
Operating profit (EBITDA)	7000

Interest	
Depreciation	-2250
Amortisation	
Net profit before tax	4750

8.4.2 Cash going into the business

The cash flow statement for this model start-up shows a radically different picture (Table 8.6). It first records the introduction of 70,000. This capital introduced is the amount of money invested by the business owners. Next it shows revenues. Revenues do not occur immediately because it takes time for the start-up to build up its organisational capacities and to get sales from its customers. **Capital introduced + revenues = total cash flows in.**

8

8.4.3 Cash going out

For money going out, Table 8.6 first shows that there are no COGS (variable costs) initially but these ramp up as production begins. Nonetheless, it does face a range of fixed costs. It also incurs capital expenditure. Like the fixed R&D costs (product development costs), this money is unevenly spent. **COGS+ fixed costs + capital expenditure = total cash flows out.**

Table 8.6 demonstrates the lumpy nature of the cash flow: rent is paid quarterly, product development expenses are incurred in the early months and marketing costs ramp up later in the year as the business gets ready for sales. COGS also show that the supplier gets paid before sales are made and revenues only appear after the start-up has made sales.

Although the P&L showed that this sample start-up made a small profit of 4750, the business is actually in deep trouble. Despite a 70,000 cash injection, by month 7 it has run out of money and has a negative cash balance of –9000. Failure looms. The cash flow projection shows month 8 is worse: it will have a negative cash balance of –32,000. Although it will be cash flow positive (have greater amounts of money coming in than going out per month) by year end, if it cannot get more cash into the business to trade through its cash deficit, the business is unlikely to survive.

8.4.4 Managing cash flow

To resolve its cash flow issues, the business has a variety of options:

1. **Introduce more capital into the business.**
2. **Reduce the cash 'burn rate' by improving cash management.** The cash 'burn' rate is the rate per month at which a business uses up its cash reserves. To reduce it, a business may try to increase sales or cut its variable and fixed costs. Ways of doing this include being shy about giving credit, keeping stock levels as lean as possible, collecting money from sales as quickly as possible and deferring capital expenditure until cash flows improve.
3. **Ask suppliers for more time to pay.** This can lead to creditor strain: suppliers, if they have to wait for too long for their money, might decide to stop supplying the start-up, creating further problems for the business.

Cash flow statements are essential. They show when a business will reach cash flow positive, help with monitoring the cash burn rate and are pivotal in addressing over-spending.

Table 8.6 Model start-up month-by-month first-year cash flow statement

	1	2	3	4	5	6	7	8	9	10	11	12	Totals
Cash in:													
Capital introduced	70,000	–	–	–	–	–	–	–	–	–	–	–	70,000
Revenues	–	–	–	–	–	–	–	–	40,000	40,000	40,000	40,000	160,000
Total cash flow in	70,000	0	0	0	0	0	0	0	40,000	40,000	40,000	40,000	230,000
Cash out:													
COGS	–	–	–	–	–	–	−10,000	−10,000	−10,000	−10,000	−10,000	-10,000	-60,000
Fixed costs:	–	–	–	–	–	–	–	–	–	–	–	–	–
Total sales and marketing costs	–	–	–	–	–	–	–	−10,000	-5000	-5000	-5000	-5000	-30,000
Total general and administrative costs	-5000	-1000	-1000	-5000	-1000	-1000	-5000	-1000	-1000	-5000	-1000	-1000	-28,000
Total personnel costs	-2000	-2000	-2000	-2000	-2000	-2000	-2000	-2000	-2000	-2000	-2000	-2000	-24,000
Total product development costs	-3000	-4000	-4000	–	–	–	–	–	–	–	–	–	-11,000
Capital expenditure	−10,000	–	–	−15,000	–	–	–	–	–	–	–	–	-25,000
Total cash flow out	-20,000	-7000	-7000	-22,000	-3000	-3000	-17,000	-23,000	-18,000	-22,000	-18,000	-18,000	-178,000
Starting cash balance	70,000	50,000	43,000	36,000	14,000	11,000	8000	-9000	-32,000	-10,000	8000	30,000	0
Monthly net cash flow	50,000	-7000	-7000	-22,000	-3000	-3000	-17,000	-23,000	22,000	18,000	22,000	22,000	52,000
Ending cash balance	50,000	43,000	36,000	14,000	11,000	8000	-9000	-32,000	-10,000	8000	30,000	52,000	52,000

Case Study: Burn baby burn

The Swedes, Ernst Malmsten and Kajsa Leander, set up boo.com to provide online shopping. It went bust after burning through $135 million in 18 months ($7.5 million a month) as it expanded from one office with 40 employees to eight offices with 400 employees. The Israeli, Shai Agassi, set up Better Place to install electric car charging points across Israel. He raised around $850 million. The cash burn rate was around $500,000 a day. Eventually, the cash dried up and Better Place went bankrupt.[7]

Entrepreneurship in Action

- Construct a first-year month-by-month cash flow statement.
- Build scenarios and estimate year 2 and beyond cash flow statements.
- Identify when your start-up gets to cash flow positive.
- What is your cash burn rate?
- What strategies are in place to make sure that the business will reach cash flow positive as soon as possible?

○ *Go to Exercise W 2.22: Is your start-up viable?*

8.5 THE BALANCE SHEET

The balance sheet is the final part of the holy trinity of financial projections. It is a snapshot of three elements: what the company owns (assets), what it owes (liabilities) and how much it is worth (owner's equity) for a given day. Assets include money that the business has, its stock, any physical assets such as machinery and buildings, and intangible assets such as patents or trademarks. Liabilities are, for example, money it owes to suppliers and loans it has made, while equity consists of what shareholders have put into the business and the earnings it has retained in the business.

The balance sheet must always balance what its assets are (use of funds) with where it got its funds from (liabilities and owner's equity). It follows this formula: **assets = liabilities + owner's equity** (Figure 8.6).

Figure 8.6 Balance sheet equation

8.5.1 Assets on the balance sheet

Assets are divided into two groups: current assets (assets that are either cash or can be converted to cash within a year) and fixed assets (assets that usually take more than a year to convert into cash). Table 8.7 shows the model start-up has total current assets of 52,000. This consists of 'cash in hand'. Other businesses, though, may have other current assets such as stock (finished goods) or Work In Progress (WIP), which are also called inventories. Table 8.7 also shows there are no customers who owe payment for a good or service. This means that there are no debtors (accounts receivable). **Cash in hand + stock + work in progress = total current assets.**

The first-year cash flow statement showed (Table 8.6) that the model start-up spent 25,000 on physical fixed assets (10,000 in month 1 and 15,000 in month 4). Similarly, the P&L (Table 8.5) showed that the annual depreciation was 2250. In the balance sheet (Table 8.7), these two figures come together to give a total for the fixed assets of 22,750 (25,000–2250). Subsequently, the total assets in the business are 74,750. **Total assets = current + fixed assets.**

Table 8.7 Model start-up first-year balance sheet

Current assets			
Cash in hand	52,000	Current liabilities	0
Stock and Work in Progress			
Debtors		Long-term liabilities	0
Total current assets	52,000	*Total liabilities*	0
		Owner's equity	
Fixed assets		Capital introduced (information from cash flow)	70,000
Property, plant & equipment (cash flow information)	25,000	Profits (retained earnings: information from P&L)	4750
Accumulated depreciation (P&L information)	-2250	*Total equity*	74,750
Total fixed assets	22,750		
Total assets	74,750	*Total liabilities and owner's equity*	74,750

8.5.2 Liabilities on the balance sheet

The model start-up does not owe any money. It has no current liabilities such as creditors (accounts payable to suppliers it owes money to). Nor does it have directors' loans or other short-term liabilities that are payable within a year. It also has no liabilities to long term creditors. Therefore, its total liabilities are zero. **Current liabilities + long-term liabilities = total liabilities.**

8.5.3 Owner's equity on the balance sheet

Owner's equity is the sum of capital invested, such as cash or shares, plus its profit and loss. The model start-up's cash flow statement (Table 8.6) showed a capital injection of 70,000, while the P&L (Table 8.5) recorded a small profit (retained earnings) of 4750. **Capital + retained earnings = owner's equity.**

The balance sheet (Table 8.7) shows that the sum of its liabilities and owner's equity is 74,750, which is equal to its assets. **Assets = liabilities + owner's equity**.

However, the cash flow statement (Table 8.5) showed that the start-up had a cash deficit in month 8 of 32,000. Because cash is king, this deficit could spell the end of the start-up. Realising this, the founder asks their mother for a loan. She agrees to lend the founder 32,000, charges no interest and asks for no equity in the business. This long-term loan (money due after 12 months) increases the model start-up's cash in hand to 84,000 by year end. Table 8.8 shows the revised balance sheet for year 1.

Table 8.8 Model start-up first-year balance sheet with the extra 32,000 loan

Assets		Liabilities and shareholders' equity	
Current assets (cash in hand)	84,000	Current liabilities	0
Fixed assets (book value)	22,750	Long-term liabilities	32,000
		Total liabilities	*32,000*
		Owner's equity	
		Capital	70,000
		Retained earnings	4750
		Total equity	*74,750*
Total assets	*106,750*	*Total liabilities and owner's equity*	*106,750*

In line with the P&L and cash flow projections, entrepreneurs may develop balance sheets for subsequent years.

8.5.4 Gearing on the balance sheet

Balance sheets show founders how much of their funding comes from long-term liabilities such as loans, how much equity they have in the business and how the two compare. This is known as 'gearing'. Table 8.8 shows the model start-up has a gearing of 45.7 per cent ((32,000/70000) × 100). Its debts (32,000) are nearly half of its capital (70,000). This looks high, and a bank may be wary of lending to the business. If banks decide the business is over-geared and too reliant on outside loans, it could also reduce its existing borrowing, forcing the start-up to find money elsewhere or close.

8.5.5 Working capital on the balance sheet

Many start-ups, particularly if they are involved in producing goods, have high percentages of their turnover locked up in debtors, their stock and work in progress. These all impact on the money to fund day-to-day activities or their working capital.

The current ratio (current assets/current liabilities) can help a business assess whether it has enough money to pay its bills. A business with 50,000 current assets and 40,000 current liabilities has a current ratio of 1.25 (50,000/40,000). Depending on the industry, this might be high. Important too is the direction of travel. Investors like to see the current ratio decline over time.

There are other ways founders can better manage their finances. Calculating stock holding days ((stocks/COGS) × 365) assesses how much a business has tied up in stock whilst working out how long customers take to pay you (debtor days = (debtors/revenues) × 365)) also helps increase working capital.

Entrepreneurship in Action

- Build your balance sheet for year 1.
- Construct a balance sheet for subsequent years.
- How 'geared' is your business?

8.6 WHAT YOU HAVE LEARNED IN THIS CHAPTER

You have learned how financial information practically aids your start-up planning. In particular, it helps assess the final three start-up questions (Workbook 2):

- What is the plan for growth?
- What does the start-up lack?
- Is the start-up viable?

However, financial information has wider implications. You have seen that developing revenue and cost models gives you a strong sense of what the options are for start-up growth and development. Similarly, you should now understand how the 'holy trinity' of financial statements – the P&L, cash flow and balance sheet – are useful in holding up a mirror to start-up assumptions.

In Chapter 9, you will be shown the four main sources of external funding for smaller businesses. But you will also learn that getting money to support a business can be difficult.

However you put these elements together, the end point should be that it gives you a narrative – captured *eventually* by a business plan – that explains where the business concept is now, where it wants to get to and how it is going to get there.

Notes

1 www.stat.ee/households.
2 www.surveysystem.com/sscalc.htm.
3 www.youtube.com/watch?v=OlBDyItD0Ak.
4 Source adapted from: *www.sec.gov/Archives/edgar/data/1511683/000104746911003874/a2203517zf-1.htm#dk41101_our_history_and_corporate_structure.*
5 www.inc.com/drew-hendricks/5-successful-companies-that-didn-8217-t-make-a-dollar-for-5-years.html.
6 www.nytimes.com/2001/05/16/business/sec-accuses-former-sunbeam-official-of-fraud.html.
7 www.fastcompany.com/3028159/a-broken-place-better-place.

CHAPTER 9

Entrepreneurial Finance

Learning Outcomes

In this chapter, you will learn:

- The sources of finance that are available to entrepreneurs.
- Why there are particular usage patterns in entrepreneurial finance.
- Why some businesses face financial constraints.
- How banks, business angels, venture capitalists and crowdfunders can support entrepreneurs.

Mini Contents List

9.1 INTRODUCTION

If the entrepreneur is the heart and brains of a start-up, finance is its life-blood. In Uganda, a randomly controlled trial gave some unemployed people $382 to set up in business while others got nothing.[1] After four years, those who had received the money earned more and had greater business assets than those who were not given the money.

A lack of finance can also constrain business growth by around 10 per cent.[2]

As this chapter shows you, entrepreneurs – in theory – have a wide range of entrepreneurial finance available to meet their start-up and growth needs but – in practice – often make very limited use of different funding sources. Similarly, you will see that some entrepreneurs face potential financial constraints.

You will also learn how four sources of external finance – banks, business angels, venture capitalists and crowdfunders – are all likely audiences for pitch decks and plans and that each have their own individual needs and aspirations. As you will see, being sensitive to these differences is crucial, particularly for working out who to ask, how much to ask and what is expected in terms of a return on this investment.

9.2 THE SOURCES OF ENTREPRENEURIAL FINANCE

Businesses require two basic forms of finance. The first is to fund short-term operational needs such as paying suppliers or employee salaries. This is called 'working capital'. The second form of finance is investment capital. Businesses need medium-and longer-term investment capital to fund the purchase of a one-off physical asset such as a car or machinery. It can also fund breaking into a new market, marketing and sales development, supporting research and development, gearing up to product launch or the hiring and training of new staff.

Funding, in theory, can either come from insider or external sources. Insider finance relates to the finance that is available to the business from the entrepreneur, their family or friends and from within the business. Entrepreneurs might fund their working and investment capital needs through their own personal savings and funding from a personal credit card or a personal bank loan. They may also turn to their family or friends to give them money, such as gifts or loans. Once a business has profits – instead of paying shareholders a share of these profits (dividends) or the entrepreneur taking money out of the business (drawings) – the entrepreneur might keep the profits in the business to fund their present and future finance needs. These retained earnings come from sales to customers. This is an extremely valuable source of funding because the business is not reliant on others to support the business.

Beyond insider financing, there exists a wide range of external sources of finance:

- **Public funders**: local, regional and national governments provide grants, 'soft' loans (repayable but often at interest rates below commercial rates), loan guarantees (guarantee by a public body to underwrite the whole or a proportion of a commercial loan if the borrower defaults) and equity finance. Many governments provide loan guarantees to encourage banks to lend to businesses without a track record (pre-revenue) or that have no collateral. Loan guarantees are not free: in borrowing money from the bank, the business still has to show to the bank that it can afford to pay back the loan. In general, governments provide finance because they want to stimulate particular policy objectives such as promoting growth or helping disadvantaged groups to take up entrepreneurship (Chapter 12, p. 305). Sources of such funding are available on government websites.

- **Banks** (pp. 224–225): typically provide overdrafts, business credit cards and loans. Credit cards can be an expensive form of finance. Like overdrafts, they mainly fund working capital needs. A loan is usually for a set period (a term loan) and is typically for funding business investment. A term loan involves paying back the amount borrowed (capital) plus interest.
- **Crowdfunders** (pp. 233–234): are a large group of people (the 'crowd') who agree to fund the entrepreneur. The crowd generally find about the entrepreneur's funding campaign via a crowdfunding platform that usually takes a payment for hosting the crowdfunding campaign. There are different types of crowdfunding: donations, rewards, loans and equity-based funding.
- **Asset financiers:** support the purchasing of fixed assets such as plants and machinery. Businesses can choose to hire purchase or lease the asset. In hire purchasing, the company pays an initial deposit, followed by regular payments until they pay off the whole amount and they own the asset. Leasing follows the same process, but at the end of the term, ownership reverts to the original provider of the asset.
- **Trade creditors:** suppliers agree to supply a good or service on account and ask for payment at a specified later date.
- **Factors and invoice discounters**: Factors buy a company's invoiced but not yet paid sales in return for a proportion of these yet unpaid invoices. Invoice discounters lend against unpaid invoices in exchange for a proportion of their value. Businesses need to have revenues to use both factors and invoice discounters.
- **Equity funders:** exchange shares in a business for cash. For example, a founder can offer 10 per cent of their company in return for an investment of $250,000. There are two main types of equity providers:

    1. Business angels (pp. 225–229): usually high net worth individuals or groups that come together to purchase a share in a business in exchange for investment in the business. Their hope is to, later on, sell their share of the business at a price much greater than they originally paid for it (a capital gain).
    2. Venture capitalists (pp. 229–233): financial intermediaries who set up a fund and seek to use the monies in the fund to buy shares in businesses with, again, the hope of later on selling their share for a capital gain.

9

Entrepreneurship in Action

- Use your financial forecasts (Chapter 8) to identify if your business faces a funding gap.
- If so, evaluate what type of funding (working and/or investment capital) you need for your business.
- If there is a gap, how much of your savings are you prepared to invest in your business?
- Can you access other sources of personal finance? Will family and friends offer you financial support?
- If you need external finance, which source is the most attractive?

9.3 DEMAND AND SUPPLY ISSUES IN ENTREPRENEURIAL FINANCE

Although, in theory, start-ups can access different sources of external finance, the reality is that 95 per cent of business founders around the world use their own funds to finance their new venture, and these savings account for 72 per cent of their total funding.[3] The next most common source of funding is from family and friends while the most likely source of external funding is bank finance.

As Figure 9.1 illustrates, these patterns hold true for start-ups in India, China and the United Kingdom (UK). Elsewhere, in countries such as the United States (USA), insider financing is the norm and external finance typically comes from a bank in the form of credit cards, loans or overdraft facilities.[4]

Figure 9.1 Sources of start-up finance for start-ups in India, China and the UK

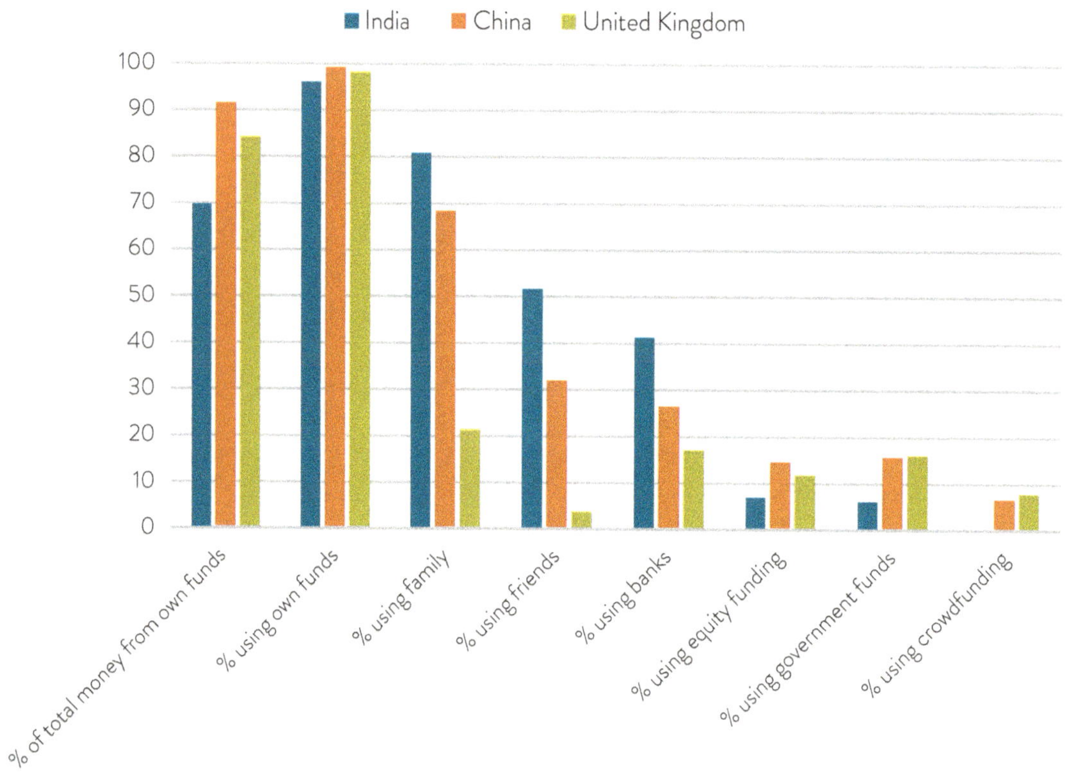

Source: GEM (2016)

Bank funding often requires personal guarantees and securities against assets such as an entrepreneur's home. Bank funding is, therefore, often tied to the creditworthiness of the start-up founder. Relatively few start-ups access equity funding, but when they do, this often makes a sizeable contribution to their overall financing.[5]

Figure 9.2 shows bank overdrafts and trade credit are among the most common sources of non-personal finance for existing businesses. This suggests that they use these facilities to address their working capital needs, such as plugging a hole in their cash flow or by providing a safety net.[6] Credit cards are the most frequently used source of external capital, despite their high-interest charges making them one of the most expensive forms of finance for start-ups and small businesses.

Figure 9.2 Sources of finance used in existing small businesses

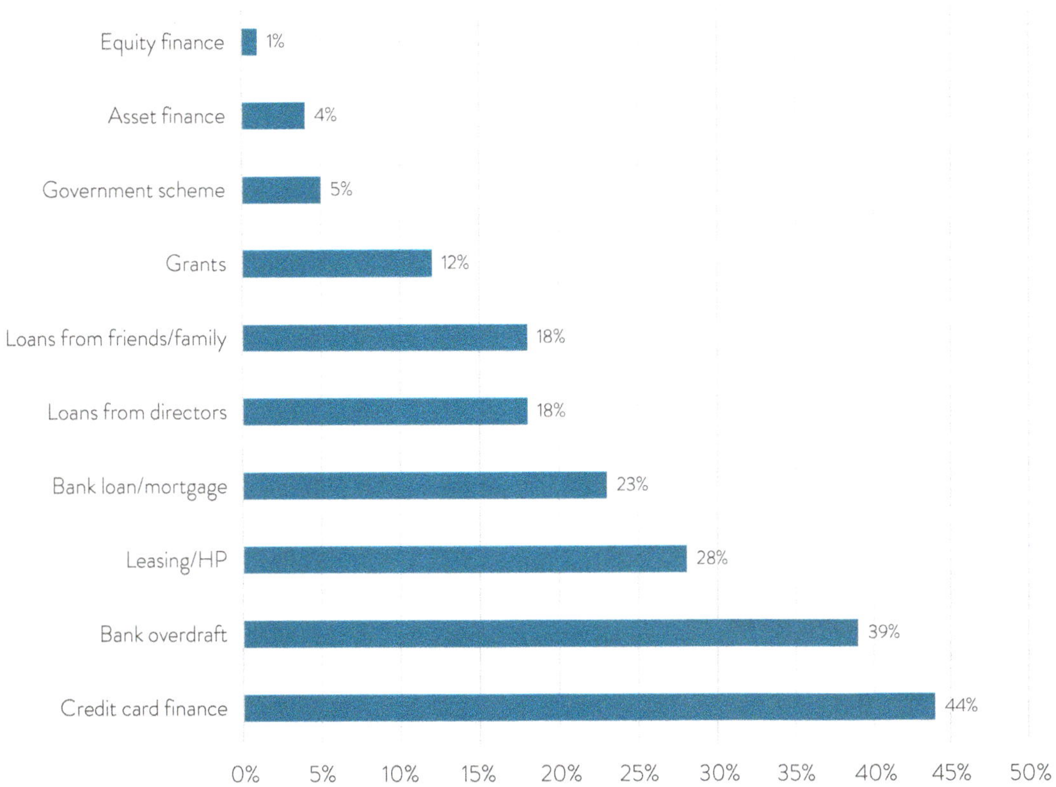

Source: Ipsos MORI (2017)

If they need investment capital, established small businesses use debt finance such as bank loans and internally funded loans from their directors or family. Few of these business use equity funders such as business angels, venture capitalists or crowdfunding finance from peer to peer (P2P) lending.

Discussion question:

- If credit cards are so expensive, why do so many existing businesses use them?

9.3.1 *The 'pecking order' preferences of entrepreneurs*

Part of the explanation for these usage patterns is the preferences of entrepreneurs. The pecking order theory of finance argues that even if different sources of money are priced identically, entrepreneurs prefer to first use their own money to fund their business.[7] Only when these personal sources and other forms of insider financing are exhausted, do start-ups turn to external finance. The pecking order theory also predicts that if a small business has to choose between external debt and equity, their choice is for debt finance.

These preferences stem from a desire for control of the business. Using existing resources involves no outsider involvement in decision-making. Debt finance is preferable to equity finance because so long as the business pays back the capital plus interest from the loan, it is theoretically free to run its own affairs. In contrast, equity finance involves ceding some or all of the control of the business to outside investors.

In practice, this means that when faced with the choice of taking on debt or finding imaginative ways of using resources, start-ups prefer to rely on a strategy of using their own money, borrowing instead of buying and begging what cannot be borrowed. Such bootstrapping involves the use of creative tactics to reduce costs and inhibit risks, such as delaying payments to suppliers, drawing on favours and borrowing equipment.[8]

Established small businesses also prefer internal over external finance. Many existing businesses decide *never* to borrow or to raise equity to fund their business. In the UK around 50 per cent of small businesses can be classed as permanent non-borrowers because they have not used external finance in the last five years.[9]

Such tactics also apply to growing businesses. Like established businesses, they prefer to use retained earnings rather than debt or equity finance.[10] They also often prefer to stay in control and stay the same size than use outside equity finance to fund business growth. In essence, they prefer to be the 'king' or 'queen' of their business even if it means missing out on being rich.[11]

Case Study: Heel the World

Fred Deegbe was fed up working for the Bank of Africa in Ghana. He wanted to set up his own business, producing hand-made shoes using skilled Ghanaian workers. His dream was to take on the existing big players in Europe and North America.

He used his own savings to start Heel the World in his spare time, running the business and sourcing workers, material and equipment while still working at the bank. Fred found it difficult to convince suppliers and investors to believe quality hand-made shoes could be made in Ghana. He was also embarrassed to tell his parents in case they thought he was crazy. Sales eventually picked up and he resigned from the bank. But instead of using his success to seek finance to expand, he decided to bootstrap the business by continuing to work out of his garage.[12]

Discussion questions:

- What are the implications of the pecking order theory on the demand for entrepreneurial finance?
- What should governments do – if anything – to promote start-ups, existing and growing businesses to switch towards debt and equity funding?

Entrepreneurship in Action

- Who can you beg and borrow from to develop your business?
- Are you willing to trade control of your business for external funding?
- What percentage share of your business would you be willing to give up to an equity investor to resolve your funding gap?

9.3.2 Information opacity

Managers of large corporates have to provide regular financial performance updates to the owners of the business. This partly reflects that the managers are essentially agents who work for the owners or principals of the business. It also reflects that owners or principals also want to know how well the management is performing. So, every year, large business managers report annual accounts. This is backed up by quarterly updates. Such information is often pored over by the media to identify how well or badly the business is doing. Sharing this information helps to address the principal-agent problem by giving shareholders (principals) the ability to monitor and hold management (agents) to account if they fail to act in their best interests.

In a start-up, this clarity is missing. Start-ups are informationally opaque.[13] At start-up, all the financier (principal) has is a sketchy plan that optimistically promises great revenues, low costs and huge margins. There are no accounts. There may be no revenues. It is unlikely that there are any tradable shares. Start-ups are also more likely to fail (Chapter 11, pp. 285–286). And without assets such as the entrepreneur's own home being available as collateral, debt financiers will worry that the start-up will default on paying back any funding given to the entrepreneur.

Alongside pecking order theory, the information opacity of start-ups helps explain why start-ups are so reliant on insider finance for their funding needs.

Assessment tip: Being less opaque

Academic writing can be dense, convoluted and full of jargon. One way of making your work easier to read is to make use of active rather than passive sentences. Active sentences introduce the person or thing responsible for an action at the start: 'Antonio Meucci was the first inventor of the telephone.' In a passive sentence, the person or thing responsible for the action comes towards the end: 'The telephone was first invented by Antonio Meucci.'

There is nothing wrong with passive sentences. Active sentences, though, are generally easier to read. Proofing tools in Microsoft Word (click on File, Options, Proofing) can identify if you are using active or passive sentences. Another way is to use specialist grammar packages to edit and review the readability of your writing. In going through your work, be brutal and remove unnecessary words.

Information, however, improves once the business posts some revenues. Having accounts helps. As time goes by, and as the business develops, it also becomes easier to identify what the business' growth trajectory, credit and risk profile are and for trust to develop between the financier and the small business.

Better information reduces information asymmetries between the financier (principal) and the small business (agent). These asymmetries come in two forms: adverse selection and moral hazard.

9.3.3 Adverse selection

This occurs when one party (the entrepreneur) has more information than another (the financier) *before* a deal is struck. Because of adverse selection, a financier might be nervous that the entrepreneur is hiding important information, much like a smoker seeking health insurance despite smoking 40 cigarettes a day.

To avoid this, the financier aims to separate out the good from the bad business through due diligence. Banks use credit scoring systems. These rely on a computer-generated credit profile that allocates points for particular attributes such as prior credit history. If the number of points (credit score) is greater than a particular threshold, the bank might decide that this 'hard' quantitative information on *prior* creditworthiness is a good indicator of *future* creditworthiness. The use of credit scoring is common.[14] These credit scores do not use gender and racial attributes in their scoring.

Beyond this, the bank offering a loan, the supplier providing trade credit or the equity funder might collect other 'hard' information from management accounts and business plans.[15] Complementing this is the collection of 'soft' information gained from taking time to develop a relationship with the entrepreneur. This 'relationship-based lending' can reduce the need for collateral, improve the prospects of getting finance and reduce interest rates costs.[16]

As Table 9.1 shows, one consequence of better information is that size (and age) matters.[17] Bigger businesses make more use of all types of external finance. Because they have a track record with suppliers, they make greater use of trade credit and have multiple sources of finance (Table 9.1: two

Table 9.1 Percentage use of external sources of finance[21]

	All SMEs	0 Employees	1–9 Employees	10–49 Employees	50–249 Employees
Currently use external finance[22]	38	33	50	64	74
Bank overdraft	17	15	21	23	27
Credit card	18	16	21	32	44
Bank loan	5	4	7	11	17
Leasing/hire purchase	8	6	11	21	25
Loans from directors, family and friends	5	4	7	6	4
Equity from directors, family and friends	2	2	2	3	4
Invoice finance	4	3	4	11	15
Grants	3	2	3	5	7
Trade credit[23]	35	30	48	66	71
Use two sources of finance[24]	10	9	13	17	21
Personal funds[25]	28	31	25	13	8
Permanent non-borrowers[26]	46	51	36	27	20

sources of finance).[18] Equally, bigger businesses are more likely to apply for finance, are confident about getting finance and ask for greater loan amounts. In contrast, more informationally opaque smaller (and younger) businesses rely more on personal funds and are more likely to be 'permanent non-borrowers' (have not sought external finance in the last five years).

9.3.4 Moral hazard

Financiers also worry about the second form of information asymmetry: moral hazard. This occurs *after* a deal is struck, usually because the financier (the principal) has failed to anticipate a change in the agent's (entrepreneur) behaviour. This happens because entrepreneurial motives are opaque and the financier cannot easily set expectations about future performance. Besides collecting information, debt providers attempt to resolve moral hazard issues by requiring security (collateral such as taking a personal guarantee on an entrepreneur's property). Asking entrepreneurs to put their own money and assets into the business (what is called 'skin in the game') is quite common: in Italy, between 55 and 83 per cent of bank loans are collateralised.[19]

Moral hazard is a particular worry for equity funders. After having conducted due diligence (controlling for adverse selection), they might find that the entrepreneur behaves differently once they have given them funding. One scenario is a growth-orientated start-up entrepreneur who has had a bare income and worked long hours to get their business off the ground. Once the equity financier gives them a substantial sum to continue to build the business, the entrepreneur might instead decide to 'work at home' and explore 'investment opportunities' in hot sandy places next to the sea.[20] This is even more likely if the equity funding is large. Venture capitalists typically offer around $2 million for a promising start-up, and this rises with successive funding rounds: the average first round of venture capital funding (sometimes called Series A) is $12 million, with this rising to $32 million (Series B), $41 million (Series C) and $98 million (Series D and beyond).[27]

At start-up, therefore, insider finance is the staple, complemented by limited amounts of public funding, crowdfunding or business angel finance (Figure 9.3). Once a business has revenues, additional sources such as bank debt finance may become more available. A post-revenue business with potential for fast growth may also gain venture capital equity funding.

Figure 9.3 Patterns in entrepreneurial finance

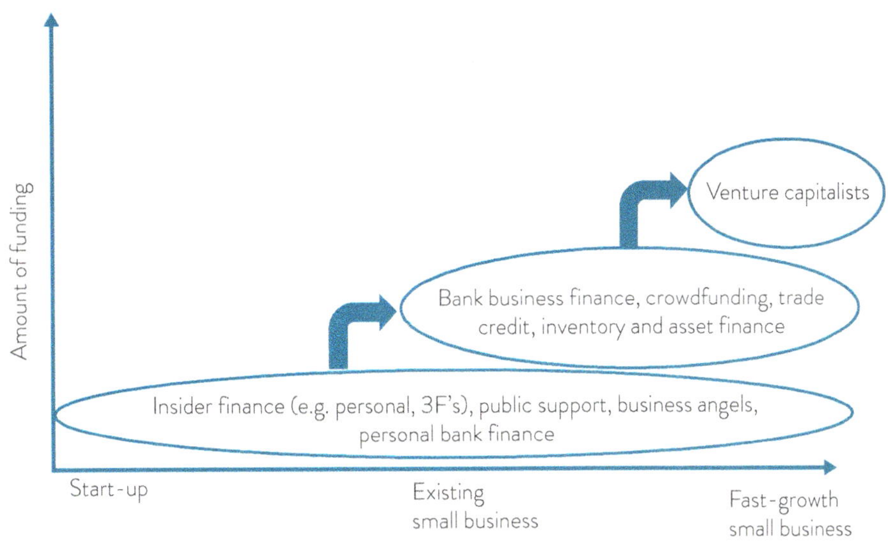

Case Study: Funding Fetchr

© Getty Images

One of the problems faced by logistics companies in the Middle East is that in densely populated areas many households lack a clear address. This makes fast, efficient and reliable 'last mile' delivery to these customers difficult. In response, Idriss Al Rifai set up Fetchr to deliver goods to customers using the GPS system on their smartphones.

But to get this disruptive idea off the ground, he needed money. He used his own savings, his wife's savings and borrowed from his mother and friends. He also went to business angels. It was still not enough. He managed to raise $600,000 but still needed another $600,000 to move Fetchr from pre-revenue to actually making sales.

So he went to a venture capitalist to raise the $600,000 of funding. The venture capitalist agreed to fund Fetchr but then at the last moment pulled out. Al Rifai was forced to take out loans just to pay himself and his employees. Eventually, he managed to close his 'seed' round of $1.2 million.

The next challenge was to raise further funding to begin to grow the business. He could not find this in the Middle East, so he went to Silicon Valley in California, where he raised $11 million (Series A funding). Subsequently, to drive international expansion across the Middle East he raised another $41 million (Series B funding).[28]

Entrepreneurship in Action

- Find out your credit score. Investigate ways in which you can improve it.
- What collateral do you have? Would you be willing to offer it as a security against investment?
- What would you do if you were given a $2 million investment in your business?

Discussion questions:

- How well does information opacity explain the market for entrepreneurial finance?
- Do you think that there are finance gaps in the provision of finance to small businesses? Do you think your government should intervene?

9.4 FINANCIAL CONSTRAINTS FACING SMALL BUSINESSES: TIES THAT BIND?

Some entrepreneurs fail to get the finance they need or can only obtain lower amounts. These financial constraints have four main consequences.

1. **It prevents talented but poor individuals from becoming entrepreneurs.**[29] Those with high entrepreneurial ability and independent wealth are more likely to get funding for their start-up. In contrast, highly talented but poor individuals are more likely to struggle to raise outside finance. This acts as a barrier to start up for poorer people and consequently chokes off entrepreneurship in society as a whole.
2. **Start-ups are under-capitalised.** In the USA, 25 per cent of new businesses begin with no start-up capital at all, while 40 per cent are started with less than $5000.[30] Women are also more reliant at start-up on internal finance than men and use about half as much external capital as men.[31] This pattern continues as the business gets older: women entrepreneurs typically use about half the external finance of men in established businesses.[32]
3. **Business costs increase.** As the banking industry has become more concentrated, financial constraints have increased for start-ups and established businesses.[33] This is particularly true in poorer countries.[34] The fear of being rejected can also be enough to discourage some businesses from applying for finance, even if they are creditworthy. The number of these 'discouraged borrowers' varies across the economic cycle and between countries but is more common among younger and smaller businesses.[35] This can lead businesses to make suboptimal investment decisions, which can cause weaker wealth and job creation.[36]
4. **Business growth is restricted and productivity falls.**[37] Many otherwise fast-growing businesses experience 'equity funding gaps', which can restrict them from growing to their potential.[38]

There is competing evidence about whether the financial constraints faced by some entrepreneurs are ties that bind. For minorities in the USA, discrimination appears to stymie the development of an opportunity-based society. In other countries, the temptation is to point to the oligopolistic market structure of banking as being behind the difficulties start-ups face in getting finance and for the existence of discouraged borrowers and equity gaps.

Academic insight: Ethnic minority discrimination in bank lending

The existence of discouraged borrowers hints at a far more pernicious problem: discrimination. Discrimination occurs when some individuals hold a prejudicial 'taste' against individuals or groups in society. In the USA, the average level of start-up capital among American blacks ($35,205) is much less than it is for American whites ($106,720).[39] Even after controlling for differences in personal and business characteristics, American blacks have lower capital levels and are less likely to get appropriate bank funding than American whites. American Hispanics also suffer similar discrimination.[40]

The evidence for ethnic discrimination in other countries is less clear. In Trinidad and Tobago, Zimbabwe and Sweden, minority-owned businesses have higher rejection rates when they apply for bank loans.[41] However, other evidence suggests that it is not ethnicity that matters but other factors such as business characteristics.[42]

The alternative argument is that the market for entrepreneurial finance is healthy: in some richer countries such as the UK about 80 per cent of small businesses get the overdraft they want from their bank and around 70 per cent get a business bank loan.[43] This is despite smaller businesses being more likely to fail and being more informationally opaque.

It is also too easy to concentrate just on the *supply* of entrepreneurial finance. On the *demand* side, small businesses are reluctant to use outside finance. Many discouraged borrowers – who are usually riskier businesses – often efficiently self-ration themselves because they realise that they are unlikely to get funding.[44] Some growth-orientated businesses do not get equity funding because they are not 'investment ready'.[45]

Discussion questions:

- What should the USA government do to address discrimination in bank lending?
- Does the market for entrepreneurial finance work well in your country?
- Is it wrong to see it as a marketplace?

Academic insight: Are women discriminated against in entrepreneurial finance?

Women business owners invest fewer resources at start-up, rely more on internal sources of funding and introduce less capital as their business grows.[46] Because finance is crucial, this has raised questions about whether or not women are discriminated against.

In some Caribbean countries, women are more financially constrained than men.[47] Similarly, in Asia and Eastern Europe, women are less likely to get a bank loan and more likely to pay higher interest rates than men.[48] In Europe, women also perceive greater financial barriers, pay higher interest rates and face higher collateral requirements.[49]

In the USA, despite clear evidence of ethnic minority discrimination, there is less evidence that women are discriminated against.[50] Once account is taken of individual attributes such as age and education and business characteristics such as size and sector, there are few differences between men and women in their application and rejection rates for funding.[51] Women also appear to be less likely to ask for finance.[52] Underlying this is that women are more likely to own a service-based business and need less finance. Women may also have different risk appetites and different business aspirations.[53]

Better understanding the contextual nature of women's financial decisions points to another perspective on gender and finance. Some studies of entrepreneurial finance start from the assumption that women face stereotypical barriers about what it takes to be an entrepreneur.[54] Because women are seen as being more risk-averse and have weaker business growth ambitions than men, they are pigeon-holed as being associated with weakness and lack. However, this 'entrepreneurial deficit' approach does not account for why women business owners use finance in particular ways and may reinforce any sexism faced by female entrepreneurs.[55]

© Getty Images

Discussion questions:

- Does seeing women as being different from men lead inevitably to magnifying small differences in their entrepreneurial behaviours?
- Should your government have a package of financial support that is for the exclusive use of women?

9.5 UNDERSTANDING THE KEY FUNDING SOURCES FOR ENTREPRENEURS

Entrepreneurs may be discouraged from applying for finance because they lack an understanding of what different funders offer to businesses and what motivates their funding decisions. As a result, business owners can waste valuable time looking in the wrong place for external finance. There are four main sources of finance that can help new and established businesses meet both their working capital and investment capital requirements: the bank, business angels, venture capitalists and crowdfunders.

9.5.1 Banks

One reason why banks get a bad name for their small business services is that their business model is poorly understood. Their business model is low risk, low returns. It is low returns because the profits from business banking largely stem from fees such as arranging an overdraft and interest payments from, for example, a bank loan.

However, banks run the risk that businesses might default on their loans, which can wipe out profits or even lead to losses.[56] A core activity for a bank is therefore to pick low-risk businesses. This can be challenging. A 'bad' borrower may go to the bank with a high-risk and high-return business proposition. Financing this is problematic for a bank. If the proposition is successful, all the bank gets is the capital and interest repayments. In contrast, the entrepreneur may walk away with a sizeable capital gain from selling their share of the business. Equally, if the proposition goes bad, it is the bank that loses its capital, and it may struggle to recover this from the 'bad' borrower.

Banks try to make sure that only 'good' businesses come forward by conducting due diligence and reviewing credit scores, business plans and management accounts. They may also ask for collateral secured against the loan such as the founder's home. This screening has roots in the use of the 'CAMPARI' mnemonic:

- **C**haracter – is the borrower respectable and honest?
- **A**bility – what is the borrower's track record?
- **M**argin – what is the percentage above base rate? How does this reflect the risks?
- **P**urpose – is the money for working or investment capital?
- **A**mount – is a realistic amount being asked for?
- **R**epayment – can the borrower fund the capital and repayments?
- **I**nsurance – is there a need for collateral? How much?

In wealthier countries, it is often practical to borrow relatively small amounts from a bank.[57] Bank funding can be preferable to equity investment because as long as a business repays the loan with interest, there is no dilution of business control. And where bank lending is automated, funding approval can be much quicker. The cost of borrowing (interest rate) may also be competitively priced. However, there are still some strings attached. Providing collateral means in practice giving up some control of the business and can increase business's fixed costs and break-even point.

Entrepreneurship in Action

- Assess your business against the CAMPARI mnemonic.
- Research the financial support on offer from banks in your local market.
- What bank offers the best support package to a start-up?
- Which bank, if any, offers a term loan to a start-up.

Alternatively, look at public sources by going to your government's website to find out what sorts of financial support it offers. Governments provide a range of financial support:

- *Grants*. Very many countries across the world provide grant funding (go to your governments website for further information). For example, Australia offers a 'Minimum Viability Product' grant to help pre-revenue innovative businesses shift from the proof of concept stage to minimum viable product stage. In Singapore, Enterprise Singapore offers a range of start-up and business development grants while in Oman the government has an SME development fund.
- *Loans*. The UK has unsecured 'start-up loans' based on creditworthiness (credit score), business viability (business plan) and personal affordability (ability to pay the loan back).58
- *Loan guarantee schemes*. Like many other countries, Nigeria offers a loan guarantee scheme in which the government underwrites some of the risks inherent in a bank lending to small businesses to encourage them to lend to companies without a track record or security.

9

9.5.2 *Business angels*

A business angel is 'a high net-worth individual investing personal funds in privately held companies, usually start-ups'.[59] In return for these investments, they get a share (equity) in the business.

The angel's business model is high-risk, high-return. Their investments are high-risk because they focus on growth potential businesses that may have an untested innovative technology, an emerging but still indistinct commercial opportunity or an incomplete entrepreneurial team. Their business model is high-return because they are hoping that by investing in a growth potential businesses they will realise a large capital gain when they come to sell their equity share.

A 'realistic' business angel who has a portfolio of investments in growth potential businesses knows that their likely returns will be skewed. In a portfolio of ten high growth potential businesses, angels expect that only one will produce 80–90 per cent of their total return. Five will return the business angel's original investment and the final four will give them nothing back.[60]

Angel finance appeals to high growth potential start-ups because they are one of the few 'stranger' sources of equity finance available. Angels – and syndicates of angels who invest together in businesses – provide large sums of funding, with average deals of €170,000 in Europe.[61] There are other benefits. It is 'patient' finance because the angels might wait between three and ten years before realising their investment.[62] And it is relatively quick, with some entrepreneurs only waiting months rather than years to see an investment. It is also 'smart' as the angel may bring invaluable contacts that strengthen the business's key strategic partnerships, as well as offering advice and assistance, and helping to leverage further business funding.

However, angel finance is rare. Fewer than five in every 100 start-ups that apply receive funding.[63] Angels are picky because they focus on sectors or geographic areas that they know well. They believe that this is likely to limit their chances of picking high growth potential businesses that fail to realise their potential. To screen potential propositions, angels often rely on a business plan. This usually leads to rejection: out of the 9640 business plans received by business angels, only 7.9 per cent (764) pitched and out of these pitches, only 31 per cent (238) of the businesses ended up getting funding.[64] Angels' common complaints include:

- Weak team or management.
- Lack of intellectual property rights and immature working prototypes for the product or service.
- Inability to identify a first customer or limited sales to date.
- An incoherent or incomplete financial model.
- Sluggish market growth.
- Immature understanding of competitors or the existence of better competitors.
- Limited plans for marketing the business.

Of these factors, the team/management is the most important reason for rejection.[65] One angel rejected a business proposition because 'You just don't believe in the people, don't feel you trust them or they may be ... not open and honest', while another stated that 'A deal killer for me is guys who come in here and ... do not demonstrate a decent understanding of the market or the competition that they're focused on'.[66]

Angels also question some entrepreneurs' approaches to funding. Many only invest in a company if a founder has invested their own money into the company. Angels can also be mystified if entrepreneurs expect to use angel funding for working capital needs rather than for investing in business growth.

One further misunderstanding is that angels just provide equity funding: the reality is that they often also provide debt funding.

Case Study: In debt to angels

AdGrok, a keyword-bidding platform for small businesses, struggled at first to raise angel finance.[67] Despite there being plenty of business angel money available in Silicon Valley, AdGrok found the angels to be more like devils. Still, AdGrok raised $470,000 from an angels syndicate.[68] In Silicon Valley, this money typically comes in the form of a loan with a nominal interest rate (convertible note) that converts into equity (shares) when a start-up raises further capital. Angels prefer convertible notes because they avoid tax issues, legal complexities and the expenses involved in new share issues.

Convertible notes can be advantageous to angel investors if they keep the valuation of the business low. If AdGrok had a pre-money valuation (before investment) of $5 million, this gives the angels a post-money valuation (after investment) of $5.47 million and an equity stake of 8.59 per cent (0.47 million /(5 million +0.47 million)). If the angels negotiated a lower pre-money value in its 'cap' or capitalisation table (an abbreviated ledger that tracks the equity ownership of a company's shareholders) of $3 million, they would receive a 13.54 per cent equity stake (0.47 million /3 million +0.47 million). However, if the cap is low, the founders will get less money when the business is sold. Despite these issues, AdGrok was reportedly sold for $10 million, leaving a healthy return for the entrepreneurial team and their angels.

Another misconception is that angels just fund businesses for non-monetary reasons such as the desire to be involved in the day-to-day running of the business. Some do. The majority of professional angel investors though focus on two key metrics:

1. Return on Investment (ROI). If a group of business angels make an initial investment of €400,000 in a business and it sells for €4 million, their ROI is ten times the initial investment. In other words, ROI is a 10x multiple.
2. Internal Rate of Return (IRR). Basically, this is the same as ROI but additionally takes account of time. If after four years the €400,000 turns into €4 million, the IRR is 323 per cent.

What really matters to business angels is the current value of a business, its value when sold, how long it will take to sell and what the ROI and IRR will be. Individual investments are part of a wider portfolio of risky and less risky investments such as savings. Angel investors aim for an IRR of around 25 per cent across their portfolio.[69]

Entrepreneurship in Action

To value a start-up, there are three common methods:

1. Price-to-Earnings Ratio (the ratio between a company's share price and its earnings). This method assumes that stock market valuations translate easily to small unproven start-ups
2. Discounted Cash Flows. This assumes a guess about cash generated and the application of some interest rate to work out what future cash is worth currently (discounted cash flow method). Many innovative businesses, though, lack cash
3. Asset Valuation. This sums physical and intangible assets such as intellectual property, which might be difficult to calculate in a start-up.

An entrepreneurial team (Tom, Dick and Harry) could use these methods to value their business. Or, because valuation is more of an art than a science, they may find out the 'going rate' for similar start-ups and adjust their valuation to their own business (Chapter 2, p. 34).

Suppose they decide to give their business a 'pre-money' valuation–before any outside person has invested – of 2 million. With their valuation, a business plan and a pitch in hand, Tom, Dick and Harry ask a group of business angels for a 250,000 investment.

After the angels have invested, the 'post-money' valuation of the entrepreneurs would be 2.25 million (pre-money valuation (2 million) + investment (0.25 million)). The equity stake for the 250,000 is 11.11 per cent (0.25 million /2.25 million). In their plan, the entrepreneurs say that *they* will sell the business in five years' time for a terminal value of 30 million, which they base on the value of other businesses in the market.

However, the more sceptical angels argue the entrepreneurs have an unrealistic valuation. This may be due to a 'hunch' about what it is worth or because they want a 30× multiple return.[70] To do so, they work out the value of the business after they have invested using this formula:[71]

- Post-money valuation = terminal value (e.g. 30 million) /anticipated ROI (30×)

Using this calculation, the angel's post-money valuation is 1 million (30 million/30) and their share is 25 per cent (investment (0.25 million)/post-money valuation (1 million)).

Tom, Dick and Harry are concerned that giving up a 25 per cent stake in their business is too much. However, the angels might say that dilution is normal and it is a 'sensible' business valuation, because if the business does need further equity to develop, both the entrepreneurs and the business angels' equity share is going to be diluted: it is better to have a thin slice of a rich cake than a whole but tiny and unsatisfying cup cake.

The entrepreneurs may further complain about the suggested 30× multiple. This ignores that this single investment is just one part of the angels' investment portfolio and the angels do not know which one is likely to be a 'home run'. Their average IRR across their portfolio should be around 25 per cent, and their ROI should be a 3× multiple. If the angels lose all of their investment on four businesses, and five more only give a modest multiple of 0.4× of their money, one has to provide a return close to 30× (4/10 × −1 + 5/10 × 0.4 + 1/10 × 30 = 3×).

However, valuations are ultimately subjective. The value of a business depends on what someone is willing to pay for it, and the presence of alternative bidders. Tom, Dick and Harry tell the angels someone else is interested in backing them, and the angels agree a new 'pre-money' valuation of the business of 1.5 million for the same angel investment of (0.25 million), the 'post-money' valuation is 1.75 million (pre-money (1.5 million) + investment (0.25 million). This gives the angels a 14.3 per cent stake (1.75 million (0.25 million/(1.5 million +0.25 million)).

The angel's shares come in the form of new shares issued. At start-up, say there were 1 million shares issued: 40 per cent to Tom; 40 per cent to Dick; and 20 per cent to Harry. At a 'pre-money' valuation of 1.5 million, each of these shares – their share price – was worth 1.5 (1.5 million/1 million). This means the issue of 166,667 new shares (investment (0.25 million)/ share price (1.5)), bringing the total of shares in the business to 1,166,667.

Figure 9.4 shows the movements in the equity shares. Some entrepreneurs also use a 'cap' or capitalisation table to track the equity ownership of a company's shareholders.

Figure 9.4 Pre- and post-valuation share ownership

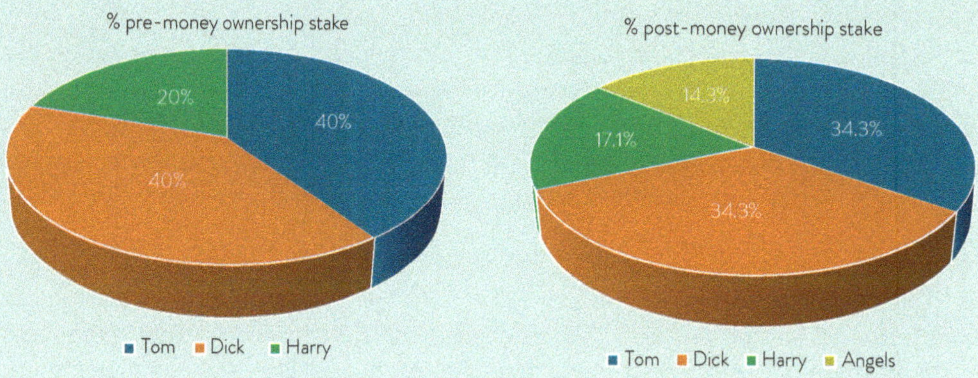

9.5.3 Post angel involvement

Angels may provide valuable tacit knowledge and contacts that can drive a business forward. Such support might come across as interference, particularly if there are strategic differences: the original owners might want to drive the business forward, while the angels may want to sell the business to realise their capital gain. Angel finance might, therefore, be impatient and lead to selling the business before it realises its full potential. Angels may also introduce anti-dilution clauses that protect their stake in the business, meaning founders have to dilute their own stakes to secure further investment.

Entrepreneurship in Action

- Investigate business angels and angel syndicates in your local market.
- Put yourself in the shoes of an angel investor. Have you clearly identified your risk–reward relationship in your business plan or pitch deck? What major risks do you face?
- For a pitch, identify: how much money you need, what it is for, what the proposed equity share is and what your valuation of the business is. What is your exit route? Is it to sell the business to a competitor (trade sale) or sell it on the public stock market (Initial Public Offer, IPO)?
- What is the minimum funding you need? What is the maximum share of equity that you are prepared to give away? What are you prepared to give away if you need extra funding later on?
- Draw up a capitalisation table that lists who owns what and any vesting agreements (Chapter 7, pp.169–170)

9.5.4 *Venture capitalists*

Like business angels, the Venture Capitalist (VC) business model is high-risk, high-return. They too focus on growth potential businesses and want to realise large capital gains. But while angels invest their own money, venture capitalists (VCs) are financial intermediaries who invest *other* people's money (Figure 9.5). They first raise a venture capital fund, then invest it in growth potential businesses and finally distribute profits to their investors. Known as Limited Partners, these investors can be pension and investment funds, governments and wealthy individuals who are looking to diversify a part of their portfolio in more risky but rewarding directions.

The VC management team are called General Partners. They can raise huge amounts of capital. Index Ventures, one of Europe's largest VCs, raised a $550 million fund for start-ups and early-stage ventures while SoftBank raised $100 billion.[72] Each fund usually lasts ten years and is focused on a particular sector. For example, the start-up Filecoin raised $52 million from VC funds focused on cryptocurrencies.[73]

As Figure 9.5 shows, once the investment fund is financed, VCs spend the first three or so years prospecting for suitable businesses.[74] This *deal generation* is usually done through their own efforts, working with other VCs who are looking to syndicate a potential deal and from professional contacts.

Next, VCs *screen* potential entrepreneurs. VCs typically undertake a lengthy process of sifting through prospects which takes anywhere from eight months to more than two years.[75] Core activities include multiple meetings with the entrepreneurial team, reviews by the VCs and conducting due diligence both on the team and on the attractiveness of the opportunity. This involves VCs looking at a range of factors such as strength of the team, their industry and entrepreneurial experience, the passion, ability and teamwork, as well as business-related factors such as the product, technology, business model and strong revenue growth potential. They also consider financial prospects (expected IRR and ROI), entrepreneurial passion and the business' fit with the fund, because they typically will only invest in industries or sectors where they believe that they have expertise.[76] Only a tiny number of companies that go through this process receive funding.[77]

Figure 9.5 Venture capital fund cycle

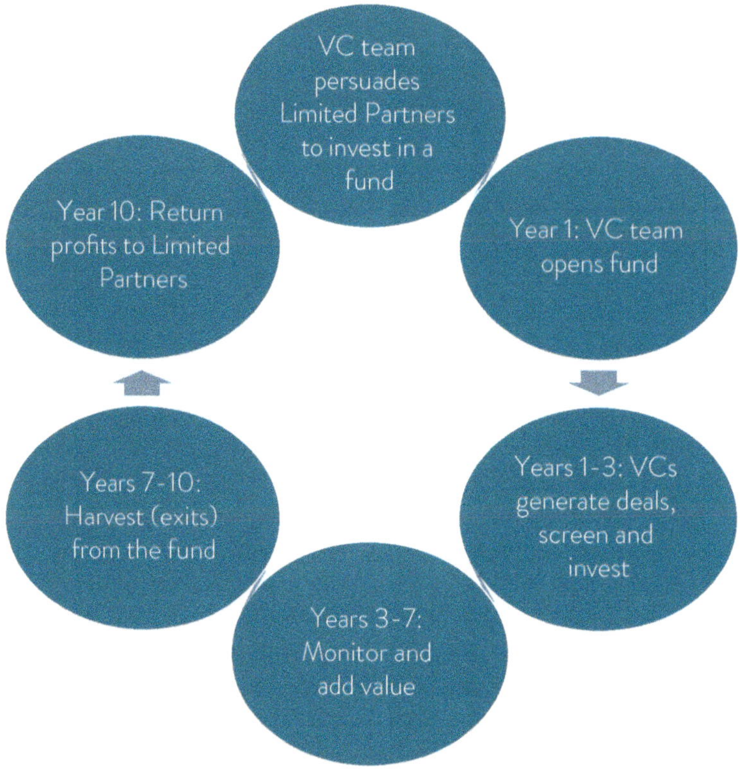

After investing in the selected businesses, VCs spend years three to seven *monitoring* and *adding value* to the business, through activities such as hiring board members and employees, connecting with customers and suppliers and providing operational and strategic advice.

Towards the end of the fund cycle, VCs look to *harvest* their investments. Their median target IRR is around 30 per cent or a 5x multiple.[78] These substantial capital gains are most likely to come from selling the business or selling its shares on the public stock market (an IPO). The US VC Sequoia Capital invested around $60 million in WhatsApp. When it was sold to Facebook, its return was around $3 billion (a 50× return).[79]

This cycle ends when the VC General Partners return fund profits to the Limited Partners. If successful, this leads to the generation of the next fund. The VC team retains 20 per cent of any profits that a fund makes above an agreed target, called carried interest.[80] They also charge a management fee of around 2 per cent of the value of the fund.[81]

9.5.5 *Disadvantages of venture capital*

If some entrepreneurs see business angels as demons, some see VCs as Satan. So-called 'Vulture Capitalists' have gained a reputation for stripping founders of their equity stake and replacing them with management board members whose primary purpose is to protect VCs' interests.

Suppose an entrepreneurial team negotiates an agreement in principle or 'term sheet' for an investment of €5 million in the first round of VC funding. Conditions of this 'Series A' deal are perhaps that it hands 50 per cent of the business to the VCs and gives them a seat on the board, with voting rights and veto powers. The VCs shares are in the form of *participating convertible preferred* shares.

Because *preferred* shares are paid out before *ordinary* shares, this means the VCs will receive their €5 million back at the point the business is sold and, crucially, before other shareholders. This mitigates the risks faced by the VC: selling the business for €5 million means they get paid first, recover all of their investment and leave the entrepreneurial team with nothing.

If preferable shares mitigate against 'downside' losses, to maximise their 'upside' gains, there are advantages in VC shares being *participating convertible* preferable shares. VCs can convert their shares into ordinary shares. If the business sells for €10 million, it can mean that the VC gets their €5 million loan back first, and then share 50 per cent of the remaining €5 million. This gives the VC 75 per cent of the proceeds from the business sale.

In fairness, this example is for a trade sale of a business.[82] A more favoured outcome is an IPO for a business. This should see entrepreneurs do better. But the reality is that almost three-quarters of entrepreneurs receive nothing when their business exits.[83]

VC money (or debt) brings with it control issues.[84] Entrepreneurs can find that their vesting rights are renegotiated, that the VC has first refusal rights over new share offers, that they can sell their shares when an entrepreneur chooses to (called 'tag along' rights) and force a sale ('drag along' rights). These matter if the business needs further injections through Series B, C and subsequent funding rounds. To protect their equity, VCs also ask for anti-dilution clauses, which may mean that the entrepreneur rather than the VC sees their equity share diluted.

If there is conflict about the business' strategic direction, VCs can seek to replace the entrepreneurial team.[85] It is also common for VCs to stage their funding to try to make sure that entrepreneurs reach certain sales or profitability milestones. Because their business model is high-risk, high-return, VCs focus on taking a business to IPO. Their next best exit outcome is a trade sale through a merger and acquisition (M&A). Table 9.2 shows the outcomes for early-stage investments by US VCs. Only around one in ten investments achieve IPO. A similar percentage achieve a cash-on-cash multiple of 10+. Focusing on high returns can mean pushing the business toward an exit.

Table 9.2 Exit routes and multiples[86]

Exit route	Percentage	Exit multiple	Percentage
IPO	9	<1	27
M&A	42	1–3	32
Failure	49	3–5	16
		5–10	13
		10+	12

Source: Gompers et al. (2016)

The VC's high-risk, high-return model does not always pay off for VC Limited Partners, some of whom might be better off investing in the general stock market.[87] Returns from VC funds may provide poor returns if incentives are weak for finding and investing in fast-growth potential businesses. If a VC fund is $500 million and the management fee is 2 per cent, VC partners will earn $10 million over the life cycle of the fund regardless of the quality of their investments. These fees can provide up to two-thirds of the gross income earned by VC partners.[88]

VC partners invest in businesses like them. Such homophily ('birds of a feather flock together') is due partly to geography. Most VC activity happens in recognised entrepreneurship centres such as Silicon Valley and London, making it more difficult for geographically remote entrepreneurs to access VC funding.[89] The entrepreneur's background is also important. VCs prefer investment opportunities from those with similar professional backgrounds to them and from experienced entrepreneurs.[90] It also helps if the entrepreneurs have similar norms, went to the same universities and schools, are male and have shared networks.[91] This may hinder the chances of fast-growth businesses run by women and minorities from getting VC funding.[92]

9.5.6 Advantages of venture capital

A VC might complain that their poor reputation among some entrepreneurs stems from a basic misconception of their motivations. They differ from banks because they are willing to take the risk of providing funding to businesses with a limited track record. Their cash injections have no impact on the cash flow of the business, thereby easing the journey across the 'valley of death' (Chapter 8, pp. 201–202). VC funding can add legitimacy to the business and help leverage other funding sources such as bank finance. Unlike angels, VCs are able to offer huge sums to early-stage businesses. This funding is patient: VCs will wait several years to realise a return and have the funds to invest repeatedly in funding rounds subsequent to Series A funding.

Equally, since VCs ten year funds are illiquid (not easy to convert to cash) and very risky, it makes sense for VCs just to focus on high-return opportunities. Without any guarantees of success, it also follows why they seek out high IRR percentages and high cash multiples. Being picky about their investments (adverse selection) helps society: an increase in the supply of VC funding led to increases in start-ups, employment and wealth (aggregate income).[93]

The ability of VCs to select, support and add value to fast-growth businesses have positive effects.[94] VC 'activism' leads to business growth and higher investment returns. Their networks can help recruitment and business development, while their expertise supports improved managerial professionalism, speeds product development and supports greater innovation towards a successful exit. Replacing the existing team can be an essential step to reach these goals. The skills needed to get a business to viability are different from those needed to scale an international business.

The common use of participating convertible preference (PCP) shares by VCs is also widely misunderstood. VCs face a real prospect of moral hazard so a PCP disciplines the entrepreneurial team to drive growth towards an IPO rather than going for a suboptimal trade sale.[95] Having a seat at the board table and staging their funding helps entrepreneurs focus on achieving agreed milestones. When a VC backed business does reach an IPO, VC firms continue to hold shares and have a positive impact on business development.[96]

Discussion questions:

- How well do moral hazard and adverse selection explain the funding selection criteria used by business angels?
- Do the advantages of VC funding outweigh its disadvantages?

Entrepreneurship in Action

- Return to your motives for starting up your business (Chapter 3, pp. 44–45 and Workbook 2 Exercise W. 2.12–13). Do these motives fit in with the ambition expected by business angels and venture capitalists?
- Identify a venture capital fund. Is it a good fit for your business' sector, profile and geography?

- If you are a social enterprise, can you find any business angel or venture capital firms that will support your aims and ambitions?
- What is the minimum funding you need? What is the maximum share of equity you are prepared to give away? What are you prepared to give away if you need extra funding later on?
- Explain why your start-up is a suitable candidate for getting to an IPO?
- Draw up a capitalisation table that lists who owns what and any vesting agreements (Chapter 7, pp. 169–170).
- Are you happy to accept a deal that involves participating in convertible preferred shares?

9.5.7 Crowdfunders

Crowdfunding is not new. In the seventeenth century, large numbers of wealthy English investors 'crowdfunded' the East India Company to exploit India's resources. At around the same time, it was common for struggling writers to ask a 'crowd' of their readers to fund the development and publication of their book in return for a copy.

However, during the past decade, the internet has created an explosion in the number of crowdfunding platforms and the volume of funding.[97] Modern day crowdfunding is defined as: 'the efforts by entrepreneurial individuals and groups – cultural, social, and for-profit – to fund their ventures by drawing on relatively small contributions from a relatively large number of individuals using the internet, without standard financial intermediaries [e.g. banks]'.[98]

In general, internet-based crowdfunding is a relationship between three parties: the business seeking funding; the intermediary; a crowdfunding platform that supports the campaign and gains a return for managing the campaign; and the audience, or crowd, that provides funding to the business. There are four basic types of crowdfunding campaigns:

1. Donations, such as gifts of money to support relief efforts after a natural disaster.
2. Preorders that offer rewards in exchange for buying a good or service before it is made.
3. Peer-to-peer (P2P) loan funding for small businesses.
4. P2P equity funding.

Danish singer Josefine Skov used crowdfunding to market and sell preorders of her new album. Her reward package ranged from a personalised email and a digital copy of the record for 20–50 Krona to writing a song for the person willing to donate between 800 and 1000 Krona.[99] Crowdfunders can also offer discounts on new products or services to those who preorder.

For P2P lending and equity funding, the most common campaign model is all or nothing. If entrepreneurs achieve their campaign's funding target, they receive all of the money, but if they fail, they get nothing.

Crowdfunding intermediaries usually charge fees for managing the project, a commission on financial transactions and a success 'fee'. They are likely to pre-screen potential businesses to ensure that they meet relevant commercial criteria. They also often ensure investors know the risks involved in crowdfunding and cannot invest above particular amounts.

Crowdfunding investors have different motivations for providing resources. Donation-based campaigns usually focus on supporting good causes and attract altruistic investors.[100] More profit-orientated investors provide loan and equity finance because they are interested in potentially higher returns, because they wish to diversify their investment portfolio and because there may be tax advantages in investing in early-stage businesses.

Choosing the correct crowdfunding platform for a campaign depends on a range of factors, such as the impetus for altruism among investors and the need for working or investment capital. A start-up seeking its first sales might choose a reward-based campaign offering tiered benefits to drive preorders. This brings in working capital and can shorten the time to break even. A post-revenue business, meanwhile, might focus on an equity campaign to get valuable investment funding.

Developing a successful crowdfunding campaign is difficult. Depending on the platform and the offer, the chances of success vary from 7 to 40 per cent.[101] Businesses need a large number of investors. This can range from an average of 85 for reward-based campaigns to 130 for those that are debt and equity-based campaigns.[102] Entrepreneurs considering crowdfunding should give careful thought to:

- **The crowdfunding platform** – what is its success rate? How does it support a campaign?
- **Previous successful campaigns** – why were they successful? A basic requirement is a professional video and a well-written, error-free explanation.[103]
- **Planning the campaign** – what is the amount of funding needed? What is the money for and what do potential backers (the crowd) get in return? Reward campaigns that use discounts to drive preordering can have a negative impact on gross margins, while peer-peer lenders often focus more on an individual's creditworthiness than the prospects for their business.[104]
- **The need for a formal pitch deck and business plan** – lending and equity crowdfunding platforms often perform due diligence on businesses to ensure that the campaign is both viable and ethical. Equally, investors want to see the entrepreneurial team and the quality of the business proposition.[105]
- **Marketing the campaign** – because campaigns are time-limited, building the community of potential backers *prior* to launch through blogs and e-marketing is key. Campaigns have a path dependency, and those that gain traction early are more likely to succeed.[106] This can be supported by updating and informing new potential backers through social media, advertising and press coverage.[107]

In addition to relatively quick injections of resources, crowdfunding can provide valuable marketing and sales insights about the viability of a product or service. However, the chances of failing to raise the money are much higher than going to a bank for a loan or overdraft. Entrepreneurs that use crowdfunding tend to do so as a last resort after they have exhausted other funding opportunities and can struggle to get follow-on equity funding if it is hard to get a large 'crowd' of investors to agree on a further round of funding.[108] Entrepreneurs also have to disclose their product or service, making them vulnerable to copycats.

Entrepreneurship in Action

- Research crowdfunding sites. Which one is most suitable for your needs? For example, besides very well-known platforms such as Kickstarter and Indiegogo, there now exist platforms that offer sharia-compliant P2P funding, such as Beehive, and dedicated social enterprise platforms, such as crowdfunder.
- What are the requirements you need to meet? One essential element is likely to be a video. Can you afford to get this professionally done? If not, how are you going to make your video stand out?

- What other costs will you incur in developing your pitch?
- Identify the 'crowd'. How do you intend to work with them prior to the launch of the campaign? How do you intend to market the campaign once it is up and running?

9.6 WHAT YOU HAVE LEARNED IN THIS CHAPTER

Finance is critical to any business. This chapter has shown you that in theory there is a range of finance available to businesses. In reality, start-ups tend to be funded initially from the entrepreneur's own resources and those of their family and friends. Established businesses also make limited use of external finance and are more likely to rely on debt finance than equity finance, while growth-orientated businesses can face challenges in accessing funding. For all of these types of business, the use of finance is influenced by pecking order preferences and principal–agent issues. These approaches help to explain why business owners prefer to self-finance and how information opacity makes it difficult for businesses to signal their quality to financiers.

Finance constraints can bind: ethnic minorities in the USA have faced discrimination in accessing bank products. However, the evidence for other countries is less clear.

You should now also have an understanding of the four main sources of entrepreneurial finance and how they operate:

- Banks follow a low-risk, low-return business model that seeks to separate out 'good' from 'bad' borrowers (adverse selection).
- Business angels and venture capitalists follow a high-risk, high-return business model that offers significant amounts of finance, as well as monitoring and value-adding services to fast-growing businesses in the hope of realising a sizeable capital gain.
- Crowdfunding finance covers a spectrum from donations and preordering models through to debt and equity-based funding.

ASSESSMENT QUESTIONS

1. What are adverse selection and moral hazard? Explain how these information asymmetries impact on the activities of a provider of finance.
2. Do entrepreneurs face financial constraints?
3. Is there evidence of discrimination in entrepreneurial finance markets?
4. Why is bank finance the most commonly used source of entrepreneurial finance?
5. Critically evaluate if either business angels or venture capitalists provide benefits to fast-growth businesses.
6. Identify the various forms of crowdfunding. For a particular type of small business, explain why a particular type of crowdfunding is the most suitable.

FURTHER READING

Berger, A. N., & Udell, G. F. (1998). The economics of small business finance: The roles of private equity and debt markets in the financial growth cycle. *Journal of Banking & Finance, 22*(6), 613–673.

Coleman, S., & Robb, A. (2009). A comparison of new firm financing by gender: Evidence from the Kauffman Firm Survey data. *Small Business Economics, 33*(4), 397.

GEM. (2016). *Report on entrepreneurial financing*. Babson College: GEM.

Gompers, P., Kaplan, S. N., & Mukharlyamov, V. (2016). What do private equity firms say they do? *Journal of Financial Economics, 121*(3), 449–76

Ipsos MORI. (2017, February). *2016 Business Finance Survey: SMEs a report by Ipsos MORI to the British Business Bank*. London: Ipsos MORI.

Metrick, A., & Yasuda, A. (2010). The economics of private equity funds. The *Review of Financial Studies, 23*(6), 2303–2341.

Mollick, E. (2014). The dynamics of crowdfunding: An exploratory study. *Journal of Business Venturing, 29*(1), 1–16.

Notes

1 Blattman, C., Fiala, N., & Martinez, S. (2013). Generating skilled self-employment in developing countries: Experimental evidence from Uganda. *The Quarterly Journal of Economics, 129*(2), 697–752.

2 Beck, T., & Demirguc-Kunt, A. (2006). Small and medium-size enterprises: Access to finance as a growth constraint. *Journal of Banking & Finance, 30*(11), 2931–2943.

3 GEM. (2016). *Report on entrepreneurial financing*. Babson College: GEM.

4 Robb, A. M., & Robinson, D. T. (2014). The capital structure decisions of new firms. *The Review of Financial Studies, 27*(1), 153–179.

5 Ibid.

6 BDRC Continental (2017, September). *SME Finance Monitor, Q2 2017*. London: BDRC Continental.

7 Myers, S. C., & Majluf, N. S. (1984). Corporate financing and investment decisions when firms have information that investors do not have. *Journal of Financial Economics, 13*(2), 187–221.

8 Winborg, J., & Landström, H. (2001). Financial bootstrapping in small businesses: Examining small business managers' resource acquisition behaviors. *Journal of Business Venturing, 16*(3), 235–254.

9 BDRC Continental (2017), ibid.

10 Vanacker, T. R., & Manigart, S. (2010). Pecking order and debt capacity considerations for high-growth companies seeking financing. *Small Business Economics, 35*(1), 53–69.

11 Wasserman, N. (2012). *The founder's Dilemmas: Anticipating and avoiding the pitfalls that can sink a start-up*. Princeton, NJ: Princeton University Press.

12 www.bbc.co.uk/news/av/world-africa-30183690/african-dream-fred-deegbe-ghanaian-banker-turned-shoemaker.

13 Berger, A. N., & Udell, G. F. (1998). The economics of small business finance: The roles of private equity and debt markets in the financial growth cycle. *Journal of Banking & Finance, 22*(6), 613–673.

14 Berger, A. N., & Frame, W. S. (2007). Small business credit scoring and credit availability. *Journal of Small Business Management, 45*(1), 5–22; Hasumi, R., & Hirata, H. (2014). Small business credit scoring and its pitfalls: Evidence from Japan. *Journal of Small Business Management, 52*(3), 555–568.

15 Kim, H., & Yasuda, Y. (2018). Accounting information quality and guaranteed loans: Evidence from Japanese SMEs. *Small Business Economics*, 1–18, https://doi.org/10.1007/s11187-018-0106-5; García-Teruel, P. J., Martínez-Solano, P., & Sánchez-Ballesta, J. P. (2014). The role of accruals quality in the access to bank debt. *Journal of Banking & Finance, 38*, 186–193.

16 Petersen, M. A., & Rajan, R. G. (1994). The benefits of lending relationships: Evidence from small business data. *The Journal of Finance, 49*(1), 3–37.

17 Andrieu, G., Staglianò, R., & Van Der Zwan, P. (2018). Bank debt and trade credit for SMEs in Europe: Firm-, industry-, and country-level determinants. *Small Business Economics, 51*(1), 245–264; Canton, E., Grilo, I., Monteagudo, J., & Van der Zwan, P. (2013). Perceived credit constraints in the European Union. *Small Business Economics, 41*(3), 701–715.

18 Mach, T. L., & Wolken, J. D. (2006, October). Financial services used by small businesses: Evidence from the 2003 Survey of Small Business Finances. *Federal Reserve Bulletin, Board of Governors of the Federal Reserve System*, pp. A167–A195.

19 BIS. (2016). *SME lending and competition: An international comparison of markets* (Research Paper No. 270). London: BIS.

20 BBB. (2017). *Small business finance markets, 2016–17*. London: BBB.

21 BDRC Continental (2017), ibid., p. 59: except where shown, data relates to Q15 All SMEs.

22 Ibid., p. 56. Q14/15 All SMEs.

23 Ibid., p. 79.
24 Ibid., p. 65.
25 Ibid., p. 67.
26 Ibid., p. 87.
27 Preqin. (2017). *Venture capital deals mark record quarter in Q2 2017*, press release, 5 July.
28 Hegazi, A. (2018). *Startup Arabia*. Santa Monica, CA: Transforma Publishing. https://endeavor.org/blog/in-the-news/uaes-fetchr-raises-11-million-series-a-round-with-participation-from-endeavor-catalyst/; https://www.crunchbase.com/organization/fetchr#section-funding-rounds.
29 Evans, D. S., & Jovanovic, B. (1989). An estimated model of entrepreneurial choice under liquidity constraints. *The Journal of Political Economy, 97*(4), 808–827; Frid, C. J., Wyman, D. M., & Coffey, B. (2016). Effects of wealth inequality on entrepreneurship. *Small Business Economics, 47*(4), 895–920; Lindh, T., & Ohlsson, H. (1996). Self-employment and windfall gains: Evidence from the Swedish lottery. *The Economic Journal, 106*(439), 1515–1526; Hurst, E., & Lusardi, A. (2004). Liquidity constraints, household wealth, and entrepreneurship. *Journal of Political Economy, 112*(2), 319–347.
30 SBA. (2014, February). *Office of Advocacy: Frequently asked questions*.
31 Coleman, S., & Robb, A. (2009). A comparison of new firm financing by gender: Evidence from the Kauffman Firm Survey data. *Small Business Economics, 33*(4), 397.
32 Ibid., p. 402.
33 Cetorelli, N., & Strahan, P. E. (2006). Finance as a barrier to entry: bank competition and industry structure in local US markets. *The Journal of Finance, 61*(1), 437–461; Han, L., Zhang, S., & Greene, F. J. (2015). Bank market concentration, relationship banking, and small business liquidity. *International Small Business Journal, 35*(4), 365–384.
34 Love, I., & Martínez Pería, M. S. (2014). How bank competition affects firms' access to finance. *The World Bank Economic Review, 29*(3), 413–448.
35 Kon, Y., & Storey, D. J. (2003). A theory of discouraged borrowers. *Small Business Economics, 21*(1), 37–49; Mac an Bhaird, C., Vidal, J. S., & Lucey, B. (2016). Discouraged borrowers: Evidence for Eurozone SMEs. *Journal of International Financial Markets, Institutions and Money, 44*, 46–55: Brown, M., Ongena, S., Popov, A., & Yeşin, P. (2011). Who needs credit and who gets credit in Eastern Europe?. *Economic Policy, 26*(65), 93–130; Chakravarty, S. and Xiang, M. (2013) 'The international evidence on discouraged small businesses. *Journal of Empirical Finance, 20*, 63–82.
36 Cowling, M., Liu, W., Minniti, M., & Zhang, N. (2016). UK credit and discouragement during the GFC. *Small Business Economics, 47*(4), 1049–1074.
37 Aghion, P., Fally, T., & Scarpetta, S. (2007). Credit constraints as a barrier to the entry and post-entry growth of firms. *Economic Policy, 22*(52), 732–779; Schmalz, M. C., Sraer, D. A., & Thesmar, D. (2017). Housing collateral and entrepreneurship. *The Journal of Finance, 72*(1), 99-132.; Krishnan, K., Nandy, D. K., & Puri, M. (2014). Does financing spur small business productivity? Evidence from a natural experiment. *The Review of Financial Studies, 28*(6), 1768–1809; Guiso, L., Sapienza, P., & Zingales, L. (2009). Does local financial development matter? In *The banks and the Italian economy* (pp. 31–66). Physica-Verlag HD.
38 Macmillan, H. P. (1931). *Committee on finance and industry: Report*. His Majesty's Stationery Office.
39 Fairlie, R., Robb, A., & Robinson, D. T. (2015). *Black and White: Access to capital among minority-owned startups* (SIEPR Discussion Paper 17-03). Stanford, CA: Stanford University.
40 Cavalluzzo, K., & Wolken, J. (2005). Small business loan turndowns, personal wealth, and discrimination. *The Journal of Business, 78*(6), 2153–2178; Blanchard, L., Zhao, B., & Yinger, J. (2008). Do lenders discriminate against minority and woman entrepreneurs? *Journal of Urban Economics, 63*(2), 467–497; Blanchflower, D. G. (2009). Minority self-employment in the United States and the impact of affirmative action programs. *Annals of Finance, 5*(3), 361–396.
41 Storey, D. J. (2004). Racial and gender discrimination in the micro firms credit market?: Evidence from Trinidad and Tobago. *Small Business Economics, 23*(5), 401–422; Raturi, M., & Swamy, A. V. (1999). Explaining ethnic differentials in credit market outcomes in Zimbabwe. *Economic Development and Cultural Change, 47*(3), 585–604; Aldén, L., & Hammarstedt, M. (2016). Discrimination in the credit market? Access to financial capital among self-employed immigrants. *Kyklos, 69*(1), 3–31.
42 Fraser, S. (2009). Is there ethnic discrimination in the UK market for small business credit?'*International Small Business Journal, 27*(5), 583–607; Raturi & Swamy (1999), ibid.
43 BDRC Continental (2017), ibid.
44 Han, L., Fraser, S., & Storey, D. J. (2009). Are good or bad borrowers discouraged from applying for loans? Evidence from US small business credit markets. *Journal of Banking & Finance, 33*(2), 415–424; Cowling et al. (2016), ibid.
45 Mason, C. M., & Harrison, R. T. (2002). Barriers to investment in the informal venture capital sector. *Entrepreneurship & Regional Development, 14*(3), 271–287.
46 Coleman & Robb (2009), ibid.
47 Raturi & Swamy (1999), ibid.; Presbitero, A. F., Rabellotti, R., & Piras, C. (2014). Barking up the wrong tree? Measuring gender gaps in firm's access to finance. *The Journal of Development Studies, 50*(10), 1430–1444.
48 Muravyev, A., Talavera, O., & Schäfer, D. (2009). Entrepreneurs' gender and financial constraints: Evidence from international data. *Journal of Comparative Economics, 37*(2), 270–286.
49 Roper, S., & Scott, J. M. (2009). Perceived financial barriers and the start-up decision: an econometric analysis of gender differences using GEM data. *International Small Business Journal, 27*(2), 149–171; Alesina, A., Giuliano, P., & Nunn, N. (2013). On the

origins of gender roles: Women and the plough. *The Quarterly Journal of Economics, 128*(2), 469–530; Bellucci, A., Borisov, A., & Zazzaro, A. (2010). Does gender matter in bank–firm relationships? Evidence from small business lending. *Journal of Banking & Finance, 34*(12), 2968–2984.

50 Blanchflower, D. G., Levine, P. B., & Zimmerman, D. J. (2003). Discrimination in the small-business credit market. *The Review of Economics and Statistics, 85*(4), 930–943; Treichel, M. Z., & Scott, J. A. (2006). Women-owned businesses and access to bank credit: Evidence from three surveys since 1987. *Venture Capital, 8*(1), 51–67.

51 Cole, R. A., & Mehran, H. (2009). *Gender and the availability of credit to privately held firms: Evidence from the surveys of small business finances* (Staff Report 383). Federal Reserve Bank of New York; Stefani, M. L., & Vacca, V. P. (2013). *Credit access for female firms: Evidence from a Survey on European SMEs* (Bank of Italy Occasional Paper 176); Kairiza, T., Kiprono, P., & Magadzire, V. (2017). Gender differences in financial inclusion amongst entrepreneurs in Zimbabwe. *Small Business Economics, 48*(1), 259–272.

52 Moro, A., Wisniewski, T. P., & Mantovani, G. M. (2017). Does a manager's gender matter when accessing credit? Evidence from European data. *Journal of Banking & Finance, 80*, 119–134; Mijid, N., & Bernasek, A. (2013). Gender and the credit rationing of small businesses. *The Social Science Journal, 50*(1), 55–65.

53 Leitch, C., & Hill, F. (2006) Women and the financing of entrepreneurial ventures: More pieces for the jigsaw puzzle. *Venture Capital, 8*(2), 159–182.

54 Marlow, S., & Swail, J. (2014). Gender, risk and finance: Why can't a woman be more like a man? *Entrepreneurship & Regional Development, 26*(1–2), 80–96.

55 Marlow & Swail (2014), ibid.

56 Storey, D., & Frankish, J. (2016). The financing of new firms: What governments need to know. *Small Enterprise Research, 23*(3), 276–292.

57 www.ukfinance.org.uk/bank-support-for-smes-3rd-quarter-2017/.

58 www.startuploans.co.uk/achievements/.

59 Gregson, G., Bock, A. J., & Harrison, R. T. (2017). A review and simulation of business angel investment returns. *Venture Capital, 19*(4), 285–311, p. 287.

60 Wiltbank, R. E. (2009). *Siding with the angels: Business angel investing-promising outcomes and effective strategies*. London: Nesta.

61 Sohl, J. (2017, May 31). *A cautious restructuring of the angel market in 2016 with a robust appetite for seed and start-up investing*. Center for Venture Research.

62 Harrison, R. T., Botelho, T., & Mason, C. M. (2016). Patient capital in entrepreneurial finance: A reassessment of the role of business angel investors. *Socio-Economic Review, 14*(4), 669–689.

63 Mason, C., Botelho, T., & Zygmunt, J. (2017). Why business angels reject investment opportunities: Is it personal? *International Small Business Journal, 35*(5), 519–534.

64 Mason, C. M., & Harrison, R. T. (2015). Business angel investment activity in the financial crisis: UK evidence and policy implications. *Environment and Planning C: Government and Policy, 33*(1), 43–60.

65 Croce, A., Tenca, F., & Ughetto, E. (2017). How business angel groups work: Rejection criteria in investment evaluation. *International Small Business Journal, 35*(4), 405–426; Maxwell, A. L., & Lévesque, M. (2014). Trustworthiness: A critical ingredient for entrepreneurs seeking investors. *Entrepreneurship Theory and Practice, 38*(5), 1057–1080.

66 Mason et al. (2017), ibid., p. 525.

67 Martinez, A. G. (2016). *Chaos monkeys: Obscene fortune and random failure in Silicon Valley*. San Fransisco: Harper Business.

68 https://techcrunch.com/2011/03/07/adgrok-raises-470k-to-be-the-turbotax-for-search-engine-marketing/.

69 Wiltbank (2009), ibid.; Gregson et al. (2017), ibid.

70 Smith, D. J., Harrison, R. T., & Mason, C. M. (2010). Experience, heuristics and learning: The angel investment process. *Frontiers of Entrepreneurship Research, 30*(2), 3.

71 Sahlman, R. (2009). *The basic venture capital formula*. Boston, MA: HBR.

72 www.nytimes.com/2016/10/14/business/dealbook/softbank-and-saudi-arabia-partner-to-form-giant-investment-fund.html.

73 www.coindesk.com/257-million-filecoin-breaks-time-record-ico-funding/.

74 Petty, J. S., & Gruber, M. (2011). "In pursuit of the real deal": A longitudinal study of VC decision making. *Journal of Business Venturing, 26*(2), 172–188.

75 Ibid.

76 Gompers, P., Kaplan, S. N., & Mukharlyamov, V. (2016). What do private equity firms say they do?. *Journal of Financial Economics, 121*(3), 449-476; Warnick, B. J., Murnieks, C. Y., McMullen, J. S., & Brooks, W. T. (2018). Passion for entrepreneurship or passion for the product? A conjoint analysis of angel and VC decision-making. *Journal of Business Venturing, 33*(3), 315–332.

77 Kirsch, D., Goldfarb, B., & Gera, A. (2009). Form or substance: The role of business plans in venture capital decision making. *Strategic Management Journal, 30*(5), 487–515.

78 Gompers et al. (2016), ibid.

79 https://techcrunch.com/2014/02/19/sequoia-and-jim-goetz-are-big-winners-in-facebooks-whatsapp-acquisition/.

80 Gompers, P., & Lerner, J. (1999). An analysis of compensation in the US venture capital partnership. *Journal of Financial Economics, 51*(1), 3–44.

81 Hall, R. E., & Woodward, S. E. (2007). *The Incentives to start new companies: Evidence from venture capital* (NBER Working Paper w13056). Cambridge, MA: National Bureau of Economic Research.

82 Kaplan, S. N., & Strömberg, P. (2003). Financial contracting theory meets the real world: An empirical analysis of venture capital contracts. *The Review of Economic Studies, 70*(2), 281–315.

83 Hall, R. E., & Woodward, S. E. (2010). The burden of the nondiversifiable risk of entrepreneurship. *American Economic Review*, *100*(3), 1163–1194.

84 De Rassenfosse, G., & Fischer, T. (2016). Venture debt financing: Determinants of the lending decision. *Strategic Entrepreneurship Journal*, *10*(3), 235–256.

85 Higashide, H., & Birley, S. (2002). The consequences of conflict between the venture capitalist and the entrepreneurial team in the United Kingdom from the perspective of the venture capitalist. *Journal of Business Venturing*, *17*(1), 59–81.

86 Gompers et al. (2016), ibid., refers to last ten years of VentureSource data.

87 Mulcahy, D., Weeks, B., & Bradley, H. (2012). *We have met the enemy … and he is us: Lessons from twenty years of the Kauffman Foundation's investments in venture capital funds and the triumph of hope over experience*. Kansas City, MO: Kauffman Foundation.

88 Metrick, A., & Yasuda, A. (2010). The economics of private equity funds. *The Review of Financial Studies*, *23*(6), 2303–2341.

89 Lutz, E., Bender, M., Achleitner, A. K., & Kaserer, C. (2013). Importance of spatial proximity between venture capital investors and investees in Germany. *Journal of Business Research*, *66*(11), 2346–2354.

90 Franke, N., Gruber, M., Harhoff, D., & Henkel, J. (2006). What you are is what you like – Similarity biases in venture capitalists' evaluations of start-up teams. *Journal of Business Venturing*, *21*(6), 802–826; Hsu, D. H. (2007). Experienced entrepreneurial founders, organizational capital, and venture capital funding. *Research Policy*, *36*(5), 722–741.

91 Terjesen, S., Patel, P. C., Fiet, J. O., & D'Souza, R. (2013). Normative rationality in venture capital financing. *Technovation*, *33*(8), 255–264; Kanze, D., Huang, L., Conley, M. A., & Higgins, E. T. (2018). We ask men to win and women not to lose: Closing the gender gap in startup funding. *Academy of Management Journal*, *61*(2), 586–614.

92 Bengtsson, O., & Hsu, D. H. (2015). Ethnic matching in the US venture capital market. *Journal of Business Venturing*, *30*(2), 338–354; Marlow, S., & Patton, D. (2005). All credit to men? Entrepreneurship, finance, and gender. *Entrepreneurship Theory and Practice*, *29*(6), 717–735.

93 Samila, S., & Sorenson, O. (2011). Venture capital, entrepreneurship, and economic growth. *The Review of Economics and Statistics*, *93*(1), 338–349.

94 Davila, A., Foster, G., & Gupta, M. (2003). Venture capital financing and the growth of startup firms. *Journal of Business Venturing*, *18*(6), 689–708; Jackson, W. E., Bates, T., & Bradford, W. D. (2012). Does venture capitalist activism improve investment performance? *Journal of Business Venturing*, *27*(3), 342–354; Bottazzi, L., Da Rin, M., & Hellmann, T. (2008). Who are the active investors?: Evidence from venture capital. *Journal of Financial Economics*, *89*(3), 488–512; Bernstein, S., Giroud, X., & Townsend, R. R. (2016). The impact of venture capital monitoring. *The Journal of Finance*, *71*(4), 1591–1622; Ragozzino, R., & Blevins, D. P. (2016). Venture-backed firms: How does venture capital involvement affect their likelihood of going public or being acquired? *Entrepreneurship Theory and Practice*, *40*(5), 991–1016.

95 Arcot, S. (2014). Participating convertible preferred stock in venture capital exits. *Journal of Business Venturing*, *29*(1), 72–87.

96 Croce, A., Martí, J., & Murtinu, S. (2013). The impact of venture capital on the productivity growth of European entrepreneurial firms: "Screening" or "value added" effect?'. *Journal of Business Venturing*, *28*(4), 489–510.

97 CCAF. (2017). *Hitting stride*. Cambridge: Cambridge Centre for Alternative Finance; CCAF. (2016). *Sustaining momentum: The 2nd European alternative finance industry report*. Cambridge: Cambridge Centre for Alternative Finance.

98 Mollick, E. (2014). The dynamics of crowdfunding: An exploratory study. *Journal of Business Venturing*, *29*(1), 1–16, 2.

99 www.booomerang.dk/projects/josefine-skov-soeger-midler-til-pladeudgivelse/.

100 Allison, T. H., Davis, B. C., Short, J. C., & Webb, J. W. (2015). Crowdfunding in a prosocial micro lending environment: examining the role of intrinsic versus extrinsic cues. *Entrepreneurship Theory and Practice*, *39*(1), 53–73.

101 www.thecrowdfundingcenter.com/data/platforms.

102 CCAF (2016), ibid.

103 Mollick (2014), ibid.

104 Kgoroeadira, R., Burke, A., & van Stel, A. (2018). Small business online loan crowdfunding: Who gets funded and what determines the rate of interest? *Small Business Economics*, *52*(6), 1–21.

105 Ahlers, G. K., Cumming, D., Günther, C., & Schweizer, D. (2015). Signalling in equity crowdfunding. *Entrepreneurship Theory and Practice*, *39*(4), 955–980; Gafni, H., Marom, D., & Sade, O. (2019). Are the life and death of an early-stage venture indeed in the power of the tongue? Lessons from online crowdfunding pitches. *Strategic Entrepreneurship Journal*, *13*(1), 3–23.

106 Vulkan, N., Åstebro, T., & Sierra, M. F. (2016). Equity crowdfunding: A new phenomena [*sic*]. *Journal of Business Venturing Insights*, *5*, 37–49.

107 Mollick (2014), ibid.; Block, J., Hornuf, L., & Moritz, A. (2018). Which updates during an equity crowdfunding campaign increase crowd participation? *Small Business Economics*, *50*(1), 3–27; Courtney, C., Dutta, S., & Li, Y. (2017). Resolving information asymmetry: Signaling, endorsement, and crowdfunding success. *Entrepreneurship Theory and Practice*, *41*(2), 265–290.

108 Walthoff-Borm, X., Schwienbacher, A., & Vanacker, T. (2018). Equity crowdfunding: First resort or last resort? *Journal of Business Venturing*, *33*(4), 513–533; Tuomi, K., & Harrison, R. T. (2017). A comparison of equity crowdfunding in four countries: Implications for business angels. *Strategic Change*, *26*(6), 609–615.

PART 4

Beyond Start-Up

CHAPTER 10

Entrepreneurial Growth

Learning Outcomes

In this chapter, you will learn:

- Why fast-growth businesses are difficult to spot.
- The five features most fast-growth businesses have in common.
- What the four main explanations for fast business growth are.

Mini Contents List

10.1 INTRODUCTION

One way of understanding entrepreneurship is to see it as a process by which start-up founders create, deliver and capture customer value. But what sets entrepreneurs such as Walt Disney, Jamsetji Tata or Coco Chanel apart is that they all came to dominate their industry. Rather than just creating, delivering and capturing value, these entrepreneurs 'cornered' value.

This journey from start-up to scale-up is very important for economic prosperity. Nokia was a sleepy and unspectacular Finnish wood pulping business until the invention of the mobile phone. By becoming a global leader in that area, it came to contribute one-quarter of Finland's economic growth. It also grew to become responsible for one-third of the country's total research and development (R&D) expenditure and generated about 20 per cent of its exports.[1]

Given the potential prize on offer, it is no surprise that bookstores groan with 'how to' guides that tell us of the simple steps necessary to grow a successful business.

The trouble is that there is no one-size-fits-all growth formula.

As you will learn in this chapter, growth is multidimensional, fleeting and almost defies prescription. Growth comes in very many flavours, such as employment or sales, and these flavours do not always go well together. Different geographical and industrial contexts, together with individual entrepreneurs' characteristics, all obscure why some companies grow larger and more quickly than others.

The good news is there are five features that fast-growing businesses have in common. The bad news is that none of them makes it any easier to identify the 'magic sauce' of business growth. However, as you will learn in this chapter, this has not stopped the development of four perspectives on business growth:

1. **Stage models** suggest that start-ups follow a life cycle and will naturally grow if they successfully navigate their growth pains or crises. These models describe the practical value of overcoming key growth challenges such as the need to shift from informal to formal business practices, and the necessity of employing more specialist workers as the business develops. These models are less clear on helping us to predict which business will grow.
2. **Strategic entrepreneurship** approaches argue that business growth stems from an entrepreneur's strategic capability to organise resources effectively and their ability to align their activities with their key sources of competitive advantage.[2] The trouble is that what works for one business may not easily work for another business.
3. **Environmental approaches** emphasise that business growth is a relative concept. Entrepreneurs compete with others and only grow if their products fit well to market needs. For example, despite facing stiff competition, the French cider producer Kupela grew very rapidly because its range of cider drinks met market demand for authentic ciders from the French Basque region.[3] However, these approaches remain largely silent on how businesses achieve product–market fit (Chapter 6, pp. 138–140).
4. **Chance-based approaches** build on the idea that being at the right place and at the right time influences growth.[4] But while luck helps explain the spotty nature of growth, it presents a dismal view of the entrepreneur, suggesting that there is very little that an entrepreneur can do to grow their business.[5]

10.2 WHY ARE FAST GROWTH BUSINESSES DIFFICULT TO SPOT?

One way of spotting fast-growth businesses is to track the fastest growing businesses for a given period. These indexes are common.[6] A follow-up task is to interview successful entrepreneurs from these fast-growth firms. A final task is to extrapolate from these case studies key lessons and apply them to the wider business population.[7]

Superficially, this approach is appealing. Entrepreneurs tell us how they grew their business, and we seek to replicate this 'magic sauce'. The trouble is that fast growth is fleeting. Very many 'iconic' entrepreneurial businesses fail to sustain growth and, in fact, often suffer a dramatic decline in performance.[8] This is also just a 'history of winners'. It is partial and biased: biased because entrepreneurs may provide inaccurate accounts of their growth (Chapter 2, pp. 36–37) and partial because high growth businesses are only understood *relative* to their competitors.[9]

Applying a standardised quantifiable measure of business growth to the whole business population is a better approach. This has led to fast-growth businesses being defined as having a minimum of ten employees and annualised employment and sales growth rates of 20 per cent over a three year period.[10]

These businesses are often called 'gazelles' or scale-ups. However, there are problems with this standard definition:

- It ignores businesses with fewer than ten workers and their contribution to job creation.[11]
- Taking a three-year growth window excludes successful businesses such as Deliveroo that took far longer to scale-up.[12]
- Measuring percentage change rather than actual change favours smaller businesses. Doubling in size from 10 to 20 equates to a 100 per cent growth rate. However, adding 10 workers to a workforce of 100 only counts as a 10 per cent increase.
- Measuring employment makes sense for policymakers interested in jobs, particularly as growth businesses tend to employ young people, immigrants and the unemployed.[13] However, entrepreneurs are more interested in financial measures such as sales or profits.[14]
- Growth measures are often not comparable with each other.[15] Fast growers begin by growing their operating profits, subsequently turn to improving their assets and revenues and only then end up growing employment.[16]
- It implies most business growth is organic, but some businesses grow by acquiring others.[17]

Assessment tip: Not all sources are the same

In planning and writing up assignments, one challenge is working out which is the most appropriate evidence to support your answer. There are two basic sources: academic writings on entrepreneurship such as journal articles, textbooks and podcasts; and evidence from other sources such as reports, newspaper articles and TED talks. Both may provide valuable information, data and insights into a topic.

However, academic sources become more important if an assignment asks you to discuss or critically evaluate your answer. Good academic sources are robust, rely on in-depth expertise and are peer-reviewed by other academics to ensure that they are rigorous pieces of work. Drawing on independent well-researched work is usually better than relying on individual anecdotes or opinions. This helps explain the tendency in academic writing to use the third person such as 'in this assignment' rather than 'in my assignment' and to avoid phrases such as 'I believe', 'I think' or 'in my opinion'.

These conventions do not always apply, so it is always useful to turn to any guidance given to you and to double-check your approach to an assignment.

Even if gazelles are spotted, there are challenges in working out their characteristics:

- **Inconsistent measures of growth characteristics.** Different studies employ different measures. An entrepreneur's ethnicity may be important if they take advantage of a rich cultural heritage that applauds business growth and uses community resources such as soft loans or mentors to grow their business. The impact of immigrant status on business growth is a similar measure. Many successful businesses in Silicon Valley have at their heart highly skilled and motivated immigrants. Born in South Africa, Tesla's founder, Elon Musk, emigrated to study in Canada before moving to the United States (USA). However, few studies measure both ethnicity and immigration status or account for generational differences.[18] Similarly, there are challenges in measuring generic background qualities, such as age and education or task-related entrepreneurial, managerial and industry experience. Even if these measures appear similar between studies, they are often measured in different ways. For example, education can be measured by whether someone has graduated from university or not and, alternatively, in terms of years of schooling.
- **Most studies are partial.** Many only consider one measure of growth such as employment or sales and only focus on one particular geography or sector.
- **Gazelles are not static.** One long-held view is that men are more likely to grow their business than women.[19] Possible reasons include: women experience discrimination, have a narrower set of business contacts than men, struggle to access finance and have greater childcare commitments that eat into the time they can devote to their business. Yet this 'female underperformance' thesis has increasingly been challenged, particular because it underestimates the different start-up sizes of male-and female-owned businesses. When these differences are taken into account, women can be just as likely to grow their business as men.[20]
- **Proxies for growth might hide underlying reasons for growth.** Limited companies grow faster than other forms of businesses, such as sole traders. However, this hides the fact that growth may be more to do with the abilities of the founding entrepreneurial team than the legal form of the business.

Case Study: Is there an identikit entrepreneur?

The identikit picture of a successful entrepreneur is an immigrant and university drop out whose high-tech start-up makes them rich.

Fitting this mould are brothers, Patrick and John Collison. They grew up in rural Ireland. Both moved as teenagers to the USA to go to university. While at university, they set up Auctomatic to help sellers on marketplaces such as eBay list their items more easily. They subsequently sold this for $5 million. Afterwards, having dropped out of university, they went on to found the online payments business Stripe in response to their frustrations in using existing payment systems. To scale Stripe, the brothers raised $450 million in successive funding rounds (seed, Series A to D), allowing them to set up offices across the globe, employ 900 people and see Stripe reach a valuation of $9.2 billion. This made both of the brothers, at least on paper, billionaires.

Not every successful founder follows the same path. One of Africa's richest entrepreneurs is Nigerian Aliko Dangote. After finishing university, he started trading in cement with money borrowed from his family. In six months, he had repaid the loan. His lucky break was that the Nigerian government ended restrictions on importing foods and goods. This allowed him to diversify into food staples such as salt, sugar, rice and flour. Instead of relying on external finance, he used his own profits to acquire competitors and to build his own manufacturing and processing plants. The strapline for Dangote's business is 'Providing your basic needs'.

Discussion questions:

- Despite the differences between Dangote and the Collison brothers, do you think that there are common entrepreneurial characteristics?
- (Chapter 2, pp. 24–27) introduced the idea that risk-taking and other personality traits are important in explaining entrepreneurial behaviour. Do you think that fast-growth entrepreneurs have particular personality dispositions?

10.3 THE FIVE COMMON FEATURES OF FAST GROWTH BUSINESSES

While gazelles remain elusive, there are five features that fast-growth businesses have in common:

1. *Fast-growth businesses are a very small proportion of the business population.* Just 2–6 per cent of companies around the world are fast-growth businesses.[21] If gazelles are rare, 'unicorns' – which are start-ups that subsequently become valued at $1 billion or more – are even rarer. In the USA, just four are born annually.[22] To put this in context, there are around 7.75 million businesses with employees in the USA.[23]
2. *Fast-growth businesses contribute disproportionately to job growth.* Fast-growth businesses create between 25 and 64 per cent of jobs globally.[24] There are similar findings for individual countries: for example, just 6 per cent of United Kingdom (UK) businesses or about 10,000 businesses were responsible for about half of all jobs created in the UK.[25]
3. *Fast growers are smaller and younger businesses.* In 1931, Gibrat formulated his law of proportionate effect. It stated that business growth is independent of size so that smaller businesses are just as likely to grow as fast as larger businesses. The reality is more nuanced.[26] To be competitive, smaller businesses have to quickly scale their operations to a size where they can compete effectively (this is called their minimum efficient scale). After this stage, growth is largely independent of size.[27] The implication is that smaller businesses add jobs quicker than larger businesses.[28] Doing so is of practical benefit: extra employees increase the chances of sales growth and business survival.[29]
   But it is not just size that matters. Younger businesses create more jobs than older businesses.[30] This again reflects the need to get to a minimum efficient scale to be credible.[31]
4. *Fast growth is 'spotty'.* Another prediction from Gibrat's Law is that growth rates are random: growth in one period does not lead to growth in the next period. This does not sit easily with the idea that growth occurs in a fairly linear and uniform way. However, while growth can beget further growth, the general pattern is that growth is haphazard.[32] Indeed, in richer countries, steady growth is unusual; more common is spotty growth.[33] For example, in Sweden, most growing businesses – like musicians in the pop charts – are 'one-hit wonders'.[34]
5. *Fast-growth businesses occur in all sectors.* There is a common misconception that fast growth is more likely for high-tech entrepreneurs such as the Collinson brothers than for those selling commodities such as Dangote. This presumes a close relationship between innovation and growth. Although there are examples of 'superstar' innovative businesses that grow quickly, growth is not more prevalent in high-technology sectors.[35] In fact, R&D intensive sectors have lower rates of high-growth businesses than non-R&D intensive sectors.[36]

There are three main reasons for this.

1. There is a great deal of uncertainty about bringing innovation to the market. This makes it difficult for an innovator to capture the benefits of a product or service. RC Cola was the first to introduce selling cola in cans, the first to introduce diet cola and the first to sell caffeine-free cola. These innovations did little to dent the market dominance of Pepsi or Coca-Cola.
2. It takes time to capture the rewards of innovation. Businesses may also fail to seize them entirely as they tend to innovate at erratic and irregular rates.[37]
3. One of the other impacts of innovation is that it can increase productivity by increasing how much a worker can produce in an hour. So, instead of adding employees, innovative businesses may do more with fewer employees, giving them low or negative employment growth.[38]

Fast-growth young businesses are incredibly important to any economy because, if nothing else, they create jobs. Fast growth, though, is dynamic and discontinuous, making it difficult to identify predictable patterns in business growth.

Discussion questions:

- What do the five common features of fast growth have for a government thinking about how it can best support fast-growth businesses?
- A bank's business model is generally low risk, low return (Chapter 9, pp. 224–225). Do you think that banks would be keen on supporting early-stage fast-growth businesses?

This has not stopped attempts to answer one of the basic questions in entrepreneurship: why is it that some businesses grow much quicker than others? The next section investigates four different approaches.

10.4 STAGE MODELS: OVERCOMING GROWING PAINS

One of the most intuitive ways of understanding growth is to see it as an organic process: a business comes into being, grows and then passes away. In order for growth transitions to occur, stage models suggest that a business has to overcome particular crises as it moves from childhood through to its adolescence and adulthood. There are a number of these life cycle models, each with varying numbers of stages.[39] Figure 10.1 and Table 10.1 show two common stage models.[40]

Larry Greiner's model (Figure 10.1) suggests that at start-up an entrepreneur is busy with product development and finding customers (growth through creativity), but as the business expands, it needs professional managers. If the business can overcome this 'crisis of leadership', it will grow until it faces its next hurdle (the crisis of greater autonomy). Subsequent growth through delegation continues until there is a crisis of control between different layers of management. And if this is resolved, the next crisis to overcome is being too bureaucratic. To grow at this stage requires a more organic strategy that embraces collaboration and strategic alliances.

Mel Scott and Richard Bruce's five-stage model (Table 10.1) identifies similar patterns.[41] At start-up, there is a flat organisational structure and a focus on commercialising the product or service and gaining traction in the market. Key challenges include achieving profitability and having basic managerial procedures in place. If a start-up overcomes these challenges (stage 2), it faces other tests if it is to grow and expand (stages 3 and 4).

Figure 10.1 Greiner's model

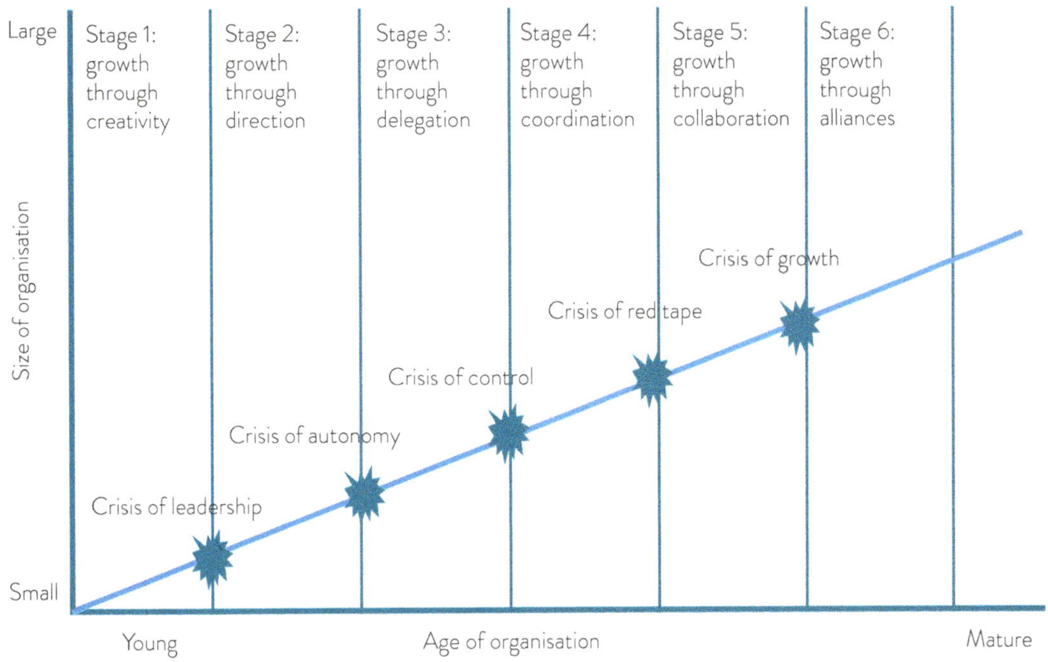

A number of criticisms can be made of stage models such as these:

- **They fail to describe the trajectory of most businesses.** The most common business fate is a quick death (Chapter 11, p. 281). Even if a business does not exit, a likely outcome for the average business is near zero growth.[42]
- **Most business owners do not have any appetite for growth.** The majority of new start-up owners seek to 'satisfice' rather than 'optimise' their business.[43]
- **Stage models downplay the role of the entrepreneur in business growth.** Most stage models argue that as a business evolves, control increasingly switches from the entrepreneur to managers. This can underplay the entrepreneur's ability to lead and their day-to-day involvement in the business. Elon Musk promised the South Australian government he could deliver a 100-megawatt lithium-ion battery in 100 days. If he failed, he would not charge them a penny. The battery was delivered ahead of schedule.
- **Business growth is unlikely to be continuous.** One period of growth may actually be followed by a period of stagnation or decline.[44]
- **Just how many stages – and crises – are there?**[45] What constitutes a crisis? Does this depend on individual circumstances? Just what are the life cycle regularities and just how do businesses transition from one stage to another? At a practical level, this presents challenges. Just what should entrepreneurs focus on? Chinese billionaire entrepreneur Jack Ma believes that focusing on a very small number of core objectives is the key to business success.[46] If this is right, stage models are unclear on which one, two or three strategic actions entrepreneurs should follow to grow.

At a practical level, there are limits to the *predictive* nature of stage models. Although they are intuitively appealing, stage models do not provide a reliable prophecy of how an individual business will grow. But they do provide a *descriptive* account of the need to develop managerial, operational and financial systems to cope with the pressures of growth.

Table 10.1 Scott and Bruce's (1987) managerial stages model

Stage	Management role	Management style	Organisation structure	Business focus	Challenges to get to next stage
1. Inception	Founder supervision	Entrepreneurial, individualistic	Unstructured	Getting product ready for market; product traction in market; getting finance	Establishing profitability; developing managerial procedures; need to delegate
2. Survival	Supervised supervision	Entrepreneurial, administrative	Simple	Getting working capital; increased competition	The danger of overtrading; the need for further delegation of tasks; external finance; overcoming increased competition; better financial information
3. Growth	Delegation/ Co-ordination	Entrepreneurial, co-ordinate	Functional (split into business areas such as finance and production), centralised (business power held at the centre)	Maintaining existing products; developing new products; maintaining financial health	Competing effectively with large businesses; financing new products while maintaining operational controls
4. Expansion	Decentralisation	Professional, administrative	Functional, decentralised (business power increasingly devolved to business units)	Obtaining long term equity finance; successfully integrating professional managers	Entrepreneurs able to cede control to professional managers; difficulties in getting staff to 'buy' into the mission of the business; greater focus on meeting customer needs
5. Maturity	Decentralisation	Watchdog	Decentralised functional/ product (split into functional business areas or by product category)	Marketing and continued differentiation of products; business succession	

Case Study: Keeping the lights on

© Getty Images

Bulb Energy founders Amit Gudka and Hayden Wood grew their renewable energy business from 15,000 to 300,000 customers in one year. But doubling customer numbers every three months had its challenges. To stay true to their vision of providing great customer service at an affordable price, they had to develop daily and weekly customer metrics to measure customer support. Otherwise, the business would quickly fall out of step with its customer and revenue growth. They also needed to pivot quickly to resolve issues when the metrics showed them that they needed to improve their performance.[47]

Entrepreneurship in Action

Eric Flamholtz and Yvonne Randle suggest there are clear symptoms of 'crises' or 'growing pains' in a business:[48]

- Staff are overstretched, unaware of what others are doing and spending too much time fighting fires.
- Managers are worried about where the business is going, feel meetings and plans are a waste of time and effort and believe the only way to get something done properly is to do it themselves.

These growing pains occur because there is a mismatch between what the business does – what they call its business infrastructure – and its revenues.[49] The infrastructure of a business consists of:

- How it manages resources, such as financial, human, technology and physical resources.
- Its operational systems, such as accounting, production and shipping, marketing and selling, and personnel.
- Management systems, such as planning, organisation, control and management development.
- Its culture – its values, beliefs and norms.

Strategic analysis and plans are essential to tackle growth pains, understand the current configuration of the business' infrastructure and to help align the infrastructure with growth.[50]

- Identify how a successful growing business overcame its growth crises or pains.
- Examine a business that did not deal well with growth. Was this a failure of alignment between the infrastructure of the business and its performance? Were there other reasons?

Discussion question:

- Do you think that there is any merit in stage model explanations for fast business growth?

10.5 STRATEGIC ENTREPRENEURSHIP APPROACHES TO GROWTH

10.5.1 *The importance of entrepreneurial teams*

One of the foremost entrepreneurship thinkers was Edith Penrose (1914–1996). She agreed with stage-based approaches that if a business is to grow, it has to develop its core capabilities and resources.[51] But she fundamentally departed from stage models in how she viewed businesses and what prompts growth. Her main problem with biological growth metaphors was that they missed the link between the motivations and activities of entrepreneurs and how their business grows.

Penrose's starting point was to argue that businesses are administrative units led by entrepreneurs who have bundles of resources that consist of the things a business buys, makes or sells, the entrepreneurial team and the staff it employs. She argued that what separates out one business from another was how the entrepreneurs chose to acquire, configure and use their resources. Penrose suggests this decision is path-dependent; in other words, history matters because an entrepreneur's past decisions influence the choices they make today and in the future.

Growth occurs if entrepreneurs find a formula that successfully combines and deploys their resources to create a source of sustainable advantage. Penrose argues that, ultimately, growth is better explained by what the business does (internal factors) rather than what happens to it in the marketplace (external factors) or because of blind luck.

Central to this is the entrepreneurial team. Better entrepreneurial teams have 'the imaginative effort, the sense of timing, and the instinctive recognition of what will catch on or how to make it catch on'.[52] They also have the skills, capabilities and competencies to use their resources to build what she called 'relatively impregnable bases'.[53] Today, these bases are more likely to be described as a company's 'sustained competitive advantage', which is a long term superiority in products or ways of doing business that competitors cannot easily duplicate.

10.5.2 Entrepreneurial orientations

This has led to a focus on entrepreneurial growth orientations. These are a prerequisite for growth.[54] It is difficult to believe that someone that starts up with no intention of growing will subsequently find themselves running or owning a large-scale business.

However, as a business expands, it may be more appropriate to talk about the entrepreneurial orientation (EO) of the business rather than the entrepreneur's personal motivation. EO is defined as 'strategic orientation, capturing specific entrepreneurial aspects of decision-making styles, methods, and practices'.[55] There are three core dimensions to EO: innovative, proactive and risk-taking.[56] Two additional dimensions are: competitive aggressiveness and autonomy (independence of activity).[57] EO is also associated with growth.[58]

Entrepreneurship in Action

There are different ways of measuring EO.[59] Below are a set of questions that have been adapted from a popular EO measure. It focuses on the three core dimensions and ranks EO on a scale of 1–7, with 1 being low on EO, and 7 being high.[60]

Innovation: The entrepreneurial team prefers...

A strong emphasis on marketing a tried-and-true offer	1 2 3 4 5 6 7	A strong emphasis on leading in innovation
Making small incremental changes to new products or services	1 2 3 4 5 6 7	Making radical changes to new products or services

Proactiveness: In dealing with its competitors, the business...

Waits for competitors to act first	1 2 3 4 5 6 7	Takes action before competitors
Lags behind in introducing new products and services	1 2 3 4 5 6 7	Focuses on being a first mover in the market
Prefers to avoid competition	1 2 3 4 5 6 7	Wants and relishes competition

Risk-taking: In general, the entrepreneurial team...

Prefers low-risk low-return business models	1 2 3 4 5 6 7	Prefers high-risk high-return business models
Believes it is better to be cautious and act slowly	1 2 3 4 5 6 7	Believes it is better to be quick and take the initiative

- Use these questions to analyse a business. Does it have a high EO? Measure this against its growth performance. What does this tell you about the relationship between EO and growth?

EO is not without criticism. Not all sectors are fast-paced and highly competitive. Some businesses grow when they cooperate and collaborate for mutual benefit. A social enterprise that wants to encourage better community values or source their goods ethically might believe being aggressively competitive is bad for business. Another issue is how businesses transition from one EO state to another. If EO is a business trait, there is little that a business can do to change its orientation. If it is a behaviour, it is unclear how businesses transform themselves to have greater levels of EO. And if it is a stable orientation, it is unclear how this fits with the fleeting and episodic nature of business growth.

Discussion questions:

- Having an entrepreneurial orientation might be necessary for growth. But is it sufficient for growth? If not, what other factors are important?
- Do you think that growth spurs the development of EO or is it the other way around?[61]

10.5.3 Growth attributes

Whilst it is difficult to work out if entrepreneurial teams cause growth or are built in response to growth, teams tend to have faster growth rates than solo entrepreneurs.[62] Likely causes of entrepreneurial team success are its collective cognitive abilities, a good balance of a range of skills, capabilities and knowledge and the ability to collaborate.[63] However, in some cases, less diverse teams run by directional rather than empowering leaders are more likely to grow.[64]

Entrepreneurship in Action

Below are four different leadership styles:

1. Entrepreneurial leadership – comes up with radical product or service improvements, new products or services, takes risks, is creative and passionate, has a vision and challenges current ways of doing business.[65]
2. Directional – sets goals, provides direction on how to achieve goals and often does the actual work.
3. Empowering – facilitates collaborative team working, provides participative goal setting and encourages individual action and opportunity recognition.
4. Adversarial – focuses on errors and mistakes, uses threats and intimidation and waits until an issue becomes a real problem.[66]

- Examine a growing business: what leadership style do its leaders follow?

Education and experience also appear to matter for growth.[67] Being better educated provides core skills and abilities and helps with accessing valuable social networks.[68] Education, though, is a form of 'generic' human capital and may be no substitute for the value of task-related 'specific' human capital such as prior managerial, sectoral and entrepreneurial experience. These 'university of life' experiences should provide core advantages because task-related experiences deepen skills, knowledge and abilities.[69] However, the evidence is mixed. No two business situations are the same, making it difficult to translate prior entrepreneurial experiences easily into a new context. Previous management experience may also be no substitute for the direct experience of owning a growth business. If earlier entrepreneurial experience is measured in isolation, it matters.[70] However, when other forms of experiences are also taken into account, it appears to have less of an impact on a growing business.

Entrepreneurship in Action

- Use LinkedIn to investigate the educational and business experience of entrepreneurs. Are they typically university graduates? Do they have direct prior experience of the industry? How many businesses have they run?

10.5.4 The importance of entrepreneurial versatility

Penrose also pointed to the importance of 'entrepreneurial versatility', which she saw as a quality of entrepreneurial imagination and vision. She argued that better teams are able to recognise their under-utilised resources, often called business slack, and identify how to use these spare resources to create new opportunities.[71]

Entrepreneurship in Action

To utilise its spare capacities, a business can vary **what** it sells or **whom** it sells to. This is the basis for the four basic strategic options for growth (Figure 10.2):

Figure 10.2 Strategic growth options

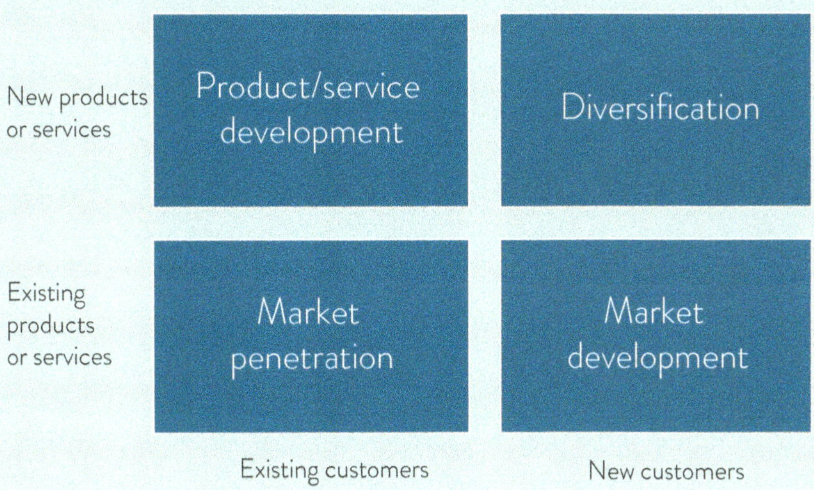

1. **Market penetration: selling more of existing products or services to existing customers.** A fast-food restaurant might do this by cross-selling (do you want a coke with your meal?) or upselling (do you want to 'go large'?). The aim is to increase market share. There are different ways of achieving this: sales and marketing through advertising, employing additional sales staff and loyalty schemes, by using penetration pricing (Chapter 8, p. 189) and by acquiring competitors. This option requires a strategic focus on executing and operations.
2. **Product or service development: selling existing customers a new product or service.** This might be an incremental change to an existing offer or the introduction of a radical new product or service. Both can be risky. Coca Cola's reformulation of its 'Classic' Coke into 'New Coke' proved to be a disaster. After a barrage of customer complaints, New Coke was dropped. Similarly, radical innovations such as Google Glasses failed. Product development requires R&D, sales and marketing expenditure, close attention to customer needs and operational capabilities.
3. **Market development: selling existing products or services to new customers.** In reaching new markets, businesses often have to consider the appropriate channels (Chapter 6, pp. 140–144) and cultural values. One of Coca-Cola's brands is Dasani. In the USA, Dasani uses municipal water and puts it through a process of reverse osmosis. It has expanded operations to the rest of the Americas and attempted to introduce it into the UK. This failed miserably. It turned out that the UK public was not prepared to pay a premium for what was essentially tap water.[72]
4. **Diversification: selling a new product or service to new customers.** This is the riskiest option. While the other three leverage existing capabilities and capacities, diversification essentially means developing a new business. Coca-Cola bought a wine business but quickly lost interest when it realised margins on wine (2–4 per cent) are much lower than soft drinks (20–30 per cent).[73]

- Analyse the strategic expansion of a fast-growth business. Did it grow by relentlessly focusing on its existing customers, changing its customers, changing what it sold or by diversifying?

Case Study: Up up and away

Like going to a garage to get a car fixed, most maintenance contracts are based on paying for repairs and servicing. However, this model incentivises the selling of spare parts, which may leave customers concerned about paying for repairs they do not need. Engine manufacturer Rolls-Royce has flipped maintenance contracts around by using an innovative 'pay per flying' maintenance contract. It only gets income from its maintenance contracts when the aircraft is flying. This incentivises the company to build reliable engines because it does not make money when they are on the ground being repaired. This has given Rolls-Royce a competitive advantage in the airline industry.

10

10.5.5 Ordinary and dynamic capabilities

Penrose's focus on entrepreneurial versatility has spawned an interest in how to transform business capabilities for growth. Every business uses its capabilities or organisational routines to organise how it buys, makes and sell its offer to customers. These 'ordinary' or operational capabilities can be a source of competitive advantage.

In fast-paced markets where it is possible to easily copy and replicate business processes,[74] ordinary capabilities can fail to provide a sustainable source of competitive advantage. In these cases, a business may need to focus more on the acquisition and retention of dynamic capabilities.[75] These are defined as 'the capabilities with which managers build, integrate, and reconfigure organizational resources and competencies'.[76] There are three core activities required to build a dynamic learning environment:[77]

- **Sensing** – being alert to opportunities inside and outside the business to create new ways of meeting customer needs.
- **Seizing** – committing resources to refine and change the mix of business models, such as incremental production or marketing shifts and the development of radical new business models.
- **Transforming** – aligning and investing in capabilities to operationalise the business model and supporting a culture to spread knowledge and learning throughout the organisation.

However, the 'sense, seize and transform' strategy mantra does not fully explain how a start-up scales up.[78] It is also difficult to distinguish between ordinary and dynamic capabilities and how a business acquires and retains its dynamic capabilities. Dynamic capabilities are likely to be unique to a particular business, making it hard for other businesses to replicate the magic sauce in a growth strategy. For instance, growth might result from being first into a market, or it might not.[79] Equally, following a cost-based strategy might lead to growth, but so too might following a differentiation strategy.[80]

Nonetheless, as a business expands it has to move away from existing customers and products to either exporting or developing its product range.[81] Strategies must also change over time or risk becoming outdated.[82] Toy seller Toys R Us built a business on massive toy stores, but wound-up filing for bankruptcy when it failed to adapt to the rise of e-commerce and growing customer demand for smaller retail settings.

Entrepreneurship in Action

Figure 10.3 shows a Business Model Canvas for a simple start-up smoothie making business (Chapter 5, Figure 5.3). It shows that this business proposes to shift from festival goers to the mass market and to develop a value proposition that explicitly involves sharing profits ethically. This business also has to change other key elements of how it does business, such as shifting from personal sales to selling through intermediaries, developing an ethical supply chain and promoting R&D.

Figure 10.3 The transition from start-up to scale-up Business Model Canvas template © Strategyzer AG; strategyzer.com/canvas

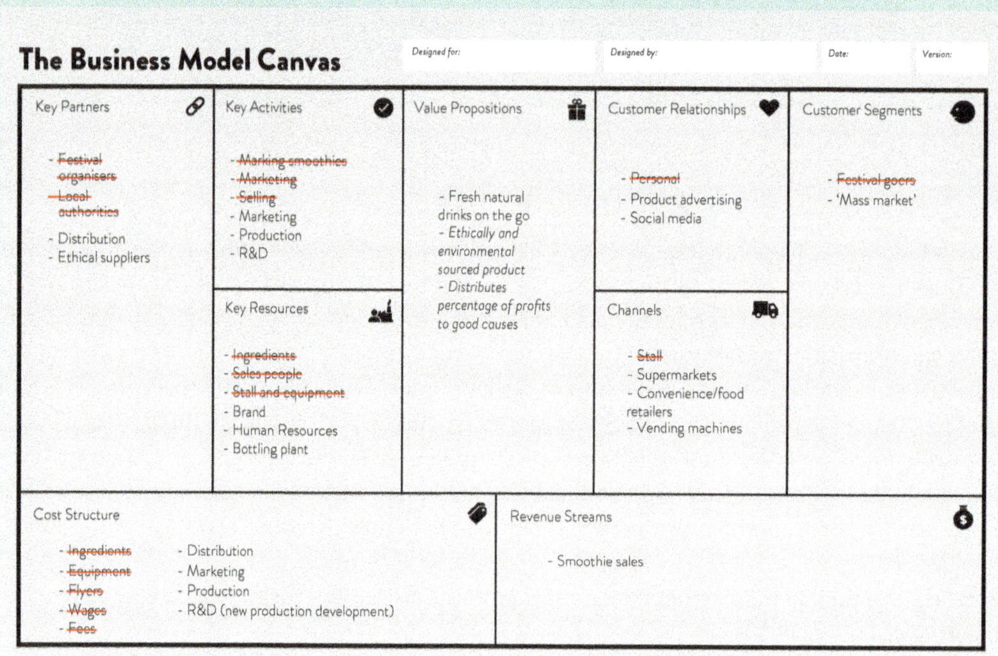

- Use the Business Model Canvas to redesign the key activities that a start-up should consider in scaling up.

Discussion question:

- Do you think that growing companies in fast moving markets can easily distinguish between their operational and dynamic capabilities?

10.5.6 The resource-based view

Penrose has also shaped the development of the resource-based view (RBV) of business growth. The RBV approach builds on three of her insights:

- Businesses are bundles of heterogeneous resources.
- Resources are relatively immobile and path-dependent.
- The entrepreneurial team directs resource usage and deployment in the business.

These resources can be defined as 'all assets, capabilities, organizational processes, firm dimensions, information, knowledge, etc controlled by a firm that enable the firm to conceive of and implement strategies that improve its efficiency and effectiveness'.[83]

From this, the RBV approach suggests growing businesses might have one or more of the following 'VRIN' attributes:

- *Valuable* – those resources or a combination of resources that allow the business to increase effectiveness and efficiency.
- *Rare* – resources that are not held by competitors.
- *Imperfectly imitable* – resources that are difficult and costly to copy.
- *Non-substitutable* – resources that have few alternative substitutes.

A key business resource is its staff. Southwest Airlines built a competitive advantage over other low-cost airlines through a customer-focused strategy that emancipated and incentivised its staff to go the 'extra mile'.

High-performance human resource practices such as training, recruitment and incentives provide key benefits for many businesses.[84] Such practices can also help small growing businesses. However, workforce development in smaller companies is often informal and occurs alongside the introduction of other managerial processes.[85] This makes it difficult to identify if training causes growth or is a response to growth.[86]

Case Study: Valve Corporation

Valve Corporation is a software company with a flat democratic organisational structure where there are no bosses and staff do not have to do what others tell them. Employees can choose their own projects, who they work with and when. They also have very high salaries and access to a range of fringe benefits such as a masseuse and subsidised restaurant. This could explain why Valve became one of the most profitable businesses per employee in the USA. An alternative view is that Valve's success is down to its being entirely self-financing and owning its own intellectual property.[87]

- Examine the human resource practices of a growing business in a particular sector. Does the way work is organised and rewarded influence growth?

Solely focusing on VRIN attributes neglects whether or not the business is sufficiently well organised to exploit its resources. It may have a unique product but lack the appropriate management systems to exploit it.

It can also be difficult to pinpoint exactly what a 'resource' actually is in RBV since 'virtually *anything* associated with the firm can be a resource'.[88] It also appears a circular argument because 'if valuable resources are defined as those increasing efficiency and/or effectiveness, and competitive advantage is defined as achieving increases in efficiency and/or effectiveness, a tautology exists'.[89]

Entrepreneurship in Action

Porter's Value Chain, a Valuable, Rare, Imitability and Organisation (VRIO) analysis, or a combination of both, can be used to understand the link between competitive advantage and the ability to deliver on this advantage[90]:

- Porter's Value Chain examines a business's core resources and identifies which resources provide a competitive advantage. Porter suggests business resources are either primary or support activities. Primary activities such as logistics, operations, marketing and sales are concerned with creating and delivering a product or service. Support activities include procurement, human resources, management and technology.
- A VRIO analysis builds on the VRIN attributes of Valuable, Rare and Imperfectly imitable to identify sources of competitive advantage and whether the business is organised to deliver on these advantages.
- Table 10.2 combines both VRIO questions with Porter's Value Chain.

Table 10.2 VRIO analysis by Porter's key Value Chain elements

Business resources	Valuable? (yes or no)	Rare? (yes or no)	Costly to imitate? (yes or no)	Organised to exploit? (yes or no)
Inbound logistics (products coming into the firm)				
Operations				
Outbound logistics (products going out of the firm)				
Marketing				
Sales				
Service				
Management				
Human resources management				
Technology				
Procurement				

- Examine a firm's resources. Are any of these valuable or rare sources of competitive advantage? How well has the business organised its resources to deliver on its competitive advantage?

One other resource concern is how to fund business expansion. Developing new products, exporting, marketing and sales all cost money. A lack of financial resources has a negative drag on business growth.[91] And while financial constraints can bind, it is not clear if external finance necessarily advantages business growth.[92] Equity finance is an obvious candidate, but this is not the only source of finance for growth. Indeed, only about 40 per cent of US public companies are Venture Capitalist (VC) backed.[93]

Penrose has stimulated an understanding of business growth that emphasises the importance of the entrepreneurial team, their capabilities and how they use and deploy their resources. These approaches lay bare the importance of entrepreneurs. How a business is run impacts on business performance.[94] Able, steadfast and resolute managers are key to encouraging innovation, and businesses that adopt better management practices are more productive.[95]

However, generalising from a single business to the wider population is unwise. The routines and culture an individual company adopts are often very specific to that business. There is also a mismatch between these strategic approaches and the empirical evidence on growth. Growth is spotty, and most growth businesses are just one-hit wonders.[96] Although high levels of EO, dynamic capabilities or having VRIO attributes are all *necessary* preconditions for growth, it is unclear if and how they are *sufficient* conditions for growth.

Discussion questions:

- Do you think that strategic approaches to growth provide a good explanation of business growth?
- If businesses benefit from particular resources, why is growth so spotty?

10.6 ENVIRONMENTAL APPROACHES TO GROWTH

While it is tempting to believe that entrepreneurs are the only authors of their success, entrepreneurial choices are made under uncertainty and are constrained by the external environment. For example, the riskiness of an industry influences the types of experience that promote growth: in low-risk situations it helps to have industry experience, but in high-risk contexts, it is better to have managerial experience.[97]

The environment can also be deterministic. Billionaire investor Warren Buffett once said: 'When a management team with a reputation for brilliance tackles a business with a reputation for bad economics, it is the reputation of the business that remains intact.'[98] This implies that no matter how talented the entrepreneurial team might be, what determines success is how favourable or munificent the environment is. After all, an Olympic gold medal-winning sailor can look decidedly ordinary if they have to sail on a windless day.

How *relatively* competitive a business is to others in their industry is also important. Roger Federer is one of the greatest tennis players ever. He won 16 tennis majors between 2003 and 2010. However, faced with competition from Rafael Nadal, Novak Djokovic and Andy Murray between 2010 and 2017, Federer won just one major. When Djokovic and Murray were both injured in the 2017 season, Federer's consistency saw him regain the world number one title.

Case Study: Finding the sweet spot

Finding a fast-moving market can prove decisive. Aged just 14, Fraser Doherty began adapting his grandmother's jam recipe to develop a range of sugar- and additive-free conserves. After sales of his jams proved popular in Scotland, he pitched them to UK supermarket buyers, who also recognised an untapped market. Early success propelled him to become one of the youngest ever millionaire entrepreneurs. When sales began to slow in his domestic market, he found new markets in South Korea and Japan.

10.6.1 Population ecology

Like stage models, population ecology theories focus on how businesses come into existence, develop and die. However, rather than concentrating on the trajectories of individual companies, they look at entire industries. They argue the richness of resources in markets and the nature of competition for them are fundamental to business birth and success.[99] If the environment is rich and there are few serious competitors, a business can grow by either following a specialist strategy that focuses on a particular niche, or a generalist strategy, such as entering different niches to spread their risk. However, in time success breeds competition for resources, which ultimately limits a business's growth potential. This limit is called density dependency. Exit is a common fate even for previously successful businesses when the way they do business or their organisational routines no longer fit their environment.

10.6.2 Evolutionary approaches

Survival of the fittest is also a key theme of evolutionary economic approaches. These stem from Schumpeter's insight that capitalism's processes are not marked by equilibrium but by 'creative destruction' (Chapter 7, pp. 177–178). 'Darwinism' may apply because some businesses offer a cost advantage or at least match the best practice in their industry.[100] This can be radical, particularly if the market is disrupted by start-ups who have superior ways of doing business that drives out existing players in the market.[101] One good example of the impact of disruptive innovation is the hard drive industry.[102] Existing firms in this industry did a decent job of developing and implementing strategies to meet customer needs until new competitors with more robust and higher-capacity solid-state drives swept their market out from under them.

Entrepreneurship in Action

- Examine a failed product or business. Analyse why it failed. How strong was the product–market fit? What could it have done to improve this fit? Was there anything it could have done to sustain an advantage over competitors?

10.6.3 Absorptive capacity

Viewing the external environment as essentially hostile underplays the importance of business collaboration and cooperation. There are three main ways of learning about the opposition: passively observing them; actively benchmarking against them; or learning with them. A business's ability to learn is known as its level of 'absorptive capacity', which is defined as 'a firm's fundamental learning processes: its ability to identify, assimilate, and exploit knowledge from the environment'.[103] Businesses with strong organisational routines and practices are better able than others to 'acquire, assimilate, transform, and exploit knowledge' for innovation and growth.[104]

Collaborating with outside parties such as universities or other businesses can stimulate new knowledge flows.[105] Such 'open innovation' can lead to entrepreneurial solutions to problems.[106] But cooperation may result in the weakening of intellectual property ownership and benefit larger businesses more than smaller businesses. Further, although higher levels of absorptive capacity appears to drive forward innovation, innovation itself does not necessarily lead to business growth.[107] Absorptive capacity's role in growth also remains unclear because the specific routines that allow individuals and businesses to access and utilise external knowledge are often underspecified.[108]

10.6.4 Location, location, location

The external business environment is shaped by its geographic contours. Either by choice or circumstance, companies can find themselves in 'entrepreneurial ecosystems', 'clusters' or 'industrial districts'.[109] All of these variations on the relationship between geography and entrepreneurship suggest that businesses benefit from being located close to each other. This clustering has three advantages.

1. **Access to specialist labour.** As Steve Jobs suggested, one of the mantras of knowledge-based growth businesses is the need to hire the best people.[110] Co-located businesses can draw on the

existing range of people with specialist skills in their area to develop the business. Areas with similar businesses also attract people with specialist skills to move to the area.

2. **Logistics and supply chain management costs savings.** Where businesses go, suppliers follow. This matters in 'fast fashion', where to keep up to date with current fashions, business source supplies closer to home so that they can quickly produce and manufacture fashionable designs.
3. **Advantages from knowledge spillovers.** These 'know how' and 'know who' advantages are geographically sensitive because knowledge is often implicit and travels poorly. To encourage innovation, some businesses provide spaces that allow different specialists to interact. Pixar Animation Studio's building was designed for managers, scientists and animators to share facilities, with the aim of fostering creativity and exchanging knowledge.

Not all fast-growth businesses are located in particular regions, but being in the right place does help.[111] It is no coincidence that business growth occurs in particular hotspots, usually grouped around urban metropolitan areas such as the European 'hot banana' (the area that runs from London through to Milan), the east and west coast of America or in the coastal areas of many Oceanic and Asian countries, such as Australia, China, India and Singapore.

Geography is also sticky. Take (West) German self-employment rates from 1925 onwards. Over this period, Germany suffered a severe recession, war and the successful rebuilding of the German economy. The regions that were entrepreneurial in 1925 stayed entrepreneurial after all these events.[112]

Case Study: Canva

Melanie Perkins and Cliff Obrecht started Fusion Books to sell yearbooks to schools in Perth, Australia. After initial success locally, they hit upon the idea of setting up Canva, an online design platform that allows people to create everything from website artwork to business cards. However, being located in Perth – one of the geographically most remote cities on earth – made access to finance difficult. So Perkins decided to go to Silicon Valley because it has the highest concentration of venture capitalists in the world. The size of this VC pool proved important as it took her three years and hundreds of rejections to get funding.[113]

Some businesses are 'born global' and start up to serve markets outside their home country.[114] Rather than first developing their offer in their local market and then tentatively looking to find the best way to export it, these companies go straight into international target markets.[115] However, most entrepreneurs do not take a strategic perspective on where they locate their business. Instead, they usually start up where they currently live.[116]

Entrepreneurship in Action

- Take a business that has grown domestically. Develop a Business Model Canvas to explore how the start-up could access a favourable export market.
- For your start-up, is it better to grow by following an incremental export strategy that focuses first on building up business domestically before turning to a favoured export market? Or is there more value in a born global approach?

10.6.5 The importance of social networks

The importance of social networks is implicit in collaborative and space-based approaches to entrepreneurial growth. Relationships and connections are not only important for spotting opportunities but also help entrepreneurs find resources and support for their business.[117] The trouble, though, is that it is difficult to pin down what role they play in business growth. Social networks can be divided into formal and informal, strong and weak ties, diverse or homogeneous (Chapter 3), Entrepreneurs also use social networks in different ways:

- Cast the net wide (a weak tie/diverse approach).
- Act as a gatekeeper, bridging between two or more networks (a structural hole approach).
- Rely on a few key family members to drive forward growth (a strong tie approach).[118]
- To make up for a lack of human or financial capital (a compensation approach).[119]

It is likely that social networks have an inverted U-shape effect on growth: there are increasing benefits up to a point in investing in them, but beyond this, it may be counterproductive.[120]

The external environment shapes business growth. What is less clear is why one business rather than another in the same environment grows. It is almost as if the entrepreneur has to be at the 'right place' and 'right time' to succeed.

Discussion questions:

- What do you think is more important to growth: finding a fertile market or having the right entrepreneurial team?
- If you choose to locate a business outside an entrepreneurial area, does this necessarily limit your growth prospects?
- If absorptive capacity is important to growth, why is growth so spotty?

10.7 RANDOM APPROACHES

Because entrepreneurship occurs under uncertainty, random or lucky events are often associated with business growth. Bill Gates argued that 'Our timing in setting up the first software company aimed at personal computers was essential to our success. The timing wasn't entirely luck, but without great luck it couldn't have happened.'[121] Luck is important because a number of factors can go right or wrong for entrepreneurs.

Case Study: Being lucky

Finnish game develops Rovio Entertainment had developed 51 relatively unsuccessful games and were on the brink of bankruptcy when they launched Angry Birds. The game debuted well on the Finnish Apple app store but its download ranking was around 600 in bigger markets. Its lucky break was to convince Apple to make it 'game of the week'. This propelled Angry Birds to be one of the most downloaded app-based games of all time.[122]

One early influential explanation for the role of luck is Jovanovic's model of 'noisy selection'.[123] He argued that entrepreneurs can only make estimates about their entrepreneurial talent once they are in business. If they find that they lack entrepreneurial talent they exit, but if they are talented they expand their business.

The process is 'noisy' because entrepreneurs might experience random shocks. Good luck might help them to grow their business but bad luck – even for the most talented – can lead them to exit. These effects are magnified in a 'winner-takes-all' market where only one business is likely to become the next Amazon, Google or Facebook. For example, if a new winner-takes-all market attracts 1000 entrants and the top ten entrants are all equally talented, the winner might be the one who has the greatest luck.

Luck can also have cumulative effects, particularly if resource accumulation and success depends on previous outcomes. For example, suppose ten women enter a snowboard slopestyle tournament where there are three rounds, and each round's score is added to the next round. First to snowboard is a rank outsider. She successfully completes her first run, achieving her best score all season. After she competes, the wind suddenly changes from a benign tailwind to a strong and variable headwind. Subsequently, all the other competitors either crash out or post scores well- below their average. The net result is that the rank outsider finds herself winning the competition because of the unassailable 'lucky' lead she built up in the first round.[124]

Gambler's ruin theory suggests that business growth outcomes are random and entrepreneurship is similar to playing roulette.[125] Over-optimistic entrepreneurs may believe they have the 'right stuff' to be successful, but in reality, the theory argues that they only achieve success because they were lucky. Having deep pockets is the only real thing that can help because access to finance means they can spin the wheel longer to increase their chances of winning eventually.

Luck does play an important role in business growth outcomes: 'the most elementary 'fact' about corporate growth thrown up by econometric work on both large and small firms is that firm size follows a random walk' (i.e. growth is largely random or stochastic).[126] Indeed, studies of business growth factors typically explain only about 4–10 per cent of why a business grows.[127]

Luck may also explain why equity financiers use a high-risk, high-return business model. Despite business angels and venture capitalists investing heavily in prospecting, screening and monitoring the growth of potential businesses, they recognise they will be lucky, even after all of this activity, to see one 'superstar' business emerge from a portfolio of investments. Moreover, although some top-performing VC funds do better, 'VC performance is mostly driven by luck'.[128]

However, humans struggle with the idea of luck. Having spent the majority of our 200,000-year history worrying where our next meal will come from or what might kill us, we are still pretty reliant on gut instincts and, indeed, 'we have no intuitive feel for the concept of randomness'.[129]

Take, for instance, an entrepreneur who one year suddenly makes a huge profit. Say they attribute this to their abilities. The next year, though, profit levels return to their long-run average. The entrepreneur is mystified and questions their abilities. However, statistically, it is common to see a 'regression to the mean' effect: a pattern of one extreme outcome surrounded by more moderate and usual outcomes. Hence, despite the entrepreneur's best efforts, profits regress to the mean average for the industry.[130]

Suggesting luck is a core determinant of business success neglects our ability to change the world. Regardless of how clouded an entrepreneur's mind is by cognitive biases, such as over-confidence or over-optimism, growth requires them to have a willingness to grow.

Furthermore, serial entrepreneurs are not just lucky, but better able to pick favourable industries and choose the right time to start up.[131] External factors also matter. The reason why some countries have greater numbers of billionaires may come down to them creating the conditions for entrepreneurs to make their own luck, through a strong rule of law, a well-educated population and market enhancing policies.[132]

Discussion questions:

- Do you think that you make your own luck?
- Do you agree with Jovanovic that people can only really estimate their level of entrepreneurial talent after they have set up a business?

10.8 WHAT YOU HAVE LEARNED IN THIS CHAPTER

10

This chapter has explained why high growth entrepreneurship is pivotal to economic wealth and prosperity. You have learned how fast-growth businesses – also called gazelles or scale-ups – create jobs across the world.

This suggests that entrepreneurship revolves not around start-ups but scale-ups.

But despite there being five common features, fast-growth businesses are rare and difficult to discern.

The chapter also showed you four perspectives on business growth:

1. **Stage models.** Although these fail to predict business development patterns, they do highlight that growth is a journey towards greater formalisation and specialisation.
2. **Strategic entrepreneurship approaches.** Penrose has stimulated interest in how motivations, capabilities and resources influence the strategy and activities of individual businesses. The appeal of these proactive business-led approaches is that they place entrepreneurs at the heart of growth and provide a number of practical ways of pursuing growth. This is attractive but does not sit easily with the spotty nature of business growth.
3. **External approaches.** A focus on the competitive and collaborative space-based nature of business growth is helpful because growth is a relative concept. Again, though, these types of approaches do not easily fit with the empirical evidence on growth.
4. **Chance.** Growth might be due to being lucky. This is dismal because it denies human agency. A more sensible approach is to recognise that although chance is important and may ultimately separate the winners from the near winners, an entrepreneur is only likely to be in contention if they have built up the motivations, skills, capabilities, knowledge and resources to be competitive.[133]

ASSESSMENT QUESTIONS

1. What role do social networks play in fast business growth?
2. What are the types of challenges faced in defining and measuring growth? What is the impact of these challenges?
3. Explain the contribution of education and experience in determining fast business growth.
4. How important are growth motivations and entrepreneurial orientations in explaining fast growth?

5. Is the external entrepreneurial environment deterministic?
6. Identify what the RBV approach is to business growth. Is it a useful approach?
7. What matters most: being in the right place, being at the right time or having the right stuff?

FURTHER READING

Baum, J. R., Locke, E. A., & Smith, K. G. (2001). A multidimensional model of venture growth. *Academy of Management Journal, 44*(2), 292–303.

Coad, A., Frankish, J., Roberts, R. G., & Storey, D. J. (2013). Growth paths and survival chances: An application of Gambler's Ruin theory. *Journal of Business Venturing, 28*(5), 615–632.

Rosenzweig, P. (2007). Misunderstanding the nature of company performance: The halo effect and other business delusions. *California Management Review, 49*(4), 6–20.

Teece, D. J. (2007). Explicating dynamic capabilities: The nature and microfoundations of (sustainable) enterprise performance. *Strategic Management Journal, 28*(13), 1319–1350.

Notes

1 *www.economist.com/node/21560867.*

2 Penrose, E. T. (1959). *The theory of the growth of the firm.* New York: Sharpe.

3 www.ft.com/content/238174d2-3139-11e9-8744-e7016697f225; www.kupela.fr/en/histoire-savoir-faire/.

4 Barney, J. B. (1986). Strategic factor markets: Expectations, luck, and business strategy. *Management Science, 32*(10), 1231–1241; Nelson, R., & Winter, S. (1982). *An evolutionary theory of technical change.* Cambridge, MA: Belknap Press of Harvard University Press.

5 Coad, A. (2009). *The growth of firms: A survey of theories and empirical evidence.* Cheltenham: Edward Elgar Publishing.

6 For example: www.thetimes.co.uk/article/fast-track-100-winners-named-j958tsq0m2m; www.afr.com/leadership/entrepreneur/financial-review-fast-100-2018-the-full-list-20181030-h179hx.

7 Peters, T. J., & Waterman, R. H. (1984). *In search of excellence: Lessons from America's best-run companies.* New York: Warner Books; Collins, J. C., & Porras, J. I. (1994). *Built to last: Successful habits of visionary companies.* New York: HarperBusiness; Collins, J. C. (2001). *Good to great: Why some companies make the leap ... and others don't.* New York: Random House; Collins, J., & Hansen, M. T. (2011). *Great by choice: Uncertainty, Chaos and luck – Why some thrive despite them all.* New York: Random House.

8 Rosenzweig, P. (2007). Misunderstanding the nature of company performance: The halo effect and other business delusions. *California Management Review, 49*(4), 6–20.

9 Ibid.

10 Eurostat/Organization for Economic Co-operation and Development (OECD). (2007). *Eurostat/OECD manual on business demography statistics.* Paris: Eurostat.

11 Daunfeldt, S. O., Johansson, D., & Halvarsson, D. (2015). Using the Eurostat-OECD definition of high-growth firms: A cautionary note. *Journal of Entrepreneurship and Public Policy, 4*(1), 50–56; Almus, M. (2002). What characterizes a fast-growing firm? *Applied Economics, 34*(12), 1497–1508.

12 https://ig.ft.com/ft-1000/2018/#methodology.

13 Coad, A., Daunfeldt, S. O., Johansson, D., & Wennberg, K. (2014). Whom do high-growth firms hire? *Industrial and Corporate Change, 23*(1), 293–327.

14 Achtenhagen, L., Naldi, L., & Melin, L. (2010). "Business growth" – Do practitioners and scholars really talk about the same thing? *Entrepreneurship Theory and Practice, 34*(2), 289–316.

15 Daunfeldt, S. O., Elert, N., & Johansson, D. (2010). *The economic contribution of high-growth firms: Do definitions matter* (Ratio Working Papers), p. 151.

16 Coad, A., Cowling, M., & Siepel, J. (2017). Growth processes of high-growth firms as a four-dimensional chicken and egg. *Industrial and Corporate Change, 26*(4), 537–554; Davidsson, P., Steffens, P., & Fitzsimmons, J. (2009). Growing profitable or growing from profits: Putting the horse in front of the cart? *Journal of Business Venturing, 24*(4), 388–406.

17 McKelvie, A., & Wiklund, J. (2010). Advancing firm growth research: A focus on growth mode instead of growth rate. *Entrepreneurship Theory and Practice,*

34(2), 261–288; Andersson, M., & Xiao, J. (2016). Acquisitions of start-ups by incumbent businesses: A market selection process of "high-quality" entrants? *Research Policy*, *45*(1), 272–290.

18 Carter, S., Mwaura, S., Ram, M., Trehan, K., & Jones, T. (2015). Barriers to ethnic minority and women's enterprise: Existing evidence, policy tensions and unsettled questions. *International Small Business Journal*, *33*(1), 49–69; Efendic, N., Andersson, F. W., & Wennberg, K. (2016). Growth in first-and second-generation immigrant firms in Sweden. *International Small Business Journal*, *34*(8), 1028–1052.

19 Cooper, A. C., Gimeno-Gascon, F. J., & Woo, C. Y. (1994). Initial human and financial capital as predictors of new venture performance. *Journal of Business Venturing*, *9*(5), 371–395; Brüderl, J., & Preisendörfer, P. (2000). Fast-growing businesses: Empirical evidence from a German study. *International Journal of Sociology*, *30*(3), 45–70.

20 Robb, A. M., & Watson, J. (2012). Gender differences in firm performance: Evidence from new ventures in the United States. *Journal of Business Venturing*, *27*(5), 544–558.

21 OECD. (2016). *Entrepreneurship at a glance 2016*. Paris: OECD.

22 https://techcrunch.com/2013/11/02/welcome-to-the-unicorn-club/.

23 www.census.gov/quickfacts/fact/table/US#.

24 Bravo-Biosca, A., Criscuolo, C., & Menon, C. (2013). *What drives the dynamics of business growth?* (OECD Science, Technology and Industry Policy Papers), p. 1; Henrekson, M., & Johansson, D. (2010). Gazelles as job creators: A survey and interpretation of the evidence. *Small Business Economics*, *35*(2), 227–244.

25 Decker, R. A., Haltiwanger, J., Jarmin, R. S., & Miranda, J. (2016). Where has all the skewness gone? The decline in high-growth (young) firms in the US. *European Economic Review*, *86*, 4–23; Deschryvere, M. (2008). *High growth firms and job creation in Finland* (ETLA Discussion Paper No. 1144); Daunfeldt et al. (2015), ibid.; NESTA. (2011). *Vital growth: The Importance of high-growth businesses to the recovery*. London: NESTA.

26 Lotti, F., Santarelli, E., & Vivarelli, M. (2009). Defending Gibrat's Law as a long-run regularity. *Small Business Economics*, *32*(1), 31–44; Almus, M. (2000). Testing "Gibrat's Law" for young firms – Empirical results for West Germany. *Small Business Economics*, *15*(1), 1–12.

27 Quatraro, F., & Vivarelli, M. (2014). Drivers of entrepreneurship and post-entry performance of newborn firms in developing countries. *The World Bank Research Observer*, *30*(2), 277–305.

28 Birch, D. (1979). *The job generation process*. Cambridge, MA: MIT Program on Neighborhood and Regional Change; Neumark, D., Wall, B., & Zhang, J. (2011). Do small businesses create more jobs? New evidence for the United States from the National Establishment Time Series. *The Review of Economics and Statistics*, *93*(1), 16–29; De Wit, G., & De Kok, J. (2014). Do small businesses create more jobs? New evidence for Europe. *Small Business Economics*, *42*(2), 283–295.

29 Coad et al. (2017), ibid.; Anyadike-Danes, M., & Hart, M. (2014). All grown up? The fate after 15 years of a quarter of a million UK firms born in 1998. *Journal of Evolutionary Economics*, *28*(4), 1–32.

30 Haltiwanger, J., Jarmin, R. S., & Miranda, J. (2013). Who creates jobs? Small versus large versus young. *Review of Economics and Statistics*, *95*(2), 347–361; Lawless, M. (2014). Age or size? Contributions to job creation. *Small Business Economics*, *42*(4), 815–830.

31 Coad, A., Daunfeldt, S. O., & Halvarsson, D. (2018). Bursting into life: Firm growth and growth persistence by age. *Small Business Economics*, *50*(1), 55–75.

32 Coad, A., Frankish, J., Roberts, R. G., & Storey, D. J. (2013). Growth paths and survival chances: An application of Gambler's Ruin theory. *Journal of Business Venturing*, *28*(5), 615–632.

33 Coad, A. (2007). A closer look at serial growth rate correlation. *Review of Industrial Organization*, *31*(1), 69–82; Satterthwaite, S., & Hamilton, R. T. (2017). High-growth firms in New Zealand: Superstars or shooting stars? *International Small Business Journal*, *35*(3), 244–261; Coad, A., & Hölzl, W. (2009). On the autocorrelation of growth rates. *Journal of Industry, Competition and Trade*, *9*(2), 139–166; Parker, S. C., Storey, D. J., & Van Witteloostuijn, A. (2010). What happens to gazelles? The importance of dynamic management strategy. *Small Business Economics*, *35*(2), 203–226.

34 Daunfeldt, S. O., & Halvarsson, D. (2015). Are high-growth firms one-hit wonders? Evidence from Sweden. *Small Business Economics*, *44*(2), 361–383.

35 Coad, A., & Rao, R. (2008). Innovation and firm growth in high-tech sectors: A quantile regression approach. *Research Policy*, *37*(4), 633–648; Acs, Z. J., Parsons, W., & Tracy, S. (2008). *High-impact firms: gazelles revisited*. Washington, DC: SBA; Henrekson & Johansson (2010), ibid.

36 Daunfeldt, S. O., Elert, N., & Johansson, D. (2016). Are high-growth firms overrepresented in high-tech industries? *Industrial and Corporate Change*, *25*(1), 1–21.

37 Geroski, P. A. (2002). The growth of firms in theory and in practice. *Competence, Governance, and Entrepreneurship – Advances in economic strategy research*., pp. 168–186.

38 Daunfeldt et al. (2016), ibid.

39 Churchill, N. C., & Lewis, V. (1983). The five stages of small business growth. *Harvard Business Review*, *61*(May–June), 30–50; Hanks, S. H., Watson, C. J., Jansen, E., & Chandler, G. N. (1994). Tightening the life-cycle construct: A taxonomic study of growth stage configurations in high-technology organizations. *Entrepreneurship Theory and Practice*, *18*(2), 5–29; Levie, J., & Lichtenstein, B. B. (2010). A terminal assessment of stages theory: Introducing a dynamic states approach to entrepreneurship. *Entrepreneurship Theory and Practice*, *34*(2), 317–350.

40 Greiner, L. E. (1972). Evolution and revolution as organizations grow. *Harvard Business Review*, *50*(4), 37–46; Greiner, L. E. (1998). Evolution and revolution as organizations grow – Larry E. Greiner responds. *Harvard Business Review*, *76*(4), 178–179.

41 Scott, M., & Bruce, R. (1987). Five stages of growth in small business. *Long Range Planning, 20*(3), 45–52.

42 Decker et al. (2016), ibid.; Bravo-Biosca, A. (2010). *Firm growth dynamics across countries: Evidence from a new database* (FORA-NESTA Working Paper).

43 Hurst, E., & Pugsley, B. W. (2011). *What do small businesses do?* (No. w17041). National Bureau of Economic Research.

44 Parker et al. (2010), ibid.; Coad et al. (2013), ibid.

45 Phelps, R., Adams, R., & Bessant, J. (2007). Life cycles of growing organizations: A review with implications for knowledge and learning. *International Journal of Management Reviews, 9*(1), 1–30.

46 https://vulcanpost.com/246691/jack-ma-success-luck-speaking-harsh-truths/.

47 www.bbc.co.uk/news/av/business-42821700/when-you-grow-quickly-it-can-be-challenging.

48 Flamholtz, E. G., & Randle, Y. (2015). *Growing pains: Building sustainably successful organizations.* New York: Wiley.

49 Ibid.

50 Ibid.

51 Penrose (1959), ibid.

52 Penrose (1959), ibid., p. 37.

53 Penrose (1959), ibid., p. 137.

54 Delmar, F., & Wiklund, J. (2008). The effect of small business managers' growth motivation on firm growth: a longitudinal study. *Entrepreneurship Theory and Practice, 32*(3), 437–457; Cassar, G. (2007). Money, money, money? A longitudinal investigation of entrepreneur career reasons, growth preferences and achieved growth. *Entrepreneurship and Regional Development, 19*(1), 89–107; Baum, J. R., Locke, E. A., & Smith, K. G. (2001). A multidimensional model of venture growth *Academy of Management Journal, 44*(2), 292–303; Baum, J. R., & Locke, E. A. (2004). The relationship of entrepreneurial traits, skill, and motivation to subsequent venture growth. *Journal of Applied Psychology, 89*(4), 587.

55 Wiklund, J., & Shepherd, D. (2005). Entrepreneurial orientation and small business performance: A configurational approach. *Journal of Business Venturing, 20*(1), 71–91, 74.

56 Wales, W. J. (2016). Entrepreneurial orientation: A review and synthesis of promising research directions. *International Small Business Journal, 34*(1), 3–15, 4.

57 Lumpkin, G. T., & Dess, G. G. (1996). Clarifying the entrepreneurial orientation construct and linking it to performance. *Academy of Management Review, 21*(1), 135–172.

58 Rauch, A. Wiklund, J., Lumpkin, G. T., & Frese, M. (2009). Entrepreneurial orientation and business performance: An assessment of past research and suggestions for the future. *Entrepreneurship Theory and Practice, 33*(3), 761–787.

59 Covin, J. G., & Wales, W. J. (2012). The measurement of entrepreneurial orientation. *Entrepreneurship Theory and Practice, 36*(4), 677–702.

60 Covin, J. G., & Slevin, D. P. (1989). Strategic management of small firms in hostile and benign environments. *Strategic Management Journal, 10*, 75–87; Miller, D. (1983). The correlates of entrepreneurship in three types of firms. *Management science, 29*(7), 770-791.

61 Eshima, Y., & Anderson, B. S. (2017). Firm growth, adaptive capability, and entrepreneurial orientation. *Strategic Management Journal, 38*(3), 770–779.

62 Stam, E., & Schutjens, V. (2005). *The Fragile success of team start-ups* (Papers on Entrepreneurship, Growth and Public Policy), p. 1705; Klotz, A. C., Hmieleski, K. M., Bradley, B. H., & Busenitz, L. W. (2014). 'New venture teams: A review of the literature and roadmap for future research. *Journal of Management, 40*(1), 226–255.

63 Brinckmann, J., & Hoegl, M. (2011). Effects of initial teamwork capability and initial relational capability on the development of new technology-based firms. *Strategic Entrepreneurship Journal, 5*(1), 37–57; Hoogendoorn, S., Parker, S. C., & Van Praag, M. (2017). Smart or diverse start-up teams? Evidence from a field experiment. *Organization Science, 28*(6), 1010–1028.

64 Hmieleski, K. M., & Ensley, M. D. (2007). A contextual examination of new venture performance: Entrepreneur leadership behavior, top management team heterogeneity, and environmental dynamism. *Journal of Organizational Behavior, 28*(7), 865–889; Amason, A. C., Shrader, R. C., & Tompson, G. H. (2006). Newness and novelty: relating top management team composition to new venture performance. *Journal of Business Venturing, 21*(1), 125–148.

65 Renko, M., El Tarabishy, A., Carsrud, A. L., & Brännback, M. (2015). Understanding and measuring entrepreneurial leadership style. *Journal of Small Business Management, 53*(1), 54–74.

66 Pearce, C. L., & Sims Jr, H. P. (2002). Vertical versus shared leadership as predictors of the effectiveness of change management teams: An examination of aversive, directive, transactional, transformational, and empowering leader behaviors. *Group Dynamics: Theory, Research, and Practice, 6*(2), 172: Zaech, S., & Baldegger, U. (2017). Leadership in start-ups. *International Small Business Journal, 35*(2), 157–177; Ensley, M. D., Hmieleski, K. M., & Pearce, C. L. (2006). The importance of vertical and shared leadership within new venture top management teams: Implications for the performance of startups. *The Leadership Quarterly, 17*(3), 217–231; Hmieleski, K. M., Cole, M. S., & Baron, R. A. (2012). Shared authentic leadership and new venture performance. *Journal of Management, 38*(5), 1476–1499.

67 Unger, J. M., Rauch, A., Frese, M., & Rosenbusch, N. (2011). Human capital and entrepreneurial success: A meta-analytical review. *Journal of Business Venturing, 26*(3), 341-358.; Mayer-Haug, K., Read, S., Brinckmann, J., Dew, N., & Grichnik, D. (2013). Entrepreneurial talent and venture performance: a meta-analytic investigation of SMEs. *Research Policy, 42*(6–7), 1251–1273; Demir, R., Wennberg, K., & McKelvie, A. (2017). The strategic management of high-growth firms: A review and theoretical

conceptualization. *Long Range Planning, 50*(4), 431–456.
68 van der Sluis, J., Van Praag, M., & Vijverberg, W. (2008). Education and entrepreneurship selection and performance: A review of the empirical literature. *Journal of Economic Surveys, 22*(5), 795–841; Barringer, B. R., Jones, F. F., & Neubaum, D. O. (2005). A quantitative content analysis of the characteristics of rapid-growth firms and their founders. *Journal of Business Venturing, 20*(5), 663–687.
69 Bosma, N., Van Praag, M., Thurik, R., & De Wit, G. (2004). The value of human and social capital investments for the business performance of startups. *Small Business Economics, 23*(3), 227–236; Ganotakis, P. (2012). Founders' human capital and the performance of UK new technology-based firms. *Small Business Economics, 39*(2), 495–515; Baum, J. R., & Bird, B. J. (2010). The successful intelligence of high-growth entrepreneurs: Links to new venture growth. *Organization Science, 21*(2), 397–412; Stam, E., & Wennberg, K. (2009). The roles of R&D in new firm growth. *Small Business Economics, 33*(1), 77–89; Eesley, C. E., & Roberts, E. B. (2012). Are you experienced or are you talented?: When does innate talent versus experience explain entrepreneurial performance? *Strategic Entrepreneurship Journal, 6*(3), 207–219; Gompers, P., Kovner, A., Lerner, J., & Scharfstein, D. (2010). Performance persistence in entrepreneurship. *Journal of Financial Economics, 96*(1), 18-32.
70 Ucbasaran, D., Westhead, P., & Wright, M. (2006). *Habitual entrepreneurs*. Cheltenham: Edward Elgar Publishing.
71 Bradley, S. W., Wiklund, J., & Shepherd, D. A. (2011). Swinging a double-edged sword: The effect of slack on entrepreneurial management and growth. *Journal of Business Venturing, 26*(5), 537–554.
72 news.bbc.co.uk/1/hi/business/3809539.stm.
73 www.forbes.com/sites/thomaspellechia/2018/03/09/after-more-than-thirty-five-years-away-from-it-coca-cola-is-getting-back-into-alcohol/.
74 Teece, D. J. (2007). Explicating dynamic capabilities: The nature and microfoundations of (sustainable) enterprise performance. *Strategic Management Journal, 28*(13), 1319–1350.
75 Ibid.
76 Adner, R., & Helfat, C. E. (2003). Corporate effects and dynamic managerial capabilities. *Strategic Management Journal, 24*(10), 1011–1025, 1012.
77 Teece (2007), ibid.
78 Ibid.
79 Robert Baum, J., & Wally, S. (2003). Strategic decision speed and firm performance. *Strategic Management Journal, 24*(11), 1107–1129; Bruton, G. D., & Rubanik, Y. (2002). Resources of the firm, Russian high-technology startups, and firm growth. *Journal of Business Venturing, 17*(6), 553–576.
80 O'Regan, N., Ghobadian, A., & Sims, M. (2006). Fast tracking innovation in manufacturing SMEs. *Technovation, 26*(2), 251–261; Siegel, R., Siegel, E., & Macmillan, I. C. (1993). Characteristics distinguishing high-growth ventures. *Journal of Business Venturing, 8*(2), 169–180; Barringer et al. (2005), ibid.
81 Golovko, E., & Valentini, G. (2011). Exploring the complementarity between innovation and export for SMEs' growth. *Journal of International Business Studies, 42*(3), 362–380.
82 Parker et al. (2010), ibid.
83 Barney, J. (1991). Firm resources and sustained competitive advantage. *Journal of Management, 17*(1), 99–120, 101.
84 Huselid, M. A. (1995). The impact of human resource management practices on turnover, productivity, and corporate financial performance. *Academy of Management Journal, 38*(3), 635–672; Rauch, A., & Hatak, I. (2016). A meta-analysis of different HR-enhancing practices and performance of small and medium sized firms. *Journal of Business Venturing, 31*(5), 485–504; Garavan, T., Watson, S., Carbery, R., & O'Brien, F. (2016). The antecedents of leadership development practices in SMEs: The influence of HRM strategy and practice. *International Small Business Journal, 34*(6), 870–890.
85 Altinay, L., Altinay, E., & Gannon, J. (2008). Exploring the relationship between the human resource management practices and growth in small service firms. *The Service Industries Journal, 28*(7), 919–937; Lopez-Garcia, P., & Puente, S. (2012). What makes a high-growth firm? A dynamic probit analysis using Spanish firm-level data. *Small Business Economics, 39*(4), 1029–1041; Sheehan, M. (2014). Human resource management and performance: Evidence from small and medium-sized firms. *International Small Business Journal, 32*(5), 545–570.
86 Wright, P. M., Gardner, T. M., Moynihan, L. M., & Allen, M. R. (2005). The relationship between HR practices and firm performance: examining causal order. *Personnel Psychology, 58*(2), 409–446.
87 media.steampowered.com/apps/valve/Valve_Handbook_LowRes.pdf.
88 Priem, R. L., & Butler, J. E. (2001a). Is the resource-based "view" a useful perspective for strategic management research? *Academy of Management Review, 26*(1), 22–40, 32.
89 Priem, R. L., & Butler, J. E. (2001b). Tautology in the resource-based view and the implications of externally determined resource value: Further comments. *Academy of Management Review, 26*(1), 57–66, 58.
90 Barney, J. B. (1995). Looking inside for competitive advantage. *The Academy of Management Executive 9*(4), 49–61.
91 Goedhuys, M., & Sleuwaegen, L. (2010). High-growth entrepreneurial firms in Africa: A quantile regression approach. *Small Business Economics, 34*(1), 31–51.
92 Parker et al. (2010), ibid.
93 Davila, A., Foster, G., & Gupta, M. (2003). Venture capital financing and the growth of startup firms. *Journal of Business Venturing, 18*(6), 689–708; Bertoni, F., Colombo, M. G., & Grilli, L. (2011). Venture capital financing and the growth of high-tech

start-ups: Disentangling treatment from selection effects. *Research Policy, 40*(7), 1028–1043; Gornall, W., & Strebulaev, I. A. (2015). *The economic impact of venture capital: Evidence from public companies* (Stanford University Graduate School of Business Research Paper), pp. 15–55.

94 Bertrand, M., & Schoar, A. (2003). Managing with style: The effect of managers on firm policies. *The Quarterly Journal of Economics, 118*(4), 1169–1208; Bowman, E. H., & Helfat, C. E. (2001). Does corporate strategy matter? *Strategic Management Journal, 22*(1), 1–23.

95 Kaplan, S. N., Klebanov, M. M., & Sorensen, M. (2012). Which CEO characteristics and abilities matter? *The Journal of Finance, 67*(3), 973–1007; Custódio, C., Ferreira, M. A., & Matos, P. (2017). Do general managerial skills spur innovation?. *Management Science, 65*(2), 459-476.; Bloom, N., Eifert, B., Mahajan, A., McKenzie, D., & Roberts, J. (2013). Does management matter? Evidence from India *The Quarterly Journal of Economics, 128*(1), 1–51; Bloom, N., & Van Reenen, J. (2007). Measuring and explaining management practices across firms and countries. *The Quarterly Journal of Economics, 122*(4), 1351-1408; Bloom, N., Genakos, C., Sadun, R., & Van Reenen, J. (2012). Management practices across firms and countries. *The Academy of Management Perspectives, 26*(1), 12–33.

96 Daunfeldt & Halvarsson (2015), ibid.

97 Dencker, J. C., & Gruber, M. (2015). The effects of opportunities and founder experience on new firm performance. *Strategic Management Journal, 36*(7), 1035–1052.

98 https://fortune.com/2012/11/19/the-wit-and-wisdom-of-warren-buffett/.

99 Hannan, M. T., & Freeman, J. (1977). The population ecology of organizations. *American Journal of Sociology, 82*(5), 929–964.

100 Nelson & Winter (1982), ibid.

101 Acemoglu, D., Akcigit, U., Alp, H., Bloom, N., & Kerr, W. R. (2013). *Innovation, reallocation and growth* (NBER Working Paper w18993). Cambridge, MA: National Bureau of Economic Research.

102 Christensen, C. M. (1997). *The innovator's dilemma. Cambridge, MA: Harvard Business School Press.*

103 Lane, P. J., & Lubatkin, M. (1998). Relative absorptive capacity and interorganizational learning. *Strategic Management Journal, 19*(5), 461–477; Cohen, W. M., & Levinthal, D. A. (1990). The implications of spillovers for R&D investment and welfare: A new perspective. *Administrative Science Quarterly, 35*(1990), 128–152; Lane, P. J., Koka, B. R., & Pathak, S. (2006). The reification of absorptive capacity: A critical review and rejuvenation of the construct. *Academy of Management Review, 31*(4), 833–863, 833.

104 Zahra, S. A., & George, G. (2002). Absorptive capacity: A review, reconceptualization, and extension. *Academy of Management Review, 27*(2), 185–203, 186.

105 Chesbrough, H. W. (2006). *Open innovation: The new imperative for creating and profiting from technology.* Cambridge, MA: Harvard Business Press.

106 Hewitt-Dundas, N., & Roper, S. (2018). Exploring market failures in open innovation. *International Small Business Journal, 36*(1), 23–40.

107 Zou, T., Ertug, G., & George, G. (2018). The capacity to innovate: a meta-analysis of absorptive capacity. *Innovation, 20*(2), 1–35.

108 Lewin, A. Y., Massini, S., & Peeters, C. (2011). Microfoundations of internal and external absorptive capacity routines. *Organization Science, 22*(1), 81–98.

109 Marshall, A. (1890). *Principles of economics.* London: Macmillan; Porter, M. E. (2000). Location, competition, and economic development: Local clusters in a global economy. *Economic Development Quarterly, 14*(1), 15–34; Martin, R., & Sunley, P. (2003). Deconstructing clusters: Chaotic concept or policy panacea? *Journal of Economic Geography, 3*(1), 5–35; Spigel, B. (2017). The relational organization of entrepreneurial ecosystems. *Entrepreneurship Theory and Practice, 41*(1), 49–72; Brown, R., & Mason, C. (2017). Looking inside the spiky bits: A critical review and conceptualisation of entrepreneurial ecosystems. *Small Business Economics, 49*(1), 11–30.

110 https://recruitloop.com/blog/steve-jobs-top-hiring-tip-hire-the-best/.

111 Acs, Z. J., Parsons, W., & Tracy, S. (2008). *High-impact firms: gazelles revisited*; Coad et al. (2014), ibid.

112 Fritsch, M., & Wyrwich, M. (2016). The effect of entrepreneurship on economic development – An empirical analysis using regional entrepreneurship culture. *Journal of Economic Geography, 17*(1), 157–189; Fritsch, M., & Wyrwich, M. (2018). Regional knowledge, entrepreneurial culture, and innovative start-ups over time and space—an empirical investigation. *Small Business Economics, 51*(2), 337–353.

113 www.bbc.co.uk/news/av/business-42614073/anyone-can-jump-in-and-design-something; https://about.canva.com/story/; www.theguardian.com/cities/2015/aug/19/where-worlds-most-remote-city.

114 Oviatt, B. M., & McDougall, P. P. (1994). Toward a theory of international new ventures. *Journal of International Business Studies, 25*(1), 45–64.

115 Johanson, J., & Vahlne, J. E. (1977). The internationalization process of the firm – A model of knowledge development and increasing foreign market commitments. *Journal of International Business Studies, 8*(1), 23–32.

116 Stam, E. (2007). Why butterflies don 't leave: Locational behavior of entrepreneurial firms. *Economic Geography, 83*(1), 27–50; Figueiredo, O., Guimaraes, P., & Woodward, D. (2002). Home-field advantage: Location decisions of Portuguese entrepreneurs. *Journal of Urban Economics, 52*(2), 341–361.

117 Brüderl, J., & Preisendörfer, P. (1998). Network support and the success of newly founded business. *Small Business Economics, 10*(3), 213–225; Hite, J. M., & Hesterly, W. S. (2001). The evolution of firm networks: From emergence to early growth of the firm. *Strategic Management Journal, 22*(3), 275–286; Stam, W., Arzlanian, S., & Elfring, T. (2014). Social capital of entrepreneurs and small firm performance: A meta-analysis of contextual and methodological moderators. *Journal of Business Venturing, 29*(1), 152–173.

118 Burt, R. S. (2000). The network structure of social capital. *Research in Organizational Behavior, 22*, 345–423.
119 Fang, R., Chi, L., Chen, M., & Baron, R. A. (2015). Bringing political skill into social networks: Findings from a field study of entrepreneurs. *Journal of Management Studies, 52*(2), 175–212; Witt, P. (2004). Entrepreneurs' networks and the success of start-ups. *Entrepreneurship & Regional Development, 16*(5), 391–412.
120 Watson, J. (2007). Modeling the relationship between networking and firm performance. *Journal of Business Venturing, 22*(6), 852–874.
121 https://buffalonews.com/1997/03/31/luck-plays-a-big-role-in-success/.
122 www.wired.co.uk/article/how-rovio-made-angry-birds-a-winner; www.pcworld.com/article/206831/the_origins_of_angry_birds.html; www.entrepreneur.com/article/226107.
123 Jovanovic, B. (1982). Selection and the evolution of industry. *Econometrica: Journal of the Econometric Society, 50*(3), 649–670.
124 Denrell, J. (2004). Random walks and sustained competitive advantage. *Management Science, 50*(7), 922–934.
125 Coad et al. (2013), ibid.
126 Geroski (2002), ibid., p. 169.
127 Coad (2009), ibid.
128 Korteweg, A., & Sorensen, M. (2017). Skill and luck in private equity performance. *Journal of Financial Economics, 124*(3), 535–562, 536.
129 Gardner, D. (2009). *Risk: The science and politics of fear* (p. 116). New York: Random House.
130 Parker et al. (2010), ibid.
131 Gompers et al. (2010), ibid.
132 Sanandaji, T., & Leeson, P. T. (2013). Billionaires. *Industrial and Corporate Change, 22*(1), 313–337.
133 Nelson & Winter (1982), ibid.

CHAPTER 11

Entrepreneurial Exit

Learning Outcomes

In this chapter you will learn:

- Why exit is not always the same as failure.
- The factors that influence entrepreneurial exits.
- The succession challenges some family businesses encounter.

Mini Contents List

11.1 INTRODUCTION

Business mortality rates are grim. A new European business has less than a 50 per cent chance of surviving to its fifth birthday party.[1] Getting through childhood is also a struggle. Only about one-third of American (USA) start-ups will reach their 11th birthday while only about one in five of them will live beyond their teenage years.[2]

However, as you will learn in this chapter, not all closures are the same. Neither are they all negative. Business exits can happen because:

1. **The business 'fails'** – the business closes involuntarily because it can no longer pay its bills and becomes insolvent, which can lead to financial penalties for the entrepreneur such as bankruptcy.
2. **The entrepreneur 'fails to make a go of it'** – the entrepreneur voluntarily decides to close the business either because it does not meet their expectations or because they fear exposure to financial losses.
3. **The business 'succeeds'** – business ownership is transferred to others, perhaps for a capital gain by selling shares in the company at a premium. Entrepreneurs can also exit successful businesses owing to their own retirement or ill health.

Both the external environment and the entrepreneur's background influence business conclusions. As you learned in Chapter 3 (p. 51), a previously unemployed founder is unlikely to succeed. If a business fails to grow beyond its initial size, it will also probably come quickly to an end.

You will also explore exits in the world's most common form of enterprise, family businesses. These businesses can be very sustainable, but they often face succession challenges in passing the business from one generation to the next.

11.2 THE DIFFICULTIES IN DEFINING AND MEASURING EXIT

Measuring if a business has passed away is difficult. The first challenge comes from the confusing range of interchangeable words used to define when a business ceases to exist, from closure, cessation, exit and termination, to conclusion, death, failure and non-survival.

There is also disagreement about whether a business 'ends' when its founder exits or when the company itself comes to an end. In the case of a sole trader, the answer is easy. Because the sole trader is the prime mover, if they depart, this usually means the termination of the business. However, a partnership may continue even if one or more partners leave. This also applies to a limited company. Limited liability companies are independent in the sense that they have their own 'persona'; able to have their own bank account, pay taxes and have responsibilities towards both their shareholders and employees. If the founding entrepreneur leaves, this is not an exit, so long as the business carries on.[3] Chapter 7, (pp. 155–156), has more information on forms of business ownership.

Having two different units of analysis creates other issues. An eBay seller's business does not end if they close their account and begin selling on Amazon. In the same way, it is common for a portfolio entrepreneur who runs several businesses at once to continue to operate after one or more of their businesses close.

Exit measurement is also data-dependent. Usually, what is counted is if the business has survived. But the trouble with (non-)survival is that there are different measures used: people who move out of self-employment, numbers of insolvencies, liquidations or bankruptcies, the closure of a bank account, involvement of a credit referencing agency or formal deregistration with a government body.

Each of these interpretations of (non-)survival produces different estimates of business death. That is not the only problem. Not all businesses are registered: for example, only about 50 per cent of USA start-ups register with the government.[4] This causes biases because registered businesses have better survival prospects than non-registered businesses.

Practically, this matters. Difficulties in tracking closures mean that business deaths are frequently under-sampled.[5] This leads to a 'survivorship bias', where individuals only look at a small subset of evidence rather than the broader picture.[6] Illusionist Derren Brown once got a TV crew to film him flipping a coin continuously for nine hours until it landed on heads ten times in a row. On his TV show, he just showed the clip of the coin landing ten times on heads; misleading his audience into thinking he could influence the outcome of a coin toss.

Just looking at the histories of 'winners' promotes entrepreneurial over-confidence. Many 'copycat' businesses close because their founders only considered the few instances of success rather than the far larger - but more difficult to see - number of others who failed with the same idea.

11.2.1 Ways of saying goodbye

Among these difficulties, three broad interpretations of business closure have emerged.[7] Table 11.1 shows that business conclusions can be equated with business failures such as bankruptcy. This has the advantage of simplicity but misses the fact that many businesses close voluntarily.

An alternative definition focuses on exit rationales, such as wanting to avoid getting into debt or because the entrepreneur believed they could not 'make a go of it'.[8] Bra business Ultimo in the United Kingdom (UK) decided to go 'bust' when it realised it was no longer competitive. Rather than getting into financial difficulties, its owners made its workers redundant and paid what it was due to its suppliers before closing its operations.

Table 11.1 Different types of exit

	'Failure'	'Failure to make a go of it'	Harvest
Definition	'Business failure occurs when a fall in revenues and/or a rise in expenses are of such a magnitude that the firm becomes insolvent and is unable to attract new debt or equity funding; consequently, it cannot continue to operate under the current ownership and management'[9]	'The cessation of involvement in a venture because it has not met a minimum threshold for economic viability as stipulated by the entrepreneur'[10]	'Harvest sale refers to a situation where the firm continues while the entrepreneur exits as majority owner. Harvest sale extracts some or all the economic value from the investment'[11]
Advantages	**Objective measure**: Bankruptcy and business dissolutions are clear instances of business closure. 'Failure' statistics can be compiled to compare different areas and countries	**Reflects reality**: Most business exits are voluntary, so this measure better reflects business exit	**Not all closures are failures**: About one-third of entrepreneurs close their business 'successfully', either because they sell it to outsiders, retire or pass it onto the next generation[12] ***Measures success:*** One goal of entrepreneurs running fast-growth businesses is to realise a capital gain from their business. This might be through their business being acquired (trade sale) or through selling shares on a stock market (Initial Public Offer)
Disadvantages	**Under-estimates the number of business exits**: About one-in-ten of the UK business population close each year but the actual rate of bankruptcies is about one in 200 businesses[13] **Stigmatises entrepreneurs**: Bankrupt entrepreneurs may find it difficult to return to entrepreneurship. This limits the pool of available entrepreneurs, particularly as only about 4–6 per cent of bankrupt entrepreneurs are fraudulent[14]	**Lack of clarity**: It not always clear if a voluntary exit takes place because of the business not meeting the entrepreneur's expectations, the fear of incurring further losses or the fear of future losses **Potential biases**: Self-reported, subjective interpretations may hide different attitudes towards 'failure': Some entrepreneurs may be loath to report their business closure, which can make it difficult to have robust international statistics on closure	**There is no death**: Focusing on successful closures means focusing on the transfer of business ownership.[15] This is not what is commonly understood by business closure

Academic insight: Closure thresholds

Ron Bridgeman has owned and run his Video World store since the 1980s. It used to make money by renting out VHS and DVD videos. But the shift to online streaming platforms such as Amazon and Netflix saw far fewer people interested in renting DVDs.[16] In response to his store not paying its way, Ron took up a full-time job alongside running his store in the evenings.

WAMO was an app designed for users to develop their own list of products that they 'Love-Want-Need'. A core benefit was the 'gamification' of the relationship between brands and brands users, who were given a challenge to go to stores or engage with companies online in exchange for discounts. WAMO's entrepreneurial team ran an 'all or nothing' (Chapter 9, pp. 233–235) crowdfunding campaign to raise £500,000 to fund its expansion. When the campaign raised £441,000, just £69,000 short of the target, its founders took the decision to close the business instead of running another crowdfunding campaign.

The types of decisions taken by Ron and WAMO were once just explained by looking at their finances. But while WAMO failed to offer enough of a return for its owners, money alone does not explain why Ron persisted with his store. Another approach is to look at switching costs. Closing WAMO was relatively easy because the owners could quickly and easily find other work. However, Ron also found it easy to find a job, but still spent his evenings running a store that failed to pay its way.

In a study by Gimeno and his colleagues, they showed that financial returns and switching costs are only part of the picture. In their study, they demonstrated that subjective performance thresholds often determine voluntary closure decisions. These are: 'the level of performance below which the dominant organizational constituents will act to dissolve the organization'.

Moreover, they showed that the: 'economic performance of the venture need not exclusively determine survival. Rather it is economic performance relative to the threshold that drives the exit decision.'[17]

These performance thresholds relate to both the human capital and to the non-monetary benefits an entrepreneur gains from their business.[18] So Ron continued with Video World because it is something that he has done for a large part of his life, he gets to meet people and he is able to offer advice on film choices. Letting go of it would be to let go of part of himself. Examples such as this one help explain why a sizeable proportion of poorly performing 'zombie' businesses hang on.[19]

In contrast, WAMO's founders saw it as a vehicle for making them wealthier. Once they found out that it would not meet their expectations, quickly closing the business was a positive outcome, particularly as they had other choices that were both feasible and desirable.[20]

Table 11.1 also shows exit can be defined as success. Success might be selling the business off for a capital gain or successfully passing it on to the next generation. Examining closure in terms of these types of 'harvest' outcomes helps because many businesses do not fail but are instead either acquired or merged with other businesses.[21] Like many entrepreneurs, venture capitalists and business angels also see exit as a positive because it unlocks the financial rewards within a business.

Assessment tip: Writing the conclusion

In academic writing, your conclusion summarises what you have said and shows how you have answered the question. This may be all that is required. But if you are asked to discuss, analyse or critically evaluate, it is your opportunity to explain what your answer means.

One way of organising this is to think of what your answer means for three communities: academics, entrepreneurs and policymakers. For entrepreneurs, it may have implications for practically starting or running a business. For policymakers, you might provide guidance on how they could improve support and assistance for entrepreneurs. Finally, for academics, your answer may be relevant to better understanding and researching entrepreneurs and their businesses. This can lead you to point to future research directions. Because much of the entrepreneurial research evidence is on richer economies, one obvious future research direction is to focus on entrepreneurial processes in poorer countries.

It pays to be cautious. All academic research has limitations. Acknowledge these in your conclusion and explain how they limit your answer. For example, if you have done a case study of a failed entrepreneur, one obvious limitation is that they may have a faulty recollection of events that led to their failure.

When writing a conclusion, it can be helpful to remember the three S's:

- Synthesise (what are your overall findings?)
- Significance (what does it mean for users?)
- Signposting (what are your limitations, and what are the future research directions?).

Entrepreneurship in Action

- Instead of looking at examples of successful start-ups or growth businesses, examine business exits for a particular sector or region. Why do businesses exit?
- Interview an entrepreneur who has voluntarily closed a business. Did their human capital and motivations influence their decision to close the business? What outside alternatives such as employment or other business opportunities influenced these decisions? Did they close the business because they were losing money or because they were worried about losing money?

Discussion question:

- What, in your view, is the best way of defining closure? - is it failure, success or a failure to make a go of it?

11.3 IS BUSINESS EXIT REALLY THAT BAD?

In South Korea, just six out of ten businesses survive their first year, and only one-quarter make it to five years old.[22] Figure 11.1 shows one-year survival rates tend to average around 80 per cent in Europe. They drop to around 60 per cent by year three and just 40–50 per cent by year five.

Figure 11.1 Business one-, three- and five-year survival rates, selected European countries

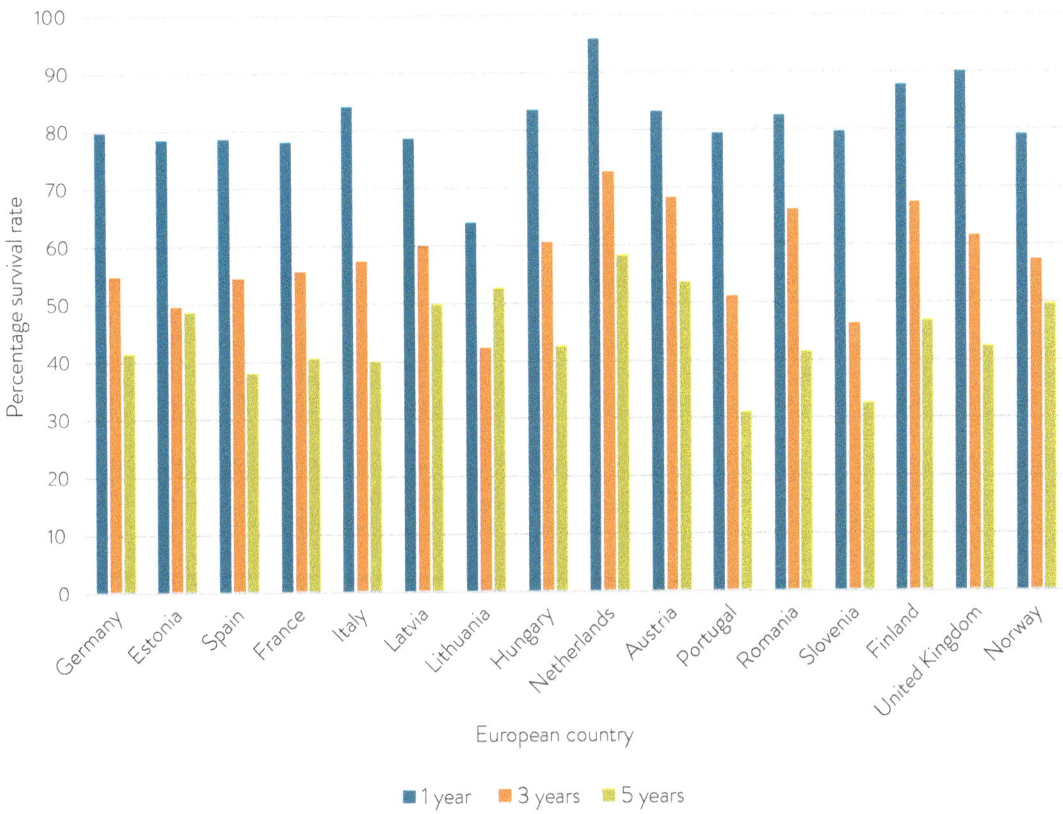

Source: Eurostat (bd_9bd_sz_cl_r2). Data compiled from Eurostat

11.3.1 The darker sides of exit

One miserable conclusion from these high mortality rates is that they represent the wasted efforts of so many people seeking to make a better future for themselves. Besides the potential of losing their income and their home, closing a business may be associated with a loss of social status and self-esteem, as well as psychological and physiological damage.[23] The fear of failure can also stop would-be entrepreneurs from considering entrepreneurship and prevent entrepreneurs from returning to entrepreneurship.[24]

Case Study: Mao Kankan

Mao Kankan set up gaming company Majoy and quickly became a famous entrepreneur in China. He later went on to become the chief executive officer (CEO) of Zhejiang Wanjia. However, this business folded, even after Kankan had put his house and car up as collateral for further loans. Kankan committed suicide soon afterwards.[25]

Exit can expose the darker side of entrepreneurship. Some of the most iconic entrepreneurs are associated with negative personality traits, such as being manipulative (Machiavellianism), lacking empathy with others (psychopathy) and having heightened self-regard (narcissism).[26] When people with this 'dark triad' or other negative personality traits fail, there can be consequences for them, for other businesses and for society.[27] Eike Batista was once one of the richest Brazilians in the world, with a fortune of around US$30 billion. Following the collapse of his oil company, his fortune nosedived, and he ended up owing $1 billion and being charged with insider dealing, market manipulation, criminal conspiracy, bribery and corruption.[28]

Case Study: The darker side of Steve Jobs

In the early 1970s, a young Steve Jobs won a contract to develop a video game from games developer Atari. Jobs persuaded his childhood friend Steve Wozniak to help him, and the pair worked for four days and nights to develop it. Jobs told Wozniak the fee was $700 and wrote him a cheque for $350. In reality, Jobs was paid $7000. Jobs also had a daughter with Christine Brennan. He denied paternity, citing he was impotent. After a paternity test, he agreed to pay $500 per month for his daughter. He was worth $200 million at the time.

Hubris can also have damaging impacts. Over-confident entrepreneurs are more likely to starve their new start-up of essential resources and, inadvertently, push it towards closure.[29]

Case Study: Fred 'the Shred' Goodwin

Before the 2008 financial crash, the Royal Bank of Scotland was one of the world's largest banks. It shares were each worth £7197. A year later, and after a £45 billion state bailout, these same shares were worth £2.07.[30] Much of the blame fell to the CEO, Fred 'the Shred' Goodwin. He earned this nickname because of his zeal for cost-cutting and his ability to 'shred' colleagues in meetings.[31] Described as 'a sociopathic bully', Goodwin reportedly exhibited 'behaviour which, arguably, bordered on the psychotic', and had a 'capricious and tyrannical management style, which discouraged dissent or challenge' that saw him spend vast sums on vanity projects.[32]

11.3.2 The spin-off benefits of exit

Business closure is a central feature of capitalism. In a capitalist economy – particularly one marked by Schumpeterian 'creative destruction' – one consequence of innovation and creativity is that the old order is destroyed. Business departures, therefore, can have positive impacts such as improving competition and promoting innovation. They signal to existing and potential companies that the business model adopted might not work and potentially free up resources for other uses.[33]

Similarly, because organisations beget organisations, many former large business employees build on their prior experiences for their own start-ups.[34] For example, four former Nokia employees established the Finnish company Piceasoft which went on to become one of Europe's leading mobile phone software providers.[35] Another example is the Jordanian business Maktoob, which was the first Arabic email service in the Middle East. Set up by Samih Toukan and Hussam Khoury, a series of other Middle Eastern businesses, such as souq.com, CashU and Payfort, were spun out from it.[36]

Other spin-off businesses that rise out of the ashes of large, small and start-up businesses can have an important role in how regional advantage occurs.[37] The 'spin-off' theory of the formation and development of regional economies suggests that what is core to regional economic development is a cluster of high performing spin-offs, seeded from a few key early businesses. This contrasts with the regional advantage resulting from localised 'agglomeration' advantages due to large pools of labour, specialist suppliers and the advantages of knowledge spillovers (Chapter 10, pp. 263–264).

Case Study: Seeding Silicon Valley businesses

William Shockley, one of the inventors of the transistor, founded his own semi-conductor business in Silicon Valley and hired eight senior engineers to work with him. When his oppressive and overbearing managerial style made him impossible to work with, the 'traitorous eight' decided to leave and form their own business, Fairchild Semiconductor. Shockley saw them as traitors because it led to the closure of his business. However, Fairchild seeded more than 90 start-up companies, such as Apple, Facebook and Google, that went on to become major public companies in their own right.[38] Helping this success was local agglomeration advantages, such as support from key local universities and finance from the venture capital industry in Silicon Valley.

11

Entrepreneurship in Action

- If you believe personality traits influence entrepreneurship, consider how susceptible you are to the traits of manipulation (Machiavellianism), self-regard (narcissism) and a lack of empathy (psychopathy). Search 'dark triad' personality test online to find free tests.[39]
- Investigate a case of an entrepreneur who behaved unscrupulously. What happened to them? Are there any attributes that are important in explaining their behaviour? What were the costs to the workers, to consumers and society?
- Write a case study of a spin-off from a large business that has closed. What does this tell us about entrepreneurial activity in a particular region or sector?

Discussion questions:

- Do you think that entrepreneurs are more likely to be successful if they have one or more of the 'dark triad' of personality dispositions?
- Should governments care if businesses fail?

11.4 WHAT FACTORS INFLUENCE BUSINESS FAREWELLS?

11.4.1 The importance of the external environment

An explanation for the 'Darwinian' rates of business mortality shown in Figure 11.1 is the lasting impact that the external environment has on survival chances. The environmental conditions new businesses face at birth 'imprint' themselves on a start-up.[40] Key also are the dynamism, uncertainty and turbulence of the external environment. Important, too, are the nature of competition and the richness (munificence) of the environment. Consequently, a business will find it easier to survive if there are few competitors for resources and the market is growing.

In contrast, if an economy is in recession, it is harder for small companies to get, retain or upsell to customers.[41] And when a country experiences political and civil unrest, it is harder for businesses to survive.[42] Even in good times, competition is a problem. If a region or an economy has high start-up rates, it tends to have high exit rates.[43] The same is true for sectors with relatively low barriers to entry. Just 50 per cent of construction, accommodation and food service businesses survive for four years in Australia, whereas two-thirds of agriculture-based businesses make it to their fifth year.[44]

Environmental influences also mark industry life cycle patterns. Evolutionary economists suggest in new industries, many entrants are seeking to develop a successful way of meeting customer needs.[45] Because of competitive pressures and the emergence of a dominant design, there is an industry 'shake-out' where many of these companies close. The few businesses left are those large enough to produce enough goods at a low enough price to make them viable (economies of scale).

Before the First World War, the early automotive industry saw a large number of entrants.[46] However, once the main features of what a car looks like and how it is made were defined, the emergence of this 'dominant design' led to an industry shake-out that left only a few key automotive manufacturers still producing cars. In mature industries, small businesses may only survive because they are able to fill strategic niches left unoccupied by larger players.[47]

Entrepreneurship in Action

- Use Porter's Five Forces (Chapter 7, pp. 172–173) to review the industry structure and the nature of competitive pressures for a business in a mature market.
- Alternatively, apply Blue Ocean thinking (Chapter 7, pp. 174–175) to identify ways in which a business could eliminate 'taken for granted' industry assumptions and/or what industry factors can be reduced or increased or created to produce new quality and cost advantages.

11.4.2 Closure liabilities

High closure rates have led to predictions about the liabilities of both size and age. There is clear evidence that the liability of smallness makes smaller business more likely to close.[48] This is regardless of whether smallness is measured by employee size or turnover levels. In Norway – as is the case everywhere else – limited companies are also more likely to survive than sole traders (Figure 11.2).[49] Equally, if a business lacks the finance to fund its business operations, such undercapitalisation will likely lead to business termination. Having capital obviously matters because 'more initial capital buys time while the entrepreneur learns to overcome problems'.[50]

Figure 11.2 Five-year survival rates of limited companies and sole traders in Norway

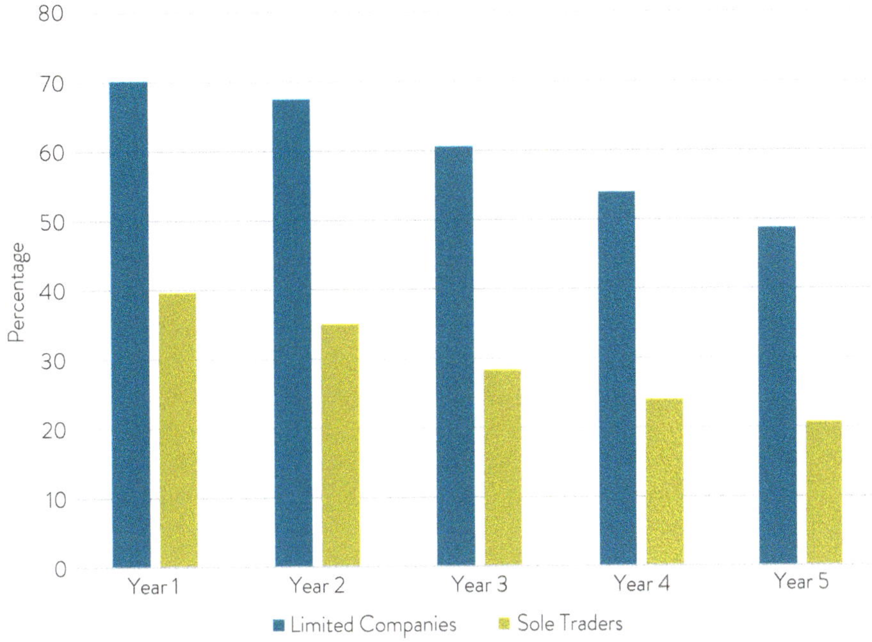

Source: Statistics Norway; www.ssb.no/en/fordem, Table 2.

Entrepreneurship in Action

- Ask an entrepreneur what types of finance they use to fund their business. This might be internal sources such as savings, retained earnings, family and friends or external sources such as banks or business angels. Ask them what they would do if they needed extra funds to help them with their working capital to fund day-to-day operational needs and investment capital to buy a new piece of capital equipment. What alternatives have they considered?
- Ask an entrepreneur about whom they turn to for advice and assistance in running their business, why they use these sources of social capital and what their experiences are of other sources of support and assistance. What extra assistance do they think they require?

11.4.3 The liabilities of aging

How business age affects closure is more ambiguous for three reasons:

1. **The 'liability of newness' – young businesses are more likely to close.** Very young businesses face the challenge of solving how they are going to develop organisational routines such as logistics, payment systems and after-sales services if they are to successfully capture, deliver and capture value. Even if a viable business model is developed, the challenge of building legitimacy and credibility with suppliers, customers and financiers remains.[51]

2. **The 'liability of adolescence' – incidences of closure follow an inverted 'U' shaped pattern (initially low, increasing after the 'honeymoon' period is over, before falling back).**[52] One explanation for this U-shaped pattern is that it takes time for a new entrant to use up their start-up resources.[53] In Jovanovic's model of noisy selection, an entrepreneur decides to set up a new business without really knowing if they have entrepreneurial talent.[54] If they do, and are not buffeted by bad luck, they continue in entrepreneurship. But if they lack talent, and are not lucky, after a while they realise that entrepreneurship is not for them. Someone might set up a restaurant, optimistically believing that they have the talent to make it work. However, after a year of failing to attract sufficient customers, working 18 hours a day and never seeing their family and friends, they might decide to close it.
3. **The 'liability of obsolescence' – older businesses are just as susceptible to closure as younger businesses.** Once established, a business develops ways of doing business or organisational routines. However, over time these routines no longer fit in with external demands.

Overall, while there is still some debate, the general drift of answers to the relative importance of the liability of newness, adolescence or obsolescence, is that very young businesses are more likely to pass away.[55]

Case Study: Pukka Food?

Celebrity chef Jamie Oliver opened a range of concept restaurants in the UK, such as Jamie's Italian and Union Jack, as part of a chain of restaurants named after him. Customers were initially attracted to his fresh approach to casual dining. However, as competition increased, tastes changed and costs went up, Oliver's restaurants kept with a complex and relatively expensive menu. Oliver was eventually left with little choice but to close his restaurant chain.[56]

Other factors such as business strategy, industrial structure and innovation ought to influence closure.[57] Of these, being innovative should improve survival chances because it provides companies with a quality or a cost advantage over their competitors.[58] The alternative view is that innovation is a risky activity, particularly if young innovators suffer from a 'liability of novelty' that makes it difficult to establish the legitimacy of the product or process to outside suppliers, customers and financiers. This liability often outweighs the advantages innovation provides and can lead to creative businesses having shorter lifespans.[59]

Entrepreneurship in Action

- Review a closed business. Was there a lack of alignment between its strategy, operations, systems and culture, and the market?

11.4.4 The importance of an entrepreneur's background

Although the environment is often important, it is not deterministic.[60] Examining what entrepreneurial characteristics allow founders to drive around the 'potholes' they face on their entrepreneurial journey may be a better way of understanding exits.

However, it can be challenging to work out which entrepreneurial characteristics are influential because studies rely on different geographies, sectors, measure closure in different ways or use different statistical techniques, such as binary logistic or hazard survival models, in their analysis.

Table 11.2 summarises studies that examine the relationship between the five main entrepreneurial characteristics and business endurance. It categorises them in terms of having a positive, non-significant or negative impact on survival.

Table 11.2 Entrepreneurial characteristics associated with business survival[61]

	Positive	Non-significant	Negative impact
Age	16	4	0
Unemployed	1	2	12
Ethnicity	0	1	8
Male	13	10	2
Education	14	11	3

Table 11.2 shows that it is inadvisable to start-up after a period of unemployment because, on average, this type of start-up is more likely to close. Unemployment, though, is a proxy for individual levels of financial, social and human capital.[62] If these forms of capital are low, the unemployed person might lack the wide range of skills and abilities to run a business (Chapter 3, p. 51) and find that they have to close. Similarly, survival prospects for younger people tend to be bleaker because they often lack financial, social and human capital, relative to those who are around 40–50 years old.

Entrepreneurial characteristics are also indicators of wider social issues. In Sweden, people from ethnic minorities often become entrepreneurs out of necessity and, subsequently, are more likely to exit self-employment and return to unemployment.[63] Men, rather than women, are more likely to survive in business. This reflects a variety of factors: discrimination, that women often enter hyper-competitive service sectors, start up with too few financial resources and the expectation that women 'ought' to perform poorly in business.[64] This is slowly changing, particularly if account is taken of women having different business expectations and being more likely to close their business voluntarily.[65]

Being better educated – to a degree – helps with survival, but this is not uniform. Those with a degree are less likely to stay in business but are also more likely to be in employment for longer.[66] The better educated are more likely to exit their business successfully through a voluntary closure than see their business go bankrupt.[67]

11.4.5 Does experience breed future success?

Table 11.3 examines how industry, managerial and entrepreneurial experience influence survival. It shows that if an entrepreneur has industry experience, business survival is more likely. Prior industry experience promotes survival because it provides valuable 'how to' industry knowledge.

Less clear-cut is if managerial experience helps. It should benefit as it provides task-based expertise in, for example, how to manage people, budgets and organise production. However, managing a business is not the same as setting up and running a business. A key task for a manager is to deliver profits and evolve existing products, while a start-up entrepreneur has to recognise the opportunity, create products and build cashflows. So entrepreneurial competencies that pull together and link the creation, delivery and capturing of value may be more beneficial.[68]

Prior entrepreneurial experience ought to be critical. Being in business before provides access to entrepreneurial competencies about how to recognise an opportunity, identify and target customers and beat the competition. This should get easier with experience if entrepreneurship is fundamentally a practical learning-by-doing activity and because 'knowledge is cumulative. What is learned in one period builds upon what was learned in an earlier period.'[69] However, Table 11.3 shows no clear link between having run a business previously and new venture survival.

Table 11.3 Experience and business survival[70]

	Positive	Non-significant	Negative impact
Industry experience	8	2	1
Management experience	2	7	0
Entrepreneurial experience	10	17	1

The fact that entrepreneurial learning might be influenced by whether or not the prior business was successful may answer this puzzle.

Prior business success ought to breed future business success since success may signal the entrepreneurial 'alertness' to viable opportunities, an ability to pick when and what opportunities to go for and to develop relevant strategic entrepreneurial competencies to take advantage of these opportunities, such as identifying and targeting key customers, competitors and suppliers.[71]

Having looked at an opportunity and tried it out by starting a business, entrepreneurs might recognise that it is not for them, particularly if it does not provide a big enough return.[72] Closure rates may be high because the only way to work out if the opportunity is there is to set up in business and, if it is not, to close it down quickly.

Past failure might also breed future business success. Famous entrepreneurs such as Walt Disney and Henry Ford ran businesses that failed. Before Bill Gates started Microsoft, he set up a company called Traf-O-Data that failed to do well, while Google was bizarrely originally called Back-Rub.

Failure provides learning opportunities for the next business: to 'learn from what works and, more importantly, from what doesn't work'.[73] Past mistakes might provide 'epiphanies' that lead to better opportunity recognition skills and the development of new resource and exploitation strategies.[74]

Because failure is often traumatic, a barrier to learning from failure might be the grief associated with the prior business failure and a range of psychological effects, including the loss of self-esteem.[75] But if these barriers are overcome, previously failed entrepreneurs report that prior failure promotes new business success.[76]

There are a number of alternative explanations for why entrepreneurial experience is not strongly associated with business survival:

- **It is hard to learn from experience.**[77] Entrepreneurial contexts are uncertain and 'simultaneous, messy and iterative'.[78] This makes it difficult to see which actions caused a business to succeed or to fail. Experienced entrepreneurs are no better at forecasting their performance than novices, and self-justification biases such as over-confidence as well as survivorship bias can lead many founders to under-sample failure and over-sample examples of success or failure.[79] This can lead them to actions that damage the current business.[80] Moreover, failure does not necessarily lead to changes in behaviour because 'the mere fact of failing [does] not result in learning effects'.[81]
- **No two business contexts are the same.**[82] Markets are dynamic, and the set of conditions that apply to one are unlikely to apply to another. Even if an entrepreneur was successful before, any lessons they have learned for success may not apply to a new context. This can lead to an entrepreneur falling into 'competency traps' whereby they simply repeat behaviours that either starve their business of necessary resources or neglect the competition.[83] Failed entrepreneurs only know what failure looks like; they have no practical experience of success.
- **Entrepreneurial 'expertise' is uncommon**. It takes about 10,000 hours to become a chess grandmaster.[84] However, as Figure 11.3 shows, three-quarters of 2.3 million small USA business owners had no prior experience of start-up.[85] Meanwhile, only about 2 per cent of entrepreneurs have set-up more than three businesses. Only a tiny fraction (0.26 per cent) have run ten or more businesses. So very few entrepreneurs are 'experts' that have repeatedly practised how to enter a market or build a sustainable business.

Like other forms of knowledge, entrepreneurial experience ought to help business survival. But successful founders are just as likely as novices to see their business close quickly.[86] For failed entrepreneurs, failure often begets failure.[87] Some may 'simply not [be] good at the entrepreneurial game'.[88]

Figure 11.3 Number of businesses owned by entrepreneurs

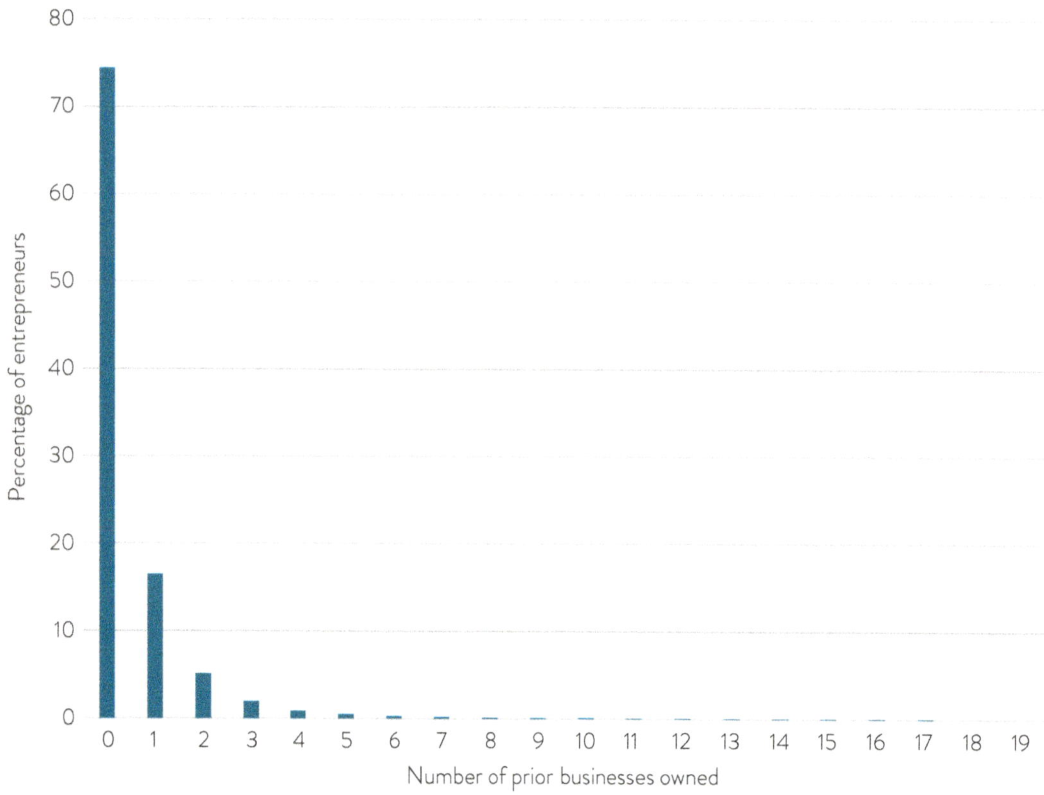

Source: Lafontaine and Shaw (2016)

Entrepreneurship in Action

- Compare and contrast three types of entrepreneur: (1) a nascent entrepreneur who is starting up for the first time; (2) an entrepreneur who has previously 'failed'; and (3) an entrepreneur who has experienced success. In what ways, if at all, do these entrepreneurs differ?

Discussion questions:

- Do you think that prior entrepreneurial success is a good predictor of future entrepreneurial success?
- Can entrepreneurs learn from past failure?
- Is business failure due to market changes or the inability of the entrepreneur?

11.5 KEEPING IT IN THE FAMILY

11.5.1 The importance of family businesses

Family businesses are part of people's everyday lives. From getting dressed in the morning (Ralph Lauren, Gap, Nike), driving to work (Volkswagen, BMW, Tata) and going shopping (Walmart, Aldi, IKEA) to buying food (Bimbo Group, Parmalat), cosmetics (Estee Lauder, L'Oréal) or drinks

(Heineken), we use products and services offered by companies run by families. We also rely on them to watch TV (News Corp, Comcast), go on holiday (EasyJet, Stena) or to look after our finances (Banco Bradesco, Frère-Bourgeois).[89]

The largest 500 family businesses in the world employ more than 24 million people and have sales of $6.8 trillion. If they were a combined economy, they would be the third-largest in the world after China and the United States.[90]

These large family businesses are important to economies such as Sweden, Belgium, Argentina and Mexico.[91] Generally, though, across the world, family businesses are small-scale 'mom and pop' operations serving local communities.

11.5.2 Family succession issues

A central imperative for a family business is surviving long enough for it to be taken over by the next generation. Some family businesses do successfully pass from generation to generation. Gunmaker Beretta (1526), Takenaka construction (1610) and brewer Molson-Coors (1774) have stayed

Case Study: 40 generations and closing

Japanese business Kongō Gumi started in 578. Over the next 1428 years, the Kongō family continued through 39 generations to build and maintain Buddhist temples despite political, economic and social crises and two atomic bombs. In 2006, bad debts led Mr Masakazu Kongō, the 40th and last generation of the Kongō family to run the business, to close it.

© Image Source/Rudi Kennard

in the same families for centuries. Succession in family-run companies can be easier than non-family businesses because:

- **They have a long-term 'patient' view of the business.** Family CEOs have longer tenure and can 'steward' the business by having longer investment horizons, being more careful with resources and being more thoughtful about how to build a sustainable future strategy.[92] A long-term orientation also promotes stable relationships with customers, suppliers and advisors and improves accountability to their workers.[93]
- **They may avoid some principal-agent problems.** In non-family businesses, the managers (the agents) can act in their own interests rather than of their shareholders (the principals).[94] It is difficult for owners to monitor such managers who may be lazy, incompetent or simply decide to play it safe. UK construction giant Carillion collapsed because of the 'recklessness, hubris and greed' of its managers who put their own interests above those of shareholders.[95] In family businesses, these problems might occur less frequently because the family both owns and manages the company, which can help drive business value. They may also be better motivated to succeed if they fear that business failure will badly affect both family finances and family relationships.[96]
- **Family businesses act as a crucible for entrepreneurship.** Children of entrepreneurs are more likely to become entrepreneurs themselves, even if they decide to leave the family business (Chapter 3, p. 55). Family businesses provide opportunities to understand what is involved in running a business, offer financial and social capital and potentially provide emotional support.

However, only 30 per cent of businesses make it to the second generation, 13 per cent to the third generation and only 3 per cent to the fourth generation.[97]

Low succession rates have to be seen in context. Most family businesses are small businesses. Since closure is a common occurrence among small businesses, it is not surprising that so few family-run companies make it through to the next generation.

However, there are particular reasons why family businesses fail to survive and why in countries such as Italy ('stables to stars to stables'), the UK ('clogs to clogs in three generations') and China ('wealth does not survive three generations'), there are proverbs describing the difficulties of family business succession. These sayings hold true for a number of reasons, such as:

- **The blood heir to a business lacks the necessary motivation or abilities to take on the business.**[98] Billionaire investment manager Warren Buffett suggested picking future managers from family heirs was like 'choosing the 2020 Olympic team by picking the eldest sons of the gold-medal winners of the 2000 Olympics'.[99] Nineteenth-century industrialist Andrew Carnegie decided to give away most of his vast fortune because he believed having wealth would give his descendants a disincentive to work hard.

Case Study: Mukoyōshi

In Japan, adoption is an accepted part of society. However, these adoptions are typically not of children but of adult men. Through a process known as Mukoyōshi, it is common for family businesses without male heirs to legally adopt sons to run their operations. Established in 718 by the Hōshi family, their ryokan (inn), Hōshi Ryokan, has been run by both blood and adopted sons for 46 generations. Likewise, the chairman of the car manufacturer Suzuki is Osamu Suzuki. He, however, was born Osamu Matsuda and was only adopted into the Suzuki family after an arranged marriage with Shoko Suzuki.[100]

This begs questions about Mukoyōshi's impact on business performance. In most other countries, if a blood heir runs the family business, the business will do less well than if they had appointed a non-family member to run the business.[101] In Japan, family businesses run by adopted sons do better than family businesses run by blood heirs. Equally, both adopted and blood heir family businesses do better than non-family businesses. Adopted heir businesses do better because the family is able to adopt very capable managers. Blood heirs also know that if they fail to perform well an adopted heir could replace them.[102]

- **Nepotism has negative side-effects**. Non-family workers or family members not destined for owning or leading the business may exert less effort because they know that they have little chance of further promotion. It may deter potential employees if they see few routes for career development. There is also sexism.[103] Some women fail to be considered for running the family business simply because they are female or fail to demonstrate 'masculine' behaviours.[104] In some societies, there is also an expectation that the first-born sons should take on the family business.[105] The danger is that this son might be temperamentally unsuited to being in charge of the business.
- **Conflict and discord**. Rather than being harmonious, family businesses can be a breeding ground for parent–child conflict, sibling rivalry or marital discord.[106] Such conflict can prevent business succession.[107] It can also impair business performance in the short-term and ultimately lead to the breakup of the business.

11

Case Study: Sitting on a gold mine?

Mining billionaire, and one of Australia's richest people, Gina Rinehart took over her father's bankrupt business and grew it to be one of the largest players in Australian mining. However, her children accused her of behaving in an 'unconscionable' way by moving assets out of this family trust, which led to a long and bitter court battle.[108]

© PhotoDisc/ Getty Images

- **Mixed incentives.** A family business must blend and balance its 'emotional logic' with its 'business logic'.[109] If the focus is more on the non-financial interests of family members – which is also called the socio-emotional wealth of the business – financial performance can suffer.[110] Equally, if the current owners are risk-averse, under-invest in innovation and rely on inward-looking management practices, there may be very little to pass on to the next generation.[111] Current generations may also find it difficult to let go of control, which can delay or even deter business succession.[112]
- **Altruism?** Some children might expect their entrepreneurial parents to gift them the family business for nothing. This ignores that children often have duties to their parents and that parents sometimes need to sell the business to fund their retirement. The average discount applied to the sale of a family business is 57 per cent.[113] So, if the business is worth 100 million pesos and the next generation cannot raise 43 million pesos, the business may need to be sold outside the family to fund the retirement plans of the older generation.

Entrepreneurship in Action

- Investigate a family business. What factors influence how long it survives? How smooth was the transfer of business ownership? If a blood heir inherited the family business, did its performance increase, stay the same or decline?

Although family businesses are central to the economic fabric of many countries, many fail to be transferred to the next generation. This might not matter, because large family businesses have been associated with acting against the interests of non-family shareholders, slower economic growth and using their status and political connections to manipulate public policy for their own ends.[114]

However, succession issues are a significant concern for small family businesses, particularly in poorer economies where family businesses' social networks often fill gaps left by missing, ineffective or corrupt institutions.[115]

In richer countries, it is more difficult to determine if family-run companies perform better than non-family ones.[116] Family businesses cannot be reduced to a simple binary of family and non-family. Focusing on this binary definition often opens a messy debate about different measures of family ownership and control, contrasts between the roles of a family CEO as opposed to a non-family CEO running a family business and different emphases on shareholder patterns and rights.[117]

Discussion questions:

- Why do you think business succession rates are low?
- Large family businesses are important in some countries. Is this a good thing?

11.6 WHAT YOU HAVE LEARNED IN THIS CHAPTER

Although business mortality rates make for grim reading, you have learned exit does not necessarily mean bankruptcy. It can instead be seen either as a failure to make a go of it or as a success.

These different interpretations suggest that there are both positive and negative effects of business conclusions. Closure might reveal the darker sides of the entrepreneurial personality, while spin-offs can create regional economic benefits.

You have also seen how the external environment and an entrepreneur's background can influence business success. Closure is more likely for smaller, younger and less well-financed businesses. Disadvantaged entrepreneurs such as those who start-up after a spell of unemployment also find it a struggle for their business to survive. Surprisingly, there is no clear association between business survival and prior entrepreneurial experience.

You should now understand that family business succession matters because family businesses are the most common type of business in the world. Family businesses potentially enjoy a number of advantages over non-family businesses. However, business succession relies on overcoming a number of barriers. Blood heirs are not always the most suitable candidates for taking over when it is time for the current owners to retire.

ASSESSMENT QUESTIONS

1. What is the best way of assessing entrepreneurial exits?
2. Identify three common factors associated with business closure. Explain which of these three factors is the most likely to explain business terminations.
3. Does the outside environment have a greater influence on entrepreneurial exits than the entrepreneur's background?
4. Does entrepreneurial experience promote business survival?
5. Discuss what factors influence family business succession.
6. Do family businesses outperform non-family businesses?

FURTHER READING

Geroski, P. A., Mata, J., & Portugal, P. (2010). Founding conditions and the survival of new firms. *Strategic Management Journal, 31*(5), 510–529.

Gimeno, J., Folta, T. B., Cooper, A. C., & Woo, C. Y. (1997). Survival of the fittest? Entrepreneurial human capital and the persistence of underperforming firms. *Administrative Science Quarterly, 42*(4), 750–783.

Gottschalk, S., Greene, F. J., & Müller, B. (2017). The impact of habitual entrepreneurial experience on new firm closure outcomes. *Small Business Economics, 48*(2), 303–321.

Mehrotra, V., Morck, R., Shim, J., & Wiwattanakantang, Y. (2013). Adoptive expectations: Rising sons in Japanese family firms. *Journal of Financial Economics, 108*(3), 840–854.

Sharma, P. (2004). An overview of the field of family business studies: Current status and directions for the future. *Family Business Review, 17*(1), 1–36.

Watson, J., & Everett, J. (1993). Defining small business failure. *International Small Business Journal, 11*(3), 35–48.

Notes

1 https://ec.europa.eu/eurostat/statistics-explained/index.php/Business_demography_statistics%23High_growth_enterprises.

2 Bureau of Labor Statistics. (2016). 'Survival rates of establishments, by year started and number of years since starting, 1994–2015, in percent', www.bls.gov/bdm/entrepreneurship/bdm_chart3.htm.

3 Coad, A. (2014). Death is not a success: Reflections on business exit. *International Small Business Journal, 32*(7), 721–732.

4 Yang, T., & Aldrich, H. E. (2012). Out of sight but not out of mind: Why failure to account for left truncation biases research on failure rates. *Journal of Business Venturing, 27*(4), 477–492.

5 Denrell, J. (2003). Vicarious learning, undersampling of failure, and the myths of management. *Organization Science, 14*(3), 227–243.

6 Denrell (2003), ibid.

7 Watson, J., & Everett, J. (1993). Defining small business failure. *International Small Business Journal, 11*(3), 35–48; Headd, B. (2003). Redefining business success: Distinguishing between closure and failure. *Small Business Economics, 21*(1), 51–61; Bates, T. (2005). Analysis of young, small firms that have closed: Delineating successful from unsuccessful closures. *Journal of Business Venturing, 20*(3), 343–358; Wennberg, K., & DeTienne, D. R. (2014). What do we really mean when we talk about 'exit'? A critical review of research on entrepreneurial exit. *International Small Business Journal, 32*(1), 4–16; Jenkins, A, & McKelvie, A. (2016). What is entrepreneurial failure? Implications for future research. *International Small Business Journal, 34*(2), 176–188; DeTienne, D. R. (2010). Entrepreneurial exit as a critical component of the entrepreneurial process: Theoretical development. *Journal of Business Venturing, 25*(2), 203–215.

8 McGrath, R. G. (1999). Falling forward: Real options reasoning and entrepreneurial failure. *Academy of Management Review, 24*(1), 13–30.

9 Shepherd, D. A., Wiklund, J., & Haynie, J. M. (2009). Moving forward: Balancing the financial and emotional costs of business failure. *Journal of Business Venturing, 24*(2), 134–148, 135.

10 Ucbasaran, D., Shepherd, D. A., Lockett, A., & Lyon, S. J. (2013). Life after business failure: The process and consequences of business failure for entrepreneurs. *Journal of Management, 39*(1), 163–202, p. 175.

11 Wennberg, K., Wiklund, J., DeTienne, D. R., & Cardon, M. S. (2010). Reconceptualizing entrepreneurial exit: Divergent exit routes and their drivers. *Journal of Business Venturing, 25*(4), 361–375, 364.

12 Bates (2005), ibid.

13 www.ons.gov.uk/businessindustryandtrade/business/activitysizeandlocation/bulletins/businessdemography/2016, figures relate to period 2010–2016; www.gov.uk/government/statistics/estimatedcompany-insolvency-rate-in-the-united-kingdom-january-to-december-2017.

14 European Commission (2014). *Commission Recommendation of 12.3.2014,* On a New Approach to Business Failure and Insolvency, C(2014).

15 Coad (2014), ibid.

16 www.theguardian.com/media/2017/jan/05/film-and-tv-streaming-and-downloads-overtake-dvd-sales-for-first-time-netflix-amazon-uk.

17 Gimeno, J., Folta, T. B., Cooper, A. C., & Woo, C. Y. (1997). Survival of the fittest? Entrepreneurial human capital and the persistence of underperforming firms. *Administrative Science Quarterly, 42*(4), 750–783, p. 750.

18 Gimeno et al. (1997), ibid.

19 Carreira, C., & Teixeira, P. (2011). The shadow of death: Analysing the pre-exit productivity of Portuguese manufacturing firms. *Small Business Economics, 36*(3), 337–351; DeTienne, D. R., Shepherd, D. A., & De Castro, J. O. (2008). The fallacy of "only the strong survive": The effects of extrinsic motivation on the persistence decisions for under-performing firms. *Journal of Business Venturing, 23*(5), 528–546.

20 McGrath (1999), ibid.; Bates (2005), ibid.

21 Daepp, M. I., Hamilton, M. J., West, G. B., & Bettencourt, L. M. (2015). The mortality of companies. *Journal of The Royal Society Interface, 12*(106), 20150120.

22 Statistics Korea. (2016). *Business demography statistics in 2016.* Seoul: Statistics Korea.

23 Singh, S., Corner, P., & Pavlovich, K. (2007). Coping with entrepreneurial failure. *Journal of Management and Organization, 13*(4), 331–344.

24 Simmons, S. A., Wiklund, J., & Levie, J. (2014). Stigma and business failure: Implications for entrepreneurs' career choices. *Small Business Economics, 42*(3), 485–505.

25 www.theepochtimes.com/successful-chinese-entrepreneur-commits-suicide_2427391.html.

26 Miller, D. (2015). A downside to the entrepreneurial personality? *Entrepreneurship Theory and Practice, 39*(1), 1–8; Boddy, C. R. (2011). The corporate psychopaths theory of the global financial crisis. *Journal of Business Ethics, 102*(2), 255–259.

27 Liu, Y., Li, Y., Hao, X., & Zhang, Y. (2019). Narcissism and learning from entrepreneurial failure. *Journal of Business Venturing*, 1–17; Box, M., Gratzer, K., & Lin, X. (2018). Destructive entrepreneurship in the small business sector: Bankruptcy fraud in Sweden, 1830–2010. *Small Business Economics*, 1–21; Hmieleski, K. M., & Lerner, D. A. (2016). The dark triad and nascent entrepreneurship: An examination of unproductive versus productive entrepreneurial motives. *Journal of Small Business Management, 54*, 7–32.

28 www.britannica.com/biography/Eike-Batista; www.nytimes.com/2017/01/26/world/americas/brazil-eike-batista.html; www.reuters.com/article/brazil-batista/brazils-cvm-fines-eike-batista-6-3-mln-for-insider-trading-idUSL1N1JA23J.
29 Hayward, M. L. A., Shepherd, D. A., & Griffin, D. (2006). A hubris theory of entrepreneurship. *Management Science, 52*(2), 160–172.
30 investors.rbs.com/share-data/share-price-chart/lse.aspx.
31 Fraser, I. (2014). *Shredded: Inside RBS: The bank that broke Britain*. Edinburgh: Birlinn.
32 Ibid., pp. xii, 72.
33 Knott, A. M., & Posen, H. E. (2005). Is failure good? *Strategic Management Journal, 26*(7), 617–641.
34 Sørensen, J. B., & Fassiotto, M. A. (2011). Organizations as fonts of entrepreneurship. *Organization Science, 22*(5), 1322–1331, 1322; Klepper, S. (2002). The capabilities of new firms and the evolution of the US automobile industry. *Industrial and Corporate Change, 11*(4), 645–666; Klepper, S., & Sleeper, S. (2005). Entry by spinoffs. *Management Science, 51*(8), 1291–1306.
35 https://www.linkedin.com/pulse/piceasoft-success-after-decline-mobile-phone-giant-andruta-ilie/; piceasoft.com/2017/12/piceasoft-wins-deloitte-technology-fast-50-award/.
36 www.jabbar.com/.
37 Klepper, S. (2010). The origin and growth of industry clusters: The making of Silicon Valley and Detroit. *Journal of Urban Economics, 67*(1), 15–32.
38 https://techcrunch.com/2014/07/26/the-first-trillion-dollar-startup/.
39 https://openpsychometrics.org/tests/SD3/.
40 Stinchcombe, A. L. (1965). Social structure and organizations. In J. G. March (Ed.), *Handbook of organizations* (pp. 142–193). Chicago: Rand McNally.
41 Geroski, P. A., Mata, J., & Portugal, P. (2010). Founding conditions and the survival of new firms. *Strategic Management Journal, 31*(5), 510–529.
42 Hiatt, S. R., & Sine, W. D. (2014). Clear and present danger: Planning and new venture survival amid political and civil violence. *Strategic Management Journal, 35*(5), 773–785.
43 Kerr, W. R., & Nanda, R. (2009). Democratizing entry: Banking deregulations, financing constraints, and entrepreneurship. *Journal of Financial Economics, 94*(1), 124–149; Honjo, Y. (2000). Business failure of new firms: An empirical analysis using a multiplicative hazards model. *International Journal of Industrial Organization, 18*(4), 557–574.
44 www.abs.gov.au/AUSSTATS/abs@.nsf/DetailsPage/8165.0Jun+2013+to+Jun+2017 (Table 3 Survival of Entries by Industry Division: June 2013–June 2017).
45 Agarwal, R., Sarkar, M. B., & Echambadi, R. (2002). The conditioning effect of time on firm survival: An industry life cycle approach. *Academy of Management Journal, 45*(5), 971–994.
46 Klepper (2002), ibid.
47 Agarwal, R., & Audretsch, D. B. (2001). Does entry size matter? The impact of the life cycle and technology on firm survival. *The Journal of Industrial Economics, 49*(1), 21–43.
48 Geroski et al. (2010), ibid.; Santarelli, E., & Vivarelli, M. (2007). Entrepreneurship and the process of firms' entry, survival and growth. *Industrial and Corporate Change, 16*(3), 455–488; Bartelsman, E., Scarpetta, S., & Schivardi, F. (2005). Comparative analysis of firm demographics and survival: Evidence from micro-level sources in OECD countries. *Industrial and Corporate Change, 14*(3), 365–391.
49 Strotmann, H. (2007). Entrepreneurial survival. *Small Business Economics, 28*(1), 87–104.
50 Cooper, A. C., Gimeno-Gascon, F. J., & Woo, C. Y. (1994). Initial human and financial capital as predictors of new venture performance. *Journal of Business Venturing, 9*(5), 371–395, 379.
51 Stinchcombe (1965), ibid.
52 Bruderl, J., & Schussler, R. (1990). Organizational mortality: The liabilities of newness and adolescence. *Administrative Science Quarterly, 35*(3), 530–547.
53 Strotmann (2007), ibid.
54 Jovanovic, B. (1982). Selection and the evolution of industry. *Econometrica: Journal of the Econometric Society, 50*(3), 649–670.
55 Caves, R. E. (1998). Industrial organization and new findings on the turnover and mobility of firms. *Journal of Economic Literature, 36*(4), 1947–1982; Thornhill, S., & Amit, R. (2003). Learning about failure: Bankruptcy, firm age, and the resource-based view. *Organization Science, 14*(5), 497–509; Bergmann, H., & Stephan, U. (2013). Moving on from nascent entrepreneurship: Measuring cross-national differences in the transition to new business ownership. *Small Business Economics, 41*(4), 945–959; Yang, T., & Aldrich, H. E. (2017). "The liability of newness" revisited: Theoretical restatement and empirical testing in emergent organizations. *Social Science Research, 63*, 36–53.
56 inews.co.uk/news/off-boil-rise-fall-jamie-olivers-empire/; www.theguardian.com/lifeandstyle/2018/feb/16/not-so-fresh-why-jamie-oliver-restaurants-lost-their-bite; www.bbc.co.uk/news/business-48352026.
57 Henderson, A. D. (1999). Firm strategy and age dependence: A contingent view of the liabilities of newness, adolescence, and obsolescence. *Administrative Science Quarterly, 44*(2), 281–314.
58 Cefis, E., & Marsili, O. (2012). Going, going, gone. Exit forms and the innovative capabilities of firms. *Research Policy, 41*(5), 795–807.
59 Hyytinen, A., Pajarinen, M., & Rouvinen, P. (2015). Does innovativeness reduce startup survival rates? *Journal of Business Venturing, 30*(4), 564–581.
60 Mellahi, K., & Wilkinson, A. (2004). Organizational failure: A critique of recent research and a proposed integrative framework. *International Journal of Management Reviews, 5*(1), 21–41.
61 Bates, T. (1995). Analysis of survival rates among franchise and independent small business startups.

Journal of Small Business Management, 33(2), 26; Cressy, R. (1996). Pre-entrepreneurial income, cash-flow growth and survival of startup businesses: Model and tests on UK data. *Small Business Economics, 8*(1), 49–58; Nafziger, E. W., & Terrell, D. (1996). Entrepreneurial human capital and the long-run survival of firms in India. *World Development, 24*(4), 689–696; Storey, D. J., & Wynarczyk, P. (1996). The survival and non survival of micro firms in the UK. *Review of Industrial Organization, 11*(2), 211–229; Gimeno et al. (1997), ibid.; Taylor, M. P. (1999). Survival of the fittest? An analysis of self-employment duration in Britain. *The Economic Journal, 109*(454), 140–155; Van Praag, C. M. (2003). Business survival and success of young small business owners. *Small Business Economics, 21*(1), 1–17; Persson, H. (2004). The survival and growth of new establishments in Sweden, 1987–1995. *Small Business Economics, 23*(5), 423–440; Bates (2005), ibid.; Harada, N. (2007). Which firms exit and why? An analysis of small firm exits in Japan. *Small Business Economics, 29*(4), 401–414; Haapanen, M., & Tervo, H. (2009). Self-employment duration in urban and rural locations. *Applied Economics, 41*(19), 2449–2461; Munoz-Bullón, F., & Cueto, B. (2011). The sustainability of start-up firms among formerly wage-employed workers. *International Small Business Journal, 29*(1), 78–102; Millán, J. M., Congregado, E., & Román, C. (2012). Determinants of self-employment survival in Europe. *Small Business Economics, 38*(2), 231–258; Boyer, T., & Blazy, R. (2014). Born to be alive? The survival of innovative and non-innovative French micro-start-ups. *Small Business Economics, 42*(4), 669–683; de Jong, J. P., & Marsili, O. (2015). Founding a business inspired by close entrepreneurial ties: Does it matter for survival? *Entrepreneurship Theory and Practice, 39*(5), 1005–1025; Coad, A., Frankish, J. S., Roberts, R. G., & Storey, D. J. (2016). Predicting new venture survival and growth: Does the fog lift? *Small Business Economics, 47*(1), 217– 241; Gottschalk, S., Greene, F. J., & Müller, B. (2017). The impact of habitual entrepreneurial experience on new firm closure outcomes. *Small Business Economics, 48*(2), 303–321; Cabrer-Borrás, B., & Belda, P. R. (2018). Survival of entrepreneurship in Spain. *Small Business Economics, 51*(1), 265–278; Nziramasanga, M., & Lee, M. (2002). On the duration of self-employment: The impact of macroeconomic conditions. *Journal of Development Studies, 39*(1), 46–73; Bosma, N., Van Praag, M., Thurik, R., & De Wit, G. (2004). The value of human and social capital investments for the business performance of startups. *Small Business Economics, 23*(3), 227–236; Dencker, J. C., Gruber, M., & Shah, S. K. (2009). Pre-entry knowledge, learning, and the survival of new firms. *Organization Science, 20*(3), 516–537; Hiatt & Sine (2014), ibid.; Meager, N., Bates, P., & Cowling, M. (2003). An evaluation of business start-up support for young people. *National Institute Economic Review, 186*(1), 59–72; Rocha, V., Carneiro, A., & Varum, C. A. (2015). Entry and exit dynamics of nascent business owners. *Small Business Economics*, 45(1), 63–84; Evans, D. S., Leighton, L. S. (1989). Some empirical aspects of entrepreneurship. *The American Economic Review, 79*(3), 519–535; Carrasco, R. (1999). Transitions to and from self-employment in Spain: An empirical analysis. *Oxford Bulletin of Economics and Statistics, 61*(3), 315–341; Andersson, P., & Wadensjö, E. (2007). Do the unemployed become successful entrepreneurs? *International Journal of Manpower, 28*(7), 604–626; Georgellis, Y., Sessions, J., & Tsitsianis, N. (2007). Pecuniary and non-pecuniary aspects of self-employment survival. *The Quarterly Review of Economics and Finance, 47*(1), 94–112; Ahn, T. (2011). Racial differences in self-employment exits. *Small Business Economics, 36*(2), 169–186; Joona, P. A. (2010). Exits from self-employment: Is there a native-immigrant difference in Sweden? *International Migration Review, 44*(3), 539–559; Asoni, A., & Sanandaji, T. (2016). Identifying the effect of college education on business and employment survival. *Small Business Economics, 46*(2), 311–324; Brüderl, J., & Preisendörfer, P. (1998). Network support and the success of newly founded business. *Small Business Economics, 10*(3), 213–225; Gompers, P., Kovner, A., Lerner, J., & Scharfstein, D. (2010). Performance persistence in entrepreneurship. *Journal of Financial Economics, 96*(1), 18–32; Aspelund, A., Berg-Utby, T., & Skjevdal, R. (2005). Initial resources' influence on new venture survival: A longitudinal study of new technology-based firms. *Technovation*, 25(11), 1337–1347; Delmar, F., & Shane, S. (2004). Legitimating first: Organizing activities and the survival of new ventures. *Journal of Business Venturing, 19*(3), 385–410; Gimmon, E., & Levie, J. (2010). Founder's human capital, external investment, and the survival of new high-technology ventures. *Research Policy, 39*(9), 1214–1226; Huggins, R., Prokop, D., & Thompson, P. (2017). Entrepreneurship and the determinants of firm survival within regions: Human capital, growth motivation and locational conditions. *Entrepreneurship & Regional Development, 29*(3–4), 357–389; Lin, Z., Picot, G., & Compton, J. (2000). The entry and exit dynamics of self-employment in Canada. *Small Business Economics, 15*(2), 105–125; Siepel, J., Cowling, M., & Coad, A. (2017). Non-founder human capital and the long-run growth and survival of high-tech ventures. *Technovation, 59*, 34–43.

62 Baptista, R., Karaöz, M., & Mendonça, J. (2014). The impact of human capital on the early success of necessity versus opportunity-based entrepreneurs. *Small Business Economics, 42*(4), 831–847.

63 Joona (2010), ibid.

64 Marlow, S., & McAdam, M. (2013). Gender and entrepreneurship: Advancing debate and challenging myths; exploring the mystery of the under-performing female entrepreneur. *International Journal of Entrepreneurial Behavior & Research, 19*(1), 114–124; Yang, T., & del Carmen Triana, M. (2019). Set up to fail: Explaining when women-led businesses are more likely to fail. *Journal of Management, 45*(3), 926–954.

65 Kalnins, A., & Williams, M. (2014). When do female-owned businesses out-survive male-owned businesses? A disaggregated approach by industry and geography. *Journal of Business Venturing, 29*(6), 822–835; Justo, R., DeTienne, D. R., & Sieger, P. (2015). Failure or voluntary exit? Reassessing the female underperformance hypothesis. *Journal of Business Venturing, 30*(6), 775–792.
66 Asoni & Sanandaji (2016), ibid.
67 Kato, M., & Honjo, Y. (2015). Entrepreneurial human capital and the survival of new firms in high-and low-tech sectors. *Journal of Evolutionary Economics, 25*(5), 925-957; Bates (2005), ibid.
68 Minniti, M., & Bygrave, W. (2001). A dynamic model of entrepreneurial learning. *Entrepreneurship Theory and Practice, 25*(3), 5–16.
69 Ibid., 7.
70 See references for Table 11.2.
71 Dimov, D. (2010). Nascent entrepreneurs and venture emergence: Opportunity confidence, human capital, and early planning. *Journal of Management Studies, 47*(6), 1123–1153; Holmes, T. J., & Schmitz Jr., J. A. (1990). A theory of entrepreneurship and its application to the study of business transfers. *Journal of Political Economy, 98*(2), 265–294; Gompers et al. (2010), ibid.; Gruber, M., MacMillan, I. C., & Thompson, J. D. (2012). From minds to markets: How human capital endowments shape market opportunity identification of technology start-ups. *Journal of Management, 38*(5), 1421–1449; Carbonara, E., Tran, H. T., & Santarelli, E. (2019). Determinants of novice, portfolio, and serial entrepreneurship: An occupational choice approach. *Small Business Economics*, 1–29.
72 Plehn-Dujowich, J. (2010). A theory of serial entrepreneurship. *Small Business Economics, 35*(4), 377–398; Kato & Honjo (2015), ibid.; Arora, A., & Nandkumar, A. (2011). Cash-out or flameout! Opportunity cost and entrepreneurial strategy: Theory, and evidence from the information security industry. *Management Science, 57*(10), 1844–1860; Grilli, L. (2011). When the going gets tough, do the tough get going? The pre-entry work experience of founders and high-tech start-up survival during an industry crisis. *International Small Business Journal, 29*(6), 626–647.
73 Smilor, R. W. (1997). Entrepreneurship: Reflections on a subversive activity. *Journal of Business Venturing, 12*(5), 341–346, p. 344.
74 Singh, S., Corner, P. D., & Pavlovich, K. (2015). Failed, not finished: A narrative approach to understanding venture failure stigmatization. *Journal of Business Venturing, 30*(1), 150–166; Singh et al. (2007), ibid.; Cope, J. (2011). Entrepreneurial learning from failure: An interpretative phenomenological analysis. *Journal of Business Venturing, 26*(6), 604–623; Cope, J. (2005). Toward a dynamic learning perspective of entrepreneurship. *Entrepreneurship Theory and Practice, 29*(4), 373–397; McGrath (1999), ibid.; Politis, D., & Gabrielsson, J. (2009). 'Entrepreneurs' attitudes towards failure: An experiential learning approach. *International Journal of Entrepreneurial Behavior & Research, 15*(4), 364–383; Byrne, O., & Shepherd, D. A. (2015). Different strokes for different folks: Entrepreneurial narratives of emotion, cognition, and making sense of business failure. *Entrepreneurship Theory and Practice, 39*(2), 375–405; Madsen, P. M., & Desai, V. (2010). Failing to learn? The effects of failure and success on organizational learning in the global orbital launch vehicle industry. *Academy of Management Journal, 53*(3), 451–476.
75 Shepherd, D. A. (2003). Learning from business failure: Propositions of grief recovery for the self-employed. *Academy of Management Review, 28*(2), 318–328.
76 Cope. 'Entrepreneurial learning from failure'.
77 Levinthal, D. A., & March, J. G. (1993). The myopia of learning. *Strategic Management Journal, 14*(S2), 95–112.
78 Brush, C. G., Manolova, T. S., & Edelman, L. F. (2008). Properties of emerging organizations: An empirical test. *Journal of Business Venturing, 23*(5), 547–566, 548.
79 Cassar, G. (2014). Industry and startup experience on entrepreneur forecast performance in new firms. *Journal of Business Venturing, 29*(1), 137–151; Invernizzi, A. C., Menozzi, A., Passarani, D. A., Patton, D., & Viglia, G. (2017). Entrepreneurial overconfidence and its impact upon performance. *International Small Business Journal, 35*(6), 709–728.
80 Ucbasaran et al. (2013), ibid.; Zollo, M. (2009). Superstitious learning with rare strategic decisions: Theory and evidence from corporate acquisitions. *Organization Science, 20*(5), 894–908.
81 Nielsen, K., & Sarasvathy, S. D. (2011). *Who reenters entrepreneurship? And who ought to? An empirical study of success after failure.* Paper presented at the DIME-DRUID ACADEMY Winter Conference 2011, Denmark, 20–22 January, p. 4.
82 Frankish, J. S., Roberts, R. G., Coad, A., Spears, T. C., & Storey, D. J. (2012). Do entrepreneurs really learn? Or do they just tell us that they do? *Industrial and Corporate Change, 22*(1), 73–106.
83 Dencker et al. (2009), ibid.; Hayward et al. (2006), ibid.; Camerer, C., & Lovallo, D. (1999). Overconfidence and excess entry: An experimental approach. *The American Economic Review, 89*(1), 306–318.
84 Gladwell, M. (2008). *Outliers: The story of success.* London: Hachette.
85 Lafontaine, F., & Shaw, K. (2016). Serial entrepreneurship: Learning by doing? *Journal of Labor Economics, 34*(S2), S217–S254.
86 Gottschalk et al. (2017), ibid.; Frankish et al. (2012), ibid.
87 Rocha, V., Carneiro, A., & Varum, C. A. (2015). Serial entrepreneurship, learning by doing and self-selection. *International Journal of Industrial Organization, 40*, 91–106.
88 Yamakawa, Y., Peng, M. W., & Deeds, D. L. (2015). Rising from the ashes: Cognitive determinants of venture growth after entrepreneurial failure.

Entrepreneurship Theory and Practice, 39(2), 209–236, 216; Nielsen, K., & Sarasvathy, S. D. (2016). A market for lemons in serial entrepreneurship? Exploring type I and type II errors in the restart decision. *Academy of Management Discoveries, 2*(3), 247–271.
89 familybusinessindex.com/#map.
90 Ibid.
91 Porta, R., Lopez-de-Silanes, F., & Shleifer, A. (1999). Corporate ownership around the world. *The Journal of Finance, 54*(2), 471–517.
92 Breton-Miller, L., & Miller, D. (2006). Why do some family businesses out-compete? Governance, long-term orientations, and sustainable capability. *Entrepreneurship Theory and Practice, 30*(6), 731–746.
93 Wilson, N., Wright, M., & Scholes, L. (2013). Family business survival and the role of boards. *Entrepreneurship Theory and Practice, 37*(6), 1369–1389; Mullins, W., & Schoar, A. (2016). How do CEOs see their roles? Management philosophies and styles in family and non-family firms. *Journal of Financial Economics, 119*(1), 24–43; Hoffmann, C., Wulf, T., & Stubner, S. (2016). Understanding the performance consequences of family involvement in the top management team: The role of long-term orientation. *International Small Business Journal, 34*(3), 345–368.
94 Villalonga, B., & Amit, R. (2006). How do family ownership, control and management affect firm value? *Journal of Financial Economics, 80*(2), 385–417.
95 House of Commons Business, Energy and Industrial Strategy and Work and Pensions Committees (2018). *Carillion*, HC 769, 16 May, pp. 3–4.
96 Miller, D., Breton-Miller, L., & Scholnick, B. (2008). Stewardship vs. stagnation: An empirical comparison of small family and non-family businesses. *Journal of Management Studies, 45*(1), 51–78.
97 Ward, J. (1988). *Keeping the family business healthy.* San Francisco: Jossey-Bass.
98 De Massis, A., Chua, J. H., & Chrisman, J. J. (2008). Factors preventing intra-family succession. *Family Business Review, 21*(2), 183–199.
99 www.nytimes.com/2001/02/14/us/dozens-of-rich-americans-join-in-fight-to-retain-the-estate-tax.html.
100 www.bbc.co.uk/news/magazine-19505088; www.scmp.com/business/companies/article/1436947/centuries-old-japanese-family-owned-inn-model-succession; www.independent.co.uk/life-style/japanese-adoption-rates-majority-adult-men-a7524301.html.
101 Bennedsen, M., Nielsen, K. M., Pérez-González, F., & Wolfenzon, D. (2007). Inside the family firm: The role of families in succession decisions and performance. *The Quarterly Journal of Economics, 122*(2), 647–691; Lemos, R., & Scur, D. (2018, January). *All in the family? CEO choice and firm organization* (CEP Discussion Paper 1528). London: Centre for Economic Performance; Pérez-González, F. (2006). Inherited control and firm performance. *American Economic Review, 96*(5), 1559–1588.
102 Mehrotra, V., Morck, R., Shim, J., & Wiwattanakantang, Y. (2013). Adoptive expectations: Rising sons in Japanese family firms. *Journal of Financial Economics, 108*(3), 840–854.
103 Glover, J. (2014). Gender, power and succession in family farm business. *International Journal of Gender and Entrepreneurship, 6*(3), 276–295.
104 Hytti, U., Alsos, G. A., Heinonen, J., & Ljunggren, E. (2017). Navigating the family business: A gendered analysis of identity construction of daughters. *International Small Business Journal, 35*(6), 665–686; Martinez Jimenez, R. (2009). Research on women in family firms: Current status and future directions. *Family Business Review, 22*(1), 53–64; Wang, C. (2010). Daughter exclusion in family business succession: A review of the literature. *Journal of Family and Economic Issues, 31*(4), 475–484.
105 Han, L., & Greene, F. J. (2016). Are "born to rebel" last-borns more likely to be self-employed? *Personality and Individual Differences, 101*, 270–275.
106 Eddleston, K. A., & Kellermanns, F. W. (2007). Destructive and productive family relationships: A stewardship theory perspective. *Journal of Business Venturing, 22*(4), 545–565.
107 De Massis et al. (2008), ibid.
108 www.afr.com/business/rinehart-family-feud-heads-to-high-court-20180531-h10t7a.
109 DeTienne, D. R., & Chirico, F. (2013). Exit strategies in family firms: How socioemotional wealth drives the threshold of performance. *Entrepreneurship Theory and Practice, 37*(6), 1297–1318, 1303.
110 Gómez-Mejía, L. R., Haynes, K. T., Núñez-Nickel, M., Jacobson, K. J., & Moyano-Fuentes, J. (2007). Socioemotional wealth and business risks in family-controlled firms: Evidence from Spanish olive oil mills. *Administrative Science Quarterly, 52*(1), 106–137; Gomez-Mejia, L. R., Cruz, C., Berrone, P., & De Castro, J. (2011). The bind that ties: Socioemotional wealth preservation in family firms. *Academy of Management Annals, 5*(1), 653–707.
111 Chrisman, J. J., & Patel, P. C. (2012). Variations in R&D investments of family and nonfamily firms: Behavioral agency and myopic loss aversion perspectives. *Academy of Management Journal, 55*(4), 976–997.
112 De Massis et al. (2008), ibid.
113 Zellweger, T., Richards, M., Sieger, P., & Patel, P. C. (2016). How much am I expected to pay for my parents' firm? An institutional logics perspective on family discounts. *Entrepreneurship Theory and Practice, 40*(5), 1041–1069.
114 Morck, R., & Yeung, B. (2003). Agency problems in large family business groups. *Entrepreneurship Theory and Practice, 27*(4), 367–382; Faccio, M. (2006). Politically connected firms. *American Economic Review, 96*(1), 369–386; Morck, R., & Yeung, B. (2004). Family control and the rent-seeking society. *Entrepreneurship Theory and Practice, 28*(4), 391–409.
115 Bertrand, M., & Schoar, A. (2006). The role of family in family firms. *Journal of Economic Perspectives, 20*(2), 73–96.
116 Gedajlovic, E., Carney, M., Chrisman, J. J., & Kellermanns, F. W. (2012). The adolescence of family firm research: Taking stock and planning for the future. *Journal of Management, 38*(4), 1010–1037; De

Massis, A., Kotlar, J., Campopiano, G., & Cassia, L. (2015). The impact of family involvement on SMEs' performance: Theory and evidence. *Journal of Small Business Management, 53*(4), 924–948; Carney, M., Van Essen, M., Gedajlovic, E. R., & Heugens, P. P. (2015). What do we know about private family firms? A meta-analytical review. *Entrepreneurship Theory and Practice, 39*(3), 513–544; Memili, E., Fang, H., Chrisman, J. J., & De Massis, A. (2015). The impact of small-and medium-sized family firms on economic growth. *Small Business Economics, 45*(4), 771–785.

117 Miller, D., Le Breton-Miller, I., Minichilli, A., Corbetta, G., & Pittino, D. (2014). When do non-family CEO s outperform in family firms? Agency and behavioural agency perspectives. *Journal of Management Studies, 51*(4), 547–572; Miller, D., Le Breton-Miller, I., Lester, R. H., & Cannella Jr., A. A. (2007). Are family firms really superior performers? *Journal of Corporate Finance, 13*(5), 829–858.

11

CHAPTER 12

Entrepreneurship Policy

Learning Outcomes

In this chapter, you will learn:

- Why governments support entrepreneurs.
- What they do to help entrepreneurs.
- Whether these policies work.

Mini Contents List

12.1 INTRODUCTION

Governments have supported entrepreneurs for a long time. The United States established its Small Business Administration in 1953. Meanwhile, the UK and many other counties actively began promoting entrepreneurship in the 1980s.[1]

However, such support is expensive.[2]

This begs questions. Questions about how governments decide to spend our taxpayer's money, what they spend this money on and if entrepreneurship policy makes a difference. This chapter shows you what the justifications and decision-making processes are that underlie these spending decisions. You will also learn about the ways governments try to help entrepreneurs. This is in two basic ways: by giving them financial incentives ('hard' support) or providing advice and assistance ('soft' support). The chapter ends by reviewing directions for entrepreneurship policy.

12.2 WHY GOVERNMENTS SUPPORT ENTREPRENEURS

There are four justifications for entrepreneurship policies:

1. **Entrepreneurs make a disproportionate contribution to job creation**. Growth businesses are central to job creation (Chapter 10, p. 247). Similarly, in recessions, the unemployed often turn to self-employment as a way of 'making' a job (a job substitution effect). So, in times of plenty or restrictions, there appear advantages in supporting entrepreneurs.
2. **Entrepreneurship contributes to economic development**. By introducing and diffusing innovations, entrepreneurs provide new ways of meeting customer needs. In this process, they rip up outdated business methods (Schumpeterian 'creative destruction'). Competition from new entrepreneurs can also force inefficient existing players out of the market or 'discipline' them so that they too have to improve their price or quality of their products and services. This results in a more efficient use of resources (productivity gains).
3. **Entrepreneurship provides diversity.** Entrepreneurs can act as agents of social change, bringing sustainable new 'businesses with a purpose' to communities, and addressing social, environmental and political problems. For example, governments in Gulf countries have developed strategies to move their countries away from a dependency on oil to other sectors. Entrepreneurship is also a productive outlet for many people: not everyone wants to spend 50 or more years working for someone else. It can also be a route out of disadvantage for those facing discrimination, such as immigrants and ethnic minorities, or those who struggle to get into the labour market, such as young people without relevant work experience.
4. **Entrepreneurs are a core political constituency.** It is hard for politicians to ignore entrepreneurs. In most countries, the self-employed make up millions of voters. In Greece, more than 1 million adults are self-employed, out of a total working population of around 3.5 million.[3]

12.2.1 The evidence-based approach

The government can take an evidence-based policy approach to decide which types of entrepreneurs to support and how. This method uses well-researched, robust evidence to:

- Identify the scale and scope of a problem by reviewing the academic evidence base or commissioning research into the problem.
- Appraise the options for solving this problem by consulting with people and by conducting research and analysis.

- Evaluate if the chosen solution actually works by conducting research to see if the solution has positive outcomes.

In an evidence-based approach, problems are called 'market failures'. These occur when the free market fails to allocate resources efficiently or in a socially balanced way. Markets can fail entrepreneurs in four main ways.

1. **Entry barriers.** In Venezuela, entrepreneurs have to complete 20 different procedures, pay nearly four times what they earn in a year and wait, on average, 230 days to set up a business. Meanwhile, in New Zealand, founders pay very limited fees, and it takes a single procedure and half a day to start a new company.[4]
2. **A lack of competition.** Without a level playing field, entrepreneurs can struggle to compete against cartels, oligopolies and monopolies. The European Commission fined Google €4.34 billion for bundling its search services because its 'practices have denied rivals the chance to innovate and compete on the merits'.[5]
3. **A lack of information.** Some individuals simply might not know about the benefits and costs of entrepreneurship. This can prevent them from becoming an entrepreneur or give them false hopes about the chances of being extremely successful in entrepreneurship. An existing small business may also be ignorant of available advice and assistance to grow.
4. **Spillover benefits.** If an entrepreneur from a poor neighbourhood becomes a role model, this can have wider positive benefits.[6] It might encourage young people to see entrepreneurship as a route out of deprivation. Business collaboration also has potential spillover benefits such as increasing knowledge about industry best practices. However, these spillover benefits and costs are not always captured by market prices.

Once research and analysis have identified a market failure, policymakers can begin looking for solutions. This often results in a cost-benefit analysis, which itemises the costs and benefits of several solutions to the market failure. Policymakers might also consult with academics, lobby groups, the public and businesses to assess the strengths and weaknesses of the policy options.

In appraising options, the starting point should be to do nothing. Doing nothing is viable because even if the problem is a big problem, the actual costs in setting up, designing and solving this problem may outweigh its benefits. A programme that targets and helps the informally self-employed into formal self-employment is attractive because it boosts social and economic inclusion. However, the actual costs of finding these 'hidden' entrepreneurs may be so high that the benefits do not justify spending taxpayers' money.

The solution with the highest net benefit to society should be implemented and allowed to run for a period of time before being reviewed. The resulting evaluation should seek to see if the programme has delivered positive outcomes, which is called the programme's 'additionality'. For example, an evaluation may reveal that free entrepreneurship leadership training leads to additionality in terms of higher productivity and job creation. In general, establishing the additionality of government intervention is not always easy because:

- The assessment of a solution's net benefits ('additionality') must also take into account what would have happened had it not been implemented (deadweight effects) and if it has negative impacts on other businesses (displacement effects).[7] Some of the entrepreneurs on a free leadership training programme would have paid for their own training even if it was not provided by the government (deadweight). Similarly, these businesses might have created jobs but only at the expense of other companies in the area losing workers (displacement).

Case Study: Unintended policy consequences

© FStop

When American (USA) policymakers launched a programme to combat discrimination and boost female self-employment in the construction industry, many husbands registered their businesses in their spouse's name to benefit from the incentives.[8] The UK's start-up loans scheme aims to ease credit constraints by offering new businesses unsecured loans of up to £25,000. However, at around 50 per cent, the rate of default for these loans was much higher than the typical default rate of 4 per cent on a bank loan.[9] In France, worker rights ramp up significantly once a business reaches 50 employees. An unfortunate aftereffect of this protection measure is that French businesses choose to stay below the 50 employee threshold. This chokes off business growth in the French economy.[10]

- Public support might crowd out private sector support. If business training is free and used by entrepreneurs, this could force private sector trainers out of business.
- Assessing the spillover benefits or wider gains to society is difficult and time-dependent. Dutch painter Vincent Van Gogh only sold one painting in his lifetime. Yet, more than 125 years after his death, Amsterdam's Vincent Van Gogh museum now attracts millions of tourists from across the world each year.
- Unless programme candidates are selected by randomly separating people into groups, it is likely those who self-select to take part will be different in some way from the wider business population. This can lead to biased results.
- Policy objectives are often poorly specified, making it difficult to determine whether they have worked.

Despite these difficulties, because governments are using public funds, governments have a responsibility to undertake evaluations to ensure taxpayers' money is spent wisely.[11]

Assessment tip: What makes for good evidence?

One short cut for evaluating academic evidence is if it appears in a 'top' journal.[12] The problem, though, is that some very good papers appear in less well-ranked journals. Another possibility is to consider a paper's citation score, but this too has its problems: recent papers generally have lower scores.

However, one way to judge a paper on its merits is to look at the quality of its evidence.

- The 'gold' standard of data collection is **Randomised Controlled Trials** (RCTs). RCTs assign people by chance into two separate groups for later comparison. One group gets the 'treatment' such as business advice and the other group gets nothing. Assigning people randomly to the two groups means that they are likely to be representative of the wider population. RCTs are also great because they compare the net benefits of a solution relative to doing nothing (the 'counterfactual'). By assigning entrepreneurs to two groups – with one given a subsidy and the other nothing – it is fairly certain that the subsidy works if those receiving it had better performance outcomes. Although RCTs are common in health, they are still rare in entrepreneurship. Entrepreneurship RCTs are more common in poorer countries. In richer countries, because RCTs are expensive and difficult to do, entrepreneurship programmes are often evaluated by sophisticated econometric techniques such as difference-in-difference and propensity score matching. These techniques attempt to mimic RCTs.
- **Longitudinal evidence** measures activities, attitudes, behaviours and outcomes over a period of time, either qualitatively or quantitatively. The great advantage of longitudinal evidence is that it can separate out the relationship between cause and effect. For instance, if a study examines staff morale before, during and after the introduction of new training, it can show if the training influences morale. Unfortunately, longitudinal evidence does not always rule out alternative explanations for causal relationships. For that to occur, an RCT is needed. Longitudinal evidence is increasingly important in entrepreneurial studies.
- **Cross-sectional evidence** collects evidence at one particular time to give a snapshot of what is occurring. It has two main problems: (1) monitoring people's opinions is a poor proxy of programme effectiveness. If entrepreneurs are given a grant or a soft loan while they are on a programme, they are unlikely to say 'sorry, I bitterly resent you giving me this money for free'. (2) It is difficult to assess the relationship between cause and effect. All that cross-sectional evidence can do is establish a correlation between two or more factors. There may be an association between training and staff morale, but it is impossible to identify if training caused changes in morale.

Entrepreneurship in Action

In designing a policy to solve a market failure, there are a number of challenges:[13]

- What is the best form of support? Is it offering finance or advice, or a mix of the two?
- Should governments provide this support directly, or should they pay the private sector to do so on their behalf? Governments are accountable for how they use our money. But private-sector companies usually have greater credibility with entrepreneurs. They are also more likely to be incentivised to do a good job because, if they fail to, they will not receive on-going work.

- Who is the support for? Is it better targeted at a particular group or should it be open to all? If it is open for everyone, how should a government fund it? If it is for a particular group, how should they actually target this group?
- How should the support be offered – face-to-face, digitally or a blend of the two?
- Should support be free? The advantage of charging is that it incentivises entrepreneurs to use the help on offer. The problem is that some entrepreneurs might really need the support but cannot afford it.
- Identify a policy problem (market failure).
- What does this evidence say about what works to solve this problem?
- Design your own solution to the problem. How would you assess it to see if it works?

12.2.2 The political economy of policy

The 'evidence-based' approach to spotting, solving and evaluating market failures offers policymakers a robust theoretical guide for spending taxpayers' money.

However, in practice, because policymaking is often a political process, it frequently resembles 'policy-based evidence' where a policy is decided first and 'evidence' is collected subsequently to back up the policy. A politician may come up with a policy out of moral conviction, from their own experience, by talking to their friends and family, listening to lobbyists and special interest groups, or because of public opinion. Having arrived at a solution, they then ask their officials to find the 'evidence' to demonstrate their idea will solve the problem.

Academic insight: English entrepreneurship policy in practice

Arshed and her colleagues have shown that England's entrepreneurship policy has used a 'policy-based' evidence approach. Policy formulation often revolved around meeting political goals: 'all the evidence in the world is irrelevant depending on what the political leadership want to do'. Similarly, policy appraisals did not follow an evidence-based approach ('the collection of evidence is politically motivated') while appraisals were usually undertaken by government officials who lacked subject expertise and were more interested in making sure that the policy looked good.[14]

Because policy design was done quickly, Arshed and her colleagues showed that little thought was given to implementation issues. Government delivery agencies had to adopt new policies, often with no real direction about how to deliver the policy or how it fitted in with other policies. Consequently, these agencies were forced to focus on 'box ticking' against policy targets rather than actually working with entrepreneurs. And, in the midst of this policy churn, actual evaluation became lost, replaced by a need to find evidence that backed up the value of the policy.[15]

A policy-based evidence approach may stem from a genuine and well-meaning interest in serving the public. But it can also be caused by politicians and government officials being more interested in their own welfare. During election campaigns, politicians may announce policies to target entrepreneurs if they believe it will improve their chances of being re-elected. Promises such as tax giveaways might aid entrepreneurs but fail to provide wider social benefits. As few stay in the same job for a long time, politicians and civil servants can also be guilty of focusing only on those policies that advance their careers, give them higher status and help them attain greater power. If so, a weak evaluation culture is likely because it avoids awkward questions about cost-effectiveness.

A more Marxist interpretation is that policymakers focus on maximising their own well-being at the expense of the public good. They introduce policies designed to serve their own family, their group or their own class interests, which opens the door for bribery and corruption.

Case Study: Corruption in Brazilian municipalities

© Alamy Stock Photo

Brazil has a long history of elected politicians and officials who have fraudulently used taxpayers' money. Estimates suggest corruption is present in 80 per cent of the country's municipalities. Diverting public funds, over-invoicing for goods and other dishonest activities led to a reduction in start-up activity. However, illicit activity can have an upside for established businesses. By bribing municipality officials, they can avoid burdensome regulations and taxes.[16]

Elected politicians ought to follow an evidence-based approach. In practice, they often appear to adopt a policy-based evidence approach that speculates on problems, picks eye-catching solutions and weakly evaluates the use of taxpayers' money. Worse still, there are examples of politicians and government officials who develop policies that serve their own self-interests.

12.3 HOW GOVERNMENTS SUPPORT ENTREPRENEURSHIP

Governments generally help entrepreneurs if they run the economy well, promote political stability, strongly and swiftly defend the rule of law and provide modern infrastructure, such as good roads and a stable supply of power.[17] Policymakers can also support new and small businesses by ensuring markets work well through competition policy, by making it easier to export goods and services, funding science and technological developments and by providing education.[18]

All of these activities taken together are sometimes called 'entrepreneurial framework conditions' or the 'rules of the game' (Chapter 3, pp. 54–57). How easy or hard a government makes doing business has a big impact on entrepreneurial activities. In countries where institutions are weak, and bribery and corruption are common, challenges in obtaining construction permits, securing a reliable source of electricity, enforcing contracts and registering property make life difficult for entrepreneurs.[19]

In others, governments actively support new and small businesses by ensuring a proportion of public contracts are awarded to entrepreneurs.[20] Another source of support is through general tax incentives or, for farmers, agricultural subsidies. These financial incentives often cost billions of dollars, euros and pounds and make up the bulk of what richer countries spend on entrepreneurship support.[21]

Entrepreneurship in Action: The Role of the State

Do you believe the 'cold bureaucratic hand' of government obstructs entrepreneurship? If so, you might think that a smaller government will reduce the regulatory costs for entrepreneurs.[22] You might see this as helpful since these costs can be a huge drain on business profits, resulting in stifled growth and innovation.[23] Moreover, you might argue burdening entrepreneurs with 'red tape' makes it difficult to start up, pushes people towards the informal economy, promotes inefficiencies, benefits self-interested groups and impedes economic growth and productivity.[24] Alternatively, you may judge that governments can be a force for good for entrepreneurs. If so, you might agree that deregulation will help poorer countries but that it will not always help richer countries.[25] Equally, you might argue that a government is necessary: someone has to set the rules of the game and do it in a smart way that balances competing interests. If you leave it to the market, you will not get the infrastructure or 'blue sky' research and development. Indeed, if it were not for governments investing in basic science, we would not have the algorithm that Google uses to drive its search engine.[26] Another argument is that governments play a critical role in making, shaping and managing markets. Without a competent referee, for example, there is potentially little chance of a carbon-free economy in the future.

- What do you think? Is your thinking based on an evidence-based or policy-based approach?

Governments have a package of support programmes to help entrepreneurs. These activities include:

- Better access to finance for start-up and growth.
- Innovation support.
- Advice, training and assistance services.
- Policies to promote social inclusion.

13.3.1 Access to finance

A lack of access to appropriate, accessible and affordable finance can constrain start-up and growth. Entrepreneurs can face financial constraints if banks struggle to separate 'good' from 'bad' borrowers, equity finance is scarce, they are easily 'discouraged' or simply unaware of available external finance (Chapter 9, pp. 221–223). Governments have sought to improve access to finance by:

- *Loan guarantee schemes.* Banks typically require an entrepreneur to have a track record as a 'good' borrower and may ask for security such as their home to guard against them defaulting on a business loan. To stimulate lending to early-stage ventures and businesses lacking security, governments across the world provide loan guarantee schemes. These guarantee to the bank that if the entrepreneur defaults on their loan, the government will give the bank back its loan. There is good evidence that these schemes can work, although they often have high default rates and unintended consequences.[27]
- *Grants or micro-loans.* Governments offer free grants and cheap micro-loans to entrepreneurs who meet particular criteria, such as being innovative start-ups or living in disadvantaged communities. These can sometimes have positive impacts, particularly in poorer countries.[28] However, they can have deadweight (would have got the money from elsewhere) and displacement effects (had a negative impact on businesses that did not receive the loan).[29] Such schemes may also promote a dependency culture because entrepreneurs might expect the government to come to their aid rather than relying on their own resourcefulness.[30]
- *Equity finance support.* Governments have set up equity programmes – either on their own or in partnership with the private sector – to improve the availability of equity finance. However, the evidence is mixed about whether these schemes work.[31]

Entrepreneurship in Action: Taxing entrepreneurs

How income tax influences people's decision to become an entrepreneur is widely debated.

Low taxation may encourage start-ups because entrepreneurs get to keep more of what they earn. You might think this is appropriate if you think that the tax system should reward entrepreneurial risk-taking.[32] You could also judge it fair because tax compliance costs are often high for entrepreneurs and they get fewer benefits from a country's social security system than employees, such as paid parental and sick leave.

Alternatively, you might argue that high tax rates encourage entrepreneurship. Because entrepreneurs self-report their income rather than having it taxed at source, being in business increases the opportunities for tax evasion (Chapter 3, pp. 47–49). Subsequently, if tax rates are high, start-ups become more likely.

The gap between self-employment and employment tax rates is another crucial aspect of this debate. You may believe that entrepreneurs should pay less tax because of the risks they face. But you may also argue that it is the role of the market to subsidise risks, not the tax system.

Large gaps between the tax rates of entrepreneurs and workers may help explain the rise of the 'gig' economy, in which workers say that they are self-employed to reduce their tax burden but actually only work for one business. It also helps their employers, who do not have to pay benefits such as pension contributions, holiday and sick pay. However, the net result is less tax is paid. This reduces the available public funding for the essential services that society needs.

Both low and high rates of income tax can encourage entrepreneurship. However, these impacts are likely to be modest and influenced by other factors, such as other business taxes and particular small business exemptions.[33]

- Do you think income taxes should be low or high for entrepreneurs?
- Do you think that the gap between the tax rates of employees and the self-employed have contributed to the rise of the gig economy?
- Who benefits from 'gig' work?

12.3.2 Innovation support

It can take 17 years and hundreds of millions of dollars to develop a new drug in the pharmaceutical industry. Even then, the chances of getting to market are only 0.01 per cent.[34] Unsurprisingly, few pharmaceutical companies and venture capitalists are willing to take on the uncertainties of very early-stage product development. As a result, this important role often falls to university research labs. Governments also play a significant role in fostering innovation. There are two reasons why:

1. **Information imperfections.** Potential entrepreneurs may have very strong technical skills but lack awareness about how to commercialise their invention. Difficulties in assessing the commercial worth of new inventions can also make it challenging to raise the finance needed for commercialising the invention.
2. **Spillover benefits.** Even if an innovation fails to achieve a commercial application, it may inspire other entrepreneurs to develop other viable and scalable products and processes based on it.

To address these market failures, governments use these solutions:

- *Innovation grants, loans and subsidies.* These usually go to research labs, businesses or third party agents such as venture capital funds. In broad terms, these schemes have a positive impact.[35]
- *Research & Development (R&D) tax credits.* To encourage businesses to spend money on innovation, one approach is to give businesses tax breaks on R&D activities to encourage them to develop new processes or products and services. This can lead businesses to produce cheaper ways of making a product or a process or develop new products and services. This helps their competitiveness. But it may also have wider spillover benefits if other businesses adopt the product or process. In general, properly designed tax breaks can work for entrepreneurs.[36]
- *Business incubators or accelerators.* These provide business development services and facilities such as subsidised office accommodation space, professional business advice and the chance to network with other start-ups or scale-ups, often in university locations.[37] However, evidence about the degree to which these spaces help entrepreneurs is inconclusive.[38]

Case Study: R&D tax credits support QPay

Zakaria Bouguettaya and Andrew Clapham established Australian start-up QPay in 2014. As a financial platform that helps university students and societies to pay for services and goods such as textbooks and events, QPay achieved revenues of $50,000 in its first year. However, in year two its revenues ballooned to $800,000. It subsequently reached $20 million in transactions and expanded rapidly outside Australia into US and UK universities. Core to its success was the development of the QPay Mastercard, which – thanks to government R&D tax incentives – the fintech company was able to bring to market a year ahead of schedule.[39]

12.3.3 Advice and assistance

Governments offer a range of support to correct information imperfections about starting up and growing a business such as:

- *Entrepreneurship education programmes.* These aim to help students of all ages appreciate what entrepreneurship is, to develop entrepreneurial skills and to improve the desirability of entrepreneurship.[40] The hope is that by fostering an 'entrepreneurial mindset' among young people, it improves their employability and prepares them for setting up their own new venture later on in life. This is important because fewer people are staying in any one role for a long time and individuals leaving education might have 15–20 jobs over their working life.[41]

  However, ambiguity remains about whether these education initiatives have a positive impact on actual entrepreneurial activity.[42] If a student takes a programme and they decide to become an entrepreneur, then the programme looks a success. However, if the same student decided that entrepreneurship was not for them, this too appears a success since the programme could have helped them reach this judgement. Another problem is that it may take 20 years before a student decides to become an entrepreneur, making it difficult to see if an entrepreneurship education programme has a positive or negative impact on outcomes.
- *Business advice and assistance.* Governments offer information and signposting services to make entrepreneurs aware of support for their business, such as available finance options or how to start exporting.[43] Simple information signposting appears to have few benefits, although targeted support for international trade can be valuable.[44] Governments also offer more customised and personalised training, counselling, consulting and mentoring to improve entrepreneurial leadership capabilities and help the business to start up and grow. More 'hands-on' business assistance can work.[45] However, in many cases, business advice and assistance provides only mixed benefits, which quickly disappear.[46]

Case Study: Role models and business support in Chile

Simón de Cirene is a Chilean not-for-profit that provides business and financial support for the self-employed. Part of this support package is offering business assistance and providing business role models. A randomised controlled trial found the provision of role models improved entrepreneurs' motivation levels and led to a 15 per cent increase in business income, particularly among those with little prior business experience. Survival rates were also higher among those who used role models. Equally, business assistance support also led to a 15 per cent increase in business income by improving management practices.[47]

12.3.4 Policies to promote social inclusion

Governments use entrepreneurship policy as a tool to support disadvantaged people and places. There are large economic imbalances across the world and groups such as women, ethnic minorities, younger people and the unemployed can all struggle to start up and grow their business. If this is due to discrimination, this presents a clear need for government intervention.

Supporting people and places opens up the potential for communities and individuals to reinvent themselves and create a route out of deprivation and poverty. However, many entrepreneurship policies are designed as part of attempts to promote equity in society. These include:

- *Place-based initiatives.* Entrepreneurship policies are often included as part of a wider mix of regional policies, such as transport and education. Their objectives may be far wider than the simple focus on entrepreneurship and can include increasing regional growth and improving social inclusion. This scope makes it difficult to see how entrepreneurship influences regional outcomes. The picture is often further confused by multiple policymakers, each with their own objectives.

  Nonetheless, governments do invest large sums of money in regionally disadvantaged areas in the hope it will create a more entrepreneurial climate. Individual programmes can help boost business performance, but often these effects are geographically uneven or lead to poor outcomes.[48]

  Governments also use a range of targeted place-based programmes such as enterprise zones. These often provide businesses with tax breaks and simplified planning restrictions, aiming to attract businesses from outside the region and to build the capacity of existing companies within the zone. There are some advantages in businesses relocating to enterprise zones. Unfortunately, these impacts can be temporary and lead to large displacement effects, such as moving entrepreneurial activity from one place to another, with no overall benefit for the region or the wider economy.[49]
- *Support for women entrepreneurs.* Nearly every country in the world provides support to help women into entrepreneurship, be it through financial assistance, business advice or a mix of the two.[50] These schemes aim to correct discrimination and close the gap between men and women in business. There have been very few evaluations of entrepreneurial support for women in richer countries. However, business training has no impact on survival outcomes for female-owned businesses in developing economies.[51]

Case Study: Egyptian entrepreneurial edutainment

Like very many other countries in the Middle East and elsewhere, Egypt has TV programmes that signpost and inform the watching public about entrepreneurship. One such programme was 'El Mashroua' ('the project'). It used the usual format of asking a group of potential entrepreneurs to complete a weekly challenge. These tasks were subsequently judged by a small panel of experienced entrepreneurs whose role was to vote off one entrepreneur each week until there was an eventual winner.

What was different about 'El Mashroua' was that researchers used a randomised controlled trial to evaluate the impact the programme had on viewers. They found that entrepreneurial 'edutainment' did little to change entrepreneurial perceptions or aspirations. However, for the less well-educated viewer, 'El Mashroua' did improve their knowledge about entrepreneurship. Women also benefited because the programme helped change some negative attitudes towards the chances of women being successful in business.[52]

- *Migrant entrepreneurship.* Support is often justified because of discrimination, to improve economic and social inclusion or to release the entrepreneurial potential of these communities. Despite the value this support might bring, there is little hard evidence that this support actually works. Much of it relies on 'best practice' reviews of migrant entrepreneurship policy rather than actual evaluations of particular schemes.[53]

- *The unemployed.* Governments often turn to supporting the unemployed into self-employment during a recession. Done successfully, these programmes could reduce social security costs. And, by providing a route back into the labour market, the hope is that they will limit the side effects of a lengthy spell of unemployment such as poor health. These schemes can work but are often expensive.[54]
- *Young people.* Integrating young people into the labour market has long-term advantages. If young people are not in employment, education or training, this imposes direct costs on society such as unemployment payments. Society also faces large indirect costs from young people being outside the labour market, such as poor health outcomes and crime. Beyond this, entrepreneurship is a way for young people to realise their ambitions and improve social and economic inclusion. Many schemes try to overcome lower financial, social and human capital among the young through financial aid, mentoring support and training. There is little evidence that these schemes provide long-term benefits.[55]

Case Study: CréaJeunes

© Getty Images/Yuri_Arcurs

Young people can suffer from multiple disadvantages. They might live in a poor neighbourhood, be unemployed and lack technical or basic education.

France's Association pour le droit à l'Initiative Economique (ADIE) established CréaJeunes in 2007 to offer long-term group training, individual coaching and financial support to help unemployed young people in some of the poorest parts of France start their own business. However, the results of an RCT showed that CréaJeunes participants had lower start-up rates, earned less if they started up, and were more likely to end up unemployed than others who were not on the CréaJeunes programme.[56]

Some individual government programmes appear to work better than others. Hard (financial) support appears to have a positive impact on entrepreneurial outcomes, particularly in innovative contexts. Less apparent is the value of soft support, such as business advice and assistance. Many policy initiatives do not just provide either soft or hard support. In poorer countries, the best way of providing entrepreneurial support appears to be by combining both hard and soft support.[57] However, in wealthier countries, this is less clear. Very few RCTs are conducted, and evaluation seldom extends beyond monitoring attendance and satisfaction levels.

Entrepreneurship in Action

Go to your government's small business website and see if you can find what sort of support it gives to entrepreneurs and small businesses. For example, countries such as the Netherlands and the United Arab Emirates have a website that lists its range of programmes, how it supports companies at different stages of the entrepreneurial journey, such as pre-start-up, start-up and growth, and what specialist assistance it provides for individual sectors or for activities such as innovation or exporting.[58]

- Are there any programmes in your own country or region that would help you start up?
- What kinds of support does your government provide for growing businesses?
- Are there programmes for particular sectors or activities such as helping to innovate or export?
- Do you think it is easy to navigate and understand your government's package of support?
- Does your government have a long-term action plan for helping entrepreneurs? Denmark has a dedicated authority that seeks to support entrepreneurship.[59] Does your government have such an agency?

12.4 DOES ENTREPRENEURSHIP POLICY WORK?

It is difficult to assess the overall impact of entrepreneurship policy for a region or a country. Different places have distinctive mixes of hard and soft support, aim their support at differing entrepreneurial groups, such as start-ups, existing small businesses and growth businesses, and choose varied ways of delivering support.

There is also a considerable amount of policy churn. One interpretation of all of this is that governments have gradually evolved over time their understanding of the role entrepreneurship plays in promoting economic development and social inclusion. So, during the past century policymakers first focused on levelling the playing field for small businesses, before gradually realising in this century that actively targeting and supporting start-ups and growing businesses is important.[60]

A less kind view of the history of entrepreneurship policy is that it is a story of constant policy flip-flops between trying to improve the start-up rate and boosting the numbers of growing businesses, mixed in with tax giveaways and the occasional regulatory bonfire.[61] With the exception of countries such as the USA, which has a stable, long-running entrepreneurship programme, in many countries what has emerged is a 'patchwork quilt', 'chaos', 'labyrinth of initiatives' or 'muddle' of entrepreneurship policy initiatives.[62] For example, there are literally hundreds of programmes to support women and migrant entrepreneurs across Europe.

The majority of reviews of entrepreneurship policy are sceptical about its cumulative overall value.[63] There is also limited evidence that entrepreneurship policy has boosted poor regional economies.[64] Despite the huge sums spent on entrepreneurship initiatives, areas that had relatively poor start-up rates in the past century still have poor start-up rates today.[65] Equally, few countries have been able to mimic Silicon Valley by creating their own Silicon Glen, Fen or Wadi.[66]

In response, there are three main ways of responding to these challenges: do nothing to support entrepreneurs; support start-ups and existing small businesses; or focus on high-growth businesses.

Besides saving billions of tax dollars, pounds or euros, there are other reasons why scrapping entrepreneurship policy entirely in favour of doing nothing at all is appealing:

12

1. **Markets work best.** Entrepreneurs make many of their decisions based on their desire for independence and autonomy (Chapter 3, pp. 44–46). If they want business advice and assistance, they go to their accountant, lawyer or financial adviser.[67] It is in the private sector's interest to provide good support because the entrepreneur can always take their services elsewhere. Having public sector support crowds out the private sector and can create a dependency culture where businesses expect governments to prop up their business. Financial incentives such as tax breaks and exemptions create distortions and unintended consequences. It is also not the role of the tax system to subsidise entrepreneurs.
2. **Costs outweigh benefits.** A core activity of any start-up is to ensure that what it provides meets customer expectations (Chapter 6, pp. 126–136). On that basis, most entrepreneurship policies are failures because they is very little take-up of these programmes among entrepreneurs. As election cycles tend to be short, initiatives are often created, duplicated and reinvented, which makes it difficult for time-poor entrepreneurs to navigate their way to the right support. And because evaluations are rare, there are few opportunities for governments to learn from previous policy experiments. This can result in a complex, bureaucratic system that is costly. Recent estimates suggest the UK government spent more than £12 billion each year on entrepreneurship policy.[68] This was more than it spent on policing.
3. **Supporting start-ups and existing small businesses does not assist with economic development.** Like most existing small businesses, the majority of start-ups only employ the entrepreneur and do not grow. They have poor productivity, operate in sectors where there is already an abundance of choice and are likely to fail.[69] Rather than competing with large businesses, they most often compete with each other, with the net result being that one small firm displaces another with no positive benefits. Most business owners have no real interest in business growth. They set up and run a business because it meets their own needs. It is not the government's role to support these individual preferences. So, in effect, 'more' is also not always 'better'.[70] Making it easier and cheaper to start up might be appealing, but one of the distinguishing features between rich and poor countries is that poorer countries have much higher levels of self-employment.
4. **Governments cannot pick winners.** Growing start-ups and existing scale-ups are difficult to spot (Chapter 10, p. 247). They exist across all sectors and may have very particular needs. They often only appear as growth businesses after they have grown. Once they have grown, there is no guarantee they will continue to.[71] If the business is growing, there are also few incentives to go to the government to speed up this growth. But failing business do have a reason to turn to the public purse, particularly if they believe that the government will help bail them out.

The second argument is that rather than cutting entrepreneurial policy entirely, support should be refocused on start-ups and existing small businesses because:

1. **No start-ups means no unicorns.** To get $1 billion valued unicorns, entrepreneurs have to start up. Improving the numbers attracted to, willing and able to start a company improves the chances of having more growth-orientated businesses.[72]
2. **Tackling discrimination.** Some groups in society face discrimination in the labour market. Once this is demonstrated, governments need to act.
3. **The need for equity.** If we want an inclusive society, we need to encourage diverse and disadvantaged communities towards entrepreneurship. Successful start-ups from these communities can also act as role models to others by signalling a way out of poverty and deprivation. Entrepreneurship policy should reflect society. Entrepreneurs make up important communities in any society, so it is right that their interests receive government support.
4. **Need to 'level the playing field'.** Entrepreneurship policies that level the playing field between large and small businesses create opportunities. Since governments cannot easily spot which businesses take advantage of these opportunities, there is value in giving support to all businesses. Since most start-ups and existing small businesses have lower levels of productivity, entrepreneurship policy should focus on where needs are the greatest.[73]

The final alternative is to target support on fast-growth businesses. Supporters of this rationale suggest this is the best approach because:

1. **Opportunity costs.** If governments have a strategic plan for improving entrepreneurial outcomes, they also know that this involves making choices about how to use scarce resources. Rather than spending valuable money on helping a 'mom and pop' store, it is better to support high potential growth-orientated businesses.[74]
2. **Importance of high growth businesses.** Many countries already have a large number of small businesses. What an economy needs are fast-growth businesses that create jobs, innovate and build economic prosperity.
3. **Smart targeting.** Only a small percentage of businesses have both the ambition and potential to grow. Finding these is not that difficult, particularly if 'big data' is used to disentangle likely growers from non-growers. Governments such as those in Nordic countries and in New Zealand have made great strides in collating administrative data on businesses. One good place to start is export-orientated businesses.[75]

In many poorer countries, improving the institutional fabric for all small businesses is often the greatest need. Deregulation to make it easier and cheaper to open, run and grow a business is important, but so too is a government that can be a fair referee, enable positive entrepreneurial framework conditions and build markets.

In richer countries, with more stable and embedded institutions, the challenge is to institutionalise an evidence-based policy culture that learns over time what works and what does not work. If governments can make a difference, developing an action plan that sets out a range of consistent long-term entrepreneurship programmes, and sticking to it, is critical.

12.5 WHAT YOU HAVE LEARNED IN THIS CHAPTER

In this chapter, you have learned that governments justify their entrepreneurship policies because they are interested in improving economic and social outcomes. You have also seen why policymakers should use an evidence-based approach that makes use of robust and reliable research to identify problems, assess and implement solutions and evaluate whether they have worked.

However, entrepreneurship policy is often in fact made using a 'policy-based evidence' approach. This is most concerning when it is apparent that policies serve the interests of a powerful minority in society.

The chapter also showed you that governments have introduced a range of policies to support entrepreneurs. Although the evaluation evidence is often thin, you have learnted that financial incentives tend to work better than business advice or assistance.

Finally, you were asked to reflect on three entrepreneurship policy options: do nothing to support entrepreneurs; offer support to all entrepreneurs; or target fast-growth businesses. You might agree with the default position of supporting new and existing entrepreneurs. Alternatively, you might see such blanket support as a poor use of scarce tax dollars, dinars or pounds since the vast majority of existing small businesses do not want to grow. Similarly, you might argue that most governments have endeavoured to make it easier to start up but also realise that subsidising people's entrepreneurial ambitions and aspirations is a poor use of taxpayer's money. This might lead you to conclude that a better way of spending scarce resources is on targeted initiatives that start and develop markets, support innovation and spur business growth.

ASSESSMENT QUESTIONS

1. Assess the case for supporting all start-ups and small businesses.
2. What is an evidence-based approach? Compare and contrast this with a policy-based approach.
3. Should we use financial incentives to support fast-growth businesses?
4. Does business advice and assistance support entrepreneurial activities?
5. Choose a disadvantaged group in society. Have entrepreneurship policies helped them?
6. Should taxes be lower for entrepreneurs?

FURTHER READING

Acs, Z., Åstebro, T., Audretsch, D., & Robinson, D. T. (2016). Public policy to promote entrepreneurship: A call to arms. *Small Business Economics, 47*(1), 35–51.

McKenzie, D., & Woodruff, C. (2013). What are we learning from business training and entrepreneurship evaluations around the developing world? *The World Bank Research Observer, 29*(1), 48–82.

Potter, J. G., & Storey, D. J. (2007). OECD *Framework for the Evaluation of SME and Entrepreneurship Policies and Programmes*. Paris: OECD.

Shane, S. (2009). Why encouraging more people to become entrepreneurs is bad public policy. *Small Business Economics, 33*(2), 141–149.

Notes

1 Greene, F., Mole, K., & Storey, D. (2008). *Three decades of enterprise culture? Entrepreneurship, economic regeneration and public policy*. London: Springer.
2 Greene et al. (2008). ibid.; Lundström, A., Vikström, P., Fink, M., Meuleman, M., Głodek, P., Storey, D., & Kroksgård, A. (2014). Measuring the costs and coverage of SME and entrepreneurship policy: A pioneering study. *Entrepreneurship Theory and Practice, 38*(4), 941–957.
3 appsso.eurostat.ec.europa.eu/nui/show.do?dataset=lfsq_pganws&lang=en; appsso.eurostat.ec.europa.eu/nui/show.do?dataset=lfsq_esgan2&lang=en.
4 www.doingbusiness.org/en/data/exploreeconomies/venezuela#; www.doingbusiness.org/en/data/exploreeconomies/new-zealand#.
5 europa.eu/rapid/press-release_IP-18-4581_en.htm.
6 Bosma, N., Hessels, J., Schutjens, V., Van Praag, M., & Verheul, I. (2012). Entrepreneurship and role models. *Journal of Economic Psychology, 33*(2), 410–424.
7 Curran, J. (2000). What is small business policy in the UK for? Evaluation and assessing small business policies. *International Small Business Journal, 18*(3), 36–50.
8 Blanchflower, D. G., & Wainwright, J. (2005). *An analysis of the impact of affirmative action programs on self-employment in the construction industry* (Working Paper w11793). Cambridge, MA: National Bureau of Economic Research.
9 www.ukbusinessforums.co.uk/articles/government-backed-start-up-loan-default-rates-reach-50.654.
10 Garicano, L., Lelarge, C., & Van Reenen, J. (2016). Firm size distortions and the productivity distribution: Evidence from France. *American Economic Review, 106*(11), 3439–3479.
11 Potter, J. G., & Storey, D. J. (2007). *OECD Framework for the evaluation of SME and Entrepreneurship Policies and Programmes*. Paris: OECD.
12 charteredabs.org/academic-journal-guide-2018/; abdc.edu.au/research/abdc-journal-list/.
13 Mole, K. F., & Bramley, G. (2006). Making policy choices in nonfinancial business support: An international comparison. *Environment and Planning C: Government and Policy, 24*(6), 885–908.
14 Arshed, N., Carter, S., & Mason, C. (2014). The ineffectiveness of entrepreneurship policy: Is policy formulation to blame? *Small Business Economics, 43*(3), 639–659, 651.
15 Arshed, N., Mason, C., & Carter, S. (2016). Exploring the disconnect in policy implementation: A case of enterprise policy in England. *Environment and Planning C: Government and Policy, 34*(8), 1582–1611.
16 Bologna, J., & Ross, A. (2015). Corruption and entrepreneurship: Evidence from Brazilian municipalities. *Public Choice, 165*(1–2), 59–77; Wellalage, N. H., Locke, S., & Samujh, H. (2019). Firm bribery and credit access: Evidence from Indian SMEs. *Small Business Economics*, 1–22.
17 Klapper, L., Amit, R., Guillén, M. F., & Quesada, J. M. (2007). *Entrepreneurship and firm formation across countries*. Washington: The World Bank; Sobel, R. S. (2008). Testing Baumol: Institutional quality and the productivity of entrepreneurship. *Journal of Business Venturing, 23*(6), 641–655; Stenholm, P., Acs, Z. J., & Wuebker, R. (2013). Exploring country-level institutional arrangements on the rate and type of entrepreneurial activity. *Journal of Business Venturing, 28*(1), 176–193; Estrin, S., Korosteleva, J., & Mickiewicz, T. (2013). Which institutions encourage entrepreneurial growth aspirations? *Journal of Business Venturing, 28*(4), 564–580; Capelleras, J. L., Mole, K. F., Greene, F. J., & Storey, D. J. (2008). Do more heavily regulated economies have poorer performing new ventures? Evidence from Britain and Spain. *Journal of International Business Studies, 39*(4), 688–704; Sanandaji, T., & Leeson, P. T. (2013). Billionaires. *Industrial and Corporate Change, 22*(1), 313–337; Besley, T., & Ghatak, M. (2010). Property rights and economic development. In Rodrik, D. & Rosenzweig, M. (Eds.), *Handbook of development economics* (5, pp. 4525–4595). Amsterdam: North-Holland.
18 Sobel (2008), ibid.; Van Landuyt, Y., Dewaelheyns, N., & Van Hulle, C. (2017). Employment protection legislation and SME performance. *International Small Business Journal, 35*(3), 306–326; Stenholm, P., Acs, Z. J., & Wuebker, R. (2013). Exploring country-level institutional arrangements on the rate and type of entrepreneurial activity. *Journal of Business Venturing, 28*(1), 176–193; La Porta, R., & Shleifer, A. (2014). Informality and development. *Journal of Economic Perspectives, 28*(3), 109–26; Chowdhury, F., Audretsch, D. B., & Belitski, M. (2019). Institutions and entrepreneurship quality. *Entrepreneurship Theory and Practice, 43*(1), 51–81.
19 www.doingbusiness.org/en/reports/global-reports/doing-business-2019; Vorley, T., & Williams, N. (2016). Between petty corruption and criminal extortion: How entrepreneurs in Bulgaria and Romania operate within a devil's circle. *International Small Business Journal, 34*(6), 797–817.
20 Glover, A. (2008). *Accelerating the SME economic engine: Through transparent, simple and strategic procurement*. London: HM Treasury; Loader, K. (2013). Is public procurement a successful small business support policy? A review of the evidence. *Environment and Planning C: Government and Policy, 31*(1), 39–55; Loader, K. (2018). Small-and medium-sized enterprises and public procurement: A review of the UK coalition government's policies and their impact. *Environment and Planning C: Politics and Space, 36*(1), 47–66; Flynn, A., McKevitt, D., & Davis,

P. (2015). The impact of size on small and medium-sized enterprise public sector tendering. *International Small Business Journal, 33*(4), 443–461; Clark III, M., & Moutray, C. (2004). The future of small businesses in the US federal government marketplace. *Journal of Public Procurement, 4*(3), 450–470.

21 Lundström et al. (2014), ibid.; Gu, Q., Karoly, L. A., & Zissimopoulos, J. M. (2008). Small business assistance programs in the United States: An analysis of what they are, how well they perform, and how we can learn more about them. *International Review of Entrepreneurship*, 8(3), 1–32; Richard, D. (2008). *Richard review on small business & government*. London: Conservative Party.

22 Hampton Report. (2005). *Reducing administrative burdens: Effective inspection and enforcement*. London: HM Treasury.

23 Eurochambres. (2009). *Counting the cost of EU regulation to business*. Brussels: Eurochambres; www.sba.gov/advocacy/impact-regulatory-costs-small-firms; https://nsba.biz/new-survey-regulations-a-major-issue-for-small-business/; Federation of Small Business. (2017). *Regulation returned: What small firms want from Brexit*. London: Federation of Small Businesses.

24 Djankov, S., La Porta, R., Lopez-de-Silanes, F., & Shleifer, A. (2002). The regulation of entry. *The Quarterly Journal of Economics, 117*(1), 1–37; European Commission. (2016). *Flash Eurobarometer 354: Entrepreneurship in the EU and beyond*. Brussels: European Commission; Barseghyan, L. (2008). Entry costs and cross-country differences in productivity and output. *Journal of Economic Growth, 13*(2), 145–167; Klapper, L., Laeven, L., & Rajan, R. (2006). Entry regulation as a barrier to entrepreneurship. *Journal of Financial Economics, 82*(3), 591–629; Dreher, A., & Gassebner, M. (2013). Greasing the wheels? The impact of regulations and corruption on firm entry. *Public Choice, 155*(3–4), 413–432.

25 Crafts, N. (2006). Regulation and productivity performance. *Oxford Review of Economic Policy, 22*(2), 186–202; Goldschlag, N., & Tabarrok, A. (2018). Is regulation to blame for the decline in American entrepreneurship? *Economic Policy, 33*(93), 5–44.

26 Mazzucato, M. (2011). The entrepreneurial state. *Soundings, 49*(49), 131–142.

27 Bertoni, F., Martí, J., & Reverte, C. (2019). The impact of government-supported participative loans on the growth of entrepreneurial ventures. *Research Policy, 48*(1), 371–384; Chandler, V. (2012). The economic impact of the Canada small business financing program. *Small Business Economics, 39*(1), 253–264; Oh, I., Lee, J. D., Heshmati, A., & Choi, G. G. (2009). Evaluation of credit guarantee policy using propensity score matching. *Small Business Economics, 33*(3), 335–351; Ono, A., Uesugi, I., & Yasuda, Y. (2013). Are lending relationships beneficial or harmful for public credit guarantees? Evidence from Japan's Emergency Credit Guarantee Program. *Journal of Financial Stability, 9*(2), 151–167; Zecchini, S., & Ventura, M. (2009). The impact of public guarantees on credit to SMEs. *Small Business Economics, 32*(2), 191–206; Riding, A., Madill, J., & Haines, G. (2007). Incrementality of SME loan guarantees. *Small Business Economics, 29*(1–2), 47–61; Lelarge, C., Sraer, D., & Thesmar, D. (2010). Entrepreneurship and credit constraints: Evidence from a French loan guarantee program. In Lerner, J. & Schoar, A. (Eds.), *International differences in entrepreneurship* (pp. 243–273). Chicago: University of Chicago Press.

28 Chen, J., Chang, A. Y., & Bruton, G. D. (2017). Microfinance: Where are we today and where should the research go in the future? *International Small Business Journal, 35*(7), 793–802; Bruton, G. D., Ketchen Jr., D. J., & Ireland, R. D. (2013). Entrepreneurship as a solution to poverty. *Journal of Business Venturing, 28*(6), 683–689; Khavul, S. (2010). Microfinance: Creating opportunities for the poor? *Academy of Management Perspectives, 24*(3), 58–72; Chliova, M., Brinckmann, J., & Rosenbusch, N. (2015). Is microcredit a blessing for the poor? A meta-analysis examining development outcomes and contextual considerations. *Journal of Business Venturing, 30*(3), 467–487.

29 McKenzie, D., & Woodruff, C. (2008). Experimental evidence on returns to capital and access to finance in Mexico. *The World Bank Economic Review, 22*(3), 457–482; Angelucci, M., Karlan, D., & Zinman, J. (2015). Microcredit impacts: Evidence from a randomized microcredit program placement experiment by Compartamos Banco. *American Economic Journal: Applied Economics, 7*(1), 151–82; Autio, E., & Rannikko, H. (2016). Retaining winners: Can policy boost high-growth entrepreneurship? *Research Policy, 45*(1), 42–55; Söderblom, A., Samuelsson, M., Wiklund, J., & Sandberg, R. (2015). Inside the black box of outcome additionality: Effects of early-stage government subsidies on resource accumulation and new venture performance. *Research Policy, 44*(8), 1501–1512.

30 Roper, S., & Hewitt-Dundas, N. (2001). Grant assistance and small firm development in Northern Ireland and the Republic of Ireland. *Scottish Journal of Political Economy, 48*(1), 99–117; Cerqua, A., & Pellegrini, G. (2014). Do subsidies to private capital boost firms' growth? A multiple regression discontinuity design approach. *Journal of Public Economics, 109*, 114–126; Islam, M., Fremeth, A., & Marcus, A. (2018). Signaling by early stage startups: US government research grants and venture capital funding. *Journal of Business Venturing, 33*(1), 35–51.

31 Cumming, D. J., Grilli, L., & Murtinu, S. (2017). Governmental and independent venture capital investments in Europe: A firm-level performance analysis. *Journal of Corporate Finance, 42*, 439–459; Grilli, L., & Murtinu, S. (2014). Government, venture capital and the growth of European high-tech entrepreneurial firms. *Research Policy, 43*(9), 1523–1543; Boyns, N., Cox, M., Spires, R., & Hughes A. (2003). *Research into the Enterprise Investment Scheme and Venture Capital Trusts* (London: Inland Revenue); Lerner, J. (1999). The government as venture capitalist:

The long-run effects of the SBIR program. *Journal of Business, 72*, 285–318; Colombo, M. G., Cumming, D. J., & Vismara, S. (2016). Governmental venture capital for innovative young firms. *The Journal of Technology Transfer, 41*(1), 10–24.

32 Fölster, S. (2002). Do lower taxes stimulate self-employment? *Small Business Economics, 19*(2), 135–145; Davis, S. J., & Henrekson, M. (1999). Explaining national differences in the size and industry distribution of employment. *Small Business Economics, 12*(1), 59–83.
Michaelas, N., Chittenden, F., & Poutziouris, P. (1999). Financial policy and capital structure choice in UK SMEs: Empirical evidence from company panel data. *Small Business Economics, 12*(2), 113–130.

33 Bruce, D. (2000). Effects of the United States tax system on transitions into self-employment. *Labour Economics, 7*(5), 545–574; Hansson, Å. (2012). Tax policy and entrepreneurship: Empirical evidence from Sweden. *Small Business Economics, 38*(4), 495–513; Gurley-Calvez, T., & Bruce, D. (2008). Do tax cuts promote entrepreneurial longevity? *National Tax Journal, 61*(2), 225–250; Georgellis, Y., & Wall, H. J. (2002). *Entrepreneurship and the Policy Environment*, St Louis: Federal Reserve Bank of St. Louis Working Paper Series (2002–019); Bruce, D., & Deskins, J. (2012). Can state tax policies be used to promote entrepreneurial activity? *Small Business Economics, 38*(4), 375–397; Clingingsmith, D., & Shane, S. (2015). How individual income tax policy affects entrepreneurship. *Fordham Law. Review, 84*, 2495.

34 Mazzucato (2011), ibid.

35 Aerts, K., & Schmidt, T. (2008). Two for the price of one? Additionality effects of R&D subsidies: A comparison between Flanders and Germany. *Research Policy, 37*(5), 806–822.
González, X., & Pazó, C. (2008). Do public subsidies stimulate private R&D spending? *Research Policy, 37*(3), 371–389; Koga, T. (2005). R&D subsidy and self-financed R&D: The case of Japanese high-technology start-ups. *Small Business Economics, 24*(1), 53–62; Kaiser, U., & Kuhn, J. M. (2012). Long-run effects of public–private research joint ventures: The case of the Danish Innovation Consortia support scheme. *Research Policy, 41*(5), 913–927; Huergo, E., & Moreno, L. (2017). Subsidies or loans? Evaluating the impact of R&D support programmes. *Research Policy, 46*(7), 1198–1214; Merito, M., Giannangeli, S., & Bonaccorsi, A. (2010). Do incentives to industrial R&D enhance research productivity and firm growth? Evidence from the Italian case. *International Journal of Technology Management, 49*(1–3), 25–48; Morris, M., & Herrmann, O. J. (2013). Beyond surveys: The research frontier moves to the use of administrative data to evaluate R&D grants. *Research Evaluation, 22*(5), 298–306; Foreman-Peck, J. (2013). Effectiveness and efficiency of SME innovation policy. *Small Business Economics, 41*(1), 55–70.

36 Dechezleprêtre, A., Einiö, E., Martin, R., Nguyen, K. T., & Van Reenen, J. (2016). *Do tax incentives for research increase firm innovation? An RD design for R&D* (Working Paper w22405). Cambridge, MA: National Bureau of Economic Research; Appelt, S., Bajgar, M., Criscuolo, C., & Galindo-Rueda, F. (2016). *R&D tax incentives: Evidence on design, incidence and impacts* (Science, Technology and Industry, Policy Papers 32). Paris: OECD; Kasahara, H., Shimotsu, K., & Suzuki, M. (2014). Does an R&D tax credit affect R&D expenditure? The Japanese R&D tax credit reform in 2003. *Journal of the Japanese and International Economies, 31*, 72–97; Sterlacchini, A., & Venturini, F. (2019). R&D tax incentives in EU countries: does the impact vary with firm size?. *Small Business Economics, 53*(3), 687–708.

37 Tamasy, C. (2007). Rethinking technology-oriented business incubators: Developing a robust policy instrument for entrepreneurship, innovation, and regional development? *Growth and Change, 38*(3), 460–473; Tavoletti, E. (2013). Business incubators: Effective infrastructures or waste of public money? Looking for a theoretical framework, guidelines and criteria. *Journal of the Knowledge Economy, 4*(4), 423–443; Bergek, A., & Norrman, C. (2008). Incubator best practice: A framework. *Technovation, 28*(1–2), 20–28.

38 Phan, P. H., Siegel, D. S., & Wright, M. (2005). Science parks and incubators: Observations, synthesis and future research. *Journal of Business Venturing, 20*(2), 165–182; Lukeš, M., Longo, M. C., & Zouhar, J. (2018). Do business incubators really enhance entrepreneurial growth? Evidence from a large sample of innovative Italian start-ups. *Technovation, 82–83*, 25–34; Ferguson, R., & Olofsson, C. (2004). Science parks and the development of NTBFs – Location, survival and growth. *The Journal of Technology Transfer, 29*(1), 5–17; Squicciarini, M. (2008). Science parks' tenants versus out-of-park firms: Who innovates more? A duration model. *The Journal of Technology Transfer, 33*(1), 45–71; Fukugawa, N. (2006). Science parks in Japan and their value-added contributions to new technology-based firms. *International Journal of Industrial Organization, 24*(2), 381–400.

39 www.businessinsider.com.au/qpay-challenger-bank-for-millennials-2018-4; www.smh.com.au/business/small-business/qpay-wins-american-express-business-explorer-grant-20171002-gyshwn.html; www.canberratimes.com.au/national/act/canberra-millennial-bank-qpay-takes-on-the-big-four-20180807-p4zw1v.html; www.startupdaily.net/2018/04/university-payments-startup-qpay-working-become-challenger-bank-millennial-market/; https://aiia.com.au/__data/assets/pdf_file/0011/85475/AIIA-case-studies-R-and-D-tax-incentive-Final-3-May-2018.pdf.

40 Peterman, N. E., & Kennedy, J. (2003). Enterprise education: Influencing students' perceptions of entrepreneurship. *Entrepreneurship Theory and Practice, 28*(2), 129–144; Thompson, P., & Kwong, C. (2016). Compulsory school-based enterprise education as a gateway to an entrepreneurial career. *International Small Business Journal, 34*(6), 838–869. Athayde, R. (2009). Measuring enterprise potential in young people. *Entrepreneurship Theory and Practice, 33*(2), 481–500; Greene, F. J., & Saradakis,

G. (2008). The role of higher education skills and support in graduate self-employment. *Studies in Higher Education, 33*(6), 653–672; Pittaway, L., & Cope, J. (2007). Entrepreneurship education: A systematic review of the evidence. *International Small Business Journal, 25*(5), 479–510; Huber, L. R., Sloof, R., & Van Praag, M. (2014). The effect of early entrepreneurship education: Evidence from a field experiment. *European Economic Review, 72*, 76–97; Souitaris, V., Zerbinati, S., & Al-Laham, A. (2007). Do entrepreneurship programmes raise entrepreneurial intention of science and engineering students? The effect of learning, inspiration and resources. *Journal of Business Venturing, 22*(4), 566–591.

41 European Political Strategy Centre. (2016). *The future of work* (EPSC Strategy Note 12). Brussels: European Political Strategy Centre.

42 Premand, P., Brodmann, S., Almeida, R., Grun, R., & Barouni, M. (2016). Entrepreneurship education and entry into self-employment among university graduates. *World Development, 77*, 311–327; Oosterbeek, H., Van Praag, M., & Ijsselstein, A. (2010). The impact of entrepreneurship education on entrepreneurship skills and motivation. *European Economic Review, 54*(3), 442–454; Nabi, G., Liñán, F., Fayolle, A., Krueger, N., & Walmsley, A. (2017). The impact of entrepreneurship education in higher education: A systematic review and research agenda. *Academy of Management Learning & Education, 16*(2), 277–299; Martin, B. C., McNally, J. J., & Kay, M. J. (2013). Examining the formation of human capital in entrepreneurship: A meta-analysis of entrepreneurship education outcomes. *Journal of Business Venturing, 28*(2), 211–224.

43 Greene, F. J., & Storey, D. J. (2004). An assessment of a venture creation programme: The case of Shell Live WIRE. *Entrepreneurship & Regional Development, 16*(2), 145–159.

44 Mole, K. F., Hart, M., Roper, S., & Saal, D. S. (2011). Broader or deeper? Exploring the most effective intervention profile for public small business support. *Environment and Planning A, 43*(1), 87–105; Munch, J., & Schaur, G. (2018). The effect of export promotion on firm-level performance. *American Economic Journal: Economic Policy, 10*(1), 357–87; Van Biesebroeck, J., Yu, E., & Chen, S. (2015). The impact of trade promotion services on Canadian exporter performance. *Canadian Journal of Economics/ Revue canadienne d'économique, 48*(4), 1481–1512; Martincus, C. V., & Carballo, J. (2010). Beyond the average effects: The distributional impacts of export promotion programs in developing countries. *Journal of Development Economics, 92*(2), 201–214.

45 Wren, C., & Storey, D. J. (2002). Evaluating the effect of soft business support upon small firm performance. *Oxford Economic Papers, 54*(2), 334–365; Lafortune, J., Riutort, J., & Tessada, J. (2019). Role models or individual consulting: The impact of personalizing micro-entrepreneurship training. *American Economic Journal: Applied Economics, 10*(4), 222–245; Rotger, G. P., Gørtz, M., & Storey, D. J. (2012). Assessing the effectiveness of guided preparation for new venture creation and performance: Theory and practice. *Journal of Business Venturing, 27*(4), 506–521; Mole, K., Hart, M., Roper, S., & Saal, D. (2008). Differential gains from Business Link support and advice: A treatment effects approach. *Environment and Planning C: Government and Policy, 26*(2), 315–334; Van Cauwenberge, P., Bauwhede, H. V., & Schoonjans, B. (2013). An evaluation of public spending: The effectiveness of a government-supported networking program in Flanders. *Environment and Planning C: Government and Policy, 31*(1), 24–38.

46 Kösters, S., & Obschonka, M. (2011). Public business advice in the founding process: An empirical evaluation of subjective and economic effects. *Environment and Planning C: Government and Policy, 29*(4), 577–604; Fairlie, R. W., Karlan, D., & Zinman, J. (2015). Behind the GATE experiment: Evidence on effects of and rationales for subsidized entrepreneurship training. *American Economic Journal: Economic Policy, 7*(2), 125–61; McKenzie, D., & Woodruff, C. (2013). What are we learning from business training and entrepreneurship evaluations around the developing world? *The World Bank Research Observer, 29*(1), 48–82; Coad, A., Frankish, J. S., Roberts, R. G., & Storey, D. J. (2016). Why should banks provide entrepreneurship training seminars? *International Small Business Journal, 34*(6), 733–759.

47 www.povertyactionlab.org/evaluation/effect-role-models-and-technical-assistance-microfirms-santiago-chile.

48 Porro, G., & Salis, V. (2018). Do local subsidies to firms create jobs? Counterfactual evaluation of an Italian regional experience. *Papers in Regional Science, 97*(4), 1039–1056; Bachtrögler, J., Fratesi, U., & Perucca, G. (2019). The influence of the local context on the implementation and impact of EU Cohesion Policy. *Regional Studies*, 1–14, https://doi.org/10.1080/00343404.2018.1551615; Bondonio, D., & Greenbaum, R. T. (2006). Do business investment incentives promote employment in declining areas? Evidence from EU Objective-2 regions. *European Urban and Regional Studies, 13*(3), 225–244; Bondonio, D., & Greenbaum, R. T. (2014). Revitalizing regional economies through enterprise support policies: An impact evaluation of multiple instruments. *European Urban and Regional Studies, 21*(1), 79–103; Čadil, J., Mirošník, K., & Rehák, J. (2017). The lack of short-term impact of cohesion policy on the competitiveness of SMEs. *International Small Business Journal, 35*(8), 991–1009.

49 Givord, P., Quantin, S., & Trevien, C. (2018). A long-term evaluation of the first generation of French urban enterprise zones. *Journal of Urban Economics, 105*, 149–161; Briant, A., Lafourcade, M., & Schmutz, B. (2015). Can tax breaks beat geography? Lessons from the French enterprise zone experience. *American Economic Journal: Economic Policy, 7*(2), 88–124; Neumark, D., & Kolko, J. (2010). Do enterprise zones create jobs? Evidence from California's enterprise zone program. *Journal of Urban Economics, 68*(1),

12

1–19; Hanson, A., & Rohlin, S. (2013). Do spatially targeted redevelopment programs spillover? *Regional Science and Urban Economics, 43*(1), 86–100; Givord, P., Rathelot, R., & Sillard, P. (2013). Place-based tax exemptions and displacement effects: An evaluation of the Zones Franches Urbaines program. *Regional Science and Urban Economics, 43*(1), 151–163; Einiö, E., & Overman, H. (2016). *The (displacement) effects of spatially targeted enterprise initiatives: Evidence from UK LEGI* (CEPR Discussion Papers, 11112). London: CEPR; Mayer, T., Mayneris, F., & Py, L. (2015). The impact of Urban Enterprise Zones on establishment location decisions and labor market outcomes: Evidence from France. *Journal of Economic Geography, 17*(4), 709–752; McKenzie & Woodruff (2013), ibid.

50 Lundstrom, A., & Stevenson, L. (2005). *Entrepreneurship policy: Theory and practice.* Stockholm: Swedish Foundation for Small Business Research.

51 McKenzie & Woodruff (2013), ibid.; Berge, L. I. O., Bjorvatn, K., & Tungodden, B. (2014). ,'Human and financial capital for microenterprise development: Evidence from a field and lab experiment. *Management Science, 61*(4), 707–722; de Mel, S., McKenzie, D., & Woodruff, C. (2014). Business training and female enterprise start-up, growth, and dynamics: Experimental evidence from Sri Lanka. *Journal of Development Economics, 106*, 199–210; Valdivia, M. (2015). Business training plus for female entrepreneurship? Short and medium-term experimental evidence from Peru. *Journal of Development Economics, 113*, 33–51.

52 www.povertyactionlab.org/evaluation/evaluating-effects-entrepreneurship-edutainment-egypt; Barsoum, G., Crépon, B., Michel, B., & Parienté, W. (2016). *Evaluating the effects of entrepreneurship edutainment in Egypt* (Working Paper).

53 European Commission. (2008b). *Entrepreneurial diversity in a unified Europe.* Brussels: European Commission.

54 Caliendo, M., & Kritikos, A. S. (2010). Start-ups by the unemployed: Characteristics, survival and direct employment effects. *Small Business Economics, 35*(1), 71–92; Caliendo, M., & Künn, S. (2011). Start-up subsidies for the unemployed: Long-term evidence and effect heterogeneity. *Journal of Public Economics, 95*(3–4), 311–331; Caliendo, M., Hogenacker, J., Künn, S., & Wießner, F. (2015). Subsidized start-ups out of unemployment: A comparison to regular business start-ups. *Small Business Economics, 45*(1), 165–190; Behrenz, L., Delander, L., & Månsson, J. (2016). Is starting a business a sustainable way out of unemployment? Treatment effects of the Swedish start-up subsidy. *Journal of Labor Research, 37*(4), 389–411; Perry, G. (2006). *Are business start-up subsidies effective for the unemployed: Evaluation of enterprise allowance.* Auckland: Auckland University of Technology; Rodriguez-Planas, N. (2010). Channels through which public employment services and small business assistance programmes work. *Oxford Bulletin of Economics and Statistics, 72*(4), 458–485; Benus, J. M. (1995). Self-employment programs: A new reemployment tool. *Entrepreneurship Theory and Practice, 19*(2), 73–85.

55 Greene, F. J. (2002). An investigation into enterprise support for younger people, 1975–2000. *International Small Business Journal, 20*(3), 315–336; Meager, N., Bates, P., & Cowling, M. (2003). An evaluation of business start-up support for young people. *National Institute Economic Review, 186*(1), 59–72; Greene & Storey (2004), ibid.

56 www.povertyactionlab.org/evaluation/small-business-training-and-loans-aspiring-entrepreneurs-disadvantaged-neighborhoods.

57 Cho, Y., & Honorati, M. (2013). *Entrepreneurship programs in developing countries: A meta regression analysis.* Washington: The World Bank.

58 www.government.nl/topics/enterprise-and-innovation/support-for-small-and-medium-sized-enterprises-smes; english.rvo.nl/; www.rvo.nl/subsidies-regelingen; www.government.ae/en/information-and-services/business.

59 https://danishbusinessauthority.dk/mission-and-vision.

60 Jurado, T., & Battisti, M. (2019). The evolution of SME policy: The case of New Zealand. *Regional Studies, Regional Science, 6*(1), 32–54.

61 Bennett, R. (2008). SME policy support in Britain since the 1990s: What have we learnt? *Environment and Planning C: Government and Policy, 26*(2), 375–397; Greene et al. (2008), ibid.; Greene, F., & Patel, P. (2013). *Enterprise 2050: Getting UK Enterprise Policy Right* (Discussion Paper 29); Wapshott, R., & Mallett, O. (2018). Small and medium-sized enterprise policy: Designed to fail? *Environment and Planning C: Politics and Space, 36*(4), 750–772.

62 Greene & Patel. *Enterprise 2050.* London: FSB.

63 Bridge, S., & O'Neill, K. (2012). *Understanding enterprise: Entrepreneurship and small business.* London: Macmillan International Higher Education; Davidsson, P. (2008). Looking back at 20 years of entrepreneurship research: What did we learn. *Entrepreneurship Sustainable Growth and Performance*, 13–26; Robson, P. J., & Bennett, R. J. (2000). SME growth: The relationship with business advice and external collaboration. *Small Business Economics, 15*(3), 193–208; Curran (2000), ibid.; Bannock, G. (2005). *The economics and management of small business: An international perspective.* London: Routledge.

64 Cravo, T. A., & Piza, C. (2018). The impact of business-support services on firm performance: A meta-analysis. *Small Business Economics*, 1–18.

65 Greene et al. (2008), ibid.; Fraser of Allander Institute. (2001). Promoting business start-ups: A new strategic formula, Glasgow: Fraser of Allander Institute; stage 1: Progress review; final report'; Williams, N., & Huggins, R. (2013). Supporting entrepreneurship in deprived communities: A vision too far? *Journal of Small Business and Enterprise Development, 20*(1), 165–180; Greene, F. J., Mole, K. F., & Storey, D. J. (2004). Does more mean worse? Three decades of

enterprise policy in the Tees Valley. *Urban Studies, 41*(7), 1207–1228.

66 Giest, S. (2017). Overcoming the failure of "silicon somewheres": Learning in policy transfer processes. *Policy & Politics, 45*(1), 39–54; Casper, S. (2007). *Creating Silicon Valley in Europe: Public policy towards new technology industries*. Oxford: Oxford University Press.

67 Bennett, R. J., & Robson, P. J. (1999). The use of external business advice by SMEs in Britain. *Entrepreneurship & Regional Development, 11*(2), 155–180.

68 Richard (2008), ibid.

69 Nightingale, P., & Coad, A. (2014). Muppets and gazelles: Political and methodological biases in entrepreneurship research. *Industrial and Corporate Change, 23*(1), 113–143; Román, C., Congregado, E., & Millán, J. M. (2013). Start-up incentives: Entrepreneurship policy or active labour market programme? *Journal of Business Venturing, 28*(1), 151–175; Acs, Z., Åstebro, T., Audretsch, D., & Robinson, D. T. (2016). Public policy to promote entrepreneurship: A call to arms. *Small Business Economics, 47*(1), 35–51; Shane, S. (2009). Why encouraging more people to become entrepreneurs is bad public policy. *Small Business Economics, 33*(2), 141–149; Vivarelli, M. (2013). Is entrepreneurship necessarily good? Microeconomic evidence from developed and developing countries. *Industrial and Corporate Change, 22*(6), 1453–1495.

70 Atems, B., & Shand, G. (2018). An empirical analysis of the relationship between entrepreneurship and income inequality. *Small Business Economics, 51*(4), 905–922.

71 Brown, R., Mawson, S., & Mason, C. (2017). Myth-busting and entrepreneurship policy: The case of high growth firms. *Entrepreneurship & Regional Development, 29*(5–6), 414–443.

72 Mason, C., & Brown, R. (2013). Creating good public policy to support high-growth firms. *Small Business Economics, 40*(2), 211–225.

73 Bloom, N., & Van Reenen, J. (2007). Measuring and explaining management practices across firms and countries. *The Quarterly Journal of Economics, 122*(4), 1351–1408.

74 Santarelli, E., & Vivarelli, M. (2007). Entrepreneurship and the process of firms' entry, survival and growth. *Industrial and Corporate Change, 16*(3), 455–488.

75 Mason & Brown (2013), ibid.

PART 5

Introduction to the Workbooks

Workbook 1 has a number of practical exercises designed to help you determine the desirability and feasibility of a start-up proposition. By the end of Workbook 1, you will have a clearer idea of whether or not to proceed with your proposition. This might be all that you need, particularly if there is no external audience or funders interested in your idea.

Workbook 2 provides a range of practical exercises to guide you through the development of a Business Model Canvas, a plan and a presentation for your start-up proposition. By the end of Workbook 2 you will have created a pitch deck and plan which comprehensively answer all 12 start-up questions identified in Chapter 5 and demonstrate the viability of your start-up.

WORKBOOK 1

START-UP DESIRABILITY AND FEASIBILITY

Learning Outcomes

In this part of the workbook you will learn:

- Whether starting up a new venture is desirable.
- If your start-up proposition is feasible.
- If you have the basis for a start-up proposition.

Mini Contents List

W.1.1 INTRODUCTION

This series of practical exercises helps you to assess whether a start-up idea is a desirable and feasible option.

It uses the 'Me, Market and Money' model (Chapter 4, pp. 80–84):

- **'Me'** focuses on your motivations, dispositions, and skills. Through these exercises, you will self-evaluate if a start-up is desirable.
- **'Market'** exercises help you to assess the competition, if there is an outline customer and if there is a 'window of opportunity'.
- **'Money'** exercises help you to start thinking about the financial and social capital needed to turn an idea into a start-up proposition.

By the end of Workbook 1, you should have a clearer idea of whether you have the basis for a start-up proposition.

Workbook 2 builds on your start-up proposition to develop a feasibility study and a pitch (Chapters 5, 6, 7, and 8).

W.1.2 ME

Reflect on your start-up dispositions, motivations and skills in the following exercises.

Exercise W.1.1: Do your personality attributes incline you towards entrepreneurship?

Entrepreneurship involves a complex set of tasks and responsibilities. To cope with these challenges, you might need particular traits and be prone to specific cognitive biases.

Score yourself on these opposing statements.

Statement 1.1: In evaluating a start-up opportunity, I am completely prepared to take risks. *Statement 1.2: In evaluating a start-up opportunity, I will only take well-informed risks.*						
Agree with statement 1.1	2	3	Neutral	5	6	Agree with statement 1.2
Statement 2.1: If my business failed, I would be likely to blame myself. *Statement 2.2: If my business failed, I would be likely to blame others or outside circumstances.*						
Agree with statement 2.1	2	3	Neutral	5	6	Agree with statement 2.2

Statement 3.1: I think that in developing a successful start-up it is better to see what happens. *Statement 3.2: I think that in developing a successful start-up it is better to plan first.*						
Agree with statement 3.1	2	3	Neutral	5	6	Agree with statement 3.2
Statement 4.1: I have high levels of self-esteem about setting up a business. *Statement 4.2: I have low levels of self-esteem about setting up a business.*						
Agree with statement 4.1	2	3	Neutral	5	6	Agree with statement 4.2
Statement 5.1: If I set up a business, I am optimistic about it being a success. *Statement 5.2: If I set up a business, I am unsure about it being a success.*						
Agree with statement 5.1	2	3	Neutral	5	6	Agree with statement 5.2
Statement 6.1: I am very confident that I would be able to set up a successful business. *Statement 6.2: I have little confidence that I would be able to set up a successful business.*						
Agree with statement 6.1	2	3	Neutral	5	6	Agree with statement 6.2
Statement 7.1: If I set up a start-up, my focus would be on maximising my return. *Statement 7.2: If I set up a start-up, my focus would be on limiting what I could afford to lose.*						
Agree with statement 7.1	2	3	Neutral	5	6	Agree with statement 7.2

The traditional view is that entrepreneurs are risk-takers (Statement 1.1), have a high locus of control (2.1) and, because they set goals, are more likely to be achievers (3.1). There is also an expectation that an entrepreneur has high levels of self-efficacy (4.1), optimism (5.1), is confident (6.1), and looks at what they can gain rather than lose (7.1).

Exercise W.1.2: what are your motivations towards entrepreneurship?

Rank each of these in order (1= highest)

In setting up a business, I would want to build a business that...	Rank
...will make me rich	
...supports my lifestyle	
...gives me flexibility and autonomy	
...gives me independence and self-fulfilment	
...provides for my family	
...actively contributes to the community	
...gets me out of what I am currently doing	
...will give me social status	
Other reason (please specify)	

Now imagine your business has come to the end of its life. What key phrase would you like it to be remembered by? Use the picture of the tombstone below and write the epitaph for your business. For example, it might say RIP [business name]. This business brought me [great satisfaction] because [It allowed me to support my community].

RIP

[.......................................]

The business brought me

[.......................................]

because

[.......................................]

Chapter 3 (pp. 44–46) showed that motivations often come in bundles and that they influence future business outcomes. People who set up out of necessity (Chapter 3, Table 3.3, p. 51) are more likely to survive in business for shorter periods. There are also performance differences between setting up out of 'love' and for 'money'.

Exercise W.1.3: what do you think about the trade-offs involved in entrepreneurship?

Becoming an entrepreneur involves potential trade-offs (Chapter 3, p. 47). You might want to be financially better off but find you have little or no money, particularly in the early start-up stages.

Equally, although you might value independence and flexibility, you still have to meet customer expectations. Entrepreneurs tend to work far longer hours than employees. However, being your own boss does have its benefits.

How much are you prepared to sacrifice to your business? Score each of these costs (1 = completely agree; 4 = Neutral; 7 = completely disagree)

I am willing to...	1	2	3	4	5	6	7
... consistently work more than 50 hours a week							
...accept that it might take a number of years for my business to be successful							
...have limited time with my family and friends							
...spend all of my savings on developing the business							
...see my business fail							

Now score each of these benefits (1 = completely agree; 4 = Neutral; 7 = completely disagree)

I would want to run my own business because...	1	2	3	4	5	6	7
...I prefer following my own schedule							
...it means that I will have a chance to do a variety of jobs in my work							
...I will gain immense satisfaction if I can grow the business							
...it will give me a chance to find a better work-life balance							

Exercise W.1.4: Do you need to be a 'jack of all trades' to be an entrepreneur?

Entrepreneurs are like party hosts who need different skills to ensure their event (business) runs well for their guests (customers). To set up a business, you might need:

- Leadership skills – the ability to motivate and influence others through networking, persuasion, and negotiation. An aptitude for delegating work effectively also helps.
- Entrepreneurship skills – the creative ability to identify customer needs, technical or market opportunities and have the management acumen to pursue opportunities.
- Organisational skills – your ability to allocate and organise resources, the financial and business literacy to monitor the vitality of the business and the management capability co-ordinate tasks.

Score your start-up skills:

Skill	Not developed	Starting to develop	Have some skills	Very strong skills
Creative thinking in solving problems				
Ability to research markets				
Ability to make decisions when faced with uncertainty				
Ability to network effectively				
Ability to evaluate and manage risks				
Negotiation and persuasion skills				
Ability to put together and understand financial information				
Ability to set goals and achieve them				
Ability to create and manage teams				
Able to market and sell products and services				

Chapter 3 (p. 50) showed that if someone was a 'jack of all trades' they were more likely to become an entrepreneur. Below are some of the functional areas of a business.

Count up (None, Some, Good) what experience you have in each of these fields.

Business area	None	Some	Good
Sales			
Marketing			
Finance & accounting			
Production & operations			
Distribution			
Human resources			

Again, the sense is that if you have a wide range of skills you are more likely to become an entrepreneur.

Exercise W.1.5: What roles does your background play in start-up?

A number of background factors may influence start-up feasibility (Chapter 3, Tables 3.3, 3.4 and 3.5). *The following questions ask you if you have the relevant background or experience to become an entrepreneur, if it matters to your start-up, and why.*

	Yes	No	Does it matter for starting up?	Why do you think this?
Do you have managerial experience?				
Do you have relevant industry experience?				
Have you set up a business before?				
Are you under 30 years old?				
In your family, is there experience of setting up a business?				
Are you the first born in your family?				
Do you have a partner?				
Are you a woman?				
Do you have any children?				
Are you currently unemployed?				
Do you have a university degree?				
Do you have a disability?				
Are you (or your parents) migrants?				

Working out how your background impacts your chances is important not just for starting up. They also are likely to influence your prospective chances of growth (Chapter 10) and survival (Chapter 11). It is important to pause and reflect on your answer to these questions by examining what – on average – happens to others.

Exercise W.1.6: What is your problem statement?

Entrepreneurs are problem solvers. *Once you have framed and reframed a problem to find out what is not working, wrong or missing, use the box below to write out your problem statement* (Chapter 4, pp. 69–75). *You should identify why this is a real problem for people.*

Exercise W.1.7: What is your idea statement?

If you have an idea (a solution to a problem), use the box below to write out your idea statement (Chapter 4, pp. 75–80). Identify the ways in which your idea is a novel and practical solution to a problem.

Exercise W.1.8: How desirable is starting up?

Ajzen's theory of planned behaviour (Chapter 2, pp. 29–30) identifies that people who are motivated towards entrepreneurship are more likely to become entrepreneurs. But there is a range of factors that influence the attractiveness of entrepreneurship.

How desirable is starting up a business? (1= totally agree; 4 = neutral; 7= totally disagree)

	1	2	3	4	5	6	7
My future career is as an entrepreneur							
If I had a good idea, I would certainly set up a new business							
If I had the money, I would certainly start up a business							
I think that my family and friends would be really supportive of my decision to start up							
I believe that I have the right skills to start a successful business							

Not all ideas are attractive. *Rank your initial perceptions about the desirability of the idea (1=not at all; 7= a great deal and don't know).*

	1	2	3	4	5	6	7	Don't know
Do you think that the idea is practical?								
Do you think that the idea is an imaginative solution to the problem?								
Is this idea something that you find attractive to you personally?								
Do you think that you have the skills, abilities and knowledge to pursue the idea?								
Do you think that your social networks would buy into your idea?								
Does the idea come at the 'right' time for you?								

W.1.3 MARKET

This section asks you or you and your team to consider if there are potential customers for your idea, who your competitors might be, and if there is a 'window of opportunity'.

Exercises W.1.9: Who is your target customer?

A creative idea might give you a competitive advantage in a market. But if an idea is completely novel, it generally takes longer to develop it into a working product or service. Customers may also be unaware of what it can do. This can mean it takes longer to educate, inform and sell your resulting product or service. *The question below asks you to self-assess the novelty of your idea.*

Is the idea (tick one box only)	Yes	No	Don't know
New to you?			
New to the market?			
Completely new?			

WORKBOOK 1

Another way of classifying your idea is to see it as an incremental or radical idea. Radical ideas are the beginnings of completely new products or services whilst incremental ideas are suggested improvements to existing products or services. Both types of idea can be for an existing market or a new market. *Place an X on the two-by-two matrix below where you think your idea should be.*

If your idea is radical and you want to sell it into a new market, the chances are that it will take longer and be more costly to develop. The advantage, however, may be that competition is lower and profits potentially higher.

To become a start-up, a necessary precondition is that there are customers for the idea. To start to identify your target customer involves working out how many people are likely to be attracted to your idea. *The question below asks you to assess if:*

The customer...	Yes	No	Don't know
... is everyone?			
... is a particular group in society?			
... is just a few people/businesses?			

As Chapter 6 (pp. 126–127) shows, if your customer is 'everyone', it is unlikely that a start-up will have the resources to reach and serve this mass market. It is better to focus on a particular customer type for your idea. You will have an opportunity to better define your customer in Workbook 2 (Exercises W.2.2–W.2.6).

Another danger is focusing too early on a target customer. If the choice of the customer is made hastily, later on, valuable time and resources will be wasted. For example, the initial target customer for Viagra was people who suffered from blood pressure problems. Its market now is men who suffer from erectile dysfunction.

One way forward is to brainstorm as many different potential target customers for your idea as you can.

Although your idea might be appealing to lots of different customer groups, the chances are that a start-up will have limited resources, making it difficult to reach all of these groups. Focusing on what group needs it most, who would be 'delighted' by the idea, who is willing and can pay for the idea are all basic ways of evaluating different target customers. *The question below asks you to make a quick assessment of what group looks the most promising. For each question, give each group a score out of 7, with 1 being low and 7 being high. Total your scores up.*

Group	A	B	C	D	E
Does your idea solve a big problem for this customer?					
Is your idea likely to 'delight' this customer?					
Is the customer willing to pay for the idea?					
Total Score					

Workbook 2 (W.2.2 Product-Market Fit) revisits this process of customer segmentation because it is important to keep questioning if a target customer is the most likely customer for your product or service.

One way of bringing all you know about the target customer together is to develop a customer vignette. This is a short portrait of your target customer. It identifies their key demographic features are such as their age, sex, location and income, and what drives their actions and behaviours such as interests and tastes. *Use the box below to either draw a picture of your target customer and/or list out their key characteristics.*

WORKBOOK 1

It is likely that this target customer will evolve and change as develop your start-up planning (Chapter 5, p. 94).

Exercise W.1.10: Who are your competitors?

Some markets are more attractive than others (Chapter 7, pp. 170–178). *Consider who your potential competitors are by answering the following questions:*

What is the alternative to the idea?... (tick one box only)	Yes	No	Don't know
... there is no alternative			
... using a product or service that is inferior			
... customers already have viable solutions available to them			

Having competitors is a good thing because it shows that there is a market for your idea.

	Yes	No	Don't know
Are there many competitors for your product/service?			
If so, can you name any of them?			

Your idea must meet an unmet need or solves a problem better than your competition. *Rank your relevant benefits in order from 1=most important.*

Lower prices	
Quality	
Service	
Location	
Newness of idea	
Technical expertise	
Other (specify)	

Explain in the box below why you think that your idea is better than what the competition offers.

If your start-up planning shows that you do not have a competitive edge over your competition, you should have serious doubts about pursuing a business idea.

Exercise W.1.11: What is happening in your market?

Some ideas are before their time. Some take years to reach the market, and others have a very short window of opportunity. Markets can go through a variety of stages too. These are all likely impact on how quickly you have to set-up and your chances of reaching profitability. *Answer the following questions to assess what is happening in the market for your idea.*

How big is the window of opportunity? (tick one box only)	Yes	No	Don't know
Days and weeks			
Less than 1 year			
Between 1 and 3 years			
Longer than 3 years			

At what stage is the market? (tick one box only)	Yes	No	Don't know
Does not yet exist			
New			
Growing			
Stable			
Declining			

Explain in the box below what implications your answers have on the development of your idea.

WORKBOOK 1

You will have to consider how quickly you enter because the opportunity may be a 'hit and home run' idea where you seek to exploit a time-based window of opportunity, build the business quickly, and exit when the business opportunity closes.

W.1.4 MONEY

This section asks you about the financial and social resources you have available to turn an idea into a start-up.

Exercise W.1.12: What financial resources do you have for a start-up?

Answer the following questions with the amount of money you have for each or say 'don't know.'

	Amount/don't know
How much spare cash do you have?	
How much do you have in savings?	
What proportion of your savings are you prepared to lose?	
How much do you need to live in an average week?	

One start-up danger is not having enough money to create a viable new venture. This 'under-capitalisation' often leads to business closure.

Exercise W.1.13: How can you bootstrap your start-up?

Use the box below to list out some ways that you might bootstrap your idea such as working from home or using second-hand equipment.

Exercise W.1.14: How can your social networks help you start up?

Write down in the box below the people that you could ask for support, assistance, money and information to help with your start-up idea. These might be family, friends or social acquaintances or work colleagues.

Now divide those your social network into those that you feel close to (strong ties) and those you know less well (weak ties) (tick yes or no). One way of distinguishing these is to decide how much trust there is between you and them. Finally, are any of these strong or weak ties a potential mentor? It is often important to have a mentor for a start-up because they can help you in developing the idea into a start-up.

Person	Strong tie? (Yes or No)	Weak tie? (Yes or No)	Mentor?

Although about half of start-ups are team-based, everyone needs some sort of support. It is also difficult to see that very many founders will have an easy start-up journey if they are not able to carry their family and friends with them, if only because these are often a primary source of financial support (Chapter 9, p. 214).

W.1.5 EVALUATING THE IDEA

Exercise W.1.15: Is starting up the right choice?

Tick below what is the best way forward for pursuing the idea.

A start-up	
Franchise	
Licencing/selling the idea	
Buying a similar business	
Don't know	

Use the box below to explain why this is the best option.

Exercise W.1.16: Is the idea really a start-up proposition?

At some point, you will have to make a go/no go decision about continuing with your idea. *The three questions below on Me, Market and Money ask you to self-assess the overall attractiveness and feasibility of your idea. For each one, tick whether they are Go, No Go or you need more information.*

	Go	No Go	Need further information
Is the idea really for me?			
Is there a customer that I believe will pay for the idea?			
Can I access enough resources to make the idea a reality?			

Exercise W.1.17: Assessing and pitching your idea

Self-assessing your start-up proposition provides insights but one way of reaching external audiences is to develop a short elevator pitch.

A basic elevator pitch format and 'Pixar' pitching are described in Chapter 4 (pp. 87–88). A simpler version is:

- *(Product or service) is (a solution) that helps (specific customers) with (a problem). This (product or service) is different because (unique solution).*

For example: 'Quikirecipe is a new food recipe app that helps single professional men who are time poor but want to eat easy to prepare nutritious food. Quikirecipe is different because it uses Artificial Intelligence to adapt recipes to fit customer needs.'

Write your own elevator pitch in the box below. One further option is to film yourself presenting it.

WORKBOOK 2

Building Your Business Model for Start-Up Pitching and Planning

Learning Outcomes

In this part of the workbook you will:

- Learn how to use the Business Model Canvas to develop answers to the 12 start-up questions.
- Build up towards a pitch and plan that provides a comprehensive understanding of all 12 questions.
- Develop a set of pitch deck slides and plan sections to demonstrate the viability of your start-up.

Mini Contents List

W.2.1 INTRODUCTION

Chapter 5 set the scene for the exercises in this Workbook. It suggested that start-up involves answering 12 core questions, such as who your customer and what are your plans for future growth.

Although there is no one way of sketching out your business model, the workbook first builds on Chapter 6 and its use of the Business Model Canvas (BMC) to help you answer these start-up questions (Chapter 5, pp. 98–99):

- Is there a market out there? and Who is the customer? (customer segments in the BMC).
- Is the business idea worthwhile? (value proposition).
- How does the business reach its customers? (customer relationships and channels).
- How does the business source, make and distribute its products and services? (key activities, resources and partners).
- How does it make money? (revenue and cost streams).

The exercises then examine the start-up questions explored in Chapter 7:

- Who are we?
- Why is this the right team?
- How is the offer different in the market?

The exercises end with considering the final three start-up questions (Chapter 8):

- What is the plan for growth?
- What does the start-up lack?
- Is the start-up viable?

W.2.2 PRODUCT–MARKET FIT

These exercises focus on building an understanding of key questions such as 'Is there a market out there?', 'Who is the customer? And 'Is the business idea worthwhile?'.

This equates to the customer segment and value proposition parts of the BMC. It also relates to the Product and Market sections used in plans. The aim is that by the end of this section, you are able to:

1. Write up your BMC customer segment and value proposition sections
2. Develop a range of pitch deck slides that explain your product and market fit
3. Write up your product and market elements for a plan

Exercise W.2.1: How big is the problem?

One way of beginning to decide on how big the problem is to split the problem market into a favoured starting geography. Many entrepreneurs start locally, often close to where they currently live. At the other extreme, some entrepreneurs are 'born globals' (Chapter 10, p. 264) with a plan to start in international markets. *Brainstorm in the box below the different problem markets your product or service would suit. Once you have done this, evaluate: a) whether it is betters to start locally, regionally, nationally or internationally and b) why your chosen location is better than possible alternatives.*

a)

b)

Go to your library website and find out what databases or sources of information it has on the market for your chosen problem. Dedicated databases such as Mintel offer you the ability to find information on market size and trends. Official statistics often provide regional and national demographic information on a country's population whilst trade associations or special interest groups often have information on changing patterns.

Collect information on the problem. Develop an infograph for your chosen problem that shows its market size and dynamics.

Adapt Figure W.2.1 for your own needs. Another version of this is shown in Figure W.2.1. If a 'problem' slide is used (Figure W.2.1.), it is usually followed by a 'solution' slide (Figures W.2.2 and W.2.8).

Figure W.2.1 The Market

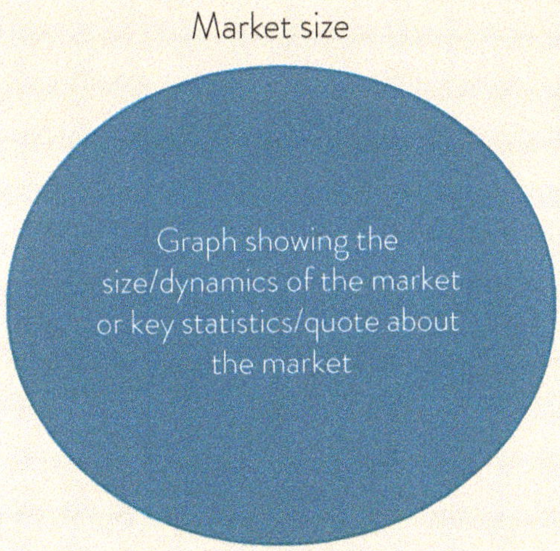

Figure W.2.2 The Problem

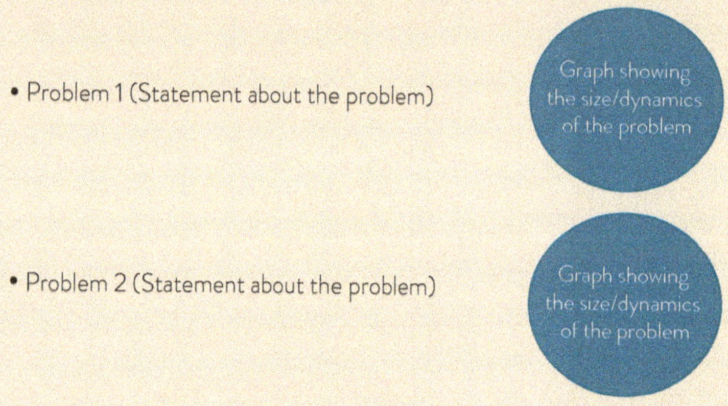

Exercise W.2.2: Who are your likely customer segments?

Most products have obvious uses. If your business idea is to develop a new type of electric charger for a phone, the market you are likely to be focused on is consumer electronics. However, some products and services can have applications in different markets. Inventions like the Post-It Note, Viagra and bubble wrap were all intended to solve problems in other markets. For example, bubble wrap was originally developed as a wallpaper.

Use the box below to brainstorm alternative ways that your product or service can be used.

Use the box below to brainstorm as many different customer segments that you think face the problem you are addressing. Remember wild solutions are welcome, as is combining and improving ideas and a lack of criticism.

Using desk research, by talking to different potential customers, or doing some mystery shopping, profile your customer segments within the total mass market for your product or service.

For a B2C (Business to Customer), complete Table W.2.1. For a B2B (Business to Business) opportunity, complete Table W.2.2.

Table W.2.1 B2C segmenting

Segment characteristics	Segment A	Segment B	Segment C	Segment D
Demography				
Geography				
Psychology				
Behaviours				

Table W.2.2 B2B segmenting

Segment characteristics	Segment A	Segment B	Segment C	Segment D
Business type				
Purchasing characteristics				
Attitudes				

Use Table W.2.3. to assess the attractiveness of the customer segments.

Table W.2.3 Evaluating customer segments

	Segment A (Rate 1–5, 5 is high)	Segment B (Rate 1–5, 5 is high)	Segment C (Rate 1–5, 5 is high)
What is the size and growth rate of the segment?			
Does the segment have a real itch (currently uses a 'workaround' to solve their problem)?			
Is the segment willing to pay for the offer?			
Is the segment easy to market and sell to?			
Is the segment guarded by a major competitor?			
Total Score			

Exercise W.2.3: What's your TAM, SAM and SOM?

In a pitch or a plan, a TAM, SAM and SOM diagram can help explain how you have used a 'top-down' and 'bottom-up' approach to arrive at your chosen target customer.

Adapt Figure W.2.3 for your own needs.

Figure W.2.3 The TAM, SAM and SOM

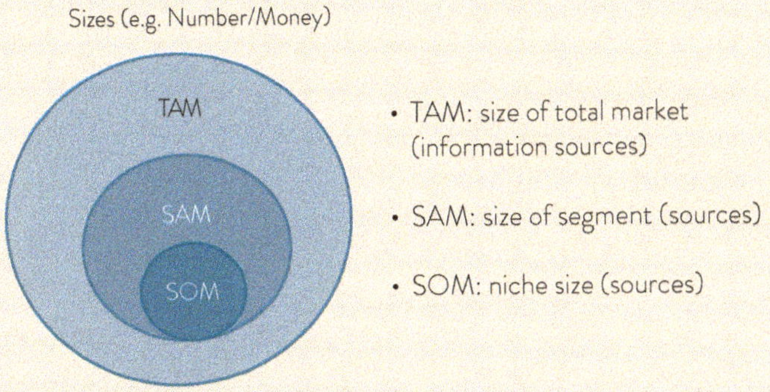

In a plan, you can include this diagram and supplement it with data and information to support your claims.

Exercise W.2.4: What is your target customer's profile?

Once you have arrived at your target customer, it is important to profile and validate these customers. A great way is by talking to them. This can involve asking them a series of situation, problem and opportunity questions.

Adapt the sample questions in the box below for your own needs:

Name of customer/alias (if the customer wants to be anonymous):

Sample situation questions:

- *How well does the potential customer fit with your customer vignette? You might prompt answers to this question by asking them about who they are (e.g. demographic factors such as their income level, approximate age, sex, geographic location), what their lifestyle is (e.g. what sorts of work do they do, how the spend their leisure time), and what the hopes and aims are. Remember personal questions can leave respondents uncomfortable so it is best to ask, if you need to, questions about age and income in terms of age or income bands.*

WORKBOOK 2

Sample problem questions:

- *How do they currently solve the problem? This might be prompted by asking questions that ask them about how they go about solving the problem – do they have a 'do it yourself' solution, do they use existing products or services, what they like about how they solve the problem, what are the problems, and what would it take for them to switch to a new solution?*

Sample opportunity questions:

- *The aim here is to work out if your proposed solution is any better than how they currently solve the problem. You might start by explaining – perhaps using diagrams – how your product or service works. Subsequently, you might want to test a range of 'guesses' about your opportunity. In doing so, it is important not to ask questions that are leading such as 'don't you think my product is fantastic'. In exploring your guesses about your business idea, you might want to work out:*
- *What are the benefits of the product or service? This can be done by asking them – perhaps using a flashcard – to rank the benefits. (Do they also have the same list of benefits and in the 'right' order?)*
- *What would it take for them to switch to a new product or service? (Do you actually have a source of competitive advantage?)*
- *How would they like to hear about it? (What is your best route to market – is it through social media or are their better ways of educating and informing the customer?)*
- *How would they prefer to buy it? (What is the best way of driving them towards a sale – how important is price and value? If they are motivated by price and your offer uses value pricing what does this say about your offer?)*
- *How do they feel about how you intend to organise delivery of the product or service to the customer? (Do they prefer to receive the product – if via the internet is this really what they want?)*

For a pitch, it is important to describe the target customer.

Depending on your preferences, either complete a customer vignette (Figure W.2.4) or a customer empathy map (Figure W.2.5).

For a plan, a vignette can also be used, if supported by relevant information and data.

Figure W.2.4 Customer vignette

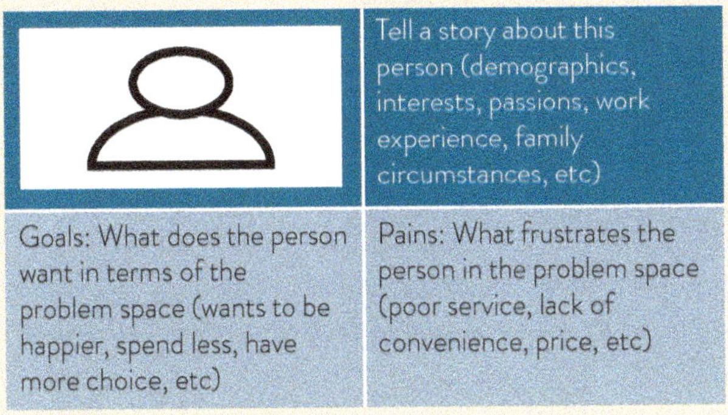

Figure W.2.5 Empathy map

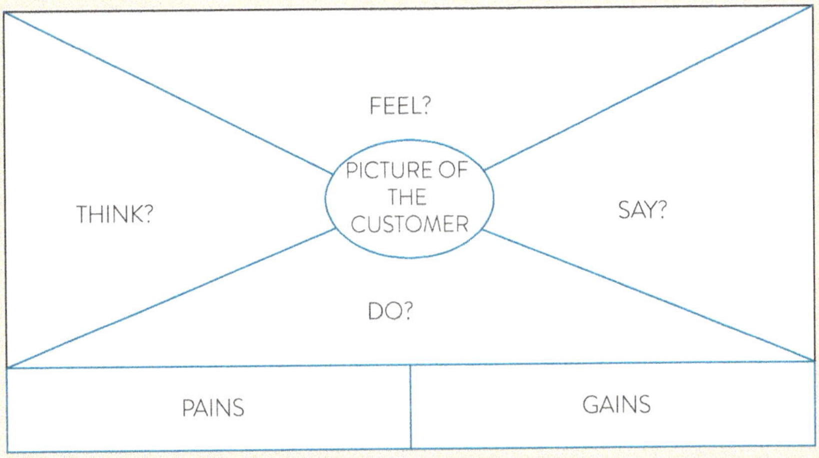

An additional exercise is to combine a customer journey with empathy mapping.

Use Table W.2.4 as a template for this activity.

Table W.2.4 Customer journey and empathy mapping

	Before	During	Afterwards
Think			
Feel			
Do			

Table W.2.4 continued

Say			
Pains			
Gains			

Exercise W.2.5: How have you validated your targeted customer?

For a pitch, a customer testimonial slide is a good way of showing that you have talked to your target customers. A testimonial is a short quote that shows their level of interest in the product or service.

Adapt Figure W.2.6 for your own needs. If your primary research is a survey, develop graphs that present relevant statistical information about your customers:

Figure W.2.6 Customer testimonials

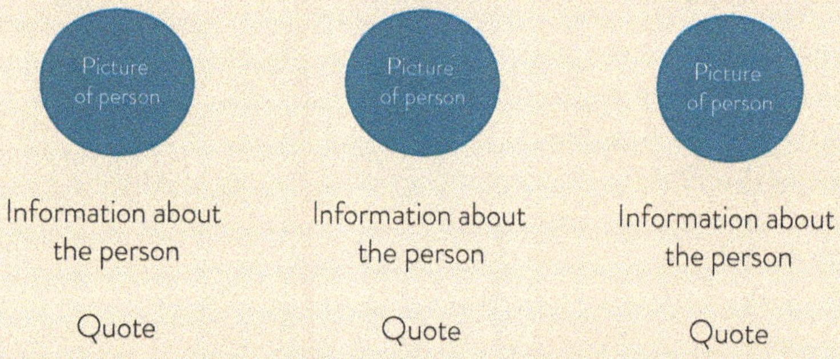

This market research can be backed up with plan appendices that detail the sample, your results and shows what are your assumptions.

Exercise W.2.6: How does your product or service work?

For a pitch, adapt Figure W.2.7 to show visually how your product or service works for the target customer.

Figure W.2.7 Product/Service demo

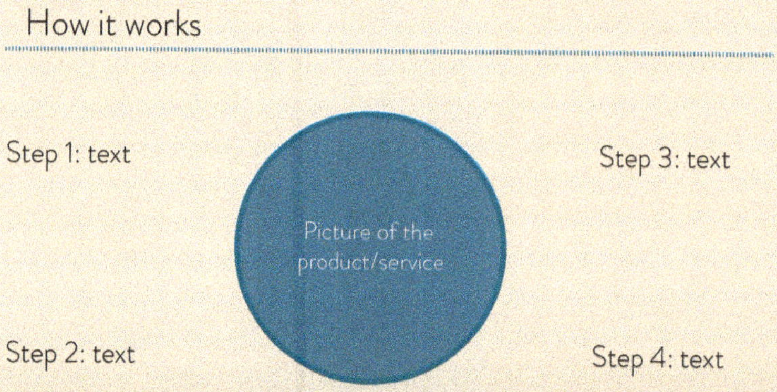

In Chapter 6 (pp. 149–150), you were shown a 'product recipe' exercise. Adapt the results of this for your plan. In the box below give a brief explanation of how your product or service works for the customer.

Exercise W.2.7: What's your value proposition?

Complete a value proposition canvas for your business.

For your pitch, you have to demonstrate that your solution either delights or resolves a genuine need for your target customer. One way of achieving this is to adapt Figure W.2.8 for your purposes.

Figure W.2.8 Solutions to problems

- Solution 1: Focus on the key first benefit
- Solution 2: Focus on the key second benefit
- Solution 3: Focus on the key third benefit

For your plan, identify the key USPs of your business idea. One way of capturing this is to adapt the product positioning statement in the box for your own purposes.

- *'For (customer niche) who (what are they looking for), the (name of product/service) is a (what is it) that (list benefits)'.*

Exercise W.2.8: Do you have product–market fit?

For your BMC, answer the questions in the box below on your customer segment:

- *For whom are we creating value?*
- *Who are our most important customers, clients, or users?*

For your BMC, answer the questions in the box below on your value proposition:

- *What value do we deliver to the customer?*
- *Which one of our customer's problems are we helping to solve?*
- *Which job are we helping the customer get done?*
- *Which customer needs are we satisfying?*
- *What bundles of products and services are we offering to each customer segment?*

For your pitch deck, there are a variety of ways of showing how your start-up has product–market fit. One way is to describe the problem (Figures W.2.1 or W.2.2), why the start-up provides a solution (Figure W.2.8) and what the market research says (Figure W.2.6: customer testimonial/market survey results). Another approach is to describe how the product or service works (Figure W.2.7) and why this solves a market problem (Figure W.2.3: TAM, SAM, SOM slide) for a target customer (Figure W.2.4: customer vignette slide) who appreciates its value (Figure W.2.6: customer testimonial/market survey results).

Decide on your pitch structure. How are you going to adapt and arrange these slides to show product–market fit?

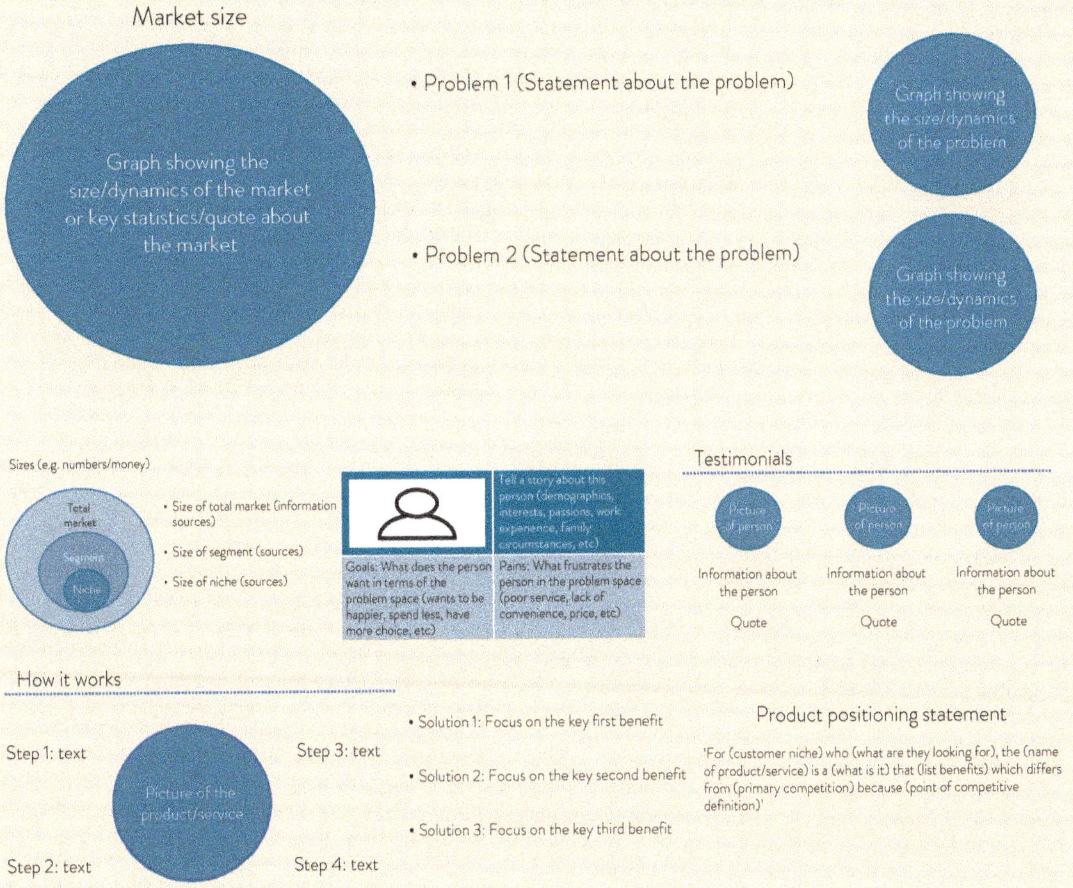

For a plan, these two basic choices also apply. The box below asks you to adopt a problem then solution approach to demonstrate your product-market. Adapt the sections to meet your own needs.

Product and customer section of the plan

- *The general profile of the market problem (size and dynamics) including TAM, SAM and SOM analysis and diagram*

WORKBOOK 2

- *How the product or service works (features and benefits)*

- *Information on customer segments/target customer (e.g. primary and secondary data and information, customer vignette diagram and analysis)*

- *If financial information is included this might detail the costs and likely revenues*

- *Appendix information (e.g. data on primary research)*

W.2.3 MARKETING AND SALES

Exercise W.2.9: How does the business reach its customers?

Start-ups have a range of ways for reaching their market.

For a pitch, adapt Figure W.2.9.

Figure W.2.9 Routes to market

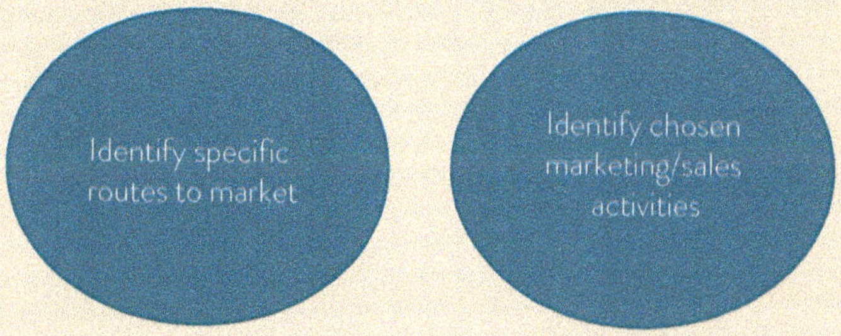

Build on this for your plan by answering the questions in the box below:

- *Identify your likely route or routes to market.*
- *Explain why this is your preferred choice. Use evidence from your primary and secondary data to support your choice.*
- *What are your likely options going forward?*

Exercise W.2.10: What is your sales strategy?

One of the main weaknesses of pitches and plans is that they fail to explain how the business will sell to customers. Most plans and pitches can identify how they will reach customers to educate and inform them about a new product or service. However, marketing alone is often insufficient. Selling is key because without sales it is difficult to see a start-up as a viable business.

One way of exploring your sales funnel is to answer these BMC questions for your chosen channel(s) and customer relationships in the boxes below:

- *Through which channels do our customer segments want to be reached?*
- *How are our Channels integrated? Which ones work best?*
- *Which ones are most cost-efficient?*
- *How are we integrating them with customer routines?*

- *What type of customer relationship does each of our customer segments expect us to establish and maintain with them?*
- *Which ones have we established?*
- *How costly are they?*
- *How are they integrated with the rest of our business model?*

For your pitch, Figures W.2.10 and W.2.11 are more explicit in identifying the start-up's sales strategy.

Use and adapt Figures W.2.10 and W.2.11.

Figure W.2.10 Sales strategy

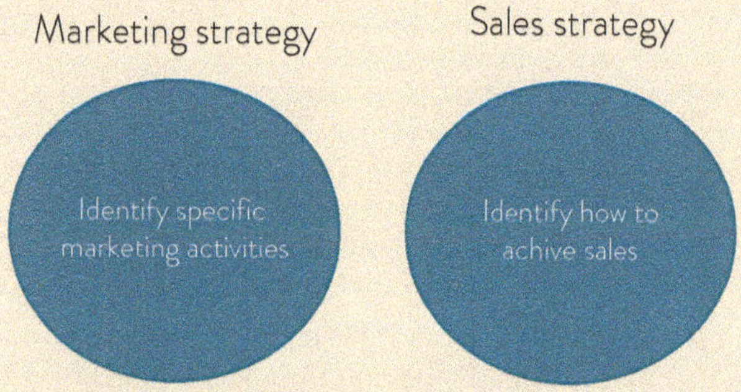

Figure W.2.11 The sales funnel

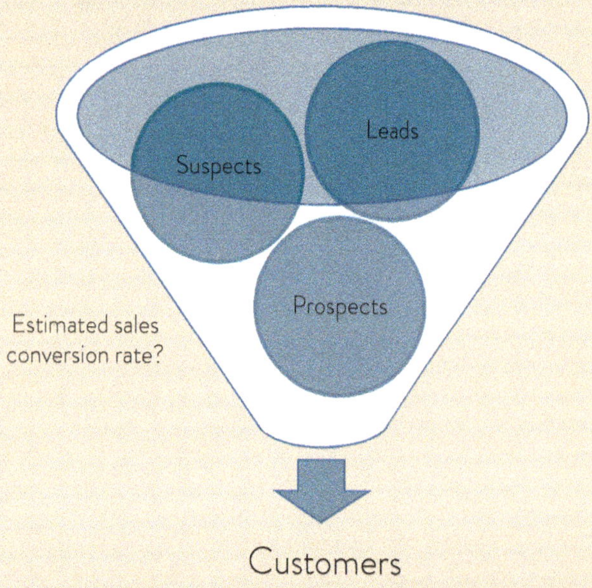

In some pitches, it may be important to identify the customer acquisition process and how you will keep and grow your customer base.

Adapt Figure W.2.12.

Figure W.2.12 Getting, keeping and growing the customer base

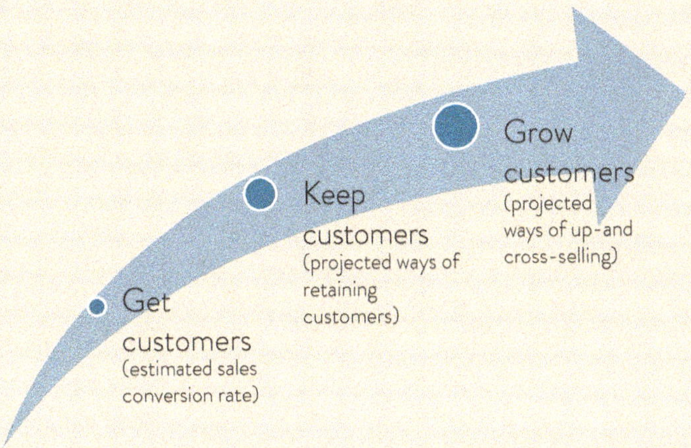

For a plan, build on your answers to the questions on routes to market to complete the section below that details your marketing and sales plan:

Marketing and sales section of the plan

- *Routes to market – how the product or service will get to the target customer.*

- *Sales strategy – how the start-up will drive the target customer down their sales funnel.*

- *If financial information is included this might include costs of sales and marketing activities.*
- *Additional information in the appendix.*

W.2.4 REVENUE MODELLING

Exercise W.2.11: How do you make money?

For your BMC, use the box below to identify your revenue streams.

- *For what value are our customers really willing to pay? For what do they currently pay? How are they currently paying? How would they prefer to pay?*
- *How many customers are you likely to reach in your first year? How much will you charge them for your product or service?*

In a pitch, a start-up has usually already explained the market problem, the solution and why this benefits a target customer. Investors are often interested in understanding how a start-up will be able to fund its development through its revenues. *Adapt one of the diagrams in Figure W.2.13 for your own uses.*

Figure W.2.13 How we make money

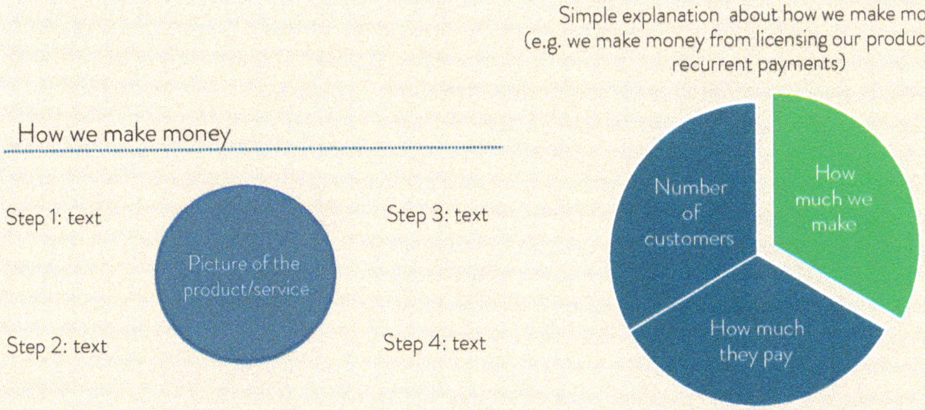

This information may be all that you need for a feasibility plan. However, these often require further information such as your break-even point and more detailed cost and revenue information. Chapter 8 and Exercise W 2.20 provide more information.

W.2.5 BUSINESS OPERATIONS AND LOGISTICS

Exercise W.2.12: How does the business source, make and distribute its products and services?

For your BMC, use the box below to identify your key resources, activities, and partners.

- *How do the delivery aspects for key resources, activities, and partners fit with your abilities to create and capture value?*
- *Who are your key suppliers?*
- *Where is the business located?*
- *If you need staff, how many and what types?*
- *If needed, how do supplies and goods get moved around?*
- *Are there any regulatory barriers you must face?*
- *Is it better to outsource some activities? What, if anything, is core to how you deliver value?*
- *How is your start-up paid?*

One other building block in the BMC is cost. In a few sentences, answer the following questions:

- *What are the most important costs inherent in our business model?*
- *Which Key Resources are most expensive?*
- *Which Key Activities are most expensive?*

Equally, from working out your business 'recipe' for your start-up 'meal' (Chapter 6, pp. 148–150) you should have some idea of how long it will take you to organise and launch your product or service.

For a pitch, a way of visually presenting this is to use a Gantt chart (Figure W.2.14) or a 'roadmap' (Figure W.2.15). A Gantt chart displays time periods across the top, such as weeks or months. Down its left side, it details activities which can be colour coded. A simple 'road map' showing the key decision points and times in the development of the start-up is an alternative way to display this information. This information can be put in both a plan and pitch to show how the start-up is expected to progress.

Adapt Figures W.2.14 and W.2.15 to show how long it will take you to launch your start-up.

Figure W.2.14 First-year Gantt chart

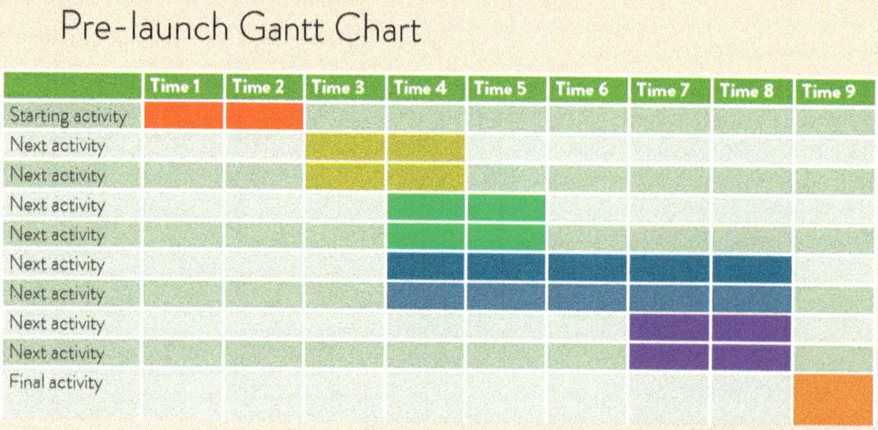

Figure W.2.15 Business progress 'roadmap'

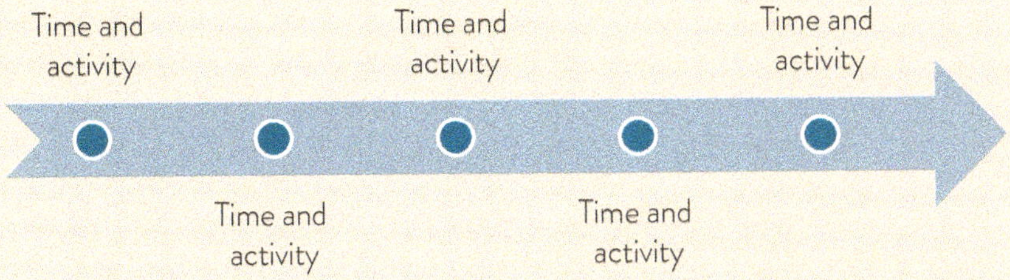

Another approach is to adapt Figure W.2.16 to show your 'recipe' for your product or service:

Figure W.2.16 How we deliver value

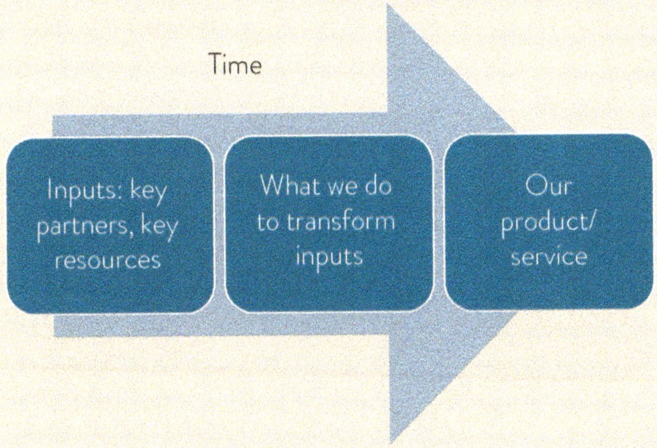

For a plan, draw your recipe for your product or service and fill in the business operations and logistics plan in the box below. Explain why these are appropriate choices.

Business operations and logistics section of the plan

- *Production and operations issues such as suppliers, raw materials, equipment and premises*

- *Logistics and distribution issues such as the use of third-party agents*

- *Timelines of activities*

- *If financial information is included this might include distribution, production and other costs*

- *Additional information in the appendix*

W.2.6 BUSINESS IDENTITY, MANAGEMENT AND TEAM

Exercise W.2.13: What are your start-up's name and logo?

One part of developing a start-up's identity is its name.

Use the box below to brainstorm different business names for your start-up. Subsequently, evaluate them. Why have you chosen this particular name?

- *Why have you chosen this particular name?*

Find out if your start-up name is already domain registered using an internet search.

Use an internet search to find out if your favoured business name is already registered with your government.

Use the box below to draw the logo for your business

Exercise W.2.14: What are your start-up's mission, mantra and summary pitch?

Exercise W 1.2 (p. 332) asked you to draw a tombstone for what you want your business to have achieved at the end of its life.

Repeat this exercise but this time ask yourself what customers or employees would say on the business tombstone.

To think through your mission, answer these four questions:

- *What do we do?*

- *How do we do it?*

- *For whom do we do it?*

- *What value are we bringing?*

For your values, brainstorm all of the values that you want your start-up to have. Evaluate your answers and shortlist those you think are your start-up's core values.

Write up your mission statement based on your vision, mission and values in the box below.

The German start-up Optionspace describes itself as the 'Airbnb for office space': matching up customers needing office space with under-used office space.[1]

Use the box below to identify the key phrase (strapline) that explains your business model.

- *Narrow this down to a 'twitter' mantra (140 characters) that captures your values and vision*
- *Write down your three-word mantra*

For a pitch, you might start it by giving an 'executive summary' of who you are and what you are doing.

One way of doing this is to adapt Figure W.2.17 for your own introductory pitch slide.

Figure W.2.17 Specimen introductory pitch slide

Often the point of a pitch is to intrigue the audience so that they enquire further about the business. One good practice is to anticipate likely questions and be able to offer additional information (see Chapter 5, pp. 110–111 for other ways of improving pitches).

For a plan, start-ups also have to think through how they are going to communicate their plan to their audience. This should be for a target audience (see Chapter 9, pp. 212–213 for further information). This might be through an introductory letter or email that provides an executive summary of the start-up proposition.

This may be repeated in a plan's executive summary. Equally, you can capture this information in a plan section on business objectives.

Use the box below to complete the executive summary and business objectives sections of a plan.

Executive summary

- *Description of start-up and its objectives (e.g. name, logo, strapline, mission statement)*

- *Information on the problem, solution and target customer*

- *What is the 'ask' – if money is needed what is it for, how will it get paid back and what is the exit route for the business (see Exercise W 2.19)*

- *What success looks like (see Exercise W 2.18)*

- *For a section on business objectives, this information can be adapted to include, for example, greater detail on the start-up's organisation structure, its mission and values, what are its hopes are for the future*

Exercise W.2.15: What is 'curve-jumping, paradigm-shifting, patent-pending' about your start-up?[22]

If your business is creative, technology, or designed based, there is often an impetus to protect your intellectual capital.

To help develop your thinking, answer the questions in the box below.

- *What sorts of protection are you using to defend your idea? Outline your sources of information to back up your claims*

- *How is your intellectual capital a barrier to entry?*

- *How are you going to exploit this intellectual property?*

- *What are your likely costs?*

In a pitch, you might include having access to intellectual property in a slide that explains the benefits of your product or service.

In your product and market section of a plan, you may include information about how you intend to exploit the advantages of access to intellectual property. This may be supported by information in the appendix which details out the specifics of the intellectual property.

Exercise W.2.16: Why is this the right team?

About half of all start-ups are team start-ups (Chapter 3, Table 3.5, p. 55). If you are a team start-up, the team's 3 'R's' (relationships, roles and rewards) are important. Table W.2.5 also suggests that your team may have weaknesses and may require outside help. *To investigate your team, fill out Table W.2.5.*

Table W.2.5 Understanding your team

Team member						
	#1	#2	#3	#4	#5	#6
Write down the names of your team members						
What is your relationship with these team members?						
What skills and knowledge do they bring to a start-up?						
What roles could they play in a start-up?						

Table W.2.5 continued

What is their equity split?						
Where is the team strong/weak?						
Who could you approach as mentors and advisors?						

For a pitch, adapt Figure W.2.18 to capture relevant information on the start-up team and its current advisors or investors.

Figure W.2.18 Pitch deck slide for the start-up team

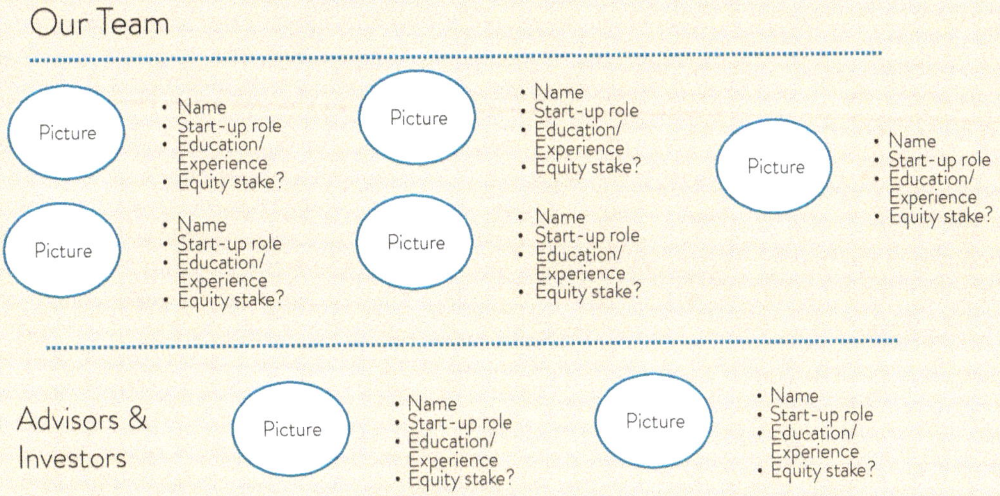

For a plan, it is often important to explain why the team is the one that is best able to drive forward the business. This matters because investors are swayed in their judgements about the start-up's chances by the quality of the team.

To show this, build the team section of your plan:

Team

- *Who is the core team, management workers and advisors; what are their strengths?*

- *What is the ownership and reward structure of the business? Why is this appropriate to take the business forward?*

- *If financial information is included this might include working out your employment costs*

- *Additional information in appendices – these could provide 'pen pictures' of why the skills, education and abilities of the team and its advisors. Another appendix can include your vesting agreement (search 'vesting agreement template' online)*

W.2.7 COMPETITION

Exercise W.2.17: How is your offer different in the market?

In plans, you still sometimes see the explicit use of models such as Porter's Five Forces or, more occasionally, the use of the Blue Ocean approach. Even when they are not evident, these tools are useful for understanding why a start-up is different.

Conduct a Five Forces or Blue Ocean analysis of your industry. Where is your source of competitive advantage? How does this relate to your strategy for developing your start-up?

Another tool that sometimes appears in both pitches and plans is the product positioning statement. In Chapter 6 (p. 139) you were asked to identify this for your product or service. You can extend this to include an awareness of your competitors:

> 'For (customer niche) who (what are they looking for), the (name of product/service) is a (what is it) that (list benefits) which differs from (primary competition) because (point of competitive definition)'

For example, for the Punkt's 'dumb' mobile phone (Chapter 6, p. 139) it might read:

> For (busy individuals) who (value their privacy), the (Punkt) is a (mobile phone) that (provides stylish, carefully designed and elegantly crafted technology) which differs from (the Apple iPhone) because (it puts time-poor people in charge of getting in touch).

Another way of demonstrating industry and market attractiveness is to redo the customer segmentation process (sometimes called TAM, SAM, SOM: see Chapter 6, pp. 131–132) but this time acknowledge that competitors are going to 'eat' into your potential market share. This takes explicit account of the fact that you will only be able to focus on 'X' per cent of the niche because existing customers are loyal to competitors.

Update your TAM, SAM and SOM and your product positioning statement to include your competitors.

In pitches and in plans, a common visual representation is a competitor benchmarking diagram that shows your start-up's benefits against your competitors. A variant of this is to offer a contrast between your start-up and the competition: 'what we can do and they can't' and (to add realism) 'what they can do but we can't'.[3] A further variation is a competitor positioning map. This has two axes that shows a particular feature/benefit of your offer. One axis might be convenience whilst the other may feature reliability. Another approach is to show on one axis the value to the customer of your product or service whilst on the other your ability to provide a unique product or service.[4] This graphically shows where your value proposition is 'high and to the right' relative to the competition.

Adapt one or more of the basic diagrams below in Figure W.2.19 for your pitch.

Figure W.2.19 Competitor benchmarking and positioning

Competitor Benchmarking

	Start-up Logo	Competitor 1 Logo	Competitor 2 Logo	Competitor 3 Logo
Feature 1	✓	X	✓	X
Feature 2	✓	✓	X	X
Feature 3	✓	X	X	✓
Feature 4	✓	✓	X	X
Feature 5	✓	X	✓	✓

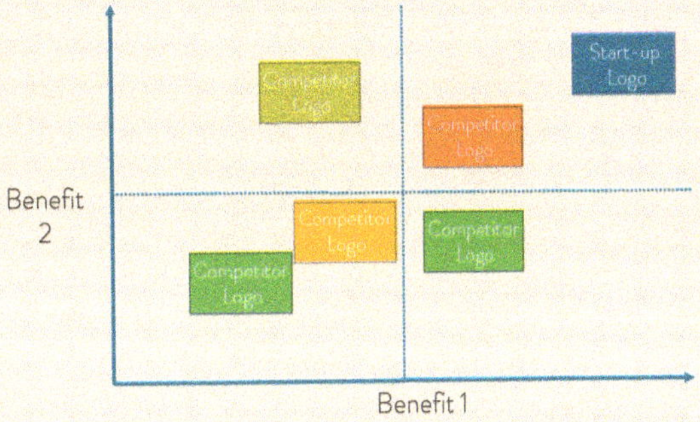

For your plan, adapt your primary and secondary information for your section on the competition.

Competition

- *The key direct/indirect competition (e.g. who they are, what they offer)*

- *Sources of current competitive advantage (e.g. competitor benchmarking and positioning diagrams)*

- *Additional information in the appendix – secondary and primary market research on competitors*

W.2.8 GROWTH AND FUNDING NEEDS

Exercise W.2.18: What's your plan for growth?

The audiences for plans and pitches often require information about what the founders see as the likely future for their business. They want to see that a start-up will grow and develop. Often they are looking for a business that is 'repeatable' and scalable.

To graphically capture your future start-up plans, adapt Figure W.2.20 for your needs. You might need to go beyond year 3 if you believe that this is a requirement of your outside audience.

Figure W.2.20 Start-up scalability

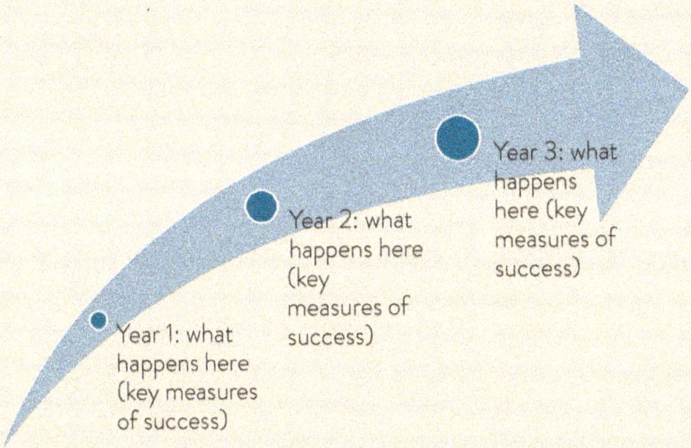

In a plan, you may have a section that identifies how you intend to grow. This might be through organic growth, franchising or via acquiring other businesses. One good place to detail your future plans is in an executive summary. You may also indicate your growth plans in your business objectives and include them in your assessment of the feasibility of the idea. This might be important because a start-up may be viable but not easily repeatable or scalable. If so, this might cause concerns to outside investors.

Use the box below to explain your growth plans. These plans may form part of your executive summary or business objectives. They also may be included in your financial section to explain your growth.

Exercise W.2.19: What does your start-up lack?

Financial projections allow you to estimate your finance 'gap' – the extra money that you might need to start up, to cross the 'valley of death' and to grow the business. This funding gap is often called your 'ask'. If you require funding, you have to think through what you want the money for, for how long, and how you will repay the funding back to the investor. Key to this is understanding if you want the money to fund operational needs or longer-term investment plans. Equally, you have to work out who you need the funding from, how long for, on what terms and why a particular financier is the appropriate sources of funding. Go to Chapter 9 (pp. 224–234) to find out more about sources of entrepreneurial finance and the business models of banks, equity financiers and crowdfunders.

Chapter 9 also identifies that financiers often want to recoup their investment. They are keen to understand how this will be done by the business. If it is a bank loan, the bank typically wants to know how their loan (capital and interest) will be repaid in full. Alternatively, if it is a crowdfunder they want to know what they will get in return for supporting your crowdfunding reward campaign or if it is a business angel or a venture capital, they want to know if the exit option is to sell the business to a competitor (a trade sale) or to sell the start-up's shares on the public stock exchange (Initial Public Offer).

If there is a need for an 'ask' and an exit plan, this might be done at towards the start of a pitch deck slide. In contrast, however, it is sometimes placed at the end of a pitch deck, once the viability of the start-up feasibility has been assessed.

Use and adapt Figure W.2.21 for your needs.

Figure W.2.21 The 'ask'

The 'ask'

- Investment amount here
- Reasons for this 'ask'
- What the investor gets in return (e.g. trade sale, IPO)

In a plan, you may have a sub-section of your financial information that identifies how much you need, what you need the money for, how long the pay back is and what it is your exit strategy. A summary of this information may appear in your cover letter or introductory email, executive summary, business objectives, start-up assessment or financial plan.

Use your financial information to identify how long and deep is your 'valley of death'.

Go to Chapter 9 and find out more about the different types of entrepreneurial finance, who is most likely to fund your financial gap, over what time period and their expectations of a return.

W.2.9 FINANCIAL PLANS AND THE GO/NO GO ASSESSMENT

Exercise W.2.20: Is your start-up viable?

For both plans and pitches, there is often a requirement to make an assessment of the viability and scalability of a new venture. One way of showing this in a plan or pitch is to use a SWOT analysis (Chapter 6, p. 108).

The founder can also make a qualitative judgement based on what they think is the balance between risks and rewards. Using their start-up planning may reveal key problems that make the business unworkable or unattractive even if there are large potential revenues. Alternatively, if the business is viable, it may not be scalable, deterring entrepreneurs from persisting with the start-up.

Financial planning can help support this assessment of whether to proceed or abandon the start-up by showing the financial health and vitality of the start-up.

In a pitch, common ways of showing viability are a slide with a SWOT analysis, break-even slide, a diagram or table that shows profit and loss information or when the business becomes cashflow positive.

For your pitch, adapt the figures in Figure W.2.22 for your needs.

Figure W.2.22 Feasibility slides

Strengths	Weaknesses
• Focus on (up to) 3 key things	• Focus on (up to) 3 key things
Opportunities	**Threats**
• Focus on (up to) 3 key things	• Focus on (up to) 3 key things

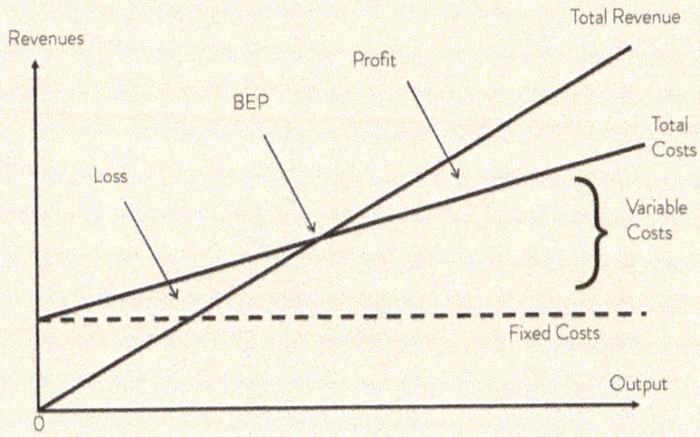

Financial Projections: Cash flow positive

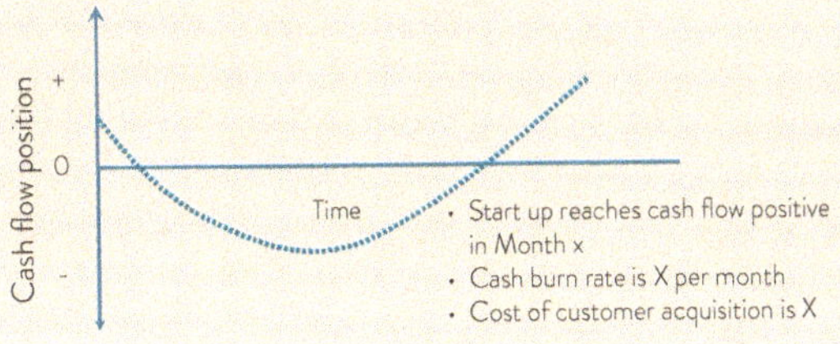

Financial Projections: P&L

	Year 1 (000s)	Year 2 (000s)	Year 3 (000s)
Revenues			
Cost of Goods Sold (COGS)			
Gross Profits Percentage			
Operating costs			
EBITA			
Break even point			

For a plan, one section can simply assess start-up feasibility to arrive at a go/no go assessment. Another option is to include this assessment as part of the section on the financial plan. This can be supported by detailed information in your appendix that demonstrates the robustness and rigour of your financial assessment of the start-up.

For your plan, use the section below to write up the financial section of your plan or to provide a go/no go assessment of your idea.

Financial Feasibility

- *Summary information on projected 1st year cashflows and P&L*

- *Financial ratios (e.g. gearing, cash burn rate)*

- *Assessment of likely start-up risks and rewards (e.g. SWOT analysis, qualitative or quantitative assessment)*

- *Additional information in the appendix – balance sheets, financial scenario plans for cashflows and P&L*

Notes

1 www.techcrunch.com/2017/03/14/germanys-optionspace-wants-to-be-an-airbnb-for-office-space/.
2 Kawasaki, G. (2004). *The art of the start: The time-tested, battle-hardened guide for anyone starting anything*. Penguin.
3 Ibid.
4 Ibid.

Index